CAMBRIDGE CONCISE HISTORIES

A Concise History of Australia

FOURTH EDITION

Australia is the last continent to be settled by Europeans, but it also sustains a people and a culture tens of thousands of years old. For much of the past 225 years the newcomers have sought to replace the old with the new. This book tells how they imposed themselves on the land, and describes how they brought technology, institutions and ideas to make it their own. It relates the advance from a penal colony to a prosperous free country and illustrates how, in a nation created by waves of newcomers, the search for binding traditions has long been accompanied by the feeling of rootlessness.

The fourth edition incorporates the far-reaching effects of an export and investment boom in the early years of the twenty-first century that lifted Australia to unprecedented prosperity. The sale of minerals and energy enabled the economy to withstand the global financial crisis of 2007–08 but there was no agreement on how the wealth was to be managed and its benefits distributed. The book describes a continuing search for solutions to climate change, the unauthorised arrival of refugees, Indigenous disadvantage and generational change.

Stuart Macintyre is an Emeritus Laureate Professor of the University of Melbourne. From 1999 to 2006 he was Dean of the Faculty of Arts, and he has served as president of the Australian Historical Association and the Academy of the Social Sciences in Australia. His books include *The Oxford History of Australia, Volume 4* (1986), *The History Wars* (2003) and, most recently, *Australia's Boldest Experiment: War and Reconstruction in the 1940s* (2015). With Alison Bashford he edited the *Cambridge History of Australia* (2013).

CAMBRIDGE CONCISE HISTORIES

This is a series of illustrated 'concise histories' of selected individual countries, intended both as university and college textbooks and as general historical introductions for general readers, travellers and members of the business community.

For a list of titles in the series, see end of book.

story

ia

Fourth Edition

STUART MACINTYRE

CAMBRIDGE
UNIVERSITY PRESS

477 Williamstown Road, Port Melbourne, VIC 3207, Australia

Cambridge University Press is part of the University of Cambridge.

It furthers the University's mission by disseminating knowledge in the pursuit of education, learning and research at the highest international levels of excellence.

www.cambridge.org
Information on this title: www.cambridge.org/9781107562431

First published 1999
Second edition 2004
Third edition 2009
Reprinted 2010, 2011, 2012, 2013, 2015
Fourth edition 2016

Cover designed by Adrian Saunders
Typeset by Integra Software Services Pvt. Ltd.
Printed in Singapore by Markono Print Media Pte Ltd

A catalogue record for this publication is available from the British Library

A Cataloguing-in-Publication entry is available from the catalogue of the National Library of Australia at www.nla.gov.au

ISBN 978-1-107-56243-1 Paperback

Aboriginal and Torres Strait Islander peoples are respectfully advised that images of deceased persons appear in this book and may cause distress.

For my daughters
MARY AND JESSIE
this is also their history

CONTENTS

ILLUSTRATIONS

MAPS

ACKNOWLEDGEMENTS

This book is part of a series of national histories published for an international readership, and successive editions have been translated into a number of foreign languages. The opportunity to explain Australia and its history to non-Australians was compelling, though when the book first appeared I became aware of the contrasting expectations of Australian readers. They look for familiar events and actors for both orientation and reassurance that this is indeed an account of their past. The overseas reader, on the other hand, has little familiarity with such local lore, and a narrative composed of it is unlikely to assist those who do not hold any prior knowledge. In subsequent revisions I have therefore provided more of these signposts while endeavouring to paint a broadbrush picture in which the detail is subordinated to the distinctive features.

A similar quandary arises from the different uses of this book. Those using it as textbook to teach Australian history expect it to encompass the principal fields of research, while other readers who feel strongly about particular causes take the amount of attention accorded them as an index of sympathies. Such weighing of proportions is inevitable, and I am aware that my emphases are indeed indicative of my own understanding and inclinations. My purpose, however, has been to present a narrative that explains why its component parts have a place in the national story and how they continue to generate discussion. I have tried to set Australian history in the context of global and regional history and to draw out comparisons with other parts of the world. This approach is intended to serve the overseas reader who perhaps has a mental image of the Australian landscape, its flora and fauna, but is dependent on a media coverage that sheds little light on the patterns of national life. I also have in mind the visitor who encounters the local practices but finds their logic difficult to follow. I hope the book assists these readers to understand what they see and hear by providing an account of how it came to be.

My predecessor as professor of history at the University of Melbourne wrote 100 years ago in his *Short History of Australia* that 'historical events, like mountain ranges, can best be surveyed as a whole by an observer who is placed at a good distance from them'. In preparing this edition I have taken the opportunity to look again at events that have now receded from the foreground and bring more clarity into the account of contemporary developments.

A concise history is necessarily dependent on a very large body of historical scholarship, and in earlier editions I acknowledged the assistance of many friends and colleagues. I have now accumulated so many layers of guidance that it would be invidious to attempt to list all my obligations. In preparing to write this edition I benefitted particularly from working with Alison Bashford on the *Cambridge History of Australia* and the nearly seventy scholars who contributed chapters to it. As before, I have learned from the undergraduates I teach and the postgraduates with whom I work, not least for sharing the questions that exercise them and the approaches to Australian history that catch their imagination.

I dedicated the first edition of the book to my two daughters Mary and Jessie, born in England, raised in Australia, who too often had their father play the pedagogue and all along were instructing him in their interests and concerns. They now live in Vancouver and Melbourne, and their children, Xuan and Tai, Rory and Hamish, in turn give me additional insights into the interplay of then and now. My wife Martha always helps me gain a better understanding of these exchanges, as well as subjects beyond Australian history.

Stuart Macintyre
February 2015

Map 1.1   Australia: the main rivers, cities and towns

I

Beginnings

How and when did Australia begin? One version of the country's origins – a version taught to generations of school children and set down in literature and art, memorials and anniversaries – would have it that Australian history commenced at the end of the eighteenth century. In 1770, after several centuries of European voyaging in the southern oceans, the English naval lieutenant James Cook sailed the length of the continent fringed by the Pacific, named it New South Wales, and claimed possession in the name of his monarch. Within twenty years the British government dispatched an expedition to settle New South Wales. On 26 January 1788 its commander, Arthur Phillip, assumed government over the eastern half of the country. The thousand officers, troops, civilian officials and convicted felons who came ashore from the eleven vessels of the First Fleet anchored in Sydney Harbour prepared the way for later immigrants, bond and free, who spread out over the continent, explored and settled, possessed and subdued it.

This is a story of a sleeping land brought to life by *Endeavour*, the name given to Cook's sturdy ship and the spirit attributed to those who followed him. The chroniclers of the First Fleet recorded how a landing party unloaded the stores, cleared a space on the wooded slopes of Sydney Cove and erected their first habitations. They were describing the advent of civilisation. The sound of an axe on wood, English steel on antipodean eucalypt, broke the silence of a primeval wilderness.

The newcomers brought with them livestock, plants and tools. They also brought a mental toolkit fashioned from the objective rationality of the Enlightenment and a corresponding belief in human capacity, the moral certainty and stern duty of evangelical Christianity, and the acquisitive itch of the market. Those ways of thinking and acting made possible the establishment of European dominion over the rest of the world. That accomplishment in turn shaped the understanding of economics, resources, navigation, trade, botany, zoology, anthropology – and history.

History served the new drive to control and order the natural world, to understand and even direct events. A new awareness of geography and chronology, of space and time as fixed and measurable, encouraged an understanding of history as a branch of knowledge independent of the standpoint of the observer, while at the same time it disclosed an insistent process of improvement and progress that legitimated the replacement of the old by the new. Seen thus, the history of Australia formed a late chapter in British, European and world history.

This version of Australia's beginning emphasised its strangeness. The plants and animals, even the human inhabitants, confounded existing taxonomies; they were both old and new. The monotremes and marsupials, warm-blooded animals that reproduced by egg or carried their offspring in a pouch, seemed to be primitive fore-runners of the placental mammal, and at the same time a bizarre inversion of nature. Hence the puzzlement of the early New South Wales judge and rhymester, Barron Field:

> Kangaroo, Kangaroo!
> Thou Spirit of Australia!
> That redeems from utter failure,
> From perfect desolation,
> And warrants the creation
> Of this fifth part of the Earth
> Which would seem an after-birth . . .

In this version of Australian history, the novelty of the place – it was New Holland before it became New South Wales – was softened by attaching its destiny to imperial origins. Colonial history took British and European achievement as its point of departure. Behind the rude improvisation on the furthest frontier of settlement of the British Empire was the inheritance of institutions, customs and expectations. A naval officer who in 1803 watched a team of convicts yoked to a cart that was sunk up to its axles in the unpromising sand hills of a southern bay comforted himself with the vision of 'a second Rome, rising from a coalition of Banditti ... superlative in arms and arts'.

That settlement was abandoned, and the officer returned eventually to England, but others stayed and reworked his anticipation. The subsequent visionaries thought of Australia not as mere imitation but as striking out anew. They believed that the unbroken horizons of this vast island-continent offered the opportunity to leave behind the Old World evils of poverty, privilege and rancour. With the transition in the middle of the nineteenth century from penal settlements to free and self-governing communities, the emphasis shifted from colonial improvement to national experimentation. With the gold rush, agricultural settlement and urban growth, minds turned from dependency to self-sufficiency, and from a history that worked out the imperial legacy to one of self-discovery.

During the nineteenth century and well into the twentieth, the sentiment of colonial nationalism served the desire to mark Australia off from Britain and Europe. Then, as the last imperial ties were severed, even that way of distinguishing the child from the parent lost meaning. In its place arose the idea of Australia as a destination for all-comers from every part of the world, which served the multicultural attitudes that formed in the closing decades of the twentieth century and further undermined the foundational significance of 1788. The blurring of origins turned Australian history into a story of journeys and arrivals, shared by all and continuing right up to the present.

But such smudging was too convenient. It failed to satisfy the need for emotional attachment and it left unappeased the pricking of conscience. The desire for a binding national past that would connect the people to the land was frustrated by a feeling of rootlessness, of novelty without depth. The longing for belonging to an indigenous culture was denied by the original usurpation. A history of colonisation yielded to a realisation of invasion.

By the end of the twentieth century it was no longer possible to maintain the fiction of Australia as *terra nullius*, a land that until its settlement in 1788 lacked human habitation, law, government or history. An alternative beginning was apparent. Australia – or, rather, the earlier landmass of Sahul, a larger island continent that extended northwards into Papua New Guinea and embraced the present island of Tasmania – was the site of an ancient way of life that had evolved over many millennia. The growing recognition of this vastly extended Australian history spoke to late-twentieth-century sensibility. It revealed social organisation, ecological practices, languages, art forms and spiritual beliefs of great antiquity and richness. By embracing the Aboriginal past, non-Aboriginal Australians attached themselves to their country.

They did so, however, not simply out of a desire for reconciliation and harmony but because they were challenged by the Aboriginal presence. The rediscovery of this longer history occurred alongside the revival of Indigenous organisation and culture, the one process feeding into the other and yet each possessing its own dynamic. For the Aboriginal and Torres Strait Islander peoples, the European invasion was a traumatic event with lasting consequences for their mode of life, health, welfare and very identity. But theirs was also a story of survival – the survival of their customs and practices and of the stories and songs through which they were maintained. The second version of Australian history, the one that begins not at 1788 in the Western calendar but at least 50,000 years before the present, is at once more controversial, more rapidly changing and more compelling.

The older history noticed Aborigines only as a tragic and disturbing presence, victims of the iron law of progress. The Latin term *Ab origines* means, literally, those who were here from the beginning: its persistence, despite attempts to find other, more specific designations such as are used for aboriginal peoples in other parts of the world, attests to their abiding presence. The remnants of this Aboriginal way of life were therefore pieced together and fitted into the jigsaw puzzle of prehistory to disclose a hierarchy of peoples at different stages of complexity, sophistication and capacity. Aboriginal traditions were of interest for the light they shed on this prehistory for, in the absence of written records, chronology and effective political authority, the Aboriginals were deemed to lack a history of their own. Denied agency in the events that began in 1788, they were no more than objects of history.

It is precisely that idea of history that is now cast into doubt by the new understanding of the Australian past. In 1992 the country's highest court found that the application of the doctrine of *terra nullius* when the British government claimed sovereignty 'depended on a discriminatory denigration of indigenous inhabitants'. Speaking six months later before an Aboriginal audience, the prime minister went further. 'We took the traditional lands and smashed the original way of life', Paul Keating stated. 'We brought the diseases. The alcohol. We committed the murders. We took the children from their mothers. We practised discrimination and exclusion.'

Keating cited these past wrongs in a spirit of reconciliation, insisting 'there is nothing to fear or lose in the recognition of historical truth'. Yet over the following decade every one of his statements was contested. His successor, John Howard, dismissed the recommendations of the Reconciliation Council. Howard's government rejected the findings of an official inquiry into the Stolen Generations of Aboriginal children taken from their parents, and restricted the operation of native title. Others have insisted that the original inhabitants of this country were a primitive people incapable of serious resistance and that the British settlement of Australia 'was the least violent of all Europe's encounters with the New World'.

Then, in 2008, thousands of Aboriginal Australians gathered in the nation's capital to watch a new prime minister, Kevin Rudd, offer an apology. 'We apologise for the laws and policies of successive parliaments and governments that have inflicted profound grief, suffering and loss on these, our fellow Australians.' His statement was televised around the nation, including at outdoor settings in remote Indigenous communities. Its declared purpose was to 'remove a great stain from the nation's soul', and open 'a new chapter in the history of this great land'.

Indigenous leaders welcomed the apology but the meaning of the new chapter was far from apparent. They were at odds over how to deal with a report written by one of them in the previous year that disclosed extensive child abuse within remote Indigenous communities; a finding that brought government intervention and imposed new restrictions on the ability of these communities to determine their own affairs. Disagreement over the intervention was accompanied by widening differences over how and by whom their disadvantage was to be overcome. Was it to be by holding onto customary practices or by accepting the need for change? Would it come from within or without? Were Indigenous peoples strong in their identity or was it romanticised by false friends to hold them in a state of dependency?

The prime minister's 2008 statement gave no answer to these questions. His new chapter rested on the assertion that by 'righting the wrongs of the past' the nation was 'moving forward with confidence to the future'. Here, as is common with such glib clichés, the wrongs are safely in the settler past, making it possible to affirm a deeper continuity. Hence, his statement was preceded by an Aboriginal welcome to country in a ceremony that now marks the opening of every new parliament. So too his opening words: 'today we honour the Indigenous peoples of this land, the oldest continuing cultures in human history'.

***

The island-continent of Australia, so the scientists tell us, formed as the great supercontinent of Pangea broke up in the remote past. First Laurasia in the north separated from Gondwana in the south. Then what would become India, Africa, South America and New Zealand broke free from Gondwana and drifted north, and later still – perhaps 50 million years ago – Australia and New Guinea did the same, until finally they stopped short of the island chain that extends from Indochina down to Timor. Although the oceans rose and fell with periods of warmth and cold, this vast land-raft was always surrounded by water. The deep channel that today separates South-East Asia from the northwest coast of Australia narrowed at times to as little as 100 kilometres, but it never closed. The sea always separated Sahul, the continental shelf that encompassed Australia, Tasmania and New Guinea, from Sunda, the archipelago that took in Malaya, Sumatra, Borneo and Java. The separation came to be known as the Wallace Line, after the nineteenth-century scientist who showed that it was a permanent zoological divide that demarcated Eurasian species from those of Australia and New Guinea.

Australia was thus isolated. It was also remarkably geologically stable. There was little of the buckling and folding of the earth's crust that elsewhere produced high mountain ranges or deep rifts. Together with the relative absence of glaciation and the infrequency of volcanic activity, this left an older, flatter landmass, rich in mineral deposits but shallow in soil covering. Weathering and erosion leached the soil of nutrients. The remarkable diversity of plants and animals that evolved and flourished in this environment had to adapt to major climatic changes. Rainforests expanded and contracted, inland lakes filled and emptied, carnivores were less durable than herbivores.

When the last ice age ended some 10,000 years ago and the present shoreline formed, Australia extended 3700 kilometres from the northern tropics to the southern latitudes, and 4400 kilometres from east to west. Much was arid plain, and much of the rain that fell on the line of mountains running down the eastern seaboard flowed into the Pacific Ocean. More than any other landmass, this one was marked by the infrequency and unreliability of rain. Twentieth-century scientists created the El Niño Oscillation Index to measure a climatic phenomenon that occurs when the trade winds that blow from the east across the Pacific Ocean fail. With that failure, warm water accumulates off the South American coast and brings fierce storms to the Americas; conversely, the colder water on this side of the Pacific reduces evaporation and cloud formation, and thus causes prolonged drought in eastern Australia. The El Niño cycle lasts from two to eight years, and climatologists can detect it in records going back to the early nineteenth century. It is probable that it has operated for much longer, and shaped the evolution of the Australian environment.

The natural historians who marvel at the rich diversity of this singular environment find in it an ingenious anthropomorphism. The plants best suited to such circumstances sent down deep roots to search for moisture, used narrow leaves and tough bark to minimise evaporation and loss of vital fluid, and scattered seeds

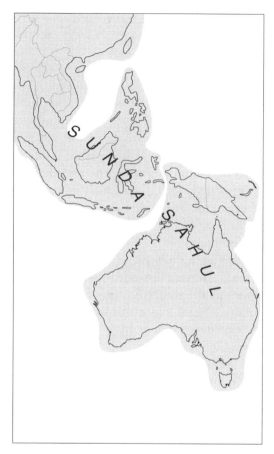

Map 1.2 Sunda and Sahul

capable of regeneration after lying for long periods on the dry earth. They were frugal in their eking out of nutrients and prodigal in their reproduction. Some of them, such as the stands of eucalypts that spread a blue haze under the hot sun, actively enlisted the assistance of the conditions by strewing the ground with incendiary material to burn off competitors and stimulate their own regeneration. In the pyrohistory of Australia, the vast and sleeping continent is reconfigured as an arena in which the gum trees triumphed by kindling a fiery vortex.

Such fires would have been ignited periodically by lightning strikes or other natural causes, but by this time there was another incendiary agent – humans. The acquisition of control over fire by *Homo sapiens* provided protection, heat, light and power: the domestic hearth became site and symbol of human society. It might well have been the sight of columns of smoke rising on the northwest shore of Sahul that attracted people on island extremities of Sunda to cross the intervening sea. We do not know when this passage occurred, why, or even how. It was probably achieved by using rafts, as the result of population pressure and at a time when the Timor Sea was low. The most recent low-point, 150 metres below present sea level, occurred about 20,000 years ago, but the evidence of occupation before then is clear. The same low-point occurred about 140,000 years ago, probably too early. In between these two approximate dates, the sea receded to some 60 metres less than today about 70,000 years ago and did not regain its present level until the last ice age ended 10,000 years ago.

The archaeological evidence for human presence in Australia remains frustratingly close to the limits of reliable dating. Arrival more than 40,000 years ago is now generally accepted; there are strong arguments for between 50,000 and 60,000 years. Furthermore, a mounting body of evidence suggests a rapid occupation of Australia, with human habitation extending from the lush tropics of the north to the icy rigours of the south, the rich coastal waterlands and the harsh interior. Whenever the first footprint fell on Australian soil, it marked a new achievement by *Homo sapiens* – maritime migration out of the African-European-Asian landmass into a new land.

The truth is, of course, that my own people, the Riratjungi, are descended from the great Djankawa who came from the island of Baralku, far across the sea. Our spirits return to Baralku when we die. Djankawa came in his canoe with his two sisters, following the morning star which guided them to the shores of Yelangbara on the eastern coast of Arnhem Land. They walked far across the country following the rain clouds. When they wanted water they plunged their digging stick into the ground and fresh water followed. From them we learnt the names of all the creatures on the land and they taught us all our Law.

The Djankawa story told by Wandjuk Marika is only one of many Aboriginal stories. Others tell of different origins, of ancestors coming from the land or from the sky, and of the mutability of humans with other life forms. This story is of origins that begin with a journey, of the signs that led the ancestors to their destination, and of the bounty of the land that sustained them.

Such creation stories are to be found for other peoples, as with the books of Genesis and Exodus in the Old Testament, but they bear lightly on the consciousness of those who still read them. Ancestral events, as recorded in stories, songs and rituals, have a marked significance in Aboriginal lives, for they express a particularly close relationship to the land. The events that occurred during the Dreamtime or the Dreaming – both English terms are used as inexact translations of that used by the Arrernte people of Central Australia: *altyerre* – created the hills and creeks, plants and animals, and imprinted their spirit on the place.

The preservation and practice of this knowledge thus affirms the custodianship of the land. Here is how a Northern Territory man, Paddy Japaljarri Stewart, explains its importance:

My father's grandfather taught me the first, and after a while my father taught me the same way as his father told jukurrpa [Dreaming], and then my father is telling the same story about what his father told him, and now he's teaching me how to live on the same kind of jukurrpa and follow the way what my grandfather did, and then teach what my father did, and then I'm going to teach my grandchildren the same way as my father taught me.

When my father was alive this is what he taught me. He had taught me traditional ways like traditional designs in body or head of kangaroo Dreaming (that's what we call marlu Dreaming) and eagle Dreaming. He taught me how to sing song for the big ceremonies. People who are related to us in a close family, they have to have the same sort of jukurrpa Dreaming, and to sing songs in the same way as we do our actions like dancing, and paintings on our body or shields or things, and this is what my father taught me. My Dreaming is the kangaroo Dreaming, the eagle Dreaming and budgerigar Dreaming, so I have three kinds of Dreaming in my jukurrpa and I have to hang onto it. This is what my father taught me, and this is what I have to teach my sons, and my son has to teach his sons the same way as my father taught me, and that's way it will go on from grandparents to sons, and follow that jukurrpa. No-one knows when it will end.

Paddy Japaljarri Stewart recorded this testimony, by tape-recorder, in his own language in 1991. He evokes the continuity of Dreaming from grandfather and father to son and grandson, down the generations and across the passage of time; yet the insistence on the obligation to preserve and transmit his three jukurrpas attests to the corrosive possibilities of secular change. He goes on to aver that the maintenance of the Dreaming has to be 'really strict', so that his family will not 'lose it like a paper, or throw it away or give it away to other families'. The overlay of new technology on customary knowledge heightens the contrast between a binding tradition and a fragile, disposable past. The history that is recorded on tape or paper, like other documents such as land titles, can be lost or surrendered to others. The history that is lived and renewed within the ties of the family remains your own.

The Aboriginal people who occupied Sahul encountered radically different conditions from those they left in Sunda. The absence of predators, for there were few carnivorous competitors here, gave them an enormous initial advantage. They spread over an extraordinary range of ecologies – tropical northern forests, Tasmanian glaciated highlands, the dry interior – and had to adjust to major climatic changes. The last cold, dry period that began 30,000 years ago reduced temperatures to 6 degrees centigrade lower than today; at its most extreme, some 20,000 years ago, rainfall was halved, reducing vegetation and creating sand dunes in the arid interior. There is archaeological evidence that some areas had to be abandoned and new techniques were required in others. The subsequent rising of the seas allowed greater use of marine resources.

Over hundreds of generations the people of this land adapted to these different, changing environments, and in turn they learned how to manipulate them to augment the food supply. As hunter-gatherers, they lived off the land with a precise and intimate knowledge of its resources and seasonal patterns. They organised socially in extended families, with specific rights and specific responsibilities for specific country, and rules to regulate their interaction with others.

Hunter-gatherer is both a technical term and something more. It refers to a mode of material life; it signifies a stage in human history. Fifty thousand years ago, when Australia was populated by hunter-gatherers, every human society in every part of the world hunted and foraged. Subsequently, the domestication of animals and sowing of crops replaced hunting and gathering in Europe, much of Asia, Africa, and the Americas. Agriculture enabled greater productivity, sustained higher population densities, gave rise to towns and the amenities of urban life. As it became possible to produce more than a subsistence, wealth could be accumulated and support a division of labour. Such specialisation fostered technological improvement, commerce and industry; it supported armies, rulers and bureaucrats who could control large political units.

When British and other European investigators first encountered the Australian Aborigines, they fitted them into a ladder of human progress on which the hunter-gatherer society occupied the lowest rung. The nineteenth-century historian James Bonwick, who wrote extensively of Aboriginal history, emphasised the Arcadian virtue of their way of life but always assumed that they were doomed to yield to European ways. For him, as for most of his contemporaries, the Indigenous people represented a primitive antiquity that lacked the capacity to change: as he put it, 'they knew no past, they wanted no future'.

More recent interpretations suggest otherwise. Prehistorians (though the persistence of this term indicates that the new sensibility is incomplete) are struck by the remarkable longevity and adaptability of hunter-gatherer societies. Demographers suggest that they maintained a highly successful equilibrium of population and resources. Economists have found that they produced surpluses, traded, made technological advances, all with far less effort than agriculturalists. Linguists are struck by the diversity and sophistication of their languages. Anthropologists discern complex religions that guided such people's lives and movements, encoded ecological wisdom, assured genetic variety and maintained social cohesion. With their egalitarian social and political structure, far-flung trading networks and above all their rich spiritual and cultural life, the celebrated French anthropologist Claude Lévi-Strauss described the Australian Aborigines as 'intellectual aristocrats'.

These reappraisals overturn the rigid hierarchy of historical progress through sequential stages, from primitive to modern, and enable us to appreciate the sophistication of a civilisation of greater longevity than any other in world history. Yet there remains the challenge to explain the apparent incapacity of the Aboriginal Australians to withstand the invasion of 1788. For all its advantages, and its capacity to meet challenges over more than forty millennia, the Indigenous population could not maintain sovereignty when confronted by British settlers. It was by no means alone in this incapacity, of course: other hunter-gatherer societies, as well as agricultural ones and even those with more extensive commercial institutions, succumbed to European conquest in the seventeenth, eighteenth and nineteenth centuries. The Australian experience points up the particular vulnerability of an isolated civilisation to external aggression.

The Aborigines were not wholly cut off from external contact. The native dog, the dingo, reached Australia some 4000 years ago; it was the first and only domesticated animal. Traders from South-East Asia were visiting the northern coast before European settlement, bringing pottery, cloth and metal tools, taking back the sea slug or trepang. Such external influences were far less significant, however, than internal processes of change wrought by the Aborigines themselves. Their arrival had almost certainly hastened the extinction of earlier megafauna. Their use of fire to burn off undergrowth and encourage new pasture for the remaining marsupials, as well as their systematic harvesting of staple plants, had altered the landscape. Their technological innovation accelerated with the development of new tools, the digging stick and the spatula, fishing net and canoe, boomerang and woomera, net and spear, hafted axe and specialised stone implements. The construction of weirs and channels to trap eels supported populations of several hundred in semi-permanent housing.

The way of life held the population at a level determined by the food that was available at the times of greatest scarcity, but it was far from a constant struggle for subsistence. The hunting of game, fishing, snaring, and harvesting of foodstuffs were part of an elaborate system of environmental management, and this essential activity was undertaken along with other activities to provide shelter

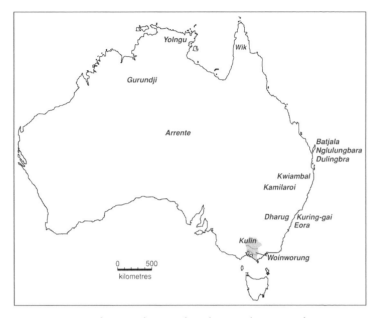

Map 1.3   Aboriginal Australia, showing location of groups mentioned in this history. (D. R. Horton (ed.), *The Encyclopedia of Aboriginal Australia*, Canberra: Australian Institute of Aboriginal and Torres Strait Islander Studies and Auslig, 1994). The editor warns that 'this map indicates only the general location of larger groupings of people which may include smaller groups such as clans, dialects or individual languages in a group. Boundaries are not intended to be exact. For more information about the groups of people in a particular region contact the relevant land councils. This map is not suitable for use in native title and other land claims.'

and clothing, renew equipment, conduct trade and communication, maintain law and order, and practise ceremony and ritual. The Aboriginal way of life is seen as affording a large amount of leisure time for cultural and artistic pursuits, but such a distinction between work and leisure separates domains of life that were conjoined. Equally, artistic expression entered into the most central forms of material practice, and Aboriginal religion encompassed all aspects of life. It is this organic character of belief and social practice that attracts so many present-day admirers of a Dreamtime wisdom:

a cosmology that prescribed the necessary knowledge of a people and saturated their every action with spiritual significance.

Did the deep respect for tradition stifle more radical transformations that might have allowed the Aboriginal people to resist the invasion of 1788? The passage of time and temporal change, so central in Western thought, do not have that status in Aboriginal ontology. If the land is primary and place immutable, then history cannot have the same determinate role. For the Europeans who took possession of the land, history exercised a powerful forward momentum of constant change and improvement. For the Aboriginals, the pattern of events was rhythmical as well as linear. The Dreamtime was not a time but a set of abiding events. In a society made up of small groups whose members set their feet carefully in the footsteps of those who had gone before, change could only be incremental.

It would certainly appear that their economy and forms of organisation set limits on the capacity to concentrate resources or mount a concerted resistance. The basic unit was the extended family, linked by intermarriage, belief and language into larger territorial groups. Europeans described such groups as tribes, but that term has now fallen into disfavour and the preferred designation is people – thus the Eora people of present-day Sydney, or the Wajuk people of present-day Perth. These peoples in turn interacted with neighbouring peoples through trade, alliance and antagonism: there were some 250 distinct language groups but most Aboriginals would have been multilingual. They came together in enlarged numbers from time to time for ceremonial occasions that were constrained in size and duration by the availability of food. Crops and herds would have relaxed those constraints and allowed greater density of settlement, larger concentrations of wealth and power, but Aboriginals did not domesticate animals, apart from the dingo, and they did not practise agriculture.

The failure to do so was not for want of precedent. The movement of humans into Sahul occurred when Australia was continuous with New Guinea, and the two countries were still joined by a neck of land near Cape York up to 8000 years ago. By that time pigs were kept and gardens cleared to grow taro in the Highlands of New Guinea. The Aboriginals of the Cape York region continued to hunt for their meat and gather their plant food. The preference – it can only have been a choice between alternatives since the Cape York Aboriginals possessed such New Guinean items as drums, bamboo pipes, and outrigger canoes – might be explained by differences of soil and regional climate.

For the rest of Australia, the environment probably made the necessary investment in agricultural production and storage uneconomic. The periodic lack of rainfall made dependence on crops too risky. The Aboriginals were mobile fire-stick farmers rather than sedentary slash-and-burn agriculturalists; they tended their plants as they visited them, fed their animals on open grassland rather than by hand, and killed their meat on the range instead of in the pen. They tracked the erratic sources of their livelihood with simplified rather than elaborate shelters, and a portable tool-kit that met their needs. This was an ingenious and closely calibrated response to a unique environmental challenge.

2

Newcomers, c. 1600–1792

The stories of the Dreaming tell of beginnings that are both specific and general. They narrate particular events that occurred in particular places, but those events are not fixed chronologically since they span the past and the present to carry an enduring meaning. By contrast, the story of the second settlement is known in minute particularity. It began with a voyage of eleven vessels that embarked with 582 male prisoners, 193 females and fourteen children, the first of 681 ships that made 1024 journeys and transported 163,000 convicts over the following eighty years.

The First Fleet left the English naval town of Portsmouth on 13 May 1787 and sailed, via Tenerife, Rio de Janeiro and Cape Town, on a marathon voyage that brought the exiles to the north shore of Botany Bay on 18 January 1788. They landed 12 kilometres to the north in a cove of Port Jackson eight days later. On a space cleared in the wooded slope that is now central Sydney, the British flag was hoisted as the commander, Captain Arthur Phillip, took formal possession of the new colony.

We have his account of the voyage and settlement, as well as other published accounts, and the official instructions, dispatches, logs, journals, diaries and letters of those who accompanied him. We know the names of every person, their status and duties, the stores they brought with them and the livestock, plants and seeds – even the books – that they brought ashore to establish the colony. We can plot the actions of the colonists with an amplitude of detail beyond almost all other similar ventures, for this was a late episode in

European expansion and the most powerful of all the European states brought an accumulated organisational capacity to it. Furthermore, the settlement at New South Wales was the bridgehead for British occupation of the whole of Australia, the landing at Sydney Cove the formative moment of a new nation that would afterwards re-enact its origins in the celebration of 26 January as Australia Day.

Yet in the marking of the anniversary, as well as the unending stream of writing on the foundation of European Australia, there is constant disputation. On the centenary of British settlement in 1888, radical nationalists attacked the official celebrations for sanitising the past of the convicts who made up the majority of Phillip's party. Fifty years later Aboriginal critics boycotted the re-enactment of the landing and declared 26 January a Day of Protest and Mourning. During the bicentenary in 1988 the official organisers arranged a passage up Sydney Harbour of ships from around the world in preference to the unofficial flotilla that retraced the voyage from Portsmouth, but this did not placate the Aboriginal protesters who flung a copy of a new bicentennial history into the waters of Sydney Cove.

As with public ritual, so with the scholarly interpretation of British settlement: its initiation, purpose, efficacy and consequences are all debated vigorously. Was it part of a larger imperial design or an improvisation? Was Australia meant to be a dumping-ground for convicts or a strategic and mercantile base? Did it begin with an 'indescribable hopelessness and confusion', as the country's most eminent historian put it, or was it a place of order and redemption? Was it an invasion or peaceful occupation, despoliation or improvement, a place of exile or hope, estrangement or attachment? The accumulation of research brings more exact knowledge of the formative events, while the passage of time weakens our connection with them and allows a multiplicity of meaning to be found. With the end of the age of European empire and revival of the Indigenous presence, the story of the second settlement of Australia is no clearer than the first.

***

The expansion of Europe began with internal conquest. From early in the second millennium of the Christian era warriors were subduing barbarian and infidel peoples in the border regions, creating new settlements and rehearsing the methods that allowed movement north into the Baltic, east over the Urals, west into the Atlantic and south down the African coast and across to East Asia. These excursions gathered pace from the fifteenth century onwards but initially involved only limited numbers. Acquisition by trade and conquest was the object, and European adventurers absorbed the knowledge (compass and gunpowder), techniques (crossbow and printing press) and products (potato and tomato) of other civilisations.

In Asia, where the Europeans encountered literate societies with highly developed economies, they established garrisons and trading depots for the acquisition of spices, coffee, tea and textiles. In the Americas they reaped windfall gains of precious bullion, and in the Caribbean they worked sugar and tobacco plantations with slave labour shipped from Africa. Only in North America and the temperate regions of South America did they settle in significant numbers: as late as 1800 just 4 per cent of European people lived abroad.

There were non-European empires, those of the Manchus in China, the Moghuls in India, the Ottomans and Safavids, Aztecs and Incas, but none of them withstood the growth of European power. They were built on large, contiguous territories with a coherent unity; the European ones were far-flung networks thrown across oceans, more mobile and enterprising. Spain, Portugal, Holland, France and Britain – the principal maritime states on the Atlantic fringe of the European peninsula – jostled and competed with each other, spurring further growth and innovation. Yet the same rivalry imposed a growing cost. Britain and France, which emerged during the eighteenth century as the two leading European powers, taxed their strength as they fought repeatedly on sea and land. From the Seven Years War (1756–63) Britain emerged victorious with control of North America and India. In the following round of hostilities, France took several of the West Indian islands and Britain lost most of North America to its own colonists in the War of American Independence (1774–83). By then France was on the verge of revolution and Britain strained under the remorseless demands for revenue and lives needed to sustain its garrison state.

The British loss of its American colonies at the end of the eighteenth century signalled a new phase of empire. Britain turned of necessity away from the Atlantic to the East, and settlement of Australia was part of its expansion in Asia and the Pacific. The same reverse also encouraged a reconsideration of how the empire should be conducted. After the conclusion of the Napoleonic Wars in 1815, there was a shift from the expensive military effort needed to protect trade monopolies, with its accompanying burden of domestic taxation, towards self-sustaining economic development and free trade. The transition was less marked in India, where the cost of expanding the empire was transferred from the British taxpayer to the local peasant, than in settler colonies such as Canada, Australia, New Zealand and South Africa.

These colonies of settlement, like the former British colonies in the United States and the Iberian colonies in Argentina and Uruguay, mark out a distinctive zone of European expansion. There was little effort in them to maintain the existing order, to enter into commercial relations with their inhabitants or recruit them as labour – and in the Australian instance the Aborigines seemed to possess no items to trade or interest in working for payment. Instead, these lands were cleared and settled as fresh fields of European endeavour. Their temperate climates were sufficiently similar to support European livestock, pasture and crops; their local biota were less diverse and less resistant to the weeds and pests the Europeans brought with them; their Indigenous inhabitants were decimated by imported diseases. Before the nineteenth century the settler colonies played a minor economic role in the European imperial system; thereafter, as large-scale industrialisation created a mass market for the primary products of their virgin soil, they became the wealthiest and most rapidly growing regions outside Europe.

An account of the colonial settlement of Australia that relies on the logic of economic and ecological imperialism leaves too much unexplained. A smallpox epidemic (probably introduced by trepang fishermen in the north) might well have carried off half the Aboriginal population in the late 1780s, but the implication that the Australian Aborigines simply disappeared with the advent of European pathogens is as unpersuasive as the suggestion that the Maori provided no effective resistance to the Pakeha in New

Zealand. It required a substantial European effort to subdue the Indigenous peoples of the regions of settlement, and no less an effort to justify their expropriation. Notions of providence and destiny dignified conquest and dispossession.

The British came to the Pacific with their sense of superiority as the inheritors of Western civility and bearers of Christian revelation enhanced by the further advantages of scientific knowledge, industrial progress and liberty. The last of these might seem an unlikely claim for a colony that began with convicts, but was no less influential for that. A Briton's freedom was based on obedience to the Crown under a system of constitutional government that safeguarded the subject's rights. The example of the American colonies and the republican doctrines proclaimed there as well as in France served as a salutary reminder of the consequences of violating such rights.

The settler societies spawned by Europe were thus extensions and new beginnings. They applied and adapted technologies with prodigious results, cultivated principles as well as plants, and sent them back to where they had come from with enhanced potency. Yet even in the United States, and the former Spanish and Portuguese colonies of Central and South America that threw off their tutelage to forge the distinctive features of the democratic nation-state, the settler-citizens remained tied to their origins. The new republics defined themselves as white brotherhoods. However much they emphasised their difference from their metropolitan cousins, whatever their conscious and unconscious adaptation to local ways, they remained estranged from the Indigenous peoples. The nation that arose on the grasslands of Australia, like those on the North American plain and the Argentine pampas, was a creole society insistent on its place in the European diaspora.

***

The British were laggards in the Pacific. The Spanish, Portuguese and Dutch preceded them into the archipelago that extends down its western fringe. Spain alone held the eastern extremity from the Strait of Magellan up to California. Between these two sides of the Pacific basin stretched 15,000 kilometres of water dotted with thousands of volcanic or coral islands, few of sufficient size or wealth to attract

European attention. They had already been navigated and settled in a series of movements that began with the human occupation of Sahul 50,000 years earlier and culminated at the beginning of the last millennium with the occupation of Easter Island in the east and New Zealand in the south.

These people of the sea practised agriculture, kept domestic animals and sustained a mosaic of polities. In 1567 the Spanish dispatched an expedition in search of gold to the Solomon Islands, but that ended in massacre and counter-massacre. In 1595 and 1605 they repeated the venture in the Solomons and Vanuatu – which Pedro de Quiros named La Australia del Espiritu Santo – with the same result. In 1606 his colleague Torres sailed west through the strait that separates Australia from New Guinea. Meanwhile the Portuguese had pushed south from India as far as Timor, and possibly to the Australian coast. After them came the Dutch, who in the seventeenth century established a trading empire in the East Indies.

The route from Holland to Batavia took the Dutch ships round the Cape of Good Hope and then east with the prevailing winds across the Indian Ocean before they turned north for Java. Given the difficulty of establishing longitude, many of their vessels encountered the western coast of Australia, sometimes with fatal consequences – the location, study and retrieval of the contents of Dutch wrecks makes Western Australia a centre of marine archaeology. By the middle of the seventeenth century the Dutch had mapped the western half of Australia, which they called New Holland, and traced some fragments of coast further east. In 1606 Willem Janszoon sailed east through the Torres Strait and unwittingly along the northeast corner of Australia. In 1642 Abel Tasman led an expedition that charted the southern part of the island now named after him, and the east side of New Zealand.

Whether these shores were part of a single land mass remained unclear. It was apparent only that the great south land was separate from the Antarctic, and that it straddled the Indian and Pacific oceans. This location continues to create uncertainty. Since 1788 the great mass of the Australian population has always lived on the eastern seaboard, facing the Pacific, and its islands have drawn them as traders and missionaries, administrators and adventurers.

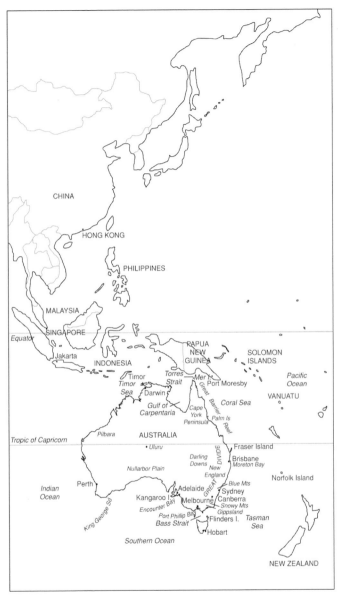

Map 2.1   Australia and the region

Australians commonly regard themselves, along with the New Zealanders, as part of Oceania, and they have liked to think they enjoy a special relation with the most powerful of all English-speaking countries on the other side of that ocean; hence they have embraced its formulation of the Pacific Rim. Yet for those who live in Western Australia, Indonesia is the nearest neighbour; the historical links with India, South Africa and even Mauritius more significant. As the balance of regional power has shifted, so Australians increasingly claim they are part of Asia and regard their earlier presence in the Pacific as a romantic interlude in tropical islands far removed from the business centres to the north.

The difference is not simply one of economic opportunity. The Pacific signifies peace, a far-flung constellation of island people living in harmony with nature, where the colonial imagination could find a soft primitivism of noble savages predisposed to friendship and hospitality. Asia, on the other hand, presented a dense tangle of peoples with polities, cultures and traditions even more deeply embedded than those of Europe. As the late-developing nation-states on the Atlantic seaboard imposed control over the older civilisations of the Eurasian continent, they hardened a distinction between the West and the East. The lands to the east of the Mediterranean became known as the Orient, the place from where the sun rose. The Orient came to stand for a whole way of life that was inferior to that of the West and yet disturbingly threatening: indolent, irrational, despotic and decayed.

Such typification of the alien other, which the critic Edward Said characterised as Orientalism, had a peculiar meaning in colonial Australia where geography contradicted history. Fascination and fear mingled in the colonists' apprehension of the zone that lay between them and the metropole. As a British dependency, Australia adopted the terminology that referred to the Near, Middle and Far East until, under threat of Japanese invasion in 1940, its prime minister suddenly recognised that 'What Great Britain calls the Far East is to us the near north.' When that threat materialised and his successor warned that 'the enemy is at our doors', he followed the United States in calling it a Pacific War.

For early European navigators, Australia was Terra Australis Incognita, the south land beyond the limits of the known world.

It was a place of mythical beasts and fabulous wealth in the imagination of those who had long anticipated it, a blank space where their fantasies could run free. Early mapmakers inscribed an indeterminate continent and decorated it with lush vegetation and barbarous splendour. Yet just as the Spanish expedition to the Solomons found 'no specimens of spices, nor of gold and silver, nor of merchandise, nor of any other source of profit, and all the people were naked savages', so Tasman reported 'nothing profitable' in the island he named Van Diemen's Land (which is now Tasmania), 'only poor, naked people walking along beaches; without rice or many fruits, very poor and bad-tempered'. Once its commercial prospects were discounted, the great south land served merely as a place of invention. In *Gulliver's Travels* (1726) Jonathan Swift located his imaginary Lilliput in South Australia, and in a final chapter he satirised the conventional account of New World settlement:

A crew of pirates are driven by a storm they know not whither; at length a boy discovers land from the topmast, they go on shore to rob and plunder; they see an harmless people, are entertained with kindness, they give the country a new name, they take formal possession of it for the King, they set up a rotten plank or a stone for a memorial, they murder two or three dozen of the natives, they bring away a couple more by force for a sample, return home, and get their pardon. Hence commences a new dominion acquired with a title by *divine right*.

It was an eerily accurate prediction of the foundation of New South Wales.

French and British interest in the Pacific revived from the middle of the eighteenth century with a renewed sense of the region's possibilities. The two countries sent a series of ships whose names – *Le Géographe, Le Naturaliste, Endeavour, Discovery, Investigator* – suggest their purpose. The ships were floating laboratories, dispatched by the respective governments in conjunction with the savants of the French Academy and the scientists of the Royal Society. They tested new navigational aids and advanced cartography to new standards. They carried naturalists, botanists, zoologists, astronomers and ethnographers; they measured, described, collected and classified flora and fauna, searching always for plants that might be propagated and utilised. They sought out the islanders

2.1 A sketch of Aborigines in canoes made in 1770, possibly by Joseph Banks. His use of art as an aid to scientific knowledge is suggested by the careful attention to boat construction and the method of spearing fish. (© The British Library Board, Add. 15508, f.10)

2.2 An idealised portrait painted by Augustus Earle and entitled *A Woman of New South Wales*. The classical beauty of the form and features contrasts with the derogatory caricature of Aborigines exposed to European vice by the same artist, which appears in the following chapter. (Augustus Earle, National Library of Australia, an2818359)

and endeavoured to learn their ways. These were men of reason hungry for knowledge rather than bullion.

The most celebrated of them is James Cook, a merchant seaman who joined the Royal Navy and led three expeditions to the Pacific. On the first (1768–71) he sailed to Tahiti to observe the transit of the planet Venus across the sun, then headed west to make a detailed

2.3 Cook is borne aloft as the hero-victim of European discovery in the Pacific, with Universal Fame on one side and Britannia on the other. (Collection of Mr G. Baker. London. Ref: B-085-007. Alexander Turnbull Library, Wellington, New Zealand)

circumnavigation of the two islands of New Zealand and trace the east coast of Australia into the Torres Strait. With only one ship, a converted collier renamed the *Endeavour*, and at just 30 metres in length, he charted more than 8000 kilometres of coastline and established the limits of the Australian island continent. On the second voyage (1772–74) he went further south into the Antarctic seas than anyone before him and tested a new chronometer to fix longitude at sea by lunar tables. On the third (1777–79) he was killed by islanders of Hawaii. Cook became a model for a subsequent generation of maritime explorers. He was a hero for his time – a practical visionary, resourceful and courageous, a man who restrained his hot temper, eschewed conjecture for accurate observation, fused curiosity and moral certainty – and for some time after he was hailed as the founder as well as the discoverer of Australia. A posthumous engraving shows him ascending to the clouds after his death with a sextant in his hand.

He had with him on the first voyage Joseph Banks, a young gentleman-scientist who would become unofficial director of Kew Gardens and make it the central collecting and distributing point in a botanical imperium, as well as the president of the Royal Society, member of the Privy Council and patron of the colony of New South Wales. There was also Daniel Solander, a pupil of the Swedish botanist Linnaeus, whose system of classification provided a framework for interpreting the hundreds of specimens gathered during the voyage. Cook's instructions were that after observing the transit of Venus he was to sail south from Tahiti, where 'there is reason to imagine that a Continent or Land of great extent may be found'; should it not be found he was to proceed west and navigate New Zealand. He did both those things, the first fruitlessly, the second superlatively, and then decided to continue west.

On 19 April 1770 the *Endeavour* sighted land at the entrance of Bass Strait on the south-east corner of the Australian mainland. As the ship coasted northwards, the country struck Banks as bare as a 'lean cow' with 'scraggy hip bones' poking through the rough timber covering. On 28 April the *Endeavour* entered a large bay fringed, according to Cook, by 'as fine meadow as ever was seen', and Banks and Solander were kept busy for a week collecting plant, bird and animal species hitherto unknown to European science. Initially they named it Sting Ray's Harbour, having caught several large stingrays during their stay, but soon decided it should be Botany Bay because of the large number of plants Banks and Solander collected there. For a further four months the company travelled north, surviving accident in the Great Barrier Reef, and marked their repeated landfalls with inscriptions cut on trees. Finally, at Possession Island off the northernmost tip of Cape York, Cook hoisted the flag, fired three volleys and laid claim to the entire eastern coast under the name of New South Wales.

The idea that Cook discovered Australia strikes many today as false as the British claim to sovereignty over it. How can you find something that is already known? His voyage to New Zealand was preceded by that of Polynesian mariners some thousand years earlier; his Australian landfall came 50,000 years after the original human presence there. Cook's description of the Aborigines, frequently quoted, attests to the European Enlightenment apprehension of the noble savage:

From what I have said of the Natives of New Holland, they may appear to some to be the most wretched people upon Earth, but in reality they are far more happier than we Europeans; being wholy unacquainted not only with the superfluous but the necessary Conveniences so much sought after in Europe, they are happy in not knowing the use of them. They live in a Tranquillity which is not disturb'd by the Inequality of Condition; the Earth and sea of their own accord furnishes them with all things necessary for life.

Those Aboriginals whom Cook encountered certainly seemed uninterested in European conveniences. The Admiralty had instructed him to 'cultivate a friendship and alliance' with the local inhabitants. This was standard practice and signified the right of the newcomers to travel and trade; it was a form of title directed at rival European powers and made no claim for title against the Indigenous owners. But the Aboriginals spurned the trinkets he offered, resisted his overtures and fired the bush where he landed: 'all they seem'd to want is for us to be gone'. Cook's presence in the Pacific as an explorer and an appropriator, his endeavour to transcend cultural difference with a mix of conciliation and force, ended with his death on a Hawaiian beach. He figures in international debates among anthropologists in a postcolonial age as a crucial test case of the limits of one culture to comprehend another. In white Australian histories Cook is a fading hero, in Aboriginal oral narratives he is a powerful and disruptive intruder. He did not so much discover Australia as make it accessible to European travel, available for British settlement.

***

The decision to settle was taken by the British government fifteen years after Cook and Banks returned with their reports of New South Wales. By this time Britain had lost its North American colonies and was no longer able to transport convicts there as it had done for most of the eighteenth century. A plan to establish a new penal colony was prepared. Initially it was to be in Africa, but when no suitable site was found there, Botany Bay was chosen in the 'Heads of a Plan' submitted to the Cabinet by Lord Sydney – the minister for the Home Office who then had responsibility for colonial affairs – and adopted in 1786.

The reasons for this choice are keenly debated. Some would have it that the purpose was to get rid of a dangerous social problem, and the farther away the better. Others contend that Botany Bay had strategic advantages. Situated on the blind side of the Dutch East Indies and equidistant from India and China, it could provide a naval base for British expansion into the Asia-Pacific region. After the loss of Nantucket in the United States, it would allow a resumption of southern whaling. Moreover, they claim, it offered two precious commodities: timber and flax. Both were in keen demand by the navy for masts, sailcloth, ropes and cordage, and Cook's second voyage had reported that both grew in abundance on Norfolk Island, which lay 1700 kilometres east of Botany Bay.

The dispute over the motives for settlement is necessarily difficult to resolve because the official documentary record is so circumstantial. The 'Heads of a Plan' provides support for both parties when it justifies the scheme as 'effectually disposing of convicts, and rendering their transportation reciprocally beneficial to themselves and the State'. The British official who probably prepared the plan coupled the availability of flax and timber with 'the removal of a dreadful Banditti from this country'. Those who argue that Australia was settled as a dumping ground for convicts see in these inauspicious origins the necessity of a new beginning. Those who hold to the geopolitical design seek a more affirmative continuity with imperial foresight.

The new colony was a product of maritime exploration, trade and penology. While the cost of imperial expansion weighed heavily on the British economy, the commercial benefits were shared unevenly. New wealth and new ways of increasing it strained the bonds of social station and mutual obligation, with a corresponding increase in crime. The government, which remained a makeshift combination of property-owning legislators, tiny administrative departments and local magistrates, responded by expanding the criminal code to make even the most minor transgression a capital offence. Between the insufficient deterrent of summary punishment by fine or infliction of pain and the intolerable recourse to wholesale execution, there was the intermediate penalty of extended imprisonment, but the ramshackle system of local prisons could not accommodate the swollen numbers of convicts. Hence the earlier recourse to transportation to the American colonies, where the felons could be put to profitable use by planters and merchants. Those who came before the assizes and were spared the gallows would now provide the basis of a new settlement.

To found a colony with convicts was a more ambitious undertaking. Since there was no one to buy convict labour, the government would have to transport and maintain them, and they were expected to become a self-sufficient community of peasant proprietors. Of the 789 who were selected, the men outnumbered the women by three to one. Since they would have to be controlled, four companies of marines were sent with them. Since there was no government, it would be a military colony, but the rule of law would prevail, courts would be established and customary rights would be maintained. Its governor, Arthur Phillip, was a naval captain, but he held a civil commission.

The First Fleet, consisting of two warships, six transports and three store ships, carried seeds and seedlings, ploughs and harnesses, horses, cattle, sheep, hogs, goats and poultry, and food for two years. An initial inspection of Botany Bay revealed that it was sandy, swampy and unsuitable for settlement; Cook and Banks had seen it in late autumn but Phillip arrived in high summer when the green cover was bleached to reveal its poverty. Immediately to the north, Port Jackson offered a superb harbour, a large stretch of sheltered water opening into smaller coves and surmounted by timbered slopes in a majestic amphitheatre; Sydney Cove had a fresh water supply. Even here, however, the land was poor and the first-sown vegetables quickly withered and died. Axes lost their edge on the gnarled and twisted trunks of the blackbutt and red gum, shovels broke on the sandstone beneath the shallow soil, stock strayed or died or was eaten. The marines refused to supervise the convicts, most of whom did not take up smallholdings but worked on public farms for rations. The women, who were encouraged to take partners, were fortunate if they found a reliable companion. Meanwhile the party that had been dispatched to Norfolk Island found the native flax could not be processed and the pine was hollow.

In October 1788 Phillip sent a ship to the Cape of Good Hope for additional supplies and reduced the ration; it returned in May 1789 with provisions but a large supply ship sent from Britain failed to arrive. The rations were reduced and reduced again, until by April 1790 the weekly distribution consisted of a kilogram of crumbling salt pork, a kilogram of rice alive with weevils, and a kilogram of old flour that the exiles boiled up with local greens. These were the hungry years when men and women fought over food and listless torpor overtook even the most vigorous. The fact that the rations were distributed equally, with no privileges for rank, alleviated resentment. Even so, the colonial surgeon wrote of 'a country and place so forbidding and so hateful as only to merit execration and curses'.

The arrival of the Second Fleet in mid-1790, with fresh supplies – though fully a quarter of its prisoners had died on the voyage and those who survived were incapable of work – and then a third fleet in the following year, eased the crisis. The cultivation of fertile soil at Parramatta on the upper reach of Sydney Harbour guaranteed survival. By the end of 1792, when Phillip returned to England, there were 600 hectares under crop, and thriving vegetable and fruit gardens. There was fish in the harbour, pasture on the Cumberland Plain. Once the newcomers adapted to the scorching summer heat – the temperature reached 44 degrees centigrade in December 1788 – the climate was benign. Bodies and minds attuned to higher latitudes, hard winters and damp, green fecundity were coming to terms with the heady smells of hot, dry scrub and the sparse canopy that filtered a dazzling brightness. The commanding officer of the New South Wales regiment that was sent in 1792 discovered 'to my great astonishment, instead of the rock I expected to see, I find myself surrounded with gardens that flourish and produce fruit of every description'.

Phillip held the colony together through the early years of desolation until kidney stones forced him back to England. He took with him in December 1792: kangaroos, dingoes, plants, specimens, drawings and two Aboriginal men, Bennelong and Yemmerrawannie. His greatest failure was in relations with the Aboriginal people of the region. He had been instructed to 'open an intercourse with the natives, and to conciliate their affections, enjoining all our subjects to live in amity and kindness with them'. He had endeavoured to comply, offering gifts as a token of goodwill and punishing any of his party who molested the inhabitants. Even when he was himself speared, in 1790, he forbade reprisals. Frustrated in his attempts to establish closer relations, he captured several Aboriginal men. The first, Arabanoo, died of the smallpox epidemic that swept the Aboriginal people of the region within a year of the European arrival. Another, Bennelong, escaped but returned to Sydney Cove following Phillip's injury to restore relations. Only when his huntsman, John Macintyre, was speared did the governor resort to indiscriminate vengeance: he ordered troops to bring back six Aboriginal heads.

That military expedition failed and Phillip returned to his fruitless endeavour to keep the peace. Not all encounters were violent. Aborigines helped the newcomers with their fishing, and exchanged their tools or weapons for hatchets, mirrors or clothing. Europeans cared for those Aborigines who sought treatment for smallpox. Such transactions occurred across a gulf of language and perception that was painfully apparent when those on one side seized the possessions or violated the customs of those on the other. The rapid breakdown in relations between the local Eora people and the newcomers continues to perplex. A distinguished Australian historian of the Aztec and Mayan cultures takes an initial meeting in Sydney Harbour when the strangers joined with the local people to dance together as emblematic of a 'springtime of trust', mutual curiosity and goodwill. The principal historian of early Sydney rejoins that the British officers introduced themselves by demonstrating the power of their muskets.

European firearms and European disease gave the invaders a lethal advantage, and the 3000 or so inhabitants of the land around Port Jackson came to shun the huddle of buildings on Sydney Cove as well as the foraging parties that spread out from them. 'Our intercourse with them was neither frequent nor cordial', wrote an officer of the marines. He thought at first that the spearing and clubbing of stragglers was caused by 'a spirit of malignant levity', but subsequent experience led him to 'conclude that the unprovoked outrages committed upon them by unprincipled individuals among us caused the evils we had experienced'. Another perceived that as long as the Aborigines 'entertained the idea of our having dispossessed them of their residences, they must always consider us as enemies'.

In striking contrast to its practice elsewhere, the British government took possession of eastern Australia (and later the rest of the continent) by a simple proclamation of sovereignty. The colonisation of North America had proceeded by means of treaties with the native population, for settlement there began on a small and tentative basis, and for some time relied on co-operation with the powerful Indian nations. Treaties were used to secure friendly relations, delineate boundaries of settlement, facilitate trade and resource exploitation, and establish military alliances against competitors – as the British, the French and the rebellious colonists jostled for control between 1763 and 1774, North American natives were signatories to no fewer than thirty treaties. None of these circumstances applied in Australia, and instead Britain relied on a legal doctrine that allowed the firstcomer to claim a vacant territory. This doctrine would become known as *terra nullius*, land belonging to nobody, and its operation would distinguish Australia from other settler societies.

We see its origins in the instructions given to Cook when he sailed in 1768 to search for the great south land: 'with the consent of the natives to take possession ... or if you find the country uninhabited take possession for His Majesty by setting up proper marks and inscriptions, as first discoverers and possessors'. From their observations along the east coast in 1770, he and Banks judged that the Aborigines were incapable of negotiating a treaty, and accordingly they hoisted the flag on its northern tip at Possession Island to proclaim dominion.

Fifteen years later, when a parliamentary committee quizzed Banks about the suitability of establishing a colony in New South Wales, he explained that there were 'very few inhabitants' along the coast and that they relied on fishing and hunting. The absence of agriculture led Banks to conjecture that the interior might be 'totally uninhabited'.

Phillip and his officers were therefore surprised by the number of Aborigines around the settlement. They quickly came to appreciate that these people had social organisation, settled localities, customary law and property rights. The whole claim of sovereignty and ownership on the basis of vacancy was manifestly based on a misreading of Australian circumstances, but his instructions did not allow for recognition of prior occupancy. The Aboriginal inhabitants of Australia were deemed to be in a state of nature without government, law or property. Not until the High Court gave its Mabo judgement in 1992 was there a legal recognition that Aborigines had owned and possessed their traditional lands. A similar recognition of prior or continuing sovereignty has yet to occur.

We do not have the direct testimony of those Aborigines who dealt with the first European newcomers, and cannot recapture how they understood their usurpation. We know from contemporary descriptions that Arabanoo, Bennelong and others were horrified by such barbarous excesses as flogging, terrified by demonstrations of musket fire, and amused by European manners and forms of hierarchy. We can only impute how they interpreted the violation of sacred sites, destruction of habitat, the inroads of disease, and their growing realisation that the intruders meant to stay. Their society was characterised by a shared and binding tradition. Familial and communal restraints imposed order, mutuality and continuity. They were confronted by a new presence in which some men wore redcoats and others worked at their command. Behind the newcomers lay a new social order in which the autonomy of the individual prevailed and a form of political organisation based on impersonal regularity. Its freedom of choice and capacity for concerted action brought innovation and augmented capacity. Its self-centredness generated social conflict, criminality and exile. Such an encounter could only be traumatic.

3

Coercion, 1793–1821

A prison situated 20,000 kilometres from the courts that sentenced its inmates was necessarily expensive. Since it was now clear that the cost would not be defrayed by the production of naval supplies, it became all the more important that this distant outpost achieve at least some measure of self-sufficiency. It had already been decided that the colony of New South Wales would be conducted as an open-air prison. To ensure that transportation served as a deterrent, the conditions would have to be punitive. To serve time without hope of eventual freedom was to shackle the human spirit in sullen despair, so to succeed the penal settlement would have to be something more.

Beyond recognition of these exigencies, the British government gave only limited direction to its new territory. In 1789 France was convulsed by a revolution from which emerged a republic that proclaimed the principles of liberty, fraternity and equality as its national ideals and international mission. In 1793 Britain joined a European alliance to put down this revolutionary threat. After a temporary peace in 1802 the former republican general, Napoleon Bonaparte, now Emperor, vanquished all his continental opponents and Britain was left as the sole obstacle to French supremacy. Until the final defeat of Napoleon at Waterloo in 1815, the war on sea and land strained British capacity to the utmost.

With the pressing demand for manpower, the number of transported convicts fell: after 4500 in the first four years, fewer than 2000 followed from 1793–1800, and barely 4000 in the succeeding decade. John Hunter, a naval captain who had served in the First Fleet and preceded Phillip back to England, did not return to succeed him as governor until late in 1795, leaving military officers to administer the colony. Hunter was succeeded in 1800 by Philip Gidley King, another naval man who had previously been lieutenant-governor of Norfolk Island, and King in 1806 by William Bligh, who had served under Cook.

As these appointments suggest, the war gave greater strategic significance to British control of the Pacific. After Matthew Flinders encountered a French expedition on the south coast of Australia during his circumnavigation of Australia in 1802, King sent a party from Sydney to occupy Van Diemen's Land (the name given to Tasmania by its Dutch navigator). Another fleet of marines and convicts sailed from London to settle Port Phillip Bay on the southeast corner of the mainland in 1803; finding the site unsuitable, it withdrew to Van Diemen's Land and joined the earlier party at Hobart on the Derwent estuary. Yet another contingent founded an additional base at Launceston on the Tamar estuary to the north of the island in 1804. In the same year King re-established a penal settlement at Newcastle, at the mouth of the Hunter River, 100 kilometres north of Sydney.

The early years in Van Diemen's Land were similar to those on the mainland. The newcomers came ashore, secured a site, unloaded supplies and established their settlement. The first crops failed and both initial sites proved unsatisfactory, so the one in the south moved downstream to Hobart and that in the north went up the Tamar River to Launceston. The stores ran low, rations were reduced and convicts were already absconding to the bush. The lieutenant-governor, David Collins, had seen it all before at Sydney Cove. He worked as unremittingly as Phillip (whom he had served as secretary) to maintain discipline, but in 1807 he himself was robbed. Yet this island had advantages over the coastal region of New South Wales: an abundance of fresh water and open grasslands that were thick with game. With hunting dogs and firearms, there was a plentiful supply of fresh meat.

This 'kangaroo economy', as a historian of the island's early decades has described it, allowed ex-convicts and convict absconders to live independent and free in the bush, for the most part harmoniously with the Aboriginal people but often preying on the homesteads of wealthy settlers. These bushrangers, as they became known, enjoyed substantial support in their defiance of authority, and the most celebrated Tasmanian bushranger, Michal Howe, posed a genuine threat to the colonial government. Styling himself 'Lieutenant Governor of the Woods', and with as many as a hundred followers, he controlled much of the hinterland before he was killed in 1818. As the same historian remarks, the association of the bush with freedom was a dramatic moment in Australian colonisation, with lasting consequences.

During these years the British exiles huddled close to the ocean. The settlements at Sydney, Hobart and Launceston were all chosen for their maritime location as well as for the promise of their hinterlands. Phillip's glowing description of Sydney Harbour – 'a thousand sail of the line may ride in the most perfect security' – emphasised the importance of this factor. The rapid creation of port facilities as well as the attention given to completing a survey of the Australian coast suggested not an occupation of the Australian continent but rather an investiture of the southwest Pacific with new stations for Britain's expanding presence east of India.

In their early activities the colonists faced outwards and only after turned inwards. As soon as 1792 the newly arrived officers of the New South Wales Corps arranged for a ship to bring trading merchandise from Cape Town; in the same year the first American trading vessel arrived at Sydney. Whales were already hunted in the Pacific for their oil, and vessels chartered for the transportation of convicts searched the southern seas as soon as they dropped their human cargo. Soon seals were being slaughtered in the Bass Strait and their pelts exported to China – sealing and whaling would contribute more to the colonial economy than land produce until the 1830s. Merchants brought pork from Tahiti, potatoes from New Zealand, rum from Bengal. They collected and re-exported sandalwood from Fiji, pearl-shell and trepang from the Melanesian islands. The tang of tar and salt air, the cry of seabirds, preceded the smell of the gumleaf and the magpie's ragged carol.

The officers of the colony had a head start in trade, though they were soon joined by enterprising ex-convicts and ambitious younger men lured from mercantile operations in other parts of the British Empire by fresh opportunity. From 1793 those responsible for the defence and administration of the colony were also eligible for grants of land, and whereas the soldiers as well as the ex-convicts received smallholdings of up to 20 hectares, there was no such limit on their superiors. The military and civil officials were also able to draw on convict labour to work their farms. Finally, they had a ready market in the government commissariat, which bought their agricultural produce for the issue of public rations.

Through their dual role as public officers and private entrepreneurs, a dual economy quickly emerged: a public sector which included the government farm and its convict workers, along with others labouring on construction projects and the provision of services; and a private sector of traders and farmers who benefited from the public largesse. Both sectors were mutually dependent on the British government, for the land it took from Aboriginal owners and gave them, for the labour it provided through transportation of convicts, and for capital injected into the colony by the Crown's expenditure on the commissariat.

The British government's direction of this extraordinary arrangement was episodic and inconsistent. From time to time it instructed the governor to augment the public farm and economise on purchases from private producers; yet governors who were expected by London to reduce outlays were understandably tempted by the opportunity to take their convicts off the rations by assigning them to the very officials on whom they relied for advice on the allocation of labour and land. The effect was to privatise the public sector, an arrangement that usually fosters cronyism and here created a clique of wealthy colleagues. By 1801 John Macarthur, the paymaster of the New South Wales Corps, had accumulated more than 1000 hectares and 1000 sheep.

Macarthur and his wife lived near Parramatta at Elizabeth Farm, named after her, where they grew wheat and kept an orchard. 'It is now spring', she wrote to an English friend in September 1798, 'and the eye is delighted with the most beautiful variegated landscape – almonds, apricots, pear and apple trees are in full bloom'. There were 1500 settlers by 1800 at Parramatta and the lightly timbered surrounding country, which Elizabeth Macarthur likened to an

'English park'. Most of it was better suited to grazing sheep and cattle than growing crops, and the large landowners on the Cumberland Plain quickly gravitated to pastoralism in preference to agriculture.

Cereal production developed along the rich river flats of the Hawkesbury, which flowed north through the Plain and on which a further 1000 colonists had settled by 1800. They were mostly ex-convicts on small blocks, who tilled the soil by hand, grew wheat and maize, perhaps ran poultry or a few pigs, lived in wattle-and-daub huts on earthen floors, and cooked their evening meals in the smoky gloom over a fire beneath a sod and bark chimney. Lacking capital, they were locked into small-scale farming and always vulnerable to the merchants' control of prices and credit. There was a high turnover of such farmers.

The pattern of settlement on the Hawkesbury placed soldiers as well as former convicts on the land. This was a well-established imperial device, used by the Romans and the Chinese long before the British adopted it to maintain security on turbulent frontiers. Raids on Hawkesbury settlers began almost immediately as the Dharuk people sought to harvest the new crops that had been planted in their old yam beds. Conflict over scarce resources quickly escalated into violence, and as early as 1795 a military expedition was sent from Sydney to kill the natives and hang them from gibbets – the earlier injunction to amity and kindness was now but a distant memory. By 1800 the war on the Hawkesbury had inflicted twenty-six British and many more Aboriginal casualties. Meanwhile Pemulwuy, the Eora man who had speared John Macintyre in 1790, mounted a sustained resistance to the colonial invasion, including an attack on Parramatta, until in 1802 he was shot down and his head placed in a barrel of spirits to be sent to Joseph Banks in England.

There was no entry for Pemulwuy in the *Australian Dictionary of Biography* until a supplementary volume appeared in 2005. During the 1960s, when the editors of that authoritative reference work were preparing the original volume in which he would have appeared, the Aborigines were regarded as no more than a minor impediment to the colonial occupation, and appeared at best as a tragic footnote in Australian history. Since then he has been elevated to the status of a hero: a novel celebrating Pemulwuy as the Rainbow Warrior appeared in 1987, an Aboriginal school in inner Sydney was named after him in 1991 and in 2010 Prince William declared he would assist the search for Pemulwuy's skull so that it could repatriated. He now figures as the first great resistance leader who sought to repel the British invasion, inaugurating a continuous struggle for Aboriginal survival.

Resistance to the incursion was undoubtedly common, but it was not the only response. Aborigines also imparted their knowledge of the land; they exchanged food and materials for British goods, and they adapted to the presence of the newcomer on the pastoral frontier. But a more sustained economic relationship would have required them to abandon their own way of life and the invader to accept their property rights over resources or to incorporate them into the labour process. Neither side was prepared to make such an accommodation.

One recurrent cause of conflict was sexual relations. From the beginning there was a gross imbalance in the proportion of male and female settlers: roughly four to one until after 1820. The promoters of the new colony had perceived this disparity as a cause of disorder, and instructed Phillip that his men might take women of the Pacific Islands as partners. During the voyage of the First Fleet, Phillip and the officers had great difficulty in separating the female convicts from the men and his encouragement on arrival of partnerships was meant to foster the civilising influence of the family. The governor also had a particular fear of male homosexuality and believed that sodomy should be punished with the utmost severity: 'I would wish to confine the criminal till an opportunity offered of delivering him to the natives of New Zealand, and let them eat him.' Since these schemes of Pacific concubinage and punishment were stillborn, the problem of lust and promiscuity weighed heavily on those responsible for the penal colony.

Phillip also thought that in time the Aboriginal men might 'permit their women to marry and live' with the convicts. As soon as the coloniser's eye turned to Aboriginal women, it perceived them as chattels. The officers' accounts of first encounters round Sydney were framed in the genteel language of civilised men confronted by women living in a state of nature, 'wood nymphs' and 'sooty sirens'

3.1 An early sketch of Aboriginal warriors was made by a draftsman on Cook's 1770 expedition. The two Gwiyagal men appear as classical heroes, resolutely defiant of the intruder. (Sydney Parkinson, National Library of Australia, an9196443)

innocent in their naked immodesty. The carefully composed writings of these educated Englishmen stressed the complete subordination of native women to their male companions, and recoiled in moral disapproval from incidents when Aboriginal men offered women to them. Sexual exchange between soldiers, convicts and Aboriginal women was common: the spread of venereal disease marked its occurrence. Yet lasting relationships were infrequent

and misunderstandings of the nature of the transaction typically a
cause of friction. Desire and affection were too often outweighed by
shame and contempt for intermarriage to form a junction between
the two peoples.

***

By the turn of the century the rudiments of a permanent presence
were evident. The 5000 British residents of New South Wales
were divided equally between Sydney and the hinterland (with a
further thousand on Norfolk Island), indicating the balance of
mercantile and agricultural activity. The colony was approaching
self-sufficiency in food, and the rapid growth of local enterprise
supported a standard of living at least comparable with that of the
parent country. This successful transplantation, achieved far more
quickly than earlier colonial foundations in North America, was
already straining the penal principles that had governed its
foundation.

In keeping with its purpose as a place of exile, Phillip had prohibited the building of all but the smallest boats, yet by 1800 there
was a busy shipyard on the western side of Sydney Cove. It had been
established as a place of punishment that would deter crime, but its
very success seemed to reward the wrongdoer: hence the jibe of the
English clergyman Sydney Smith that 'the ancient avocation of
picking pockets will certainly not become more discredited from
the knowledge that it may eventually lead to the possession of a
farm of a thousand acres on the River Hawkesbury'.

Moreover, the conditions that governed the convicts' lives apparently confirmed them in their incorrigibility. Samuel Marsden, the
censorious colonial chaplain, complained to Governor Hunter in
1798 that 'riot and dissipation, licentiousness and immorality ...
pervaded every part of this settlement'; Hunter himself reported that
'a more wicked, abandoned and irreligious set of people have never
been brought together in any part of the world'. For Jeremy
Bentham, the penal reformer who was pressing the British government to adopt his scheme of building a new kind of prison there, one
designed so that the inmates could be brought to penitence by
constant supervision, the scheme of transportation was deficient in
both economy and moral effectiveness.

All these judgements were informed by values and assumptions that entered into every observation about the convicts and which still pervade the arguments of even the most insistently objective historians. Those sympathetic to the convicts draw heavily on popular ballads and broadsides as well as the protests of contemporary humanitarians to present them as victims of a harsh penal code and brutal regimen; in his vast panoramic evocation of *The Fatal Shore* (1987) Robert Hughes portrays early Australia as a place of banishment, exile, privation and death – as a gulag. Those cliometricians who seek to establish the character of the convicts from penal records find them to be criminals. The economic historians who are more interested in the convicts as a workforce reconfigure the same records and find the same people to possess skills that they put to good use. Feminist historians of the 1970s took the masculine preoccupation with the immorality of the female convicts as indicative of an oppressive patriarchy, yet subsequent champions of female achievement reconstructed their life stories to show them as exemplary mothers. Each of these schools of interpretation seeks to release the convicts from the shackles of prejudice, yet every attempt is caught inextricably in the tangle of language and imagery used to describe them.

The convicts who arrived in the early years were mostly English; one-fifth were Irish and there was a sprinkling of Scots. Most had been convicted of a property offence, and brought only a few meagre possessions. Among them were Henry and Susannah Kable, both in their twenties, who met in Norwich Gaol and took their baby with them on the First Fleet. Their plight aroused sympathy and a parcel of clothes was bought for the young family by public subscription. The clothes disappeared during the voyage, and in the first civil action in the colony they were awarded compensation. The Kables were unusually successful – Henry became a constable and later a merchant – but this case established a crucial precedent. The transportees were not felons 'dead in law' as the eminent eighteenth-century jurist Blackstone put it, but subjects of the Crown with legal rights.

In these foundation years, also, the essential conditions of their treatment were established. Those on public labour drawing public rations worked until the early afternoon, when they were free to work on their own account to pay for lodgings, since the government did not provide them with accommodation, and to buy drink or tobacco or other solaces. Those who were assigned to a master received food and lodging from him, and again often a further income – the records of storekeepers reveal convict purchases extending to elegant clothes. In both cases discipline was enforced by the lash; floggings of up to 500 strokes could be administered but only on the order of a magistrate. For the recalcitrant there were further sanctions including removal to the special penal settlement established at Newcastle in 1804. Supplementing these deterrents was the inducement of a 'ticket-of-leave' that entitled the well-behaved convict to work on his own account, which was an innovation of Governor King. Those female convicts who did not have partners or were not assigned to domestic service performed lighter labour; though some were flogged in the early years, their usual punishment was confinement.

Upon the expiry of a sentence or by early pardon, the convict was emancipated. By 1800, two-thirds of the New South Wales colonists were free, but most of them were former convicts, and that status was not easily expunged. Even those who did not bear scars on their backs still carried an indelible stigma in the eyes of the respectable. The division between the 'exclusives' and the 'emancipists' – those who came free and those who were transported – troubled all aspects of public life in a confined, intimate society and persisted into the next generation and beyond until the numbers and attitudes of the 'native born' finally prevailed.

The responses of convicts evade easy judgement. The historians who seek to 'normalise' the convict experience stress the comparative advantages of fresh opportunity, superior climate and diet, demographic vigour, and the paradoxical restoration of rights with fresh force in a regimen where rules had to substitute for rank and custom. There is much in these claims: some convicts accumulated substantial wealth, most ate better, their children were more successful, and they had a keener sense of their entitlements than the agricultural labourers and urban poor who remained in the United Kingdom.

Yet how can the tyranny of the lash be weighed in these calculations? How might the desolation of those separated from loved ones, the lack of recourse from arbitrary decision and the sheer hopelessness of fate be tallied? From the earliest years some convicts simply bolted into the bush or ventured onto the ocean in frail craft. George Bass, the surgeon and sailor who in 1797 first navigated the strait (named after him) that separated Van Diemen's Land from the mainland, found five escapees marooned on an island there and set them back to the Australian coast to walk the 700 kilometres back to Sydney. The remains of some absconders were recovered, while others lived for long periods with Aboriginals. In 1791 a party of twenty-one convicts set off north from Parramatta and when a settler asked where they were going, answered 'to China'.

The officers who related this ridiculous enterprise interpreted the convicts' answer as evidence of childish ignorance, as perhaps those who gave it intended. Gaoler and gaoled communicated across a gulf of mutual antagonism: against the formally declared and forcibly imposed authority, the felons had their own private communication, the 'flash' language of old lags, and associated methods of withholding themselves even as they outwardly obeyed. Patterns of compliance and resistance drew on the official regulations, on rights set down in British law and also on the less tangible but sometimes more compelling notions of entitlement embedded in popular custom. Convicts used their knowledge of the rules to appeal against excessive treatment or insufficient rations. They engaged in collective protest by withdrawing their labour, damaging property and making shows of dumb insolence or theatrical protest, as with the group of female convicts who turned about to pull up skirts and smack their buttocks before a governor.

There was some safety in numbers, but in 1804 the most numerous and overt challenge to penal rule brought savage retribution. Irish convicts sentenced for their part in the rebellion there in 1798 rose up on a government farm at Castle Hill and led 300 men first to Parramatta and then to seek support from the farmers of the Hawkesbury. The rebels were overtaken by troops and their uprising put down. A score or so were butchered on the spot, eight hanged, and more flogged in an effort to obtain information.

***

A second uprising followed four years later, which became known as the Rum Rebellion. It shed no blood and was conducted by the officers of the New South Wales Corps, who overthrew the governor, William Bligh. He had been sent in 1806 to impose order and brought with him a considerable reputation as a naval disciplinarian – a quarter-century earlier Bligh had provoked the celebrated mutiny of the crew of the *Bounty* and then directed eighteen men in an open boat halfway across the Pacific to salvation.

Upon his arrival in Sydney the new governor quickly antagonised the regimental officers with his high-handed manner, which included the reissue of an order that forbade the barter of spirits for food or wages. This trade had begun in 1792 when a group of officers bought a consignment of rum. It was commonly used as a means of payment and often blamed for ruining emancipist farmers. Governors Hunter and King had tried to curb the trade in spirits, and King had sent back to London one of its instigators, John Macarthur, for wounding a superior officer in a duel. 'This rich Botany Bay perturbator', as King described Macarthur, soon recovered his fortunes. He adroitly resigned his commission, persuaded influential British patrons of the potential of the wool samples he took back with him, and returned with an order that he be granted a further 2000 hectares.

Had Bligh's dispute been restricted to the officers' trade in rum he might well have prevailed. But he caused greater resentment with his insistence on control of Crown land. Despite the absence of legal title, convicts and officers alike fenced off and improved their allotments, and Bligh's decision to impose greater order on the patchwork Sydney streetscape by eviction and demolition of residences violated the colonists' insistence on their property rights. When Bligh fell out with Macarthur, impounded his trading schooner and put him on trial, he was accused of trampling on constitutional liberties. The military officers placed the governor under house arrest until he agreed to return to England – an undertaking he immediately broke and instead took up residence in Hobart. Meanwhile the commanding officer assumed the title of lieutenant-governor and Macarthur

3.2   In 1808 the officers of the New South Wales Corps overthrew the governor, William Bligh. This cartoon, alleging that
soldiers found Bligh hiding under his bed at Government House,
was displayed in Sydney by the victorious junta. (Mitchell
Library, State Library of New South Wales, a128113)

styled himself 'Secretary to the Colony'. The members of this junta
helped themselves to additional land and labour.

London could scarcely ignore such a challenge to the constituted
authority. It recalled Bligh and dispatched Lachlan Macquarie, a
military man with his own regiment to replace the discredited New
South Wales Corps. Even before the conclusion of the Napoleonic
Wars in 1815 resulted in a wave of new transportees, Governor
Macquarie effected a substantial consolidation of the colony – as
was often the case in the British Empire, it was the local crisis that
was the trigger of expansion. Governor Macquarie was a planner
and a builder. He established a bank and introduced a currency.
He laid out Sydney afresh and embarked on a major programme of
public works: roads, bridges, a lighthouse on the South Heads, new
barracks for the soldiers and also for the male and female convicts, a

hospital (financed by a licence fee on the importation of spirits) of sufficient substance that part of it still serves as a house of parliament. Macquarie planned in straight lines and built in Georgian symmetry.

Three years after his arrival the Europeans found a route across the mountain range that ran down the eastern seaboard and hemmed them in. While from the coast it appeared as a dark blue line on the horizon of the Cumberland Plain, this fretted plateau presented a maze of towering escarpments. Macquarie soon had a road constructed to the new town of Bathurst on the other side, which provided access to rich grazing country. The tiny Van Diemen's Land settlements of Hobart and Launceston simultaneously thrust north and south into a corridor of fertile land that was well suited to both agriculture and pastoralism, and well served by waterways. From 1816–20 there was a rapid increase in the arrival of convicts. The population of the mainland colony reached 26,000 by 1820, that of the island offshoot 6000.

Macquarie, a Highland bonnet laird turned professional soldier, was a benevolent despot who regarded New South Wales as a place for 'the reformation, as well as the punishment, of the convicts'. This required an improved discipline (hence the construction of the convict barracks) but also the chance to make amends, for 'when a man is free, his former state should no longer be remembered, or allowed to act against him'. The governor used freely his prerogative to pardon convicts for good conduct; he continued to provide them with grants of land on the expiry of their sentences, and favoured their agriculture over the pastoral interests of the large landowners.

Macquarie was especially indulgent towards educated and successful emancipists, such as the surgeon William Redfern, the architect Francis Greenway, the merchant Simeon Lord, and the poet laureate Michael Robinson. The appointment of such men to official positions and entertainment of them at the governor's table scandalised the exclusives, as did Macquarie's discouragement of the free settlers drawn after 1815 by the increasing prosperity of the colony: 'Is there no way to get to New South Wales but by stealing?' asked a British treasury official in 1820. Nor was Macquarie daunted by the constitutional impropriety of his decision that ex-convict lawyers could appear before the new Supreme Court, despite the opposition of the judge who presided over it. 'This country should be made the home and a happy home to every emancipated convict who deserves it', he insisted.

Discipline and reformation required public morality and personal restraint. Macquarie prohibited nude bathing and unseemly behaviour. He refused to sanction cohabitation with convict women, and the increased opportunities he allowed reformed males locked women more tightly into marriage and domesticity. He enforced the Sabbath. This active enlistment of Christianity in the colonial project marked a break with the past, for even though Phillip, Hunter and King had paraded unwilling congregations of convicts to listen to sermons on obedience, the early governors did so not out of piety (leading officials in both Sydney and Hobart lived openly with convict mistresses) but rather because the Church of England was an arm of the state.

The clergymen who tried to reform their charges made little progress. Male convicts were known to use Bibles and prayer books to make playing cards; women convicts turned tracts into hair curlers. A Spanish priest who visited the colony in the early years was startled by the absence of a church. 'The first thought of colonists and of Government in our colonies', he remarked, 'is to plant the cross and erect the edifices of religion'. The foundation years in New South Wales, on the other hand, fostered a military chaplaincy style of religion that was perfunctory in its forms and had little to do with personal faith.

That emerged with new forms of ministry. In 1798, eleven missionaries arrived from Tahiti, rebuffed in their attempt to convert the Polynesians. They were members of the London Missionary Society, founded three years earlier by Nonconformist denominations to minister to the heathens. The advent of Methodist and Congregationalist preachers brought a less formal and hierarchical religion with a stronger emphasis on individual conversion and salvation. Whereas Samuel Marsden, the leading Anglican minister and by now a wealthy landowner, thundered from the magistrate's bench as well as from the pulpit against the depravity of the felons, these Nonconformists sought to reclaim the sinner to godliness. There was also an acceptance of the right of Catholics to practise their devotions. As early as 1803 King allowed an Irish convict to exercise his clerical functions, though that privilege was withdrawn in the following year when the priest was suspected of using the mass to plan the Castle Hill rising. In 1820, two new priests came voluntarily from Ireland with official permission to fulfil their compatriots' religious obligations.

Marsden was himself a proselytiser. Through the Anglican Church Missionary Society he hoped to convert the Pacific Islanders and personally led a mission to the North Island of New Zealand in 1814. The Maoris, as a 'very superior race of men', might be weaned from their savage vices and brought to Christianity through an appreciation of the advantages of civilisation, which would be apparent if they were instructed in agriculture and commerce. Trade and the gospel made unreliable partners in Marsden's settlement at the Bay of Plenty, but he saw little chance of the Aborigines adopting such practices and did not participate in the training farm that Macquarie established for them in the same year or the Native Institution that was founded to educate their children and conducted by a Congregational missionary.

'It seems only to require the fostering hand of time, gentle means and conciliatory manners to bring these poor unenlightened people into an important degree of civilization', the governor assured the minister for the colonies. Macquarie instituted an annual gathering or 'Congress' of Aborigines at Parramatta. It began in 1814 with a distribution of roast beef, plum pudding, tobacco, clothing and blankets as symbols of his gift of Christian civilisation, and also with the presentation of breastplates to select Aboriginal men in an effort to provide them with a visible badge of authority.

These attempts to incorporate the Aborigines came as the pressure of colonial expansion brought renewed conflict. By 1816 Macquarie resorted to a punitive expedition that took fourteen lives. While he was still 'determined to persevere in my original plan of endeavouring to domesticate and civilise these wild rude people', it was apparent that this could only be done by removing and remaking them. The Aboriginal women who attended the Congress of 1816 cried when a dozen children from the Native Institution, clad in neat

3.3 The first known portrait in oils of an Aboriginal was exhibited by Augustus Earle in 1826. It shows Bungaree, a man of the Kuring-gai people, whom the early governors valued as a mediator; Macquarie had presented him with a breastplate as 'King of the Blacks'. The artist poses Bungaree in the grand manner with the fort at Sydney Harbour in the background. A subsequent lithograph divested him of his dignity by including an Aboriginal woman with pipe and alcohol in a squalid Sydney street. (Augustus Earle, National Library of Australia, an2256865; an6016167-2)

suits and dresses, processed with Mrs Macquarie and the missionary's wife. Those tears flowed well into the twentieth century.

By this time the governor's own problems were falling in upon him. He had brought regularity and direction to the conduct of the colony. He had insisted that it should be a place of reclamation as well as punishment, and balanced the demands of exclusives with the needs of the emancipists. Pastoralists still received land and labour, for Macquarie assigned the majority of transportees, but they were not allowed to monopolise opportunity so that the nine-tenths of the population who had begun as or were descended from convicts held roughly half the wealth. But the numbers that disembarked after 1815 swamped the assignment system. With more convicts on the governor's hands, expenditure mounted.

Macquarie's local critics, who alleged that he favoured the fallen over the free and enterprising, joined officials in London who condemned the cost of his public works. In 1819 London dispatched J. T. Bigge, the chief justice of the colony of Trinidad, to conduct an inquiry into New South Wales. Before Bigge presented the first of his reports in 1822, Macquarie resigned.

***

In 1803 Matthew Flinders reached Sydney after charting the Australian coast for the British Admiralty. Since his ship, the *Investigator*, was unfit for further service, he embarked for England in a schooner, but it too proved unserviceable on the voyage across the Indian Ocean, and he called at French Mauritius for assistance. By this time France was again at war with Britain, and the governor of Mauritius detained him until 1810. Thus it was not until 1814 that Flinders' account of *Voyage to Terra Australis* appeared, and a further three years before Macquarie's eye lighted on a passage in it: 'Had I permitted myself any innovation upon the original name, it would have been to convert it into AUSTRALIA; as being more agreeable to the ear.'

At the end of the year Macquarie suggested that the name should be adopted for the whole of the island-continent in preference to the common designation of New Holland, which strictly applied to only the eastern half. On 26 January in the following year he honoured the thirtieth anniversary of the colony's foundation with a public holiday and celebratory ball. Anniversary Day became an annual festival, the *Australian* the name of the insistently independent newspaper founded in 1824 to advance the interests of the emancipists.

The British had occupied only a small part of the southeast of Australia. In Van Diemen's Land they congregated on the central plain; in New South Wales they extended north and south along the coast, west into the transalpine slopes. Sealers and other adventurers ventured further, but the mainland settlement was contained in a 150-kilometre arc around Sydney. While by this time the invaders outnumbered the Aboriginals of Van Diemen's Land, in New South Wales they still constituted a minority. There were many Aboriginal peoples who had still not encountered the white man, seen his livestock and crops, or heard the sound of his musket. Yet they were marked by the advent of the intruder as surely as the smallpox scars of those who survived the spread of the diseases the colonists brought with them. The settlement thus far constituted a bridgehead for the far more rapid expansion that would follow, its tell-tale signs of denuded sealing grounds, missing stands of timber and soil already impoverished by overcropping an augury of the devastation still to come.

A settler empire, according to an American geographer, meant 'the permanent rooting of Europeans in conquered soil', a transplantation of technology, institutions and mental habits such that 'settler colonies took on a life of their own to a degree quite unparalleled by any other type of imperial holding'. The process of plantation was clearly apparent in Australia, but so too was the accompanying process of settler colonists attaching themselves to the new place. The life that was emerging blended what was brought with what was found. 'It is certainly a new world, a new creation. Every plant, every shell, tree, fish and animal, bird, insect different from the old', wrote Thomas Palmer, a Unitarian minister transported from Scotland for sedition. His experience was also different. He was free from the usual restraint, allowed to engage in trade and shipbuilding, and even to send back his criticisms of Governor Hunter. Everything was topsy-turvy, and even the attempts to faithfully reproduce familiar institutions brought hybrid results. A vigorous and often rancorous society had emerged in which captivity meant freedom, and the gentleman chafed while the outcast enjoyed the governor's favour. Then, with the arrival of commissioner Bigge, the Empire struck back.

4

Conquest, 1822–1850

Within a month of landing at Sydney, John Bigge was in dispute with Lachlan Macquarie over the appointment of the emancipist surgeon, William Redfern, to the magistracy. Over the next fifteen months of his inquiry the commissioner reached conclusions about the future of the Australian colonies sharply at odds with those of the governor. The two men were divided by background, training, temperament, and expectations of empire. Macquarie, a career soldier, always viewed New South Wales as a 'penitentiary or asylum on a grand scale'. It was destined to grow from a penal to a free society and 'must one day or other be one of the greatest colonies belonging to the British Empire', but that would depend upon the rehabilitation of its convicts under his tutelage. Bigge, a cool and systematic younger man, brought a lawyer's judgement and a tendency to weigh local circumstances by English standards.

The two men belonged to different generations, represented different eras. Macquarie, in his late fifties, spanned the collapse of clan society in the Scottish Hebrides and the remaking of his nation into north Britons in the service of the Empire. He combined the eighteenth-century values of reason and sentiment with the habit of command, and the regularity he sought was one tempered by paternalism and patronage. Now, after his forty years of military service, the Empire was at peace. The defeat of Napoleon left Britain free from external threat, and the enormous effort of war could be diverted into commerce and industry. Through a series of political and administrative reforms the imperial state reduced its fiscal burden and increased its efficiency. The engrossment of wealth by restrictive regulation and exclusive trading gave way by degrees to an open market in which all could participate. Free trade and the maxim *laissez faire*, let things be, became by the middle of the nineteenth century the guiding principles of British policy.

As the logic of the market took hold, it entered into every aspect of human life. A social order based on rank and station, in which relationships were personal and particular, yielded to the idea of society as an aggregation of autonomous, self-directed individuals, everyone seeking to maximise their own satisfaction or utility. The Utilitarians, the group of single-minded reformers led by Jeremy Bentham who reshaped public policy, propounded a simple behavioural algorithm: given appropriate institutional stimuli, the impulse of the human actor to pursue pleasure and avoid pain would be channelled into choices conducive to the general benefit.

Bigge, as a public official committed to the rule of law and still in his mid-thirties when the wartime emergency ended, was an early agent of the corresponding transformation of colonial policy. In criminology, as in political economy and most branches of social policy, the effect was to reconstruct the subject as an object of bureaucratic administration: precise, uniform and efficient. The wrongdoer must be deterred. Bigge was accordingly to inquire into the prospects of New South Wales both as a gaol and a colony, to rein in its costs and make it more profitable. Above all, his instructions from the minister for the colonies emphasised that transportation should be rendered 'an object of real terror'.

His three reports, presented in 1822 and 1823, suggested how punishment could be reconciled with profit. Deterrence called for greater severity in the punishment of convicts through greater regularity. They should not be given special indulgences or allowed to earn money in free time to spend on town pleasures, but instead be assigned to rural labour under strict supervision. They should not receive land grants on expiry of their sentences but continue to work for a living. They should not be admitted to positions of public responsibility but rather remain in a subordinate status. Bigge's recommendations on the penal system simultaneously defined the future development of the colony. It would rest on free settlers who would possess the land, employ the convicts and grow wool – John Macarthur had caught his ear. It would require a system of government suitable for free subjects of the Crown: a legislature to curb the governor's arbitrary powers and a judiciary to safeguard the rule of law.

With the implementation of these recommendations the colonial presence in Australia was transformed. Pastoralism flourished, and the greatly increased numbers it attracted burst the limits of settlement. Explorers and surveyors opened up the interior, and new colonies were planted on the southern and western coasts. Relations between Aboriginals and settlers on the vastly extended frontier deteriorated into endemic violence. Stricter supervision of the greatly increased numbers of convicts exacerbated conflict between the emancipists and the exclusives. The restraints on rule by decree opened up a three-cornered contest for power between these two groups and the governor. Australia was incorporated into an empire of trade, technology, manners and culture, while at the same time its own distinctive forms became clearer.

***

The internal exploration of the country proceeded rapidly after the crossing of the Blue Mountains in 1813. A series of expeditions from 1817 followed the inland river system that drained from the western plains of New South Wales into the Murray, and by 1830 traced that river to its outlet on the south coast. Northern ventures pushed from the Hunter Valley through the high country of New England onto the Darling Downs in 1827 and well into Queensland by 1832. A journey south to Port Phillip was made in 1824, in 1836 the grasslands of Western Victoria were traversed and in 1840 a route through the Snowy Mountains into Gippsland was found. By this time the topography and resources of southeast Australia had been ascertained.

The explorers are central figures in the colonial version of Australian history. Celebrities in their own time, they were commemorated afterwards with statues and cairns, celebrated in school textbooks – even today, schoolchildren trace the paths of their

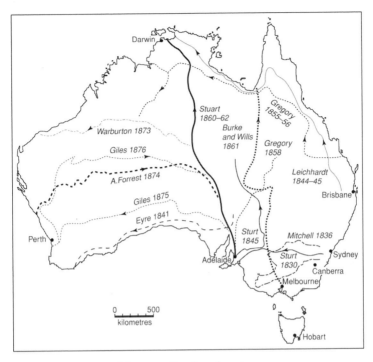

Map 4.1   Land exploration.

journeys onto templates of an empty continent. They figured as exemplary heroes of imperial masculinity: visionary individuals who penetrated into trackless wilderness, survived attacks by savage and treacherous natives, endured hunger and thirst in their endeavour to know the land. More recent writing has undermined this heroic status. The epic version of exploration history left out the role played by sealers and drovers, travellers and outcasts who often preceded the explorer. When John Wedge, the assistant surveyor of Van Diemen's Land, made his journey of discovery into the mountainous southwest in 1826, he discovered the hideout of a bushranger. When Thomas Mitchell, the chief surveyor of New South Wales, reached the Victorian coast in 1836, he found a collection of whalers' huts and nearby a family farm.

The celebrants of exploration also minimised the role played by Aboriginal guides. Mitchell employed three of them, and while he exulted in 'a land so inviting and still without inhabitants', scarcely a day passed without him recording in his diary an encounter with the owners of that land. Once the Aboriginal presence is acknowledged, the idea that the explorers were engaged in a process of discovery yields to the realisation that they were superimposing their own form of knowledge for their own purposes. Thomas Mitchell recorded in his journals an affray on the Murray River in 1836: the Aborigines 'betook themselves to the river, my men pursuing them and shooting as many as they could ... Thus, in a short time, the usual silence prevailed on the banks of the Murray, and we pursued our journey unmolested'.

Major Mitchell was a Scottish career soldier who brought the survey techniques he had learned on the Spanish battlefields of the Napoleonic Wars. Some of the epic feats of land exploration in the nineteenth century were performed by Britishers born too late to win martial glory. For them the conquest of unknown territory was proof of manhood in imperial service – a tradition that continued right up to the eve of the First World War with Robert Scott's dash to the South Pole in 1912. In Australia it culminated with an equally vainglorious expedition from the south to the north coast, led by an Anglo-Irish adventurer, Robert O'Hara Burke, who perished in Central Australia in 1861. By then the locals were achieving greater success. They travelled more lightly in the outback, had fewer preconceptions, adapted equipment to local conditions.

The pastoral occupation proceeded apace. During the 1820s stockholders moved out of the Cumberland Plain, over the Blue Mountains and along the inland creeks and rivers. To contain them in 1829 the governor declared nineteen counties that stretched some 200 kilometres from Sydney, these constituting the limits of location in New South Wales. In Van Diemen's Land the lines of settlement north and south of the estuarine bases met in 1832 and quickly broadened. Sheep numbers on the mainland increased from 120,000 in 1821 to 1 million in 1830, and from 170,000 to another million in the island colony. Production of other livestock, especially cattle, and cultivation of cereals also increased rapidly, but these were for domestic consumption while wool was exported and in the next two decades sheep surpassed all other instruments of the

European economy. They were the shock troops of land seizure. New South Wales flocks numbered 4 million in 1840 and 13 million in 1850. By then there were some two thousand graziers operating on a crescent that stretched more than 2000 kilometres from Brisbane down to Melbourne and across to Adelaide.

Australian sheep produced wool for British manufacturers to spin and weave. The mechanisation of textile production began the industrial revolution that turned Britain into the workshop of the world. While Lancashire's cotton industry was the more spectacular, the mill towns of Yorkshire turned out ever-increasing quantities of woollen cloth, garments, blankets and carpets that consumed ever-increasing volumes of fine wool. Between 1810 and 1850 British imports of fleece increased tenfold. First Spain and then Germany catered to this growing demand, but as Australian producers improved the quality of their wool with the introduction of the Merino breed, they captured an increasing share of the British market – one-tenth in 1830, a quarter in 1840, half by 1850. By then sales of Australian wool amounted to over £2 million per annum, more than 90 per cent of all exports. Here was the staple that sustained Australian prosperity for a century.

It was produced in circumstances that allowed newcomers to achieve rapid success: plentiful land at minimal cost, a benign climate that required no handfeeding in winter, a high-value product that could absorb transport costs. Such opportunities attracted army and naval officers discharged after the Napoleonic Wars, and younger sons of gentry families in England and Scotland who sought their own estates. An entrant required some initial capital to buy stock; he then hired labour and drove his animals to the edge of settlement; laid claim to an area that might extend 10 kilometres or more; arranged his flocks under the care of shepherds who pastured them by day and penned them by night; put rams to the ewes to build up numbers; clipped the fleece, washed and pressed, and dispatched it for sale.

There were fortunes to be made in this first, heady phase of the pastoral industry, but it was a young man's calling and not one for the faint-hearted. Drought, fire or disease might ruin the most resolute. A downturn in British demand at the end of the 1830s caused prices to tumble, and millions of sheep had to be boiled down for tallow. The insecurity of conditions, as well as the absence of land title, kept the pastoralist's eye fixed on speedy returns so that beyond improvement of stock lines, there was little effort to increase efficiency or conserve resources. Stock quickly ate out native grasses. The cloven hoof hardened the soil and inhibited regrowth. Patches of bare earth round the stockyards, eroded gullies and polluted water-courses marked the presence of the pastoral invader.

So did the signs of human loss, the ruined habitats and desolate former gathering places of the Aboriginal inhabitants, the skulls and bones left unburied on the sites of massacres, and the names that became associated with some of them. There was 'Slaughterhouse Creek', on the Gwydir River of northern New South Wales, where perhaps sixty or seventy were 'shot like crows in the trees' in 1838; 'Rufus River' on the lower Murray where the water ran red in 1841; and other such places that recorded past atrocities with chilling frankness: 'Mount Dispersion', 'Convincing Ground', 'Fighting Hills', 'Murdering Island', 'Skull Camp'. White settlers sometimes suppressed the memory of such disturbing events and sometimes preserved it in local lore, so that in a pub conversation in rural New South Wales 170 years later an old hand could relate how the first-comers had 'rounded all the blackfellas up at the top of the gorge, and shot at them till they all jumped off'.

Aboriginal versions of these encounters have an additional dimension. Their stories are at once specific and cumulative, telling of particular events at particular places and of their larger meaning. 'Why did the blackfellows attack the whites?' the South Australian commissioner of police asked Aboriginal survivors after the Rufus River affray. 'Because they came in blackman's country', he was told. Far from obliterating the Indigenous presence, the white onslaught produced an enlarged awareness of a pattern of conquest that began with the first British landfall. 'You Captain Cook, you kill my people', expostulated a Northern Territory stockman in the 1970s.

The violence was on such a scale that white colonists spoke during the 1820s and 1830s of a 'Black War' – but uneasily, for the conflict did not lend itself to a romance of heroes and martial valour; the predominant attitude was one of 'fear and disdain'. Talk of a frontier war was quickly abandoned, and has resurfaced only recently as the Aboriginal presence in Australian history has been more fully restored. In 1979 the historian Geoffrey Blainey suggested that the Australian War Memorial should incorporate a recognition of Aboriginal–European warfare. In 1981 the pre-eminent white historian of frontier contact, Henry Reynolds, argued that the names of the fallen Aborigines be placed on our memorials and cenotaphs 'and even in the pantheon of national heroes'.

Some historians query the emphasis on frontier violence and destruction, and suggest that the martial interpretation fails to understand Aboriginal actions in their own terms. The pastoral incursion was undoubtedly traumatic. Indigenous populations shank dramatically (one national estimate suggests from 600,000 to fewer than 300,000 between 1821 and 1850), but disease, malnutrition and infertility were the principal causes. Aboriginal survivors responded to this disaster with a variety of strategies, and accommodation was one of them. During the 1830s and 1840s they incorporated themselves into the pastoral workforce as stock workers, shepherds, shearers, domestic servants and sexual partners. There was loss, but there was also persistence.

The idea of a Black War attests to the extent of Aboriginal resistance. In Van Diemen's Land, where in a single month of 1828 there were twenty-two inquests into settlers killed by Aborigines in the outlying district of Oatlands, the governor declared a state of martial law. After parties of bounty hunters failed to quell the threat, he ordered 3000 men to form a cordon across the island and drive the Aborigines southwards to the coast. This Black Line, 200 kilometres in length, captured just one man and one boy, and even while it was moving down the island during 1830, four more settlers were killed and thirty houses plundered.

More than five hundred soldiers were employed in Van Diemen's Land as part of the futile Black Line in 1830 and afterwards for punitive purposes. The governor of the infant colony in Western Australia led a detachment of the local regiment into the Battle of Pinjarra of 1834, when perhaps thirty of the Nyungar were shot, and military garrisons were deployed in the other new settlement in South Australia as late as 1841. Alternatively, the governors deployed forces of mounted police, and subsequently mounted native police. The mobility and firepower of such paramilitary forces were difficult to withstand, and the enlistment of Aborigines allowed the British to follow the common imperial device of using conquered peoples to overrun the remaining independent societies. Under the command of Major James Nunn, the mounted police of New South Wales conducted a 'pacification' expedition during 1838 that inflicted heavy casualties on the Kamilaroi people of the northern plains.

Yet these set-piece encounters again give a misleading impression of the conflict. When trained men fell on assemblies of Aborigines in open country, the firearm prevailed over the spear, especially after the repeater rifle replaced the musket. Aboriginal warriors had no fortifications, and made little use of their enemies' military technology. In contrast to the Maori, who tied up 20,000 British troops in New Zealand for twenty years, they could not sustain a formal warfare of massed battle. They quickly learned to avoid such encounters, and typically used their advantages of mobility and superior bushcraft to conduct guerilla resistance. Destruction of livestock and surprise attacks on pastoral outstations exacerbated the fear and insecurity of white settlers 'waiting, waiting, waiting for the creeping, stealthy, treacherous blacks'.

The result was a particularly brutal form of repression conducted by the settlers themselves. The most notorious instance occurred in 1838 near the Gwydir River at Myall Creek in northern New South Wales, when a group of stockmen riding in pursuit of Aboriginals wanted for spearing cattle came instead upon a party of Kwiambal people, mostly women and children, who had taken shelter with a hutkeeper. There was goodwill between the men of the station and the Kwiambal, who cut bark, helped with the cattle and were allowed to keep up their hunting of game; several of the Aboriginal women had formed relationships with the white men. There was foreboding and irresolution among the station hands when the white vigilantes took the Aborigines into the bush and butchered the entire party. There was bombast from the murderers when they returned alone, and then furtive guilt as they returned to try to destroy the remains of their victims. We know about the Myall Creek massacre

4.1   Guns against spears – mounted troopers do battle with
Aboriginal warriors across a creek. This portrayal of a violent
encounter on the pastoral frontier suggests that the invaders
will prevail, though the adversaries are more evenly matched
than they would be after repeater firearms replaced the musket.
(Charles Mundy, *Our Antipodes*, London: Richard Bentley,
1852)

because the station overseer reported it at a time when the governor
had been put on notice by the British government that such atrocities
were not to be condoned. He brought those responsible to trial, and
when a Sydney jury found them not guilty, ordered a retrial.

Seven of the murderers were eventually convicted and executed,
an outcome that astounded most colonists. The official response
to the Myall Creek massacre was quite exceptional, both in the
decision to prosecute and in the availability of white witnesses
prepared to give evidence against them. Since Aborigines could not
swear on oath that they would tell the truth, they were unable to
testify against those who did them injury. The ostensible even-
handedness of British justice – proclaimed by Lieutenant-Governor
Arthur of Van Diemen's Land in a message board that depicted first
a black spearing and then a white shooting, each treated as crimes
and each punished – rested on a fundamental inequality. In both
panels it was the white man who prescribed the rules and meted out
the punishment. The Aboriginal rejoinder to such one-sided justice

4.2   George Arthur, the lieutenant-governor of Van Diemen's Land, issued this pictorial proclamation in the same year that he declared martial law. The upper panels promote inter-racial amity, the lower ones indicate the penalties for violence. Arthur himself appears in official dress as the embodiment of authority and justice. (Tasmanian Museum and Art Gallery)

was delivered in the year that Arthur conducted his Black Line: 'Go away, you white buggers! What business have you here?'

Earlier encounters between Aborigines and colonists had established the fundamental incompatibility of two ways of life. The Aborigines had tried through negotiation and exchange to incorporate the Europeans into their ways, but the Europeans had little desire to assimilate into Aboriginal society. Even so, the restricted nature of colonial settlement up to the 1820s left open the possibility of some form of coexistence. The rapid extension of the pastoral frontier removed that possibility since it resulted in a succession of sudden, traumatic encounters. There was still room for both peoples, for the Europeans spread along open grasslands, leaving the more heavily timbered higher slopes, and some initial accommodation based on mutual exchange of goods and services did occur. But Aborigines were loath to accept the occupation of their hunting ranges and despoliation of their waterways, while pastoralists commonly responded to stock losses with unilateral action aimed at nothing less than extermination of the original inhabitants. The colonial authorities, having set this lethal chain reaction in motion, were unable to prevent the spread of killing.

There were some whites who recoiled before the enormity of their compatriots' actions, who perceived that such inhuman conduct compounded the unjust expropriation, and who warned that 'the spot of blood is upon us'. The evangelical activists who campaigned against slavery in Britain's plantation colonies, and secured its abolition in 1833, mounted a similar case against the abuses committed in the settler colonies. In both instances they proclaimed a sacred duty to protect, convert and redeem 'the untutored and defenceless savages'. The agitation led to the establishment of a select committee of the House of Commons, which found in 1837 that the colonisation of South Africa, Australia and British North America had brought disastrous consequences for the native people: 'a plain and sacred right', an 'incontrovertible right to their own soil', had been disregarded.

The British government was already concerned by reports of massacres and the use of martial law against the natives of the Australian colonies. 'To regard them as aliens with whom a war

4.3 In 1929 Lieutenant-Governor Arthur commissioned George Robinson to make contact with the remaining Aborigines of Van Diemen's Land and persuade them to settle on a reserve. Benjamin Duterrau's 1840 painting, *The Conciliation*, shows a man of peace and compassion. Despite his promises to the Aborigines of Tasmania, Robinson arranged for them to be deported to Flinders Island. (Tasmanian Museum and Art Gallery)

can exist', the minister for the colonies wrote to the governor of New South Wales in 1837, 'is to deny that protection to which they derive the highest possible claim from the sovereignty that has been assumed over the whole of their ancient possessions'. He insisted that the Aborigines be protected.

None of the schemes of protection was successful. In Van Diemen's Land, Lieutenant-Governor Arthur had already commissioned a local tradesman, George Robinson, to round up the remaining Aborigines. Robinson's 'friendly mission' employed Aboriginal companions to succeed where the Black Line had failed. Between 1830 and 1834 he conciliated and captured the last defiant Aborigines and placed them on Flinders Island, in Bass Strait, where their numbers declined until the survivors were returned to a reserve near Hobart in 1847. Similar reserves or mission stations were established on the mainland during the 1820s and 1830s, usually by Christian missionary societies with government support. Some well-wishers, including the judge who presided over the trial of the Myall Creek murderers and who had earlier experience at the Cape Colony, wanted larger reserves on which the natives might be settled and protected from the perils of white civilisation.

Settlement was a word of many meanings. The Aborigines were to be settled so that colonial settlement could proceed unhindered: indeed, one of the Myall Creek culprits announced that he and his mates had 'settled' the 'blacks'. The governors of New South Wales, however, preferred incorporation to segregation and appointed white protectors to accompany Aborigines in their wanderings and help settle them. George Robinson became the chief protector of Aborigines in the Port Phillip District, sometimes able to curb the worse abuses, powerless to prevent the continuing encroachment on their lands.

Another course of action was possible. The settlement of the Port Phillip District began in 1835 when a group of entrepreneurs from Van Diemen's Land led by John Batman crossed Bass Strait. In return for a payment of blankets, tomahawks, knives, scissors, looking-glasses, handkerchiefs, shirts and flour, and an undertaking to pay a yearly rent, they claimed to have received 200,000 hectares from the Kulin people. This unofficial and contrived agreement fell a long way short of the treaties negotiated by British colonists with indigenous people in New Zealand (it was more like the 'trinket treaties' arranged in the American West), but did suggest some acknowledgement of Aboriginal ownership. The minister for the colonies dismissed the arrangement on the grounds that 'such a concession would subvert the foundation on which all property rights in New South Wales at present rest'.

It was at this point that the official policy of Aboriginal protection succumbed to the land hunger of the settlers. Settlement on the mainland had hitherto been restricted to the nineteen counties. Its boundaries were already transgressed and 1836 Governor Bourke charged annual payments for those depasturing stock beyond the limits of settlement. This licence system ran counter to the official policy of concentrating settlement, but Bourke argued that 'sheep must wander or they will not thrive, and the colonists must have sheep or they will not continue to be wealthy'.

Batman and his colleagues had no licence, so theirs was an illegal settlement, but it occurred at the very time Mitchell reported the rich grasslands south of the Murray. Rather than evict the trespassers, Bourke came down to the squatters' camp, named it Melbourne, and allowed a frenzied land rush that by 1842 extended pastoral leases over more than half the district. A recent historian sees this decision as conceding 'the right of settlers to live where they chose' and thereby determining 'the conquest of Australia'. The paradox was that at the very moment when the Colonial Office in London was emphasising the need to protect the indigenous people, its local administrators allowed settlers to invade their land – indeed, it is likely that the £20 million the British government paid at this time as compensation to slave-owners provided much of the capital for the pastoral invasion. Try as the colonial authorities might to follow instructions to restrain violence, they were simply incapable of policing the vastly extended zone of dispossession.

In 1836 the Colonial Office also insisted that the new colony proposed for South Australia must respect the 'rights of the present proprietors of the soil', and its commissioners stipulated that the land should be bought and a portion of purchase price paid to the Aborigines. The South Australian settlers ignored these conditions. Similarly, the warning of the governor in his proclamation of the colony that he would 'punish with exemplary severity all acts of violence and injustice which may be practiced or commences against the Natives' gave way within four years to summary execution of two Aboriginal men identified on the basis of hearsay as responsible for killing a party of shipwrecked colonists. An early pastoralist in South Australia said that those who were displaced for sheep 'were looked upon as equally detrimental with wild dogs'.

Within five years the Aboriginal people on the outskirts of the new settlements at Melbourne and Adelaide were reduced to beggary. In Sydney their numbers dwindled and by the 1840s most were camped near the heads at Botany Bay. An old man there, 'Mahroot', told an

4.4 An 1839 depiction of Aborigines in Sydney, degraded by alcohol. The male figure still wears a breastplate, but his ragged clothing and dissolute appearance declare that the earlier effort to incorporate Aborigines into the colonial order had failed. (Mitchell Library, State Library of New South Wales, a1528625)

English visitor of the changes he had witnessed: 'Well Mitter ... all black-fellow gone! all this my country! pretty place botany! Little pickaninny, I run about here. Plenty black-fellow then, corrobbory; great fight; all canoe about. Only me left now, Mitter – Poor gin mine tumble down, All gone!'

White town-dwellers complained of the riotous dissipation and drunken squalor of these Aboriginal residents. White artists caricatured them as semi-naked figures who sprawled over public spaces with tobacco, alcohol, mangy dogs and neglected children, shameless in their vices and incapable of responding to the virtues of civilisation. Such representations of Aboriginal depravity established the victims as responsible for their fate, but there were alternative and far more disturbing images of the wild and untamed native. Captivity narratives circulated of white men who fell into the hands of Aborigines and returned to a state of nature, or of white women who survived their ordeals in the wild.

The most celebrated of these was Eliza Fraser, who survived a shipwreck in 1836 and for fifty-two days lived with the Nglulungbara, Batjala and Dulingbra peoples on an island off the coast of central Queensland. Her 'Deliverance from the Savages', as the title of one of many contemporary publications put it, dwelt on the killing of her husband and male companions, and the sexual degradation of an unprotected white woman. Fraser herself appeared as a sideshow attraction in London's Hyde Park, telling her tale of barbarous treatment, and the episode has formed the basis for a novel by Patrick White, paintings by Sidney Nolan, music by Peter Sculthorpe and several films.

***

By such means the land was taken, settled and possessed. To make it productive and profitable there were the convicts. Between 1821 and 1840, 55,000 convicts landed in New South Wales, and 60,000 in Van Diemen's Land where transportation continued for a further decade. The great majority were assigned to masters and most served out their time in rural labour. There was keen demand for them since a pastoral station needed large numbers of shepherds, stockmen and hutkeepers, and bond labour could be made to endure the isolation and insecurity that deterred free labour. Convicts, who cost no more than their keep, underwrote the rapid growth and high yields of the pastoral economy.

Assignment was now accompanied by a far tighter regulation. Convicts were no longer allowed free time at the end of the day or permitted to receive 'indulgences'. As Bigge had recommended, there were fewer pardons and no more land grants to convicts on the expiry of their sentences. Officials exercised a closer control over the treatment of assigned convicts and the magistrates before whom they were brought for breach of the rules. Lieutenant-Governor Arthur in Van Diemen's Land went furthest in his construction during the 1820s and 1830s of an elaborate system of supervision documented in 'Black Books' that set out a full record of every felon's behaviour 'from the day of their landing until the period of their emancipation or death'. His regimen was less brutal than that of his predecessors, though one convict in six was still flogged annually, but perhaps more chilling in its bureaucratic regularity.

As the convict system was made more regular and its caprices smoothed out, so the opportunities to circumvent its rigours were closed. That made it less, not more, normal.

Those who broke the rules were subjected to further punishment, now carefully graduated in severity: first, flogging or confinement, then consignment to public works or the chain gang, and finally secondary transportation to one of the special penal settlements set well away from civilisation. These settlements multiplied rapidly: Port Macquarie, up the coast from Newcastle, in 1821, and Moreton Bay, further north, in 1824; Macquarie Harbour on the west coast of Van Diemen's Land in 1822, and Port Arthur, on the southeast corner of the island, from 1832. Norfolk Island was also used for the same purpose from 1825. Such sites were chosen for their isolation, and the natural beauty of the locations only emphasised the horrors attached to their reputations. Macquarie Harbour was approached through a narrow and treacherous entrance, Hell's Gates, and its inmates had to cut down the giant eucalypts from the rainswept hills and haul them to the water's edge. Port Arthur, where the stonework still stands in the lush green surrounds of the Tasman Peninsula as a major tourist attraction, has served as a prison, asylum, boys' prison and, in 1996, the site of a gun massacre.

Moreton Bay, where eventually the city of Brisbane arose, had a death rate of one in ten. Its commander, Captain Patrick Logan, was killed in 1830 by Aborigines at the instigation, it was claimed, of the convicts he mistreated. A popular ballad celebrated the event:

> For three long years I've been beastly treated;
> Heavy irons each day I wore;
> My back from flogging has been lacerated,
> And of times painted with crimson gore.
> Like the Egyptians and ancient Hebrews,
> We were oppressed by Logan's yoke,
> Till Kind Providence came to our assistance,
> And gave this tyrant his mortal stroke.

Norfolk Island's new commander in 1846, John Price, began by hanging a dozen mutineers and was accused by his own chaplain of 'ferocious severity' that included chaining men to a wall in spread-eagle position with an iron bit in the mouth. Some years after Price left Norfolk Island to become inspector-general of prisons at Melbourne, a group of men fell on him and beat him to death.

The infamies of Norfolk Island and other penal settlements undoubtedly achieved their deterrent purpose in Britain. Earlier complaints that exile to Botany Bay resulted not in penitence but pleasure were replaced in the 1830s with an image of New South Wales and Van Diemen's Land as sites of close confinement and desperate extremity. This reputation, however, strengthened the hand of the evangelical critics. They publicised the scandals that emerged from the penal settlements to clinch their argument that the convict system was immoral and unnatural. Along with campaigns against slavery and oppression of native peoples in other parts of the Empire, the anti-transportation movement worked on a humanitarian conscience that was more sensitive to pain, more susceptible to reports of moral degradation. It also fostered the pejorative British attitudes towards the Australian colonies that affronted the colonists, and possibly contributed to a lingering condescension: well into the twentieth century a prickly Australian could be accused of 'rattling his chains'.

Within Australia there was a reluctance to acknowledge the convict stain. The gothic horrors of Macquarie Harbour, Port Arthur and Norfolk Island were lodged subsequently in the popular imagination through the writing of Marcus Clarke (who based a character in the novel *His Natural Life*, 1874, on Price), William Astley (who wrote of the same events during the 1890s in *Tales of the Convict System* and *Tales of the Isle of Death*), and more recently in Robert Hughes' epic *The Fatal Shore*. Against such dark and brooding imagery contend the revisionist historians, who point out that most convicts never experienced secondary punishment. Their emphasis on the utility of the convict worker and normality of the convict experience within a comparative framework of global movements of labour in the nineteenth century is now in turn challenged by cultural historians fascinated by the otherness of the convicts. A recent study has noted their ethnic diversity. They came from Antigua and Barbados, China and India, Madagascar and Mauritius; they included Maori warriors and Aboriginal men punished for night raids and pitched battles, bushranging, and even pauperism.

Women, who constituted one-sixth of all the transportees, have particular salience in these reworkings of convict history, because they emerge in them as actors in their own right. Earlier historians assessed the female convicts according to their performance of particular social functions, usually posed in moral or economic terms. Were these women 'damned whores' or virtuous mothers, robust human capital or a wasted resource? Given the dual subordination of convict women, to the state and to men, such questions could hardly resolve the contradictions of their condition. The female transportees brought valuable qualities – they were younger, more literate and more skilled than the comparable female population of the British Isles – but had a minor role in the pastoral industry and were usually employed in indoor work. They played a vital demographic role – they were more fertile than those whom they left behind – but the assignment system made it difficult for them to marry.

Mary Sawyer, a female convict in Van Diemen's Land, applied to marry a free man in 1831. Her record showed a series of misdemeanours – she was insolent, she had absconded, she had been 'tipsy' – and she was refused permission to marry until she had been 'twelve months in service free from offence'. Two years later Sawyer was back in detention. Since the authorities were reluctant to send females to the places of special punishment, there was a heavy reliance on special 'female factories' built at Parramatta, Hobart, and then other centres. These served as places of secondary punishment but also as refuges for the unemployed and the pregnant, and provided the women with a space to assert their own rough culture.

The convict system cast a long shadow over societies that were ostensibly moving towards civic normality. In keeping with Bigge's recommendation that the Australian colonies should be places of free settlement, the British government constrained the governor with a legislative council to authorise his measures and an independent court to ensure that they were not repugnant to English law. The first legislative council was a primitive affair of just seven appointed members, and Macquarie's immediate successors were slow to grasp that they no longer possessed an absolute authority. In 1826 Governor Ralph Darling altered the sentence of the court against two soldiers who had stolen to obtain a discharge, and ordered that they be worked in chains. The death of one of them brought condemnation of the governor's actions by the press, which he attempted to suppress with a law that the chief justice disallowed. Several years later, Darling had one newspaper editor imprisoned under new legislation, which the Colonial Office disallowed. Other restrictions included the exclusion of former convicts from jury service, a slight that provoked the emancipist poet Michael Robinson to propose a toast at the Anniversary Day dinner on 26 January 1825, 'The land, boys, we live in'.

By this time a line of cleavage was apparent between those who wished to preserve political authority and social esteem for the wealthy free settlers and those who sought broader, more inclusive arrangements. The division was no longer simply one between exclusive and emancipist, for a new generation of those born in the colony had come of age – hence the common designation of 'currency lads and lasses' (in reference to locally minted money) as opposed to the 'sterling' or 'pure merinos' (since they flaunted their unsullied pedigrees and pastoral wealth). The most prominent of the currency lads was William Charles Wentworth, the son of a convict mother and highwayman father, who had agreed to come out as a colonial surgeon instead of as a convict, and prospered under Macquarie as a trader, police commissioner and landowner. His son was educated in England and returned in 1824 with a keen resentment of the exclusives after rebuff in a suit for the daughter of John Macarthur. Darling described Wentworth as a 'vulgar, ill-bred fellow'; he denounced Darling as a martinet.

Through the newspaper he helped establish, the *Australian*, Wentworth agitated for an extension of freedom, an unfettered press, a more inclusive jury system, a more representative legislature. These objectives were gradually won against the lingering restrictions in a society where so many strangers were suspect – a Bushranging Act introduced in 1830 gave such extraordinary powers of arrest that even the chief justice was apprehended while walking near the Blue Mountains. A partly elected legislature, which was conceded in 1842, had to await the cessation of transportation, for reasons the minister for the colonies made clear: 'As I contemplate the introduction of free institutions into

New South Wales, I am anxious to rid that colony of its penal character.'

More than this, the popular movement that gathered force in the 1830s asserted the equal rights of all colonists, regardless of origin or wealth. It sought to break down the disparities and distortions that pastoralism generated in combination with transportation, and to replace a social hierarchy in which a rich oligopoly controlled land and labour with a more open and inclusive society that would allow all to share in the bounty. Its members styled themselves Australians or natives, and that term signified an attachment to place – the freedom they sought was for the colonisers, not the colonised – but their movement also drew on the growing numbers of new arrivals. From 1831 the British government used revenue from sale of land to subsidise the passage of a new class of 'free' migrants seeking a fresh start. They arrived in New South Wales in increasing numbers – 8000 in the 1820s, 30,000 in the 1830s – and chafed at the restrictions they encountered.

The new land laws replaced grants with sale by auction and generated sufficient revenue to finance a substantial scheme of assisted migration. It altered the balance of population movements among the settler societies: whereas in 1831, 98 per cent of emigrants from the British Isles crossed the Atlantic to the United States or Canada, in 1839 a quarter of them chose Australia. A further 80,000 free settlers landed in New South Wales during the 1840s. Sale of land also weakened the arbitrary character of colonial rule, for it replaced the grace-and-favour system of land grants with the impersonal operation of an open market.

The engrossment of land continued, however, because the pastoralists moved beyond the official limits of settlement to occupy their runs by simply squatting on them – that term of disparagement originally applied to former convicts who gleaned a living on 'waste land', but it soon came to designate a privileged class of large landholders: the 'squattocracy'. Bourke's introduction of pastoral licences in 1836 was followed by further regulations that restricted the tenure of squatters, but the British government set aside this threat to their privileges when, in 1847, it provided fourteen-year leases. A hapless governor who tried to compel the pastoralists to pay for their runs remarked that 'As well might it be

4.5 Emigration as a remedy for poverty. In this English celebration of the colonies, the sullen discontent of the poor during the 'hungry forties' is contrasted with familial plenty across the seas. The references to Chartism, socialism and legal repression emphasise the contented harmony of colonial life. (*Punch*, 1848)

attempted to confine the Arabs of the Desert ... as to confine the Graziers or Woolgrowers of New South Wales within any bounds'. With the introduction of leases the squatters legitimated their illegal occupancy and turned possession into property. The buying and selling of land as a freely tradable commodity turbocharged the economies of the settler colonies.

The rapid expansion of the frontier made effective supervision of convict assignment increasingly difficult, while the use of land revenue to subsidise migration rendered it increasingly superfluous. By the late 1830s the pressures for the abandonment of penal transportation were thus becoming irresistible. A parliamentary committee in London gathered evidence of the iniquity of the convict system, and its 1837 report deemed transportation an 'inefficient, cruel and demoralising' punishment that turned colonists into 'cruel and hard-hearted slave-owners'. The government suspended transportation to New South Wales in 1840.

An attempt to revive it in 1849 brought indignant colonial protest and final abandonment.

That left Van Diemen's Land as the destination for criminal exiles. The island colony (its administration was separated from New South Wales in 1825) had, in any case, a higher proportion of transportees and a smaller proportion of free settlers: three-quarters of the population in 1840 consisted of convicts, ex-convicts and their offspring. The gap between the exclusive and the felon was wider, more poisonous in its effects. The eagle-eyed Governor Arthur kept a far closer control than his mainland counterparts, extending to a law in 1835 that imposed special penalties on convicts, ticket-of-leave men and even expirees.

The pastoral gentry built country seats of impressive grandeur and planted the amenities and institutions of English landed society, as if to ward off the raw novelty of life on a distant island where the brooding hills and sombre forests pressed in upon them. The finest of all colonial artists, John Glover, built his house on the northeast plain on a property of 3000 hectares. He painted it in 1835 with

4.6 John Glover was a successful English artist who settled in Australia in 1831. His 1835 painting *A View of the Artist's House and Garden in Mill Plains, Van Diemen's Land* domesticates the landscape with European plants. (Art Gallery of South Australia)

orderly rows of imported flowers and shrubs in the foreground, the eerie native growth behind. His farm scenes of Arcadian tranquillity reconstructed a familiar English world. Yet the veneer of civilisation was thin and the rapid increase in convict numbers during the 1840s – more than 25,000 were added to a population of fewer than 60,000 – increased the demand to remove the criminal incubus and start anew. With its abandonment of transportation in 1853, Van Diemen's Land became Tasmania.

***

One reason for the stagnation of Tasmania during the 1840s was that so many of its enterprising residents crossed Bass Strait for the Port Phillip district on the mainland. While the British government rejected the land grab that John Batman and his colleagues negotiated with the Aboriginals in 1835, it had thrown open the district to settlement. A stream of over-landers who followed Thomas Mitchell's route from New South Wales quickly joined the over-straiters to spread over the rich grasslands. By 1841 the district contained 20,000 settlers and 1 million sheep, and by 1850 the population reached 75,000 Europeans and 5 million sheep. Land in the principal settlement of Melbourne at the head of Port Phillip Bay was already attracting speculative English investment.

The rectangular grid design of the new town, laid out on Bourke's instructions in 1837, marked a break with the older settlements of Sydney and Hobart. They were dominated by their garrisons and barracks, an improvised and irregular streetscape marking out the administrative, commercial and residential quarters, with the well-to-do commanding the higher spurs and the lower orders huddled close to the water's edge. Melbourne, by contrast, was a triumph of utilitarian regularity, a series of straight lines imposed on the ground that allowed investors to buy from the plan.

Two other new settlements used commerce as the basis of colonisation. The first of them, the Swan River Colony, began with an eye to the threat of French occupancy: in 1826 the governor of New South Wales sent a party to King George's Sound on the far south-west corner of Australia to forestall that possibility and a naval captain, James Stirling, to explore the principal river further up the western coast. The decision in 1829 to annex the western third of Australia and create a colony on the Swan River favoured a group of well-connected promoters who were allocated land in return for their contribution of capital and labour. They created a port settlement, Fremantle, at the mouth of the Swan, and a township, Perth, further up where the river widened, but their hopes of agricultural bounty were soon dashed. By 1832, out of 400,000 hectares that had been alienated just forty were under cultivation.

The failure of the original expectations stemmed partly from the poor soil and dry climate, but most of all from shortage of labour: the 2000 who arrived in the foundation years scarcely increased for a further decade. In 1842 an Anglican clergyman visited one of the colony's original promoters. His cousin, Robert Peel, had been a minister in the government that authorised the colony and was now the prime minister. Yet Thomas Peel, the proprietor of more than 100,000 hectares, was living in 'a miserable hut' with his son, mother-in-law and a black servant. 'Everything about him shows the broken-down gentleman – clay floors and handsome plate – curtains for doors and piano forte – windows without glass and costly china.'

Such a fate had been predicted by a perceptive, if erratic critic, Edward Gibbon Wakefield, when the Swan River Colony was proposed. Writing in 1829 from Newgate Prison in London (where he was imprisoned for eloping with a young heiress) a work that he passed off as a *Letter from Sydney*, Wakefield observed that cheap land made labour expensive since the wage-earner could too easily become a proprietor. His own scheme of 'systematic colonisation' would set a higher price on land to finance migration and ensure an adequate labour supply – like Bigge, he sought to replicate the British class structure, only he would replace the convict depot with the labour exchange. Land, labour and capital could be combined in proper proportions by providing that settlement was confined and concentrated. 'Concentration would produce what never did and never can exist without it – Civilization.'

An accomplished mesmerist, Wakefield appealed to both Utilitarians and political economists with his idea of harnessing self-interest and social improvement in model communities created

by private initiative with a self-regulating division of labour, generous provision of parks, churches and schools, and the greatest
measure of freedom. Systematic colonisation was implemented in
six separate New Zealand settlements. It was first attempted in
South Australia.

The Province of South Australia, established in 1836, distributed
power between the Crown and a board of commissioners responsible for survey and sale of land, and selection and transport of
its migrant labour force. While the principal settlement, Adelaide,
and its surrounds were carefully laid out by William Light,
the surveyor-general, the arrangement soon succumbed to land
speculation, and South Australia reverted to the status of an
ordinary Crown colony in 1842. It recovered, nevertheless, with
fertile wheatlands surrounding the indented coast, and rich copper
deposits. By 1850 the white population passed 60,000. The colony
fulfilled its founder's expectations in other ways: it was a free
colony, untainted by convicts, and with a measure of self-
government; it was familial, with a closer balance of male and
female than any other Australian settlement; and it offered religious equality, so that Nonconformist denominations imparted an
improving respectability to its public life.

With the British settlement in the central portion of Australia, the
whole of the continent was formally taken up. The increase in
colonial population – 30,000 in 1820, 60,000 in 1830, 160,000 in
1840, 400,000 in 1850 – reveals a quickening tempo, as does the
spread of settlement after 1820 beyond the original narrow enclaves
in the southeast. Yet the dispersal remained limited. A Queensland
outpost got under way only after the Moreton Bay penal colony was
abandoned in 1842 and the district thrown open to settlement; the
white population in 1850 was just 8000. Attempts to establish new
colonies further north invariably failed, and the white population
above the Tropic of Capricorn was negligible. After sixty years of
endeavour, two-thirds of the white population still lay within the
southeast corner of the mainland. The same proportion has held
ever since.

Already 40 per cent of the population lived in towns. The
preference for contiguity was a pronounced feature of the older
penal settlements and even stronger in the new, voluntary ones.

The graziers of New South Wales might roam like the Arabs of the desert, but the less favoured clung to the comforts of the oasis. For all the attempts of the governors after the Bigge report to send convicts up-country, they drifted back to more congenial surrounds such as The Rocks area of inner Sydney with its rough conviviality and networks of support. Isolation in the bush had its own measure of freedom, and generated its own fraternity of mateship, but isolation reduced choice and increased exposure. Life in The Rocks was rowdy and violent, most children were born out of wedlock and there was a constant turnover of residents, but this very fluidity shielded the inhabitants from surveillance and control. In the free colonies a different logic produced a similar result. There was no desire for anonymity here but rather a hunger for sociability that would soften the emotional rigours of separation and ease loneliness. A fabric of voluntary associations – civic, religious and recreational – was quickly created in Adelaide, Melbourne and Perth to incorporate their residents into community life.

In the penal colonies such institutions were more likely to be imposed from above. For as long as the convict system lasted these colonies had to be administered because they could not be trusted to govern themselves, and those who were subjected to such control were less inclined to submit themselves willingly to its operation. In the absence of representative assemblies, people turned for protection from over-zealous officialdom to the courts, so that political debate was displaced into arguments over legal rights. The custodians tried persistently to civilise these colonies and plant the institutions that would redeem their inhabitants, yet every one of the civilising devices they employed was distorted by the coercive purpose to which it was put.

The family was one such device. In 1841 Caroline Chisholm, the wife of an army officer, established a female immigrants' home in Sydney to rescue single women from the mortal sin to which they were so perilously exposed. She accompanied them into rural areas and placed them in domestic employment under suitable masters in the hope that matrimony would follow. To end the 'monstrous disparity' between the sexes and rescue the colonies from 'the demoralising state of bachelorism' was her aim, so that 'civilization and religion will advance, until the spire of the churches will guide the stranger from hamlet to hamlet, and the shepherds' huts become homes for happy men and virtuous women'. In this scheme of 'family colonisation' the women were to serve the men as wives and mothers in order to reclaim them to Christian virtue; as she put it, they were pressed into service as 'God's police'.

Religious worship was in turn promoted in New South Wales by the Church Act of 1836, which subsidised the building of churches and the stipends of ministers. Similar legislation was extended to Van Diemen's Land in the following year. The measure was significant for its recognition of all denominations (it was less than a decade since Catholics in the United Kingdom had been allowed to participate in public life), and confirmation of religious freedom. It brought a rapid growth of church activity, and the fact that Methodists, Congregationalists and Baptists used that term in preference to the more traditional 'chapel' declared their claims to parity. There would be no confessional state in Australia, nor the customs and traditions that shaped community life in Europe. Here religion was more institutional and faith a matter of personal belief and commitment.

In 1848 a minister in New South Wales reported the saying 'No Sunday beyond the mountains'; it was used, he said, by men as they descended from the Blue Mountains onto the western plains. Yet provision for worship had increased five-fold since the introduction of public subsidies. Often it meant no more than a small timber box on the main street of an infant settlement, or a primitive church built of slabs in a freshly cleared paddock where tree-stumps outnumbered gravestones. The church brought people together in common purpose and encouraged a range of voluntary activity.

Public assistance also encouraged denominational rivalries. While the Church of England made the most of the subsidies, since it could draw on support of wealthy adherents to qualify for them, the local hierarchy was reluctant to accept its loss of privileged status. The Anglicans continued to think of themselves as the church of the establishment, with the strengths and weaknesses of that orientation. Catholics remained sensitive to slights, a feeling intensified by their status as both a religious and a national minority that was over-represented among the needy. The English Benedictine who was sent as vicar-general in 1832 wrestled with the Irish temper of his charges, but his attempt to recruit English priests failed. Without priests there could be no sacraments, and the inability to sustain the faith exacerbated resentment. John Dunmore Lang, the leading Presbyterian minister, was an implacable foe of both the episcopal denominations but particularly hostile towards Catholicism. Others who shared his vision of a godly nation also tried to impose a civic Protestantism on public life.

In this formative period the churches also worked out their local forms of government, and the patterns of support. The Anglicans had most adherents, something less than half, followed by the Catholics, about a quarter. Presbyterians, Methodists, and other Nonconformists made up the remainder. Though there were significant variations between the colonies, these proportions would persist for at least a century. The growth of Christian worship came from a low base. Anglican, Catholic and Presbyterian alike complained of the neglect of the Sabbath, the profanity, and immorality, and shared with the less numerous Nonconformist evangelicals a preoccupation with sin. Alongside the ballads and broadsides that proclaimed defiance of conventional morality –

> Land of Lags and Kangaroo,
> Of possums and the scarce Emu,
> The Farmer's pride but the Prisoner's Hell,
> Land of Sodom – Fare-thee-well!

– there were some contrite convict statements. Typically composed in narrative form as moral tracts, these confessional works described the wretched degradation of penal life, told of the blessed moment when the sinner became conscious of God's grace, then recorded the good works and purposeful endeavour that brought sobriety, industry, and happiness after the convert put aside vicious habits and dissolute associations. Such homilies only emphasised the heathen character of the mass of the felonry.

The colonists drew also on the arts of civilisation. In prose and verse, art and architecture, they marked the course of progress,

order and prosperity. Landscape painting contrasted the primitive
savage with the industrious swain, the sublime beauty of nature with
the divided fields and picturesque country house. Didactic and epic
odes celebrated the successful transformation of wilderness into
commercial harmony:

> Now, mark, where o'er the populated Plain
> Blythe Labour moves, and calls her sturdy Train;
> While, nurs'd by clement skies, and genial Gales,
> Abundant Harvests cloathe the fruitful Vales.

The imagery was neoclassical, casting back to the ancient civilisations to affirm the course of empire and suggesting how through
successful imitation the colonists were participating in universal
laws of human history to fulfil their destiny. Hence Wentworth's
'Australasia', submitted for a poetry prize while he was a student in
Cambridge in 1823:

> May this, thy last-born infant, – then arise,
> To glad thy heart, and greet thy parent eyes;
> And Australasia float, with flag unfurl'd,
> A new Britannia in another world.

The neoclassical sought to affirm and renew a received model of
social order that was organic and hierarchical. Through restraint
and regularity it endeavoured to dignify the harsh circumstances of
involuntary exile and brutal conquest, to elevate colonial life, and
instruct the colonists in the arts and sciences. As the coercive phase
of the penal foundations gave way to emancipation and free settlement, the neoclassical model yielded to the Utilitarian project of
moral enlightenment. The emphasis here was on schemes of secular
as well as spiritual improvement, temperance, rational recreation,
cultivation of the mind and the body. It found expression in the
pastoral romance of the bush, where the merry squatter achieved
freedom and fulfilment in a way of life that was no longer imitative
but distinctive and new.

   The very names that the settlers placed on the land suggest a
similar emergence of new from old. The principal settlements were
named after members of the British government (Sydney, Hobart,
Melbourne, Brisbane, Bathurst, Goulburn) or birthplace (Perth) or

royal birthplace (Launceston) or consort (Adelaide). Harbours and ports were more likely to honour local figures (Port Macquarie, Darling Harbour, Port Phillip, Fremantle). Familiar names were transferred to some localities (the Domain, Glebe), some were simply descriptive (The Rocks, the Cowpastures, the Cascades, the Swan River) and some evocative (Encounter Bay) or associational (Newcastle). There were few Aboriginal names in the early years of settlement (Parramatta, Woolloomooloo, though Phillip named Manly after one) but they were more common by the 1830s (Myall Creek). By then the obsequious habit was in decline. Rather than seek favour with official patrons in London, the locals proclaimed their places of origin. Hence the regional clusters of English, Scottish, Irish, Welsh and, from the 1840s, even German place-names.

These ethnic identities found their way into work and worship. The maintenance of networks, the searching out of compatriots and the reproduction of customs were a natural response to the anonymities of resettlement. With some outlying exceptions (such as the German Lutheran community in the Barossa Valley of South Australia), however, none of the national groupings formed a genuine enclave. All of them were porous, allowing for movement, interaction and intermarriage. The display of Cornishness, for example, was more the advertisement of particular qualities and attributes well suited to work in the copper mines of South Australia than of any irredentist impulse. The ersatz Scottishness that compounded Burns suppers and Highland games was a secondary identity for those who chose to practise it. A Saint Patrick's Day procession through the streets of Sydney began in 1840, not as a protest but 'to demonstrate the respectability, loyalty and community spirit of affluent Irish emancipists'.

The same impulse was apparent in the commercial centres of the new colonies, where land was bought and sold, and the owner built as he chose. The symmetrical balance of Georgian and Regency design used, with local adaptations, in Sydney and Hobart, succumbed in Melbourne and Adelaide to a multiplicity of styles – medieval Gothic, renaissance revival and the round-arched Italianate – which proclaimed the new measure of civic freedom and autonomous identity.

Between 1822 and 1850 the Australian colonies relaxed coercion by the state for reliance on the market and its associated forms of voluntary behaviour. The transition was accompanied by violent expropriation, and the convict experience left its own legacy of bitter memories. Yet the outcome was a settler society characterised by high rates of literacy, general familiarity with commodities, productive innovation, and impressive adaptation to the challenge of uprooting and starting anew. What began as a place of exile had become a location of choice.

5

Progress, 1851–1888

At the end of 1850 Edward Hargraves returned to Sydney from a year on the other side of the Pacific. He was one of the 'fortyniners' who had converged on California in search of gold. Although unsuccessful in that quest, Hargraves was struck by the similarity between the gold country there and the transalpine slopes of his homeland. In the summer of 1851 he crossed the Blue Mountains to Bathurst and washed a deposit of sand and gravel from a waterhole to disclose a grain of gold in a tin dish. 'This is a memorable day in the history of New South Wales', he told his companion. 'I shall be a baronet, you will be knighted, and my old horse will be stuffed, put into a glass-case, and sent to the British Museum.' Hargraves named his place of discovery Ophir and set off back to Sydney to claim a reward from the governor.

Hargraves was not the last Australian miner to engage in self-promotion or seek public recognition and reward. He was not even the first colonist to find gold: shepherds had picked up nuggets from rocky outcrops, and a clerical geologist collected many such specimens. In 1844 this scientist showed one to Governor Gipps and claimed that he was advised, 'Put it away, Mr Clarke, or we shall all have our throats cut.' This again was one of the tall tales spun from the precious metal. The colonial authorities were certainly worried that buried treasure would excite the passions of the criminal class and distract men from honest labour. Faced with the fact of a local rush, however – and within four months of Hargraves trumpeting his success, one thousand prospectors were camped on

Ophir – they devised an appropriate response. There would be commissioners to regulate the diggings and collect licence fees, which entitled the holder to work a small claim. The same pragmatic policy was extended to the Port Phillip District (which in July 1851 was separated from New South Wales and renamed the colony of Victoria) when the rush spread there three months later.

The deposits of gold in southeast Australia were formed by rivers and creeks that flowed down the Great Dividing Range and left large concentrations of the heavy sediment in gullies as they slowed where the gradient flattened. Much of this gold was close to the surface and could be dug with pick and shovel, washed in pans or simple rocking cradles. Together with the licence system, the alluvial nature of the goldfields allowed large numbers to share in the wealth. There were 20,000 on the Victorian diggings by the end of 1851, and their population peaked at 150,000 in 1858. The diggers worked in small groups, for the surface area of a claim was often no larger than a boxing ring, and moved on as soon as they had exhausted the ground below.

During the 1850s Victoria contributed more than one-third of the world's gold output. With California it produced such wealth that the United States of America and the United Kingdom were able to back the expansion of their monetary systems with gold to underwrite financial dominance. The gold rush transformed the Australian colonies. In just two years the number of new arrivals was greater than the number of convicts who had landed in the previous seventy years. The non-Aboriginal population trebled, from 430,000 in 1851 to 1,150,000 in 1861; that of Victoria grew sevenfold, from 77,000 to 540,000, giving it a numerical supremacy over New South Wales that it retained to the end of the century. The millions of pounds of gold bullion that were shipped to London each year brought a flow of imports (in the early 1850s Australia bought 15 per cent of all British exports) and reinforced the proclivity for consumption. The goldfields towns also provided a ready market for local produce and manufactures. In this decade the first railways were constructed, the first telegraphs began operating and the first steamships plied between Europe and Australia.

'This convulsion has unfixed everything,' wrote Catherine Spence, an earnest young Scottish settler in Adelaide when she visited

5.1 The writer and photographer Antoine Fauchery worked for two years on the Victorian fields in the early 1850s. His carefully composed tableau of alluvial prospectors, with shovels and pan, conveys the excitement of the early gold rush. (La Trobe Picture Collection, State Library of Victoria)

Melbourne at the height of the 'gold fever'. 'Religion is neglected, education despised, the libraries are almost deserted; ... everybody is engrossed by the simple object of making money in a very short time.' Many shared her concern. Gold acted as a magnet for adventurers from all round the world, with a preponderance of single men who imbued the diggings with masculine excitement. Most of them were British but there was a substantial proportion of 'foreigners': Americans, with a knowledge of water-races and a fondness for firearms; French, Italian, German, Polish and Hungarian exiles who had been swept up in the republican uprising of 1848 that shook the thrones of Europe. The Chinese, 40,000 of them, made up the largest foreign contingent and were subjected to ugly outbreaks of racial violence.

At the head of Port Phillip Bay, where most goldseekers disembarked, heaps of abandoned possessions alongside the forest of masts testified to the exorbitant prices for accommodation and transport. Seamen jumped their ships, shepherds left their flocks, servants quit their masters and husbands their wives to seek fortunes with pick and shovel. Small wonder that critics saw the gold rush as a ruinous inundation and denounced the mania that turned settlers into wanderers, communities into mobs.

These fears came to a head as the surface gold at Ballarat was worked out and the diggers, who now had to labour for months in wet clay to reach the deep leads, became resentful of the bullying and corruption associated with the collection of the monthly licence fee. Agitators such as the Prussian republican Frederick Vern, the fiery Italian redshirt Raffaelo Carboni, and the blunt Scottish Chartist Tom Kennedy, harangued them:

> Moral persuasion's all a humbug,
> Nothing convinces like a lick in 'the lug'.

They came together in a Reform League under the leadership of an Irish engineer, Peter Lalor, to declare that 'the people are the only legitimate source of all political power'. At the end of 1854 a thousand men assembled at Eureka, on the outskirts of Ballarat, and unfurled their flag, a white cross and stars on a blue field, to proclaim their oath: 'We swear by the Southern Cross to stand truly by each other, and fight to defend our rights and liberties.'

Troops from Melbourne overran the improvised stockade on the slopes of the Eureka goldfield and killed twenty-two of its defenders. But the rebels were vindicated. Juries in Melbourne refused to convict the leaders put on trial for high treason; a royal commission condemned the goldfields administration; the miners' grievances were remedied and even their demands for political representation were soon conceded, so that within a year the rebel Lalor became a member of parliament and eventually a minister of the Crown.

The Eureka rebellion became a formative event in the national mythology, the Southern Cross a symbol of freedom and independence. Radical nationalists celebrated it as a democratic uprising against imperial authority and the first great event in the emergence of the labour movement. The Communist Party's Eureka Youth League invoked this legacy in the 1940s, and the industrial rebels of the Builders' Labourers Federation adopted the Eureka flag in the 1970s; but so did the right-wing National Front, while revisionist historians have argued that the rebellion should be seen as a tax revolt by small business. More recently, the open-air museum at Ballarat has recreated 'Blood on the Southern Cross' as a sound-and-light entertainment for tourists.

Rebellion might be too strong a term for a localised act of defiance. Like the officials who overreacted, its celebrants saw it as a belated counterpart to the Declaration of Independence of the American colonists eighty years earlier, without which a transition to nationhood was incomplete. Even a conservative historian writing in the early years of the Australian Commonwealth called it 'our own little rebellion'. Long before then, however, the Southern Cross had been hoisted anew as an emblem of protest, the Eureka legend incorporated into radical action.

The Victorian gold rush was followed by subsequent discoveries and further rushes. Forty thousand headed for the South Island of New Zealand in the early 1860s, and as many more crossed into New South Wales when fresh finds occurred there. Next came major discoveries up in Queensland, including Charters Towers in 1871, the Palmer River in 1873 and Mount Morgan in 1883, and over the Coral Sea into the Pacific islands. Then there was a movement into the dry Pilbara country of north-western Australia and further south on the Nullarbor Plain, where major finds at Coolgardie in 1892 and Kalgoorlie 1893 completed an anti-clockwise gold circuit of the continent. Meanwhile, in 1883, rich lodes of silver and lead had been found inside the circle by Charles Rasp, a sickly German boundary rider, on a pastoral station in far western New South Wales that became the mining town of Broken Hill; he died a rich man.

The mineral trail was marked by land stripped bare of trees to line the workings and fuel the pumps and batteries, by polluted waterways, heaps of ransacked earth and deposits of mercury and arsenic – and also by churches, schools, libraries, galleries, houses and gardens. The impulse to atomistic and single-minded cupidity that dismayed Spence when the hunt for gold began was quickly tempered by collective endeavour and civic improvement. The repeated movements drew on an accumulation of knowledge and skill, though in the process there was a perceptible change. Later mining fields offered more limited opportunities close to the surface.

Their greatest wealth lay deeper in reefs that required expensive machinery and more complex metallurgical processes. So the lonely prospector gave way to the mining engineer, the independent digger to the joint-stock company and wage labour.

Mining communities are always beset by a consciousness of impermanence that is inherent in their dependence on a non-renewable resource. The transformation of the gold rush into an industry created nostalgia for a past heroic era. It was captured in 1889 by a young poet, Henry Lawson, who had grown up on the diggings:

> The night too quickly passes
> And we are growing old,
> So let us fill our glasses
> And toast the Days of Gold;
> When finds of wondrous treasure
> Set all the South ablaze,
> And you and I were faithful mates
> All through the Roaring Days.

The mateship of the roaring days was kept alive in sentiment and action. The goldfields were the migrant reception centres of the nineteenth century, the crucibles of nationalism and xenophobia, the nurseries of artists, singers and writers as well as mining engineers and business magnates. The country's great national union of bush workers had its origins on the Victorian goldfields. Its founder was William Guthrie Spence, as earnest and improving as his compatriot and namesake who had lamented the gold frenzy.

***

The gold rush coincided with the advent of self-government. In 1842 Britain granted New South Wales a partly elected legislative council, a concession it extended to South Australia, Tasmania and Victoria by 1851 when the last of these colonies was separated from New South Wales. In 1852, as ships laden with passengers and goods departed British ports for Australia on a daily basis, the minister for the colonies announced that it had 'become more urgently necessary than heretofore to place full powers of self-government in the hands of a people thus advanced in wealth and prosperity'. He therefore invited the colonial legislatures to draft constitutions for representative government, and in the following year his successor allowed that these could provide for parliamentary control of the administration under the Westminster system of responsible government.

The colonies proceeded accordingly, and in 1855 the British parliament enacted the constitutions of New South Wales, Tasmania and Victoria. South Australia received its constitution in 1856 and Queensland was separated from New South Wales in 1859 and similarly endowed. Henceforth the colonies enjoyed self-government along the lines of the British constitution: the governors became local constitutional monarchs, formal heads of state who acted on the advice of ministers who in turn were members of, and accountable to, representative parliaments. The imperial government retained substantial powers, however. It continued to exercise control of external relations. It appointed the governor and issued him instructions. Any colonial law could be disallowed in London and governors were to refer to the Colonial Office any measure that touched the imperial interest, such as trade and shipping, or threatened imperial uniformity, such as marriage and divorce.

These restrictions were of less immediate concern to the colonists than the composition of their parliaments. Following the British model of the Commons and the Lords, they were to consist of two chambers: an Assembly and a Council. The Assembly would be the popular chamber, elected on a wide masculine franchise. South Australia provided at the outset that all men could vote for the Assembly and the other colonies followed in the next few years. The Council was to be the house of review and a bulwark against excessive democracy.

But how? Those who feared unfettered majority rule favoured the installation of a colonial nobility, a device mooted earlier in Canada and now proposed for New South Wales by the ageing William Wentworth with support from a son of John Macarthur, but ridiculed by a fervent young radical, Daniel Deniehy. Since Australians could not aspire to the 'miserable and effete dignity of the worn-out grandees of continental Europe', this 'Boy Orator' supposed that it would be consistent with 'the remarkable contrariety which existed at the Antipodes' that it should be favoured with a 'bunyip aristocracy' – the bunyip being a mythical monster. As for John Macarthur's son, Deniehy proposed that he must surely become an earl and his coat of arms would sport a rum keg on a green field.

Deniehy's mockery helped defeat the proposal. New South Wales and Queensland fell back on an upper house consisting of members appointed for life by the governor. As the governor acted on the advice of his ministers, this proved a less reliable conservative brake than was created in South Australia, Tasmania and Victoria, where the upper house was elected on a property franchise. Since those Councils had to agree to any change to their unrepresentative composition, they proved impregnable to the popular will. Furthermore, since the constitutions gave the Councils near equality with the Assemblies in the legislative process (in contrast to Westminster, where the relationship between the two houses of parliament was tilting in favour of the representative branch of the legislature), the men of property were able to veto any popular measure that threatened their interests.

The frequent legislative deadlocks produced occasional but grave constitutional crises, notably in Victoria where advanced liberals mobilised widespread support for reform in the 1860s and again in the late 1870s. The insistence of the Colonial Office that the governor maintain strict neutrality in the first of these confrontations strained the limits of self-government. George Higinbotham, the unbending champion of the colonial liberals, asserted that the governor was bound to take the advice of his ministers and claimed that the instructions of the Colonial Office meant that 'the million and a half of Englishmen who inhabit these colonies, and who during the last fifteen years have believed that they possessed self-government, have really been governed during the whole of that time by a person named Rogers', Sir Frederic Rogers being the permanent head of the Colonial Office. Since lesser men shrank from the consequences of Higinbotham's obduracy, his efforts to put an 'early and final stop to the unlawful interference of the Imperial government in the domestic affairs of this colony' were unavailing.

These flaws were obscured in the first, heady phase of self-government by the rapid advance of democracy. In the 1840s a popular movement had formed in Britain around democratic principles embodied in a People's Charter. Chartism terrified that country's rulers and many Chartists were transported to Australia. Yet in the 1850s four of the six demands of the Chartists were secured in the three most populous southeastern colonies. Their Assemblies were elected by all men, in secret ballots, in roughly equal electorates, and with no property qualification for members. While the fifth Chartist objective of annual elections found little support, most colonies voted every three years, and by 1870 Victoria embraced the sixth demand, payment of members.

The people governed, and yet they remained dissatisfied with the results, for in their triumph they had created a new tribulation – the popular politician. As their representative he was expected to serve them, and constituents importuned their local member to make the government meet their needs. They demanded roads, railways and jobs for their boys. The member of parliament in turn pressed these claims upon the ministry and, if they were not satisfied, sought to install a more amenable alternative. Under such pressures democratic politics was bedevilled by patronage and jobbery. Elections took on the nature of auctions in which candidates outbid each other with inflated promises. Ministries formed and dissolved in quick succession as the result of shifting factional allegiances. Parliamentary proceedings became notorious for acrimony and opportunism. Public life was punctuated by revelations of corruption, vitiated by cynicism.

Colonial politics, then, operated as a form of ventriloquism whereby the politician spoke for the people. Those who made a career from this activity were artful, theatrical and above all resilient – none more so than Henry Parkes, five times premier of New South Wales between 1872 and 1891, who had arrived as a young English radical and ended as the arch-opportunist 'Sir 'Enery', several times bankrupt and a father once more at the age of seventy-seven. If, in principle, the system of government was democratic and the parliamentarians were servants of the people, then the working of the representative institutions left a gulf between the state and its subjects. The politicians shouldered the blame for this unpalatable paradox and Australians quickly developed a resentment of the inescapable necessity of politics. They erected grandiose parliamentary buildings to express their civic aspirations and despised the flatterers and dissemblers they installed there.

The colonial state grew rapidly. In the 1850s it inherited a restricted administrative apparatus of officials, courts, magistrates and local police, which proved quite inadequate for the fresh demands created by the gold rush, and was almost immediately expected to perform important new functions. In addition to the maintenance of law and order, colonial governments embarked on major investment in railways, telegraphic and postal communications, schools, urban services and other amenities. They continued to spend heavily on assisted immigration. They employed one in ten of the workforce, and their share of colonial expenditure rose from 10 per cent in 1850 to 17 per cent by 1890.

The public provision of utilities, in striking contrast to the pattern of private enterprise in the United States, is held up as an exemplar of national difference between dependence on the state and entrepreneurial initiative. The circumstances that confronted the Australian colonies allowed no alternative. They sought to develop a harsher, more thinly populated land by creating the infrastructure for the production of export commodities. The colonial governments alone could raise the capital, by public borrowing on the London money market, and alone could operate these large undertakings. More than this, they were expected to foster development in all its publicly recognised forms – economic, social, cultural and moral – for this was an age that believed in progress as both destiny and duty.

The enhanced role of the colonial state had further effects. When the colonies took charge of their own affairs, they became competitors for immigration and investment. The separation of Queensland from New South Wales in 1859, followed by boundary adjustments in 1861 and the allocation of the Northern Territory to South Australia in 1863, completed the parcelling up of the continent. Except for the transfer of the Northern Territory to a new federal government and the excision of the Australian Capital Territory in 1911, these divisions have remained. The devolution made for important differences in public policy (symbolised by the adoption of different railway gauges) and accentuated regional variations of economy and demography, though a common constitutional, legal and administrative heritage was always apparent.

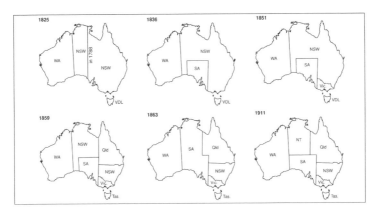

Map 5.1   Boundaries of states and territories (NSW: New South Wales; NT: Northern Territory; Qld: Queensland; SA: South Australia; Tas.: Tasmania; VDL: Van Diemen's Land; Vic.: Victoria; WA: Western Australia). In 1911 the Australian Capital Territory was excised from New South Wales.

Self-government also created highly centralised polities. The colonies had previously followed the English practice of appointing local magistrates to conduct local courts, supervise the police, grant licences to publicans, control public works and generally act as the eyes and ears of the administration. Local school boards were responsible for the provision of education. Now these activities were turned over to centralised agencies and funded by colonial revenue rather than from rates. Local initiative languished. Although urban and rural authorities were established on an elective basis, they were mere statutory creations of the colonial legislatures, so that local government remained a stunted creature with residual responsibilities. The police station, the courthouse, the post office and the school, all were agencies of a bureaucratic hierarchy controlled from the capital city by regulation and inspection, post and telegraph, in a career structure that ensured uniformity.

***

The issue that dominated the first colonial parliaments and animated colonial politics was the campaign to unlock the lands. The former

Chartists who flocked to the goldfields brought with them a hunger for the freedom and independence of an agricultural smallholding, as did Irish tenants, Americans seized with the doctrines of Jeffersonian democracy, and other Europeans with memories of rural communities broken up by commercial landlords. Those who came to Australia found that its fertile southeast corner was occupied by several thousand pastoralists who were meanwhile entrenching their privileges in the unrepresentative upper houses of the colonial parliaments. The campaign to gain access to the land was therefore simultaneously a campaign to democratise the constitutions.

In Victoria a Land Convention formed in 1857, under a banner with the motto *vox populi* inscribed on a Southern Cross, to protest against a bill that would renew the tenure of the squatters. In 1858, when the Council rejected electoral reform, the Convention assembled a crowd of 20,000 to march on Parliament House and nail to it a sign, 'To let, the upper portion of this house'. In New South Wales the Council's rejection of a land reform proposal provided the Liberal premier with the justification to purge that nominee chamber of its diehard conservatives.

If the land campaign was a source of contention and a means of confronting the inequality of wealth and power, it was inspired by a dream of agrarian harmony.

> Upset squatterdom domination,
> Give every poor man a home,
> Encourage our great population
> And like wanderers no more we'll roam;
> Give, in mercy, a free scope to labour
> Uphold honest bold industry,
> Then no-one will envy his neighbour,
> But contented and happy we'll be.

The land reformers envisaged a society of self-sufficient producers that would channel the energies of the people into productive contentment. It would replace the vast tracts of grassland with crops and gardens, the squalid huts of the shepherds with smiling homesteads, the restlessness of the single man with the satisfactions of family life, the improvised pleasures of the bush shanty with the amenities of civilisation. The yeoman ideal that exerted a powerful influence from this time until well into the next century was an essentially masculine one. It anticipated what a liberal newspaper described in 1856 as a 'pleasant, patriarchal domesticity' with the patriarch 'digging in his garden, feeding his poultry, milking his cow, teaching his children'. That his wife was likely to undertake most of these tasks was passed over. Having acquired the right to govern the state, men assumed equal rights to govern their families.

Selection Acts were passed in all colonies, beginning with Victoria in 1860 and New South Wales in 1861. They provided for selectors to purchase cheaply up to 250 hectares of vacant Crown land or portions of runs held by pastoral leaseholders. Their immediate effect was the opposite of that intended by the land reformers. Squatters kept the best parts of their runs, either by buying them or using dummy agents to select them on their behalf. By the time the loopholes in the early legislation – some of them the result of bribery and some inadvertent – were closed, the squatters had become permanent landowners. The genuine selectors, meanwhile, struggled to earn a living as farmers on holdings that were often unsuited to agriculture. Lack of expertise, shortage of capital and equipment, and inadequate transport defeated many of them.

Those who survived found the yeoman ideal of self-sufficiency turned women and children into unpaid drudges who worked long hours in primitive conditions and subsisted on a restricted diet. A selection had to be cleared by axe, the felled trees cut up and stacked around tree-stumps so that they could be burnt; then it had to fenced, ploughed and put under crop. The need to supplement income with wage labour took men from their homes, separated families and delayed the development of their farms. The father of the bush poet Henry Lawson took up a selection, but his mother worked it, and he wrote of

Land where gaunt and haggard women live alone and work like men
  Till their husbands, gone a-droving, will return to them again.

Perhaps half of the selectors gave up the unequal struggle. The remainder persisted, adapted and survived. The family farm became one of Australia's most resilient institutions.

A revival of bushranging in the 1860s drew on the discontent of the rural poor, and the young men who joined Ned Kelly, the most legendary bushranger of them all, were sons of struggling or unsuccessful selectors. The Kelly gang cultivated local celebrity in the rugged country of northeast Victoria as flash larrikins who stole horses as casually and as recklessly as latter-day delinquents steal cars – until in 1878 they ambushed a police patrol and killed three officers. The gang's subsequent exploits were the stuff of legend: a series of audacious bank robberies; a long statement of self-justification that joined the ancestral memories of Ned's Irish convict father to the grievances of an oppressed rural underclass; the beating of ploughshares into body-armour for a final shootout when the gang sought to wreck a train carrying police from Melbourne; and then Ned's studied defiance through his trial and passage to the gallows. His supposed final words, 'Such is life', ensured immortality.

Just as the Kelly gang sang the ballads that commemorated earlier gallant bushrangers, so they too became folk heroes. Sympathisers sustained them in mountain hideouts beyond the reach of the railway, local informers operated a bush telegraph by word of mouth to set against the electronic telegraph of the authorities. More than this, the symbolism of making agricultural implements into helmets and breastplates proved irresistible to journalists and press photographers who carried the story to a national audience, as well as to the writers, artists, dramatists and film-makers who have repeatedly reworked it. Vicious killer or social rebel, Ned Kelly is a product of a countryside on the cusp of modernity.

Those selectors who prospered did so as commercial producers who bought additional land, hired extra labour and combined farming with grazing. Agricultural success came first in the 1870s among wheatgrowers of South Australia and western Victoria, where the advent of the railway and adoption of farm machinery made for productive efficiency. Other farms were hacked out of the dense rainforests along the eastern coast: those in the south used the cream separator and refrigerator to establish a dairy industry, while in the north a thriving sugar industry emerged on plantations. The area of cultivated land increased from less than 200,000 hectares in 1850 to more than 2 million by the end of the 1880s.

Wool production also increased tenfold, and from a much larger base. By the early 1870s it once more led gold as the country's leading export, and sales to Britain during the 1880s amounted to one-tenth of the national product. The increased output was facilitated by substantial investment in improvements, which in turn was made possible by the newly secured property rights. Larger sheep with heavier and finer fleeces grazed on better pastures that were now fenced and watered by dams and underground bores. Before 1850 a traveller could have proceeded through the pastoral crescent of eastern Australia without opening a gate. Now lines of posts spanned with fencing wire marked the grazier's transition from squatter to landowner. The enclosed paddocks were dotted with the ghostly trunks and limbs of trees devoid of leaves, killed by ringbarking to augment the pasture; the native wildlife was losing out to imported flora and fauna such as thistles and rabbits, which would become serious pests.

For the time being, the owner rejoiced in the remaking of the habitat. His simple homestead was replaced by a grand residence and probably a townhouse in the capital city where he educated his children and spent part of the year. Architects assisted him to proclaim his success in a sprawling vernacular form or an opulent reproduction of the baronial style, and decorators filled it with art and furnishings from the old country. Behind this imposing edifice were the manager's quarters, and a small village of workshops, yards, dams, gardens and accommodation for the workforce as well as the woolshed – misleadingly named, for it was a great hall with stands for fifty shearers or more to strip the fleece that afforded these wool-kings their dynastic comforts.

Wool prices remained high until the mid-1870s and then turned down. Caught in a cost-price squeeze, the graziers responded by increasing production, pushing further inland into the arid grassland and saltbush and mulga country beyond. Abandoned properties testified to the perils of excessive optimism. Newcomers pressed too far into Queensland in the 1860s, too far north in South Australia in the 1870s, and too far west in New South Wales in the 1880s. These advances ended in retreat. Cattle could survive in the low-rainfall zone – they could walk further to water, were less vulnerable to attack by dingo, and could be driven long distances to market – but they were less profitable since experiments with canning and refrigeration had yet to succeed, and beef producers were still restricted to the domestic market.

The movement into the interior brought a revival of exploration and yielded new heroes in a more grandiose, high-Victorian mode of epic tragedy. In 1848 the German Ludwig Leichhardt, famous for an earlier overland journey to the Northern Territory, set off for the west coast from Queensland and disappeared with six companions; among the conjectures of his fate in the wilderness is Patrick White's novel *Voss* (1957). In the same year Aborigines speared another explorer, Edmund Kennedy, in the far-north Cape York Peninsula.

In 1860 Robert Burke, an officer on the Victorian goldfields, and William Wills, a surveyor, were seen off at Melbourne on a lavishly appointed expedition to cross the continent from south to north. Scattering equipment behind them, they reached the muddy flats of the Gulf of Carpentaria but died of starvation on the return journey at Coopers Creek, near the border of Queensland and South Australia. The colonists made heroes of them in verse and art, and there have since been histories, novels, plays and several films. Their remains were brought back to Melbourne to lie in state before a funeral that attracted more than 50,000 mourners. The pencilled diary of their final days holds pride of place in Victoria's state library. A statue was unveiled in Melbourne in 1865, the first great monument to inhabitants of that city; its repeated relocation attests to an uncompleted journey.

It was a South Australian, John Stuart, who succeeded in the following year and his return journey was a near-run thing, with partial paralysis and temporary blindness – but unlike Burke and Wills, whose bodies were recovered for a state funeral, Stuart left Australia embittered at the lack of recognition. His journey provided the route for the Overland Telegraph line, completed in 1872, which established direct electronic communication from Europe; the repeater stations became bases for prospectors and pastoral pioneers in Central Australia. Further expeditions traversed the Gibson Desert to the west and the Nullarbor Plain that stretched between Adelaide and Perth. Alexander Forrest's journey from the north coast of Western Australia to the Overland Telegraph found grazing lands in the Kimberley district that were taken up in the 1880s by overlanders from Queensland such as the Durack family.

Another South Australian explorer in the spinifex country of the western desert crested a hill some 300 kilometres from the Overland Telegraph in 1873 and saw a great monolith more than 2 kilometres long and 350 metres high. The explorer named it Ayers Rock, after the colony's premier. In 1988 it was returned to the traditional owners and its original name of Uluru was restored. Red in colour, it transmits a spectacular light at sunrise and sunset. For its owners it is a sacred place, and for the many tourists who now flock to Uluru and the New Age visitors who journey there as a spiritual pilgrimage, it is the epicentre of the country's Red Heart. It is also a place of mystery and dark secrets. The disappearance there in 1980 of a baby, Azaria Chamberlain, joined the powerful tradition of the child lost in the bush to rumours of devil worship and ritual sacrifice at a site of sinister mystery.

These are recent transformations. Earlier European Australians spoke not of a Red Centre but a Dead Centre. The inland frontier of settlement was known as the 'the outback' or the 'Never-Never', a place of confrontation with inhospitable nature. In 1891, the year before he hanged himself with his stockwhip, the drover and poet Barcroft Boake wrote of the city comforts provided to absentee pastoralists by the men and women of the outback:

> Out on the wastes of the Never Never –
> That's where the dead men lie!
> There where the heat-waves dance for ever –
> That's where the dead men lie!

In contrast to the westward occupation of North America, the European occupation of Australia was never completed, the inland frontier never closed.

As they moved north, the Europeans encountered further challenges. Geographically, the upper third of the Australian continent above the Tropic of Capricorn presents extreme variations of landforms, rainfall and habitat: from the arid northwest coast, across stretches of red sand dunes, claypans, baked floodplains and broken, rocky country to the dense rainforests, mangrove beaches and coral reef that run along the eastern shore. Physically, the region called into question the coloniser's capacity to adapt: habituated to a temperate climate, newcomers were slow to shed their flannel underwear, Crimean shirts and moleskin trousers, or give up their diet of meat, flour and alcohol. Psychologically, it confronted them with the presence of other people more at home in an alien environment. On both sides of the Torres Strait and Coral Sea, where European Australia converged with Asia and the Pacific, the white man was outnumbered.

Apart from the Aboriginal people of the north, Malays, Filipinos and Japanese worked in the pearling industry on the northern coast, and Afghan cameleers carried goods to mining camps. The Chinese were the most numerous and encountered the greatest hostility. For more than a century they were the largest non-European ethnic group in Australia, different in appearance, language, religion and customs. Nearly 100,000 came to Australia during the second half of the nineteenth century as part of a much larger movement that encompassed the Pacific Rim. A common arrangement was for compatriots in Australia or Hong Kong to sponsor their passage and the loan to be repaid through fraternal associations. Some returned to China but the majority put down roots or else moved on to new destinations, for these sojourners were as restless and enterprising as their European counterparts.

The effectiveness of this arrangement and the industry of the Chinese newcomers created resentment. 'We want no slave class amongst us', a Melbourne newspaper insisted in 1855. Bowing to popular pressure, the Victorian government imposed special entry taxes on Chinese immigrants and appointed protectors to segregate them on the goldfields, though this did not prevent a major race riot in 1857. The New South Wales government introduced similar restrictions after another attack on a Chinese encampment there in 1861. From this time onwards there was a racist strain in popular radicalism.

The Chinese accompanied the gold rush into north Queensland in the 1860s and the Northern Territory in the 1870s, and moved into horticulture, commerce and service industries. Gold in turn took European Australians into New Guinea, and the British government was startled to learn in 1883 that Queensland claimed its eastern half. London disallowed the action but annexed the southeast territory of Papua after Germany took the northeast segment. Earlier, in 1872, Queensland's northern border had been extended into the Torres Strait to encompass islands that were rich in pearl, trochus, turtle-shell, trepang and sandalwood. The trade in these items extended both east and west, from Broome across to the outer Coral Sea, and proceeded along quite different lines from resource industries in the south. The work was performed by local or imported labour, using systems of employment developed on the beach communities of the Pacific.

Whereas pastoralism spread workers thinly over grasslands and agricultural selection spawned the family farm, the labour needs of the more intensive enterprises in the north called for different arrangements. Whether the white man was incapable of sustained physical effort in the tropics, as contemporary science suggested, or simply unwilling to become a plantation labourer, it was clear that some other source was needed. The sugar plantations that were established in north Queensland from the 1860s used the Pacific islands as a labour reserve. At first they drew on the New Hebrides (Vanuatu), whence the common term 'kanakas'; later they turned to the Solomons and other island groups off the east coast of New Guinea for men and women to clear the forest, plant and weed the cane, then cut, crush and mill it into sugar. Sixty thousand of them were brought to Australia over forty years, some voluntarily and some at the point of a gun. Initially they worked as indentured labourers under close restriction for a fixed term and returned with European goods; by the 1880s a sizeable proportion settled with a substantial measure of freedom as part of the local working class.

Well-publicised cases of abuse brought growing criticism of the Pacific Island labour trade from humanitarians in the south. The ruthless behaviour of the 'blackbirders' who recruited the islanders, the harsh discipline of the planters, the high mortality rate and low rates of payment suggested a form of bond labour akin to slavery. A comparison might be drawn with penal transportation, which resumed in Western Australia between 1850 and 1868, for this too incurred the odium of eastern colonists. That the Western Australians had invited London to send convicts to remedy their labour shortage did not remove the stigma. But the west could be seen as a delinquent laggard on a recognised path of a development – it used convicts to construct public works and foster pastoralism and agriculture – whereas the plantation economy of the north suggested a more polarised and regressive social order. More than this, it threatened the growing concern for the racial integrity of Australia.

The Aborigines of the north played little part in the plantations but were substantially involved in maritime and other resource industries such as woodcutting. Through links with Torres Strait and Melanesian islanders, they were incorporated into the colonial economy far more extensively than further south. Their recruitment into the pastoral industry followed a process of invasion that was even more fiercely contested than that which had gone before and more shocking to the invader because it cost the lives of white women and children.

'There is something almost sublime in the steady, silent flow of pastoral occupation over northern Queensland', wrote the governor of that colony in 1860. 'The wandering tribes of Aborigines retreat slowly before the march of the white man, as flocks of wild-fowl on the beach give way to the advancing waves.' Yet a settler family of nine at Fraser's Hornet Bank Station was massacred in 1857, and nineteen at Cullinlaringo (inland from Rockingham) in 1861. Soon the sheep were giving way to cattle, but still the fighting continued. At Battle Mountain, in far west Queensland, as many as 600 Aboriginal warriors confronted settlers and native mounted police in 1884. During the 1880s perhaps a thousand Aborigines were killed in the pastoral district of the Northern Territory.

So difficult was the European occupation of the north, and so demanding the circumstances of pastoralism there, that the occupiers had no alternative but to employ Aboriginal labour. The incorporation of Aboriginal communities into the open-range cattle industry gave participants a significant role. They constituted a pool of labour from which pastoralists drew drovers, servants and companions, who sustained them and maintained their enterprise. The lot of these Aboriginal workers has generated debate. Descendants of the pastoral pioneers recalled them as wayward children and later critics of racial inequality saw them as oppressed and exploited. More recently, as the northern cattle industry has declined, historians have drawn on the memories of Aboriginal informants to suggest how Aboriginal men and women 'workin' longa tucker' managed both the land and the stockowners as well as the stock.

Further south, Aborigines were becoming wards of the state. Prior to self-government it was the Crown that stood between settlers and indigenous peoples; freed of that restraint, the colonial parliaments pushed them aside for agricultural settlement. The Victorian Board of Protection, established in 1859, regarded them as victims to be protected by confinement: 'they are, indeed, but helpless children whose state was deplorable enough when this country was their own but is now worse'. Edward Curr, a pastoralist and sympathetic student of *The Australian Race: Its Origins, Languages, Customs* (in four volumes, 1886–7), told a subsequent inquiry that 'The blacks should, when necessary, be coerced, just as we coerce children and lunatics who cannot take care of themselves'. At Coranderrk, in the upper Yarra Valley, 2000 hectares were provided in 1863 as a self-contained rural settlement under the direction of a white manager. Its residents ran stock, grew crops, operated a sawmill, a dairy and a bakery, but days were set aside for hunting and artefacts were produced for white purchasers in an early version of cultural tourism.

The urge to collect was premised on an anticipation of imminent disappearance. In Tasmania, the death in 1869 of an Aboriginal man who was taken (and believed himself) to be the last man of his people resulted in a macabre contest for possession of his skull between the local Royal Society and a doctor working for the Royal College of Surgeons in London. His widow, Truganini, was greatly disturbed by the mutilation and anxious that her body be protected from the men of science, but when she died seven years later, her remains were soon exhumed and the skeleton put on display at the Tasmanian museum in 1904. In novels, plays, films and postage stamps she appeared as the 'last Tasmanian', the representative of a sad but inevitable finality. Seventy years later Truganini's skeleton was restored to the Tasmanian Aboriginal community; it was cremated and the ashes were scattered over the waterway her people had occupied. A British museum returned a

shell necklace belonging to her in 1997, and the Royal College
of Surgeons in London repatriated her hair and skin for burial
in 2002.

Among those who lived at Coranderrk was Barak, a man of the
Wurundjeri clan of the Woi-worung people, who as a small boy had
witnessed the signing of Batman's 'treaty'. Those associations
were now regarded as quaint antiquities, for the custodial regime
obliterated the territorial divisions of the Indigenous peoples and
submerged their distinct identities, languages and social structures
into the common category of Aborigines. Given the Christian name
William and the title of the 'last king of the Yarra Yarra tribe', Barak
produced drawings of aspects of traditional life: corroborees, with
figures in possum-skin cloaks; hunting, with men pursuing emus,
echidnas, snakes and lyrebirds; ritual fighting between warriors
wielding boomerangs and parrying-shields. These closely patterned
drawings embodied an ordered social structure integrated with the
natural world.

5.2   William Barak (Wurundjeri c. 1824–1903) drew many
versions of the corroboree. At the top of the drawing are two
rows of dancers with boomerangs. Below them are two fires
and in the lower section seated spectators keep the time by
clapping, with two men standing over them in possum-skin
cloaks. The design echoes the rhythmical pattern of the ceremony. (*Ceremony*, 1898. National Gallery of Victoria)

Corroborees were not permitted at Coranderrk; in 1887 the governor wished to see one but had to settle for a drawing by Barak. But this was not the only form of Aboriginal self-representation. In 1868 Thomas Wills, the inventor of Australian Rules football and a survivor of the Cullinlaringo massacre, took a team of Aboriginal cricketers from western Victoria to England. They alternated displays of their prowess with bat and ball with exhibitions of boomerang throwing and dancing. Whether by imitation of the white man's ways or maintenance of their own, a powerful syncretism was resisting absorption and extinction.

***

Up to 1850 the increase in the European population of Australia matched the decline in the Aboriginal population. After 1850 the number of inhabitants rose rapidly, to over three million by 1888. A torrent of immigration during the first, heady years of the gold rush slowed to an irregular stream that again flowed rapidly in the 1880s. The rate of natural increase was also high: a woman who married in the 1850s was likely to bear seven children; one who married in the 1880s, five. Mortality declined with improved sanitation. Although one in ten babies died before the age of one and epidemics of infectious disease were still common, Australia was (with New Zealand and Sweden) the first country to reach a life expectancy of fifty years. Three million humans were more than the land had ever supported and required a more single-minded exploitation of its resources than had previously been attempted.

It was achieved by continuous improvement in the production of commodities for overseas markets. That improvement was in turn made possible by transfers of capital, labour and technology. The heavy investment by British financiers in the pastoral industry and the ready subscription of British savings to public loans raised by the colonies to finance railways and other utilities allowed for a rapid build-up of the capital stock. The decision of ambitious individuals and families to try their luck in Australia brought new skills and energies. The introduction of new methods and techniques to pastoralism, agriculture, mining and smelting stimulated a more general dynamic of adaptation and modification.

Sustained over three decades, the cumulative effect of these improvements brought remarkable material prosperity. Over thirty years an annual economic growth rate of 4.8 per cent was sustained. Australians earned more and spent more than the people of the United Kingdom, the United States, or any other country in the second half of the nineteenth century. The necessities of life were cheaper, opportunities greater, and differences of fortune less pronounced. Not all shared in the bounty. Low wages and irregular earnings pinched the lives of those without capital or work skills, but the capacity to set the working day at just eight hours indicated an economy operating well above subsistence level. First won by building workers in Melbourne in 1856, the eight-hour day was never general. It served rather as a touchstone of colonial achievement.

In the global economy created by European expansion, the imperial powers commanded the resources and exploited the populations of Africa, Asia and Latin America for their own benefit. In these colonies of sojourn, the European coloniser was concerned to extract raw materials for his factories; the colonised peoples were at the mercy of changes in technology and products, and the gap was widening. By contrast, settler colonies such as Australia were able to close the gap, to increase local capacity and enjoy its benefits.

The efficiency gains of rural industries left the majority of the workforce free to pursue other activities. Some processed food and made household goods, some were employed in construction, and some in the widening range of service industries. An increasing number went into workshops that produced a growing range of items formerly imported from Britain. The growth of towns was a distinctive feature of these prodigious settler colonies. Even during the gold rush and the wave of agricultural settlement that followed, two out of every five colonists lived in towns of 2500 or more inhabitants. By the 1880s towns held half the population, a far higher proportion than in Britain, higher also than in the United States or Canada. Even smaller towns supported a range of urban amenities: hotel, bank, church, newspaper, flourmill, blacksmith and stores. No less than international trade, the Australian town created an economy of market-minded specialist producers.

5.3 Shearers at work on a station near Adelaide. These men use blade shears, which were replaced by machine shearing at the end of the century. Some 50,000 men were employed during the shearing season. (State Library of South Australia, B 18259)

In every colony the capital city consolidated its dominance. It was the gateway, the rail terminus and the principal port, the place where the newcomer disembarked and, after the gold rush, usually stayed. It was the commercial, financial and administrative hub, and used its political leverage to augment control over the hinterland. Brisbane, Sydney, Melbourne, Hobart, Adelaide and Perth, each one of them coastal cities established before the settlement of their inland districts, were separated from each other by at least 800 kilometres and movement between them was by sea. Perth, the most isolated, was still hardly more than a township with 9000 inhabitants in 1888; Hobart languished with 34,000. Brisbane and Adelaide had grown into large regional towns of 86,000 and 115,000 respectively. Melbourne, with 420,000, and Sydney, with 360,000, were the behemoths. Of the North American cities, only New York,

Chicago and Philadelphia exceeded Melbourne. Work began in 1888 on a building in its business centre that rose 46 metres, and Melbournians liked to claim it was the highest in the world; a more likely ranking is that it was the third-highest.

Each of the colonial capitals presented the visitor with its own appearance and atmosphere: torpid Perth on the sunlit estuary of the Swan River; trim Hobart beneath a brooding mountain; vigorous Brisbane with airy bungalows in lush sub-tropical splendour; the orderly cottages of Adelaide framed by spacious parklands; Sydney's crooked sandstone terraces on the slopes around its majestic harbour; the ornate iron lacework on the rows of houses set out on the flat grid of Melbourne. Pressed for an admiring response to these various places, the visitor was more likely to register their common features. Each metropolis sprawled over a large area with low population densities. Each was surrounded by extensive suburbs, linked to the centre by public transport and served by other utilities, though all but Adelaide lacked sewerage and the primitive sanitation was noisome during the long summers.

The houses were more spacious than those of older cities (four rooms or more was now the norm) and there was already a preference for the single-story cottage or bungalow on a substantial allotment. Half or more were owned by their occupants. This generous residential provision absorbed a high proportion of private capital and cost the occupiers a considerable part of their incomes, but food was cheap and families took pleasure in their own house and garden. The small scale of most enterprises, the infrequency of large factories and the absence of the crowded tenements typical of the great nineteenth-century cities with their teeming masses of peasants-turned-proletarians, all testified to the modest comfort of the Australian commercial city.

Such reflections would scarcely satisfy the colonial need for affirmation. The colonists of the New World, as they increasingly thought of themselves, wished both to emulate and surpass the models of the old. The cities were their showplaces, and they expected the increasing numbers of celebrities, travel writers and commentators who came out to Australia to praise their achievement. 'Marvellous Melbourne', a title conferred by a visiting British journalist, embarked during the 1880s on a heady boom. Its pastoralists had expanded across the Murray River into the southern region of New South Wales and spearheaded the Queensland sugar and cattle industries. Its manufacturers took advantage of protective tariffs to achieve economies of scale in the largest local market and sell to other colonies. Its merchants created plantations in Fiji and demolished kauri forests in New Zealand. Its financiers seized control of the rich Broken Hill mine, its stock exchange buzzed with flotations on other minefields. The ready availability of foreign investment inflated a speculative bubble of land companies and building societies.

There was a strong Scottish presence among Melbourne's business class and, in the words of an emigrant Scot, 'There are few more impressive sights in the world than a Scotsman on the make.' Single-minded in the pursuit of wealth, these calculating men marked their success with flamboyant city offices and suburban palaces. Morally earnest, they worshipped in solid bluestone churches and raised stately temperance hotels. Confident and assertive, they assumed their capacity to guide social progress and took pleasure in sport and display. An unsympathetic observer suggested that,

> In another hundred years the average Australian will be a tall, coarse, strong-jawed, greedy, pushing talented man ... His religion will be a form of Presbyterianism, his national policy a Democracy tempered by the rate of exchange. His wife will be a thin, narrow woman, very fond of dress and idleness, caring little for her children, but without sufficient brain power to sin with zest.

That observer was Marcus Clarke, a literary bohemian who complemented the boastful achievements of Marvellous Melbourne with the exotic images of low life in Outcast Melbourne. The squalor and crime of the inner-city slums, the gambling dens of Chinatown, the dosshouses and brothels of the lanes and alleyways, all just a short distance from the clubs and fashionable theatres, provided bohemians and moral reformers alike with a repertoire of city life as compelling in cosmopolitan ambience as the stock exchange or the sporting oval. Fergus Hume's crime novel, *The Mystery of a Hansom Cab* (1886), became an international bestseller with its interplay of the bright daytime respectability of Marvellous Melbourne and the shadowy nightlife of Outcast Melbourne, both in their own ways

5.4   The man of the house at ease with a magazine while the woman reads the Christmas mail. The lush fernery frames the verandah of their urban villa and the light clothing emphasised the summer warmth of the antipodean setting. (*Illustrated Sydney News*, 23 December 1882)

places where people cast off their pasts to assume new identities: 'Over all the great city hung a cloud of smoke like a pall.'

The same process of reinvention was apparent in those more intimate literary products of a settler society: the diary and the letter. Mail was the chief link between separated kith and kin. It cost sixpence to send a letter home, and took months for it to reach its destination, but 100,000 were sent back monthly during the 1860s and as many arrived from Britain and Ireland. At both ends of the oceans, a circle of family, friends and neighbours formed at the arrival of the mail to share the news from the other side of the world.

Uncollected letters at the colonial post offices bore mute testimony to the fragility of these threads. Death, disgrace or despair might terminate communication with relatives back home; alternatively, a long silence might be broken decades later by a dispatch from the backblocks or even a dramatic reunion. Newcomers moved freely in colonial society and quickly formed new associations, so that half of all Irish brides who married in Victoria in the 1870s took a non-Irish husband. It was the same with patterns of residence. The 1871 census revealed just one electoral district in which Catholics (and that religion was almost synonymous with Irish descent) made up more than half the population. In Australia the English, Scots, Welsh and Irish lived alongside each other.

The effects were apparent in patterns of speech. First-comers spoke in British regional dialects, but their children shared a distinctive nasal twang and flat pronunciation. School inspectors noted how these young Australians elided syllables, dropped aitches, turned –ing endings into –en, and were incorrigible users of diphthongs: hence a cow was a 'caow', take became 'tike', and you would 'hoide' rather than hide. The lack of social or geographical differentiation spoke eloquently of a fluid, mobile society.

Many from the old country mistook these speech patterns for those of working-class Londoners. The novelist Charles Dickens, who had a keen ear for Cockney, did not. He used Australia as a device to dispatch a redundant character, including two of his own sons. For Arthur Conan Doyle, at the century's close, it offered a ready supply of enigmatic returnees suitable either as victim or culprit, whom Sherlock Holmes invariably detected through their recourse to the shrill cry of 'cooee' (a piercing call supposedly adopted from the Dharug people east of Sydney) or some other colonial hallmark. The lost inheritance of the antipodean exile and the windfall legacy from a long-forgotten colonial relative became a stock-in-trade of fictional romance.

Within Australia, the restless motion of arrival and departure presented particular problems for those in dependent relationships: special laws and special arrangements were needed for deserted mothers and children. Colonists responded to these uncertainties by reproducing the familiar forms of civil society. Here they displayed a marked preference for voluntarism, not so much a check on government as a supplementation of it. For all their reliance on state support in the pursuit of economic development and material comfort, they built their economy and satisfied their needs through the market. The market rewarded those who helped themselves and encouraged exchanges based on self-interest; when extended to other areas of social life in a settler society committed to advanced democracy, the impulse for gratification opened an enlarged space for personal choice.

The freedom of the individual, however, was premised on the expectation that it would be exercised responsibly. If the law of supply and demand threatened social cohesion, it was abrogated: hence the appeal of the eight-hour day as a protection of labour against excessive toil. That expressive national phrase 'fair dinkum' derives from the English midlands, where 'dinkum' means an appropriate measure of work. 'Fair dinkum' and 'fair go' took on wider meaning in Australia to mark out a normative code that applied more widely to other aspects of social interaction.

The social norms were expressed most fully in voluntary dealings where individuals approached each other as equals united in common purpose. Voluntarism combined the expectation of individual autonomy with the need for mutuality that was all the more urgent in a land of strangers. Clubs and societies provided for their interests and recreations, sporting associations for their games, lodges for companionship, learned societies for the advancement of knowledge and literary societies for its display, mechanics' institutes for self-improvement, friendly societies and mutual benefit organisations for emergencies.

The family, the most intimate form of association, was bound tightly. Both the reduction in the numerical imbalance of men and women, and the continuing legal and economic imbalance between the sexes, made for high rates of family formation. Holy wedlock was now the norm, reinforced by laws that controlled a wife's property and offspring, and provided few opportunities for her to escape an oppressive husband. The couple's fortunes usually depended upon his capacity as a provider and hers as a domestic manager. Yet even within this unequal partnership the voluntary principle still operated. Both bride and groom chose each other freely and quickly established autonomy from parents and in-laws in their own household. In the colonial family, furthermore, the wife typically played a more active role and was more closely involved in crucial decisions. Children, similarly, carried greater responsibilities and enjoyed greater licence.

Even in worship the same tendencies were apparent. It was already established that there was no official religion in Australia, and that all were entitled to worship as they chose. This was in part a recognition of ethnic diversity: the overwhelming majority of Catholics were Irish, most Presbyterians Scottish, and they demanded equality of status with the Church of England. The colonies had formerly encouraged the activities of the principal Christian denominations with financial support, but even this form of religious assistance was now withdrawn under challenge from the voluntarists.

Yet this was a period of religious growth. Both church membership and church attendance increased markedly from the 1860s. The visiting English novelist, Anthony Trollope, was struck by the popularity of worship in Australia and thought it indicative of the prosperity of the colonists and a corresponding desire for respectability: 'decent garments are highly conducive to church-going', he wrote. A similar impetus was apparent in church building, as the principal denominations raised large places of worship in stone or brick, with spires and ornamentation. A religion of sentiment flourished, as hymn singing spread and sermons became more intense. This fervour in turn stimulated a range of Christian missions and charities, while it promoted an ethic of self-discipline, industry, frugality and sobriety.

Australia became a fertile field for the new methods of revivalism pioneered by Moody and Sankey, and overseas evangelicals toured the colonies to preach before mass gatherings. The major denominations had little need of these influxes of international expertise since they maintained close links with their parent churches. Anglicans continued to recruit their bishops from England and

address them as 'my lord'; they built big in the Gothic style, introduced choirs, surplices, organs and church decoration. Now led by
Irish bishops, Catholics responded enthusiastically to Pope Pius IX's
proclamation of papal infallibility, and their work was assisted by
the introduction of a number of male and female orders from France
and Spain as well as Ireland. Catholicism in Australia was a religion
that stressed discipline and obedience under clerical guidance. As the
faith of a minority group with little fondness for British rule, it was
also a strong force for Australian nationalism.

The evangelical religion of the dissenters became the majority faith
of active Christians during the second half of the nineteenth century.
Their more localised, less hierarchical forms of government, and the
greater involvement of their laity made for higher rates of worship. In
Victoria and South Australia, where Presbyterians, Methodists,
Congregationalists and Baptists were strongest, they exerted a powerful influence on society at large: pubs and shops closed on Sunday,
few trains ran and public amusements were prohibited. Yet even this
stern puritan discipline was under challenge. As early as 1847 the poet
Charles Harpur detected an 'individualising process' at work in colonial religious life that could not be stopped. The growing challenge of
science and reason weakened the hold of dogma. Some clung to their
religion, some cast it off, and others felt the loss of faith as a painful
but inescapable necessity. The crucial point was that all these alternatives were available. By 1883 even the devout George Higinbotham
could see no alternative but to 'set out alone and unaided on the
perilous path of inquiry'.

Up to the middle of the century the churches had been the
chief providers of education; henceforth the state assumed that
role. It entered the field primarily because of the failure of church
schools – in 1861 only half the children of school age could read
and write – but the withdrawal of state aid was hastened by
rancorous denominational particularism. The creation of an alternative system of elementary education – secular, compulsory and
free – was prompted by a desire to create a literate, numerate,
orderly and industrious citizenry. 'The growing needs and dangers
of society', declared Higinbotham in 1872, demanded 'a single
centre and source of responsible authority in the matter of primary

education'; it must of necessity be the responsibility of the state. The provision of state schools in every suburb and bush settlement made a heavy call on public outlays; the teachers and administrators comprised a substantial part of the public service. Centralised, hierarchical and rule-bound, the education departments were prototypes of the bureaucracy for which Australians demonstrated a particular talent.

The universities that were established in Sydney (1850), Melbourne (1853) and Adelaide (1874), similarly, were civic institutions, established by acts of parliament, supported by public appropriations and controlled by lay councils. Melbourne even prohibited the teaching of theology. Their founders hoped that a liberal education in a cloistered setting would smooth rough colonial edges and elevate public life. In practice the universities quickly developed a more utilitarian emphasis on professional training. Preparation of lawyers, doctors and engineers became the chief justification of a restricted and costly higher education.

For that matter, the expectation that the 'common', 'public' or 'state' school (the various cognomens conveyed a wealth of meaning) would redeem the rising generation of colonial children, enhance their capacity and nurture a common purpose proved illusory. Some teachers brought the centrally prescribed curriculum to life. Some pupils caught from it a spark that fired their imaginations. For the most part, however, the government school operated as a custodial institution. The ringing of the bell and marking of the roll instilled habits of regularity. Ill-trained and hard-pressed teachers drilled their charges in the rudiments of reading and writing, instructed them with moral homilies and released them into the workforce in their early teens.

Nor was the goal of a common education – secular, compulsory and free – ever achieved. Catholics shunned what the Archbishop of Sydney described as 'an infidel system of education', and made extraordinary sacrifices to construct their own system. Mother Mary MacKillop – who in 1866 helped found the Order of Josephites, dedicated to the education of the Catholic poor, especially in the outback – became an inspiration for this mission. Her refusal to submit to authority brought temporary excommunication and an episcopal antagonism that persisted throughout her life, but she has since been elevated into a national hero. In 1995 Pope John Paul II visited Sydney to celebrate her beatification, and in 2010 Mary McKillop became Australia's first and only saint. The Protestant schools operated at the other end of the social ladder by filling the gap between elementary and higher education for the well-to-do.

The state persisted, nevertheless, in its promotion of a common culture. Museums, galleries, libraries, parks, botanical and zoological gardens were among the sites of rational recreation and self-improvement. While imitative of established models (Melbourne's public library began with a blanket order for all the works cited in Gibbon's *Decline and Fall of the Roman Empire*, its gallery with plaster casts of classical friezes and statuary), the civic emphasis gave such institutions a distinctive character, at once high-minded, didactic and popular. Their public function in turn shaped cultural forms. The privately commissioned portraits and domestic paintings of earlier colonial artists gave way to the romantic landscapes of Conrad Martens and Eugène von Guérard and the monumental history canvases of William Strutt. The proliferation of commercial

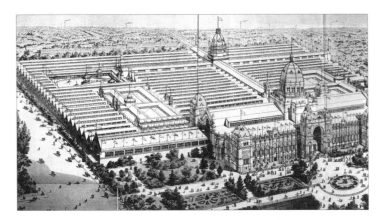

5.5   The Melbourne international exhibition of 1880–81 was the grandest of all the colonial exhibitions, with two million visitors. The temporary pavilions were subsequently removed, leaving the principle domed building as a lasting monument to 'Marvellous Melbourne'. (National Library of Australia)

theatre, sport and other recreational activities testified to the extent of discretionary expenditure as well as the time and space to enjoy it. From 1877 England and Australia began playing regular cricket matches. The first Australian victory on English soil in 1882 gave birth to a mock obituary to England's supremacy and thus the Ashes, which are the world's oldest international sporting contest.

An English visitor to Melbourne in the late 1850s was struck during her morning perambulations by the sight of a newspaper on every doorstep. By 1888 there were six hundred of them with circulations that ranged from a few hundred to 80,000. The newspaper extended the process of voluntary association far beyond the limits of the public assembly and the spoken word. It exploited technological improvements – the overseas telegraph, the mechanised press, cheap pulp-based paper and rapid, regular transport – to reach a mass audience. It was itself a commodity and enabled buyers and sellers to operate in a market that was no longer confined to a place. It both reported events and interpreted them, mobilised the public as a political force and constituted the reader as a sovereign individual.

The power of the press was unmistakable: more than one Victorian premier submitted the names of his ministers for the approval of David Syme, the majority owner of the Melbourne *Age*. Some thought of journalism as constituting a fourth estate of government; though since the colonies lacked lords spiritual and temporal, their newspapers might claim a higher precedence. Even this was not enough for Syme: a lapsed Calvinist and trainee for the ministry, he exercised stern moral vigilance over every aspect of colonial life. 'What a pulpit the editor mounts daily', the *Age* boasted, 'with a congregation of fifty thousand within reach of his voice.' A forthright secularist, land reformer and advocate of protection, he was the most advanced in his liberalism, but other newspaper owners with similar Nonconformist connections lent their support to schemes of material and moral progress as befitted a property-owning democracy. John Fairfax, the owner of the *Sydney Morning Herald*, was a Congregational deacon, and John West, its most notable editor, had been a minister in the same church. So too was the founder of the Adelaide *Advertiser*.

The colonies marked their progress in bricks and mortar, but also in amenities, achievements and anniversaries. In 1888 Sydney marked the centenary of the arrival of the First Fleet with a week of celebrations. There was a civic procession and a banquet with portraits of Wentworth and Macarthur looking down on the table of dignitaries. A statue of Queen Victoria was unveiled in the city and a new Centennial Park opened in swampy land to the south. Parcels of bread, cheese, meat, vegetables and tobacco were distributed to the poor, though not to the Aborigines. 'And remind them we have robbed them?' was Henry Parkes' sardonic retort to this suggestion. Parkes himself wanted to raise a pantheon in the new park to house the remains of the nation's honoured dead and the relics of both European and Aboriginal Australia, but his idea met a fate similar to William Wentworth's earlier call for a colonial peerage. 'We have not advanced to that stage of our national life when we have any great heroes to offer', observed a radical critic.

Parkes also proposed that New South Wales be renamed Australia, but this too was mocked into oblivion: one Victorian suggested 'Convictoria' would be more apt. Victoria responded later in the year with a Centennial Exhibition, the most ambitious and expensive of these exercises in colonial promotion modelled on London's Great Exhibition of 1851. Two million visitors entered the pavilions where every imaginable kind of produce was on display, along with decorative and applied arts. There was also a cantata that dramatised the colonial progress from rude barbarity to urban splendour:

> Where the warrigal whimpered and bayed
> Where the feet of the dark hunter stayed
> See the wealth of the world is arrayed
> Where the spotted snake crawled by the stream
> See the spires of a great city dream
> Is it all but the dream of a dream?

Such affirmative comparisons of then and now were a stock-in-trade of colonial writing. That a note of uncertainty should be struck in the centennial year and at the very height of colonial vainglory suggests a remarkable foresight.

6

Reconstruction, 1889–1913

The Jondaryan station occupied 60,000 hectares of grazing country in the Darling Downs district of south Queensland in the 1880s, and employed seventy hands. Twice a year, in late spring and early autumn, some fifty contract workers would assemble there and cut away the fleece of more than 100,000 sheep. They lived in primitive quarters close to the shearing-shed, where six days a week from sunup to sundown they bent down over the ewes and plied their shears. Charges for rations and fines for improperly shorn sheep or other infractions were deducted from their earnings. In the late 1880s the Queensland shearers formed a union to secure better pay and conditions, and by December 1889 it had enrolled 3000 members. The union demanded that pastoralists employ union members only; the Darling Downs employers refused.

The shearers gathered at Jondaryan in September 1889 and set up camp till the manager acceded to their demands. The manager sought non-union labour to break the strike: as one shearer put it, the station 'got a lot of riffraff from Brisbane who "tommy-hawked" the wool off somehow'. But when the wool bales were railed to Brisbane for shipment to England, the waterside workers refused to handle them and declared the wool would 'stay there till the day of judgement and a day or two after' if the owners of Jondaryan did not concede the union conditions. The station manager met with other members of the Darling Downs Pastoralists Association in May 1890, which sent representatives to a conference in Brisbane of pastoralists and shippers who agreed they would employ only union shearers. Only then were the 190 bales of Jondaryan wool released for shipment.

The victory of the Queensland Shearers Union encouraged the Australian Shearers Union, which covered the southern colonies. It too was challenging the tyranny of the wool kings and pressing for exclusion of non-union labour from the woolsheds. But the pastoralists and shipowners were determined to resist the union demands, and responded to the alliance of rural and urban workers with their own union of employers. 'The common saying now is the fight must come', announced the president of the Sydney Chamber of Commerce in July 1890, 'and most employers add the sooner the better'. The fight came in the following month when the shipowners told the recently formed Marine Officers Association that, before its wage claims could be discussed, the association's Victorian members must end their affiliation with the Melbourne Trades Hall Council. The marine officers walked off their ships, the waterside workers refused to load them, the coalminers refused to supply coal to the bunkers, the colliery owners locked them out and the pastoralists broke off negotiation with the shearers.

The Maritime Strike, as it became known, spread further. The owners of the Broken Hill silver and lead mine locked out their workers; the Labour Defence Committee brought out the transport workers who linked the wharf and the railhead to the factory and the shop; the gas stokers, who provided the city with its power and illumination, refused to work with coal cut by strikebreakers. A city without light! What forces of disorder might that release? 'The question' for Alfred Deakin, the chief secretary of Victoria, 'was whether the city was to be handed over to mob law and the tender mercy of roughs and rascals, or whether it was to be governed, as it had always been governed, under the law in peace and order'. He called out the part-time soldiers of the local defence force, who confronted union pickets at the port of Melbourne and were instructed by their commander that if necessary they should 'fire low and lay them out'. In Sydney the government of Henry Parkes sent special police with firearms to Circular Quay to clear a passage for wool-drays through a menacing crowd. In Queensland, where the pastoralists seized the opportunity in early 1891 to renege on

6.1   In this contemporary depiction of the Maritime Strike, Capital and Labour confront each other across a precipitous divide. Capital appears as an overbearing Mr Fat, Labour as a lean and resolute working man. (*Bulletin*, 16 August 1890)

their earlier agreement with the shearers, Samuel Griffith as premier also called out the defence force and read the Riot Act.

The employers, the police, the troops and the courts broke the great Maritime Strike before the end of 1890. In 1891 and again in 1894 the pastoralists once more defeated the shearers; the mine-owners of Broken Hill repeated their victory in 1892 and the coal-owners theirs in 1896. Other, less organised workgroups simply crumbled before their employers' demands: perhaps one in five wage-earners belonged to a union in 1890 but by 1896 scarcely one in twenty did. The confrontation between the workers, with their demand for a 'closed shop', and the employers, who insisted on 'freedom of contract', had ended with a decisive victory for the latter. The colonial governments' interpretation of 'law and order' ensured that all attempts to prevent the introduction of non-union strikebreakers failed.

Yet the events of the early 1890s had a lasting effect. The unrest in the cities frightened liberal politicians such as Deakin and Griffith into alarmed repression. The conflict in the countryside resulted in a far more draconian punishment. The Southern Cross flag flew over the camps of striking shearers, who in revenge for their victimisation burned grass, fences, buildings and even riverboats. The bush was put under armed occupation, the ringleaders rounded up and imprisoned for sedition and other crimes. An era of liberal consensus that reconciled sectional interests in material and moral progress had passed.

One reason for the alarm was the suddenness of this polarisation of employer and employee. Local associations of masters and craftsmen in particular trades had dealt with each other for decades within a shared framework of mutual obligations and shared values. Then, in the late 1880s, new unions sprang up to enrol all workers in their industries, and proclaim solidarity with other workers, not just here but around the world – in 1889 the Australian unions subscribed £36,000 to the strike fund of the London dockers. Employers formed their own combinations and they too abandoned the language of moral suasion for the rhetoric of confrontation. An illusion of harmony gave way to open antagonism as the two sides faced each other across the barricades of class warfare.

The liberals were not alone in their disillusionment. For Henry Lawson, a boy from the bush who had recently joined his mother in Sydney and was caught up in the radical fervour, the attack on workers was shocking and the response defiant:

> And now that we have made the land
> A garden full of promise,
> Old greed must crook his dirty hand

And come to take it from us.
But Freedom's on the wallaby,
She'll knock the tyrants silly,
She's going to light another fire,
And boil another billy.
We'll make the tyrants feel the sting
Of those that they would throttle;
They needn't say the fault is ours
If blood should stain the wattle.

His mother, Louisa Lawson, had fled an unhappy marriage and published Henry's first verse in her magazine, the *Republican* – its mission, 'to observe, to reflect, and then to speak and, if needs be, to castigate'. For mother and son, the need was urgent.

For William Lane, an English migrant who edited the newspaper of the Queensland labour movement, the defeat was final. He had come to Australia as a place of redemption from 'the Past, with its crashing empires, its falling thrones, its dotard races'. Now the serpent of capitalism had invaded the Edenic new world, and the racial and sexual integrity of *The Workingman's Paradise* (as he entitled his novel of the strike) was defiled. In 1893 Lane set sail with more than two hundred followers to start anew in Paraguay, where his messianic puritanism soon brought discord in the socialist utopian settlement he called New Australia. One of Lane's followers was a young schoolteacher, Mary Cameron, linked romantically to Henry Lawson before she sailed across the Pacific:

O, women of New Australia,
As our hands were clasped this day,
We knew that the Lord was with us
And had led us all the way.

She returned in 1902 as Mary Gilmore and accompanied her husband to his family's rural property. Writing sustained her from this 'descent into hell', and in 1908 she became the contributor of a woman's page for the principal union paper, the *Australian Worker*. As poet, commentator and correspondent, Mary Gilmore fashioned herself into a national bard.

For W. G. Spence, the founder of the Australian Shearers Union, the actions of 1890 revealed a different lesson. As he set them down in his memoirs, they brought about *Australia's Awakening*. First

6.2   The bush poet, Henry Lawson, is shown humping his swag with waterbag and billy. Although Lawson had gone briefly up-country in the summer of 1892–93, he lived most of his adult life in Sydney. (Frank Mahony, National Library of Australia, an12114346)

there was stirring of Australian manhood into the fraternity of unionism, which elevated mateship into a religion 'bringing salvation from years of tyranny'. Then came the industrial war, 'which saw the Governments siding with the capitalists', and revealed the true nature of both. This revelation in turn 'brought home to the worker the fact that he had a weapon in his hand' that could defeat them and bring final emancipation: the vote. Within a year of their defeat in the Maritime Strike, the trade unions of New South Wales formed a Labor Electoral League that won thirty-five of the 141 seats in the Legislative Assembly. Similar organisations emerged in the other colonies and came together at the end of the decade as the Australian Labor Party. By 1914 the Labor Party had experience of government nationally and in every state. Spence himself wrote *Australia's Awakening* from the federal parliament.

It was a dramatic reversal of fortune. Long before the British Labour Party achieved more than token representation, even while the socialist parties of France and Germany were still contending for full legitimacy, the stripling Australian Labor Party won a national electoral majority. Union membership recovered to one-third of all wage-earners by 1914, a level unprecedented in any other country. That precocious success stunted the Australian labour movement. The achievement of office while still in its infancy turned the Labor Party into a pragmatic electoral organisation. Its socialist founders either moderated their principles or were pushed aside. Its inner-party rules, designed to ensure democratic control, were used to consolidate the dominance of the politicians. As early as 1893 the Queensland shearer Thomas Ryan, who had been charged with conspiracy in 1891 and elected to parliament in 1892, proclaimed the results: 'The friends are too warm, the whiskey too strong, and the seats too soft for Tommy Ryan. His place is out among the shearers on the billabongs.'

Ryan had been chosen as the Labor candidate by workers gathered under a spreading ghost gum tree that stood at the entrance to the railway terminus at Barcaldine in central Queensland, where just a year earlier striking shearers and shed-hands congregated to read the jeremiads of William Lane. It was known as the Tree of Knowledge and its forbidden fruit was parliamentarism. The tree stood for more than a century, a hallowed symbol of Labor mythology, until in 2006 it was poisoned. But when Ryan returned to his workmates, there was no lack of volunteers to take up the burden of parliamentary duties.

The creation of a political party out of the wreckage of a crushing industrial defeat presaged a new force that would soon impel the earlier political groupings, liberal and conservative, to form a single anti-Labor Party. Henceforth politics was organised on class lines and the mobilisation of class loyalties affected every aspect of public life. The differences so clearly expressed in the events of the Maritime Strike produced a solidarity that was almost tribal in its intensity, the workers determined that they should prevail, the capitalists adamant that they should not. Alfred Deakin predicted accurately in 1891 that 'the rise of the labour party in politics is more significant and more cosmic than the Crusades'.

The wave of strikes and lockouts occurred as the years of prosperity and growth ran out. Wool prices had been slipping since the 1870s (the drive of the pastoralists for greater productivity underlay the conflict in that industry). There was an increased reliance on British investment both for government expenditure on public works and for private urban construction. Both were marked by excessive optimism, cronyism and dubious business practice, for the same promoters were active in the cabinet and the boardrooms, and easy credit fuelled the land boom that reached its peak in Melbourne.

By 1890 the cost of servicing the foreign debt absorbed 40 per cent of export earnings. The London money market took fright in that year when several South American governments defaulted, and refused new loans to Australia. Then some of the riskier land companies failed and the drain on bank deposits quickened into a run. In the autumn of 1893 most of the country's banks suspended business, plunging commerce and industry into chaos. To add insult to injury, many of Melbourne's land boomers used new laws to escape their creditors. A deep suspicion of the 'money power' was a lasting legacy of the depression of the 1890s.

Between 1891 and 1895 the economy shrank by 30 per cent. As employers laid off hands, the number of unemployed reached a third of the workforce and this at a time when there was no public provision of income support. Charities provided assistance to women and children, and work schemes were created for men, but these were pitifully inadequate to cope with the need. Some fled to Western Australia, where the discovery of new gold deposits brought fresh British investment and attracted 100,000 easterners. Some tramped the bush in search of work or handouts. Those who went 'on the wallaby', the expressive phrase Henry Lawson had used, rolled their possessions in a blanket to form a swag. In these hard times a distinction was drawn between the swagman who was prepared to work for a feed and the sundowner who arrived at the end of the day seeking a free supper.

A sharp decline in rates of marriage and childbirth indicated the extent of poverty and insecurity. Immigration came to a halt after 1891: there was a net inflow of just 7000 during the rest of the decade. Australian incomes did not regain their pre-depression level until well into the following decade. An entrenched caution and aversion to dependence were additional long-term effects of the depression.

After depression came drought. From 1895 to 1903 a run of dry years parched the most heavily populated eastern half of the continent. The land was already under pressure as the result of heavy grazing and repeated cropping. After supporting human life for tens of thousands of years the country had been conquered and remade in less than a century. The sudden change of land use from subsistence to gain and the introduction of new species and practices determined by an international flow of credit, supplies and markets brought drastic environmental simplification, imbalance and exhaustion.

The signs were already apparent in habitat destruction by exotic plants and animals. By the 1880s rabbits, which had ruined pastoral properties in Victoria, South Australia and New South Wales, spread north into Queensland, and in the 1890s they crossed the Nullarbor Plain into Western Australia. When drought killed off the last of the ground cover, the land was bare. Dust storms swallowed up dams and buried fences. The largest of them in late 1902 blotted out the sky, covering the eastern states with a red cloud that even crossed the Tasman to descend on New Zealand, 3000 kilometres to the east. Between 1891 and 1902 sheep numbers were halved.

***

Discord, depression, drought. The horsemen of the apocalypse rode over the continent and trampled the illusions of colonial progress. Yet from these disasters arose a national legend that maintained a powerful hold on succeeding generations. It was created by a new generation of writers and artists who adapted received techniques into consciously local idioms. In their search for what was distinctively Australian they turned inwards, away from the city with its derivative forms to an idealised countryside. This countryside was no longer a tranquil Arcadian retreat. In the paintings of Tom Roberts and Fred McCubbin it was a landscape of dazzling light. In the ballads and stories of Henry Lawson it was harsh and elemental.

The green tones of the pastoral romance gave way to the brown of the bush, the squatter and his homestead to the shearer, the boundary rider, and other itinerant bush workers whom a visiting Englishman described in 1893 as 'the one powerful and unique national type produced in Australia'. With the nomad bushman were associated fierce independence, fortitude, irreverence for authority, egalitarianism and mateship – qualities that were no sooner suppressed in the war against the bush unions than they were claimed for the nation at large.

The weekly *Bulletin* magazine was the chief medium of this national self-image. Founded in 1880, it practised an exuberant and irreverent mockery of bloated capitalists, monocled aristocrats and puritan killjoys, while it championed republicanism, secularism, democracy and masculine licence. From 1886, when the *Bulletin* threw its pages open to readers, thousands of the beneficiaries of mass education were drawn into an enlarged republic of letters. Here Lawson and A. B. Paterson jousted in verse, the one a refugee from the horrors of the outback, the other a pastoralist's son turned city lawyer who extolled its majestic plenitude – though Paterson also wrote 'Waltzing Matilda', the song of the tragic swagman who probably plunged into the billabong to evade the troopers because he was an organiser of the striking shearers. Here too appeared Steele Rudd, with his bucolic jocularity at the expense of the hapless Dad and Dave on their selection; Barbara Baynton, a selector's wife, who wrote of the malevolence of the bush and the brutality of its men; and John Shaw Neilson, who span songs of spare beauty out of his grim lot as a failed selector's son.

The outback is never kind to women and children. Lawson's laconic irony sustains the idealism and sentimentality of masculine bonding, but his most powerful stories tell of women with absent husbands who are left to fight the terrors of the bush. Nature in Australia has a dark side that defies ordinary logic and eventually drives its human victims mad. Just nineteen years old, Miles Franklin related *My Brilliant Career* (1901) as a rebel against her fate as the daughter of a dairy farmer: 'There is no plot in this story', she explained, 'because there has been none in my life'. Joseph Furphy, failed selector, bullock-driver and finally a wage-worker in his brother's foundry, opened *Such Is Life* (1903), the most complexly nomadic of the novels of the period, with the sardonic exultation 'Unemployed at last!' He sent the manuscript to the editor of the *Bulletin* in 1897 with the characterisation: 'temper democratic: bias, offensively Australian'. Yet even Lawson, the most gifted of the radical nationalist writers, soon retreated into the platitudes of 'The Shearers' (1901):

> No church-bell rings them from the Track,
> No pulpit lights their blindness –
> 'Tis hardship, drought and homelessness
> That teaches those Bushmen kindness.
> They tramp in mateship side by side –
> The Protestant and 'Roman' –
> They call no biped lord or 'sir',
> And touch their hats to no man!

The bush legend was just that, a myth that enshrined lost possibilities, but one that could be tapped repeatedly for new meaning. Even in the 1980s it allowed an unsophisticated crocodile hunter to triumph over hard-boiled New Yorkers in a Hollywood feature film.

Crocodile Dundee was the creation of a street-wise former maintenance worker on the Sydney Harbour Bridge. The bush legend of the 1890s was shaped by men who clung to the city despite their dissatisfactions with its philistine respectability. Lawson had grown up in the bush but his knowledge of the outback derived from a brief foray in the summer of 1892–93 into southwest Queensland. 'You have no idea of the horrors of the country here', he wrote to his aunt; 'men tramp and beg and live like dogs'. The *plein air* artists of the Heidelberg school ventured just a few kilometres beyond the suburbs of Melbourne to set up camp and paint the scrub. Tom Roberts executed the iconic pastoral work, 'Shearing the Rams', in his city studio after a short trip up-country. Charles Conder used Sydney Harbour and its adjacent waterways for his impressionist paintings. The *Bulletin* was known as 'the bushmen's bible', but it was created and produced in Sydney by alienated intellectuals who projected their desires onto an imagined rural interior and allowed city readers to partake vicariously in the dream of an untrammelled masculine solidarity.

All settler societies have their frontier legends. Whether it be the sturdy independence found in the American West by Frederick Jackson Turner, or the escape from bondage that Boers commemorated in their Great Trek, white men attach themselves to the land in a nationally formative relationship. In challenging such myths, revisionist historians do not dispel the aura of national origins so much as rework them to discover alternative foundations. Thus the Australian feminist historians who contested the misogyny of the legend of the nineties still saw the nomad bushman as emblematic, only they interpreted his freedom as a repudiation of domestic responsibilities. The masculinity the *Bulletin* celebrated was a licence to roam. Its writers and cartoonists mocked those who would hobble the lone hand: the nagging housewife, the prim parson and the assembled forces of wowserdom (wowser was an expressive local term for those who sought to stamp out alcohol, tobacco and other pleasures). The principal contest at the turn of the century, these feminist critics suggest, was not the class conflict between capitalists and workers but rather the more elemental conflict between men and women.

The women's movement that emerged alongside the labour movement at the end of the century shared many of its assumptions. Early feminists such as Louisa Lawson dwelt, as did early socialists, on the progressive character of Australian society. They celebrated the egalitarianism of Australian men and the comparatively good position of women. They also regarded Australia as free of the Old World evils of class, poverty or violence, and correspondingly free to explore novel possibilities. Just as local republicans drew on American precedents, agrarian radicals on the ideas of Henry George and socialists on the writings of Edward Bellamy, so the women's movement was strongly influenced by the Woman's Christian Temperance Union, which crossed the Pacific in the early

1880s. The movement sought to advance women and reform society by purifying domestic and public life of masculine excess. It thus pursued a range of measures – temperance, laws against gambling, control of prostitution, an increase in the age of consent, prevention of domestic violence – to protect women from predatory men. Conscious of their lack of political power, these women campaigned for female suffrage, and between 1894 and 1908 they won the right to vote for the national and every colonial legislature.

The leaders of this suffrage movement were educated and independent women. Rose Scott in Sydney, the elegant daughter of a Hunter Valley pastoralist, and Vida Goldstein in Melbourne, whose mother's family were substantial landowners, acquired organisational skills in public philanthropy that they then applied to the cause of sexual emancipation. For both of them it was a full-time activity that precluded marriage and motherhood. Mary Gilmore explained her own lapse from participation in the campaign as the consequence of domesticity:

> I gang nae mair t' lecture ha'
> I sit nae mair 'neath Mistress Scott;
> I mak' a denner jist f'r twa,
> An' sit beside a bairnie's cot.

There were strains, also, between the feminists of the labour movement, who sought a more equal partnership to redeem the working-class family from hardship, and the more assertive modernism that would remove familial impediments to autonomy. Higher education, professional careers, less constrictive clothing and even the freedom of the bicycle were among the hallmarks of the 'new woman'.

The appearance of the new woman signalled a contest as fierce in its conduct and far-reaching in its consequences as that fought out between labour and capital. It did not give rise to a new political party, and all early attempts by women to win parliamentary representation failed, for the sex war was fought on a different terrain. The leader of the Labor Party announced in 1891 that his comrades had entered the New South Wales legislative assembly 'to make and unmake social conditions'; the women's movement stayed out of parliament to remake the family and sexual conditions. In both cases a fierce assault brought home the illusory character of customary expectations. A heightened consciousness of distinctive interests produced a movement that sought to recover just entitlements with novel demands. The labour movement fought for the rights of labour, the women's movement for control of women's bodies.

An infamous rape case in 1886 on wasteland at Mount Rennie in Sydney, close to the site of the Centennial Park, served as the Jondaryan incident in this contest between the sexes. A sixteen-year-old orphan girl searching for work was waylaid by a cab driver, taken there and pack-raped by eighteen youths. There was an upsurge in such crimes in the 1880s, suggestive of heightened sexual tension, and they involved young men known as larrikins, distinctive in their flash clothing and brazen defiance of authority. 'We seldom get through a march without being covered in flour or eggs', complained an officer of the Salvation Army in 1883.

Larrikin pushes formed in the inner industrial suburbs, comprising both boys and girls who worked in casual, unskilled employment. Occupations such as street-selling, scavenging and running messages, which exposed youths to the temptations of the city, aroused middle-class fears that the city was being taken over by the most bestial forms of humanity. The Mount Rennie rapists were prosecuted, four hanged, and seven others sentenced to hard labour for life. A Methodist minister regarded the outrage as evidence of the 'vile lowering tendencies' of Australian youth; the defiant *Bulletin* insisted that 'if the prisoners' deed deserved so frightful a penalty, where is there "a man of the world" who would go unwhipped?' The Mount Rennie case was as unusual and as controversial as the Myall Creek case fifty years earlier.

Those who sought to curb the animal instincts of men extended their campaign to crimes against women within the home. From denouncing the evil of domestic violence they moved to question the very basis of marriage as a trade in sexual labour, and to demand that women should have control over their fertility. Here they were swimming with the demographic tide – there was a marked decline in marriage during the depression decade, and an even sharper decline in reproduction – though that did not prevent the men who conducted a royal commission on the birthrate in 1903 from blaming women for neglecting their national duty as breeders and domesticators.

Women had an effective response to that accusation. The interests of the nation would best be served by ensuring that children were born voluntarily and raised in homes purged of men's irresponsibility and excess. It was for this reason that feminists sought to restrain the men who frittered their earnings on gambling, tobacco and alcohol, and returned from the pub to tyrannise their dependents. Masculinity had to be tamed of its selfish, aggressive qualities in order for the lone hand to be brought to his duty as a reliable breadwinner and helpmate. Femininity had to be heeded for its superior moral status to purify the family circle and exalt national life. Not all Australian feminists followed this domestic logic to its extreme conclusion of separate spheres. They still argued for women's rights of education, employment and public participation. They also created their own voluntary associations that infused civic life with nurturing maternalist values celebrated by the Woman's Christian Temperance Union:

> Queen of the Home, true friend and helpmeet,
> Guide and mother of the race;
> Wide her sphere, and great her mission.
> Naught her influence can efface.

The contest between the sexes at the turn of the century did not displace men from positions of dominance in politics, religion and business, but it decisively altered their prerogatives.

***

The labour and the women's movements were movements of protest. With the end of an era of uninterrupted growth, the belief in progress faltered. The failure of existing institutions to maintain harmony fractured the liberal consensus. An optimism grounded in common interests and shared values yielded to disillusionment and conflict. Socialists and feminists called on the victims of oppression to rise up against the masters and men who exploited and abused them. The goal was to reconstruct society and heal the divisions of class and gender; the effect was to mobilise powerful collectivities with separate and distinctive loyalties – socialism and feminism were universal in scope and international in operation. In response to these challenges an alternative collectivity was asserted: that of the nation. It was institutionalised during the 1890s through a process that produced a federal government with restricted powers, but behind that limited compact lay the stronger impulses of tradition and destiny. Out of the crisis of colonial coherence, a binding Australian nationhood was created.

Australians can hardly be accused of rushing into federation. The process can be dated back to the early 1880s, when the designs of the French and Germans in the southwest Pacific alarmed the colonies, but New South Wales' suspicion of Victoria prevented anything more than a weak and incomplete Federal Council. In 1889 the aged and previously obstructive premier of New South Wales, Henry Parkes, made a bid for immortality as the father of Federation by issuing a call for closer ties. That brought representatives of the colonial parliaments to a Federal Convention in Sydney in 1891.

6.3   Edmund Barton and Alfred Deakin were the leaders of the federal movement in New South Wales and Victoria, and the first two prime ministers of the new Commonwealth. Barton sits on the left in the marmoreal dignity, while Deakin's informal pose suggests a more mercurial temperament. (Tosca, National Library of Australia, an22948286)

They drafted a constitution, but their colonial parliaments failed to approve it.

Federation revived when the colonies authorised the direct election of delegates to a new convention and agreed in advance to submit its proposals to popular referendum. The second Federal Convention met from 1897 to 1898, but only the four southeast colonies proceeded to referenda and only three produced the necessary affirmative vote. Further concessions were required before New South Wales did so in a second referendum and the outlying colonies of Queensland and Western Australia joined in. The proclamation of the Commonwealth on 1 January 1901 in Centennial Park, Sydney, came more than a decade after Parkes had appealed to 'the crimson thread of kinship'.

For Alfred Deakin, the leading Victorian who pursued union as a sacred duty and prayed frequently for the fortunes of Federation, 'its actual accomplishment must always appear to have been secured by a series of miracles'. For Edmund Barton, the champion in New South Wales and the first national prime minister, the winning of 'a nation for a continent and a continent for a nation' was a surpassing achievement. It touched the easy-going Barton as no other cause, and when he launched the Yes campaign in the first referendum he declared that 'God means to give us this Federation'.

If Federation was sacred, it was not beholden to organised Christianity. Cardinal Patrick Moran, the Catholic Archbishop of Sydney, provoked fierce Protestant opposition when he stood for the Federal Convention. The convention did bow to a torrent of church petitioners and acknowledge in the preamble to the constitution that the people were 'humbly relying on the blessing of Almighty God' when they formed their Commonwealth, but section 116 of that constitution excluded any establishment of religion. Moran withdrew from the ceremony inaugurating the Commonwealth because the Anglican primate had precedence in the procession.

The constitution blended the British system of responsible government with the American model of federalism: the colonies (henceforth States) assigned certain specified powers to a bicameral national parliament, the House of Representatives representing the people and the Senate the States, with the government responsible to the popular lower house. Much of the protracted federal debate was taken up with enumerating those powers and balancing the fears of the less populous States with the ambitions of the more populous ones. All of the States made elaborate calculation of the effect of the union on their own fortunes. Merchants, manufacturers and farmers considered how they would fare when Australia was turned into a common market. As Deakin recognised, 'Few were those in each colony who made genuine sacrifices to the cause without thought or hope of gain.'

Nor did the colonists wrest independence from imperial control. During this period the British government encouraged the settler colonies of Canada, New Zealand, Australia and South Africa to amalgamate into more coherent and capable dominions, self-governing in their internal affairs while consistent in their imperial arrangements. The new designation, Dominion, was adopted in 1907 at a colonial conference in London that determined these gatherings would henceforth be known as imperial conferences. So London fostered Australian federation, the Colonial Office shaped its final form, and the Commonwealth constitution took legal force as a statute of the British parliament.

That fact alone alienated local republicans, while the process of Federation was initiated too early for members of the labour or women's movement to participate and shape it. In contrast to the earlier confederations of the United States and Germany, Australia undertook no war of independence or incorporation. Unlike the Italians, it experienced no Risorgimento. The turnout in the federal referenda was lower than for parliamentary elections; in only one colony, Victoria, and that narrowly, did a majority of eligible citizens cast their votes in favour of Federation.

Yet for the federal founders and for those present-day patriots who would revive the civic memory, those plebiscites were all-important. They installed the people as the makers of the Commonwealth and popular sovereignty as its underlying principle – a principle the courts have now come to recognise in their interpretation of the constitution. According to this view, the politicians had been entrusted with the national task but botched it. The work of the first Federal Convention of 1891 languished in the colonial parliaments. Then came an unofficial gathering in 1893 at the Murray River town of Corowa, on the New South Wales-Victoria border, of representatives of local federal leagues and branches of the influential Australian Natives Association, a voluntary society restricted to those born in the country. The gathering devised the alternative procedure that would bring success: the people themselves would elect the makers of a new federal arrangement, the people would adopt it, the people would be inscribed in its preamble and included in the provisions for its amendment. This was a unique achievement. In the words of one celebrant, it was 'the greatest miracle of Australian political history'.

Perhaps it was, but it was also expressive of national prejudices. The unofficial gathering at Corowa was orchestrated by politicians. The man who proposed the new approach there and enunciated the principle 'that the cause should be advocated by the citizen and not merely by politicians' was himself a politician. All but one of the delegates elected to the second Federal Convention had parliamentary experience; two-thirds had ministerial experience, a quarter as premiers. Federation was an inescapably political act but one that Australians, with their disregard for politics, preferred to see otherwise.

These people were Australians but that national identity was itself undergoing reconstruction. The new nation was shaped by external threat and internal anxiety, the two working together to make exclusive racial possession the essential condition of the nation-state. The external threat came initially from rival European powers. France, Germany, Russia and now the United States and Japan were expanding their overseas territories. The Australian colonies, which had their own sub-imperial ambitions in the region, pressed Britain to forestall the interlopers, but Britain was already feeling the strain of its imperial burden.

The maintenance of the British Empire absorbed an increasing effort. As Britain faced sharper competition from the ascendant industrial economies, it turned to easier fields in its colonies and dominions. But cheap colonial produce, ready Dominion markets and lucrative careers in imperial administration imposed their own cost. A free-trade empire required a large military expenditure and the cost of the Royal Navy constituted an effective levy on the cheap imports that sustained the workshop of the world. That cost increased as European powers stepped up the pace of the arms race and Britain was forced to concentrate more of its naval strength closer to home.

It therefore expected its settler Dominions to become more self-sufficient. In 1870 it had withdrawn the last garrisons from Australia, leaving the colonies to raise their own troops; an adverse British report in 1889 on the capacity of these militia forces was one stimulus for Federation. The Royal Navy remained as the final guarantor of Australian security, and forts constructed at the entrance of major ports were meant to hold off an attacking force until relief arrived. In 1887, the colonies agreed to meet part of the cost of a British squadron in Australian waters.

If the Empire no longer extended to the antipodes as securely as the nervous settlers wanted, they must offer themselves in its overseas service. They had begun to do so in the 1860s as volunteers alongside British troops and pakeha in a war against the indigenous Maori. Their next act of assistance, to a British expeditionary force in Sudan in 1885, was insubstantial and inglorious. The contingents sent to South Africa between 1899 and 1902 was more substantial – 16,000 Australian troops assisted the British in putting down Dutch settlers there – but scarcely earned martial glory. Again in 1900 the colonies sent a contingent to China to assist the international forces quell a rebellion against the European presence. All four of these overseas wars, it should be noted, began as local risings against foreign control and in all four the Australians fought on the imperial side against national independence.

The last of them was the least remarked and probably the most eloquent of Australian fears. By the early twentieth century the premonition of a new, awakening Asia displaced Europe as the source of military threat in the national imagination. A rash of invasion novels appeared at this time in which the country was no longer besieged by French or Russian battleships but rather overrun by hordes of Orientals. The fear was fed by the growing power of Japan, which imitated Western economic and military techniques to defeat China and occupy Korea in 1895. An Anglo-Japanese treaty in 1902, which allowed Britain to reduce its own naval strength in the Pacific, increased the Australian concern.

The Japanese navy's destruction of a Russian fleet in 1905 increased it further. Thwarted in his efforts to increase the British presence in the Pacific, Alfred Deakin as prime minister invited the 'Great White Fleet' of the United States to visit Australia on its global voyage in 1908. A popular verse captured the sentiment:

> Not heedless of your high descent,
> The grand old Anglo-Saxon race,
> To check with stern, unflinching mace
> The swarming, hungry Orient.

In the following year Australia decided to acquire its own fleet and in 1910 it introduced compulsory military training.

More than this, the Australian fear of invasion played on the Asian presence in Australia. There had been earlier explosions of racial violence, most notably against the Chinese on the goldfields, though their enterprise brought success and substantial community acceptance. Antagonism revived in 1888 with the arrival of a vessel from Hong Kong carrying Chinese immigrants who were turned away under threat of mob action from both Melbourne and Sydney. The controversy touched national sensitivities since Hong Kong was a British colony, and the Colonial Office was antagonistic to immigration restriction based on overt racial discrimination. For nationalists, the alien menace therefore served as a reminder of imperial control; hence the adoption by the *Bulletin* in this same year of the slogan 'Australia for the Australians'. For trade unionists, the Chinese were cheap labour and a threat to wage standards. For ideologues such as William Lane, they were sweaters and debauchers of white women. Even the high-minded Alfred Deakin judged that the strongest motive for Federation was 'the desire that we should be one people, and remain one people, without the admixture of other races'.

Yet racial exclusion did not require a break with Britain, nor did it rely on Commonwealth legislation. Racism was grounded in imperial as well as national sentiment, for the champions of the Empire proclaimed the unity of the white race over the yellow and the black. Charles Pearson affirmed a white brotherhood in a global survey of race relations to claim that 'we are guarding the last part of the world in which the higher races can live and increase freely for the higher civilization'. Pearson, a costive English intellectual who migrated to Australia for his health and practised both education and politics with a melancholic rectitude, sounded the alarm in a book that he proposed to call *Orbis Senescens* – for he was convinced that civilisation was exhausting the vitality of the European peoples.

His London publisher thought that title too gloomy so it appeared in 1893 as *National Life and Character: A Forecast*, and impressed the future American president Theodore Roosevelt with the urgency of its warning. Alfred Deakin, Pearson's former pupil, shared his fears and claimed the visit of the Great White Fleet showed that 'England, America and Australia will be united to withstand yellow aggression'. Australians did not invent this crude xenophobic terminology – it was, after all, an imperial bard who warned of 'lesser breeds without the law' – but their inclination to overlook the multiracial composition of the Empire was a domestic indulgence that only a dutiful Dominion could afford.

In 1897 the Colonial Office persuaded the Australian premiers at a conference in London to drop explicit discrimination against other races in favour of an ostensibly non-discriminatory dictation test for immigrants, a device used by other British Dominions to achieve the same result. Since a foreigner could be tested in any European language, the immigration official need only select an unfamiliar one to ensure failure. This was the basis of the Immigration Restriction Act passed by the new Commonwealth parliament in 1901, but by then Asian immigration was negligible. White Australia was not the object of Federation but rather an essential condition of the idealised nation the Commonwealth was meant to embody.

Deakin spelt it out during the debate on the Immigration Restriction Act:

The unity of Australia is nothing, if that does not imply a united race. A united race means not only that its members can intermix, intermarry and associate without degradation on either side, but implies one inspired by the same ideas, an aspiration towards the same ideals, of a people possessing the same general cast of character, tone of thought ...

The founding conference of the federal Labor Party adopted White Australia as its primary objective; in 1905 it provided the rationale with its commitment to 'The cultivation of an Australian sentiment based upon the maintenance of racial purity and the development in Australia of an enlightened and self-reliant community'.

Ideals, character, tone of thought, sentiment, enlightenment, self-reliance, community. These virtues sound as desirable at the beginning of the twenty-first century as they were at the beginning of the last. The dissonance comes from their association with racial exclusiveness. We might better grasp their plausibility if we transfer them from race to culture. Our recognition of other ethnic groups, and respect for their language, beliefs and customs, is a pluralist one purged of biological undertones of genetic determinism, but we still expect their subordination to a shared and binding culture.

White Australia was therefore an ideal, but it was also a falsehood. The Immigration Restriction Act was used to turn away non-European settlers, but it left substantial numbers of Chinese, Japanese, Indians and Afghans already here. Commonwealth legislation passed in 1901 provided for repatriation of Pacific Islanders from the Queensland sugar industry, but long-term residents were allowed to stay as the result of protests. New immigrants from Java and Timor were allowed to enter the pearling industry. Non-European traders, students and family members continued to land at Australian ports. Since racial uniformity was an illusion, the promise of equality was also a lie. Discriminatory laws denied naturalisation to non-Europeans, excluded them from welfare benefits, shut them out of occupations, and in some States refused them land tenure.

The impact of these policies was especially marked in northern Australia. The population living above the Tropic of Capricorn at the turn of the century was about 200,000. Half were Europeans, though they were concentrated in the Queensland ports of Townsville, Mackay and Cairns, and the mining town of Charters Towers, and elsewhere showed little sign of increase. Some 80,000 were indigenous, mostly in the vast hinterland, and another 20,000 were Asians and Pacific Islanders. Europeans constituted but a small minority in the thriving multiracial communities of Broome, Darwin and Thursday Island, off the tip of Cape York, which did more business with Hong Kong than any Australian city.

It was the southern visitor who found the multiracial north so shocking. A contributor to the Sydney *Worker* complained how he was forced to travel with 'two Chows, one Jap, six kanakas' on his passage to Cairns. A correspondent to the *Bulletin* wrote in disgust of the situation at Townsville with 'kanakas on sugar plantations ... blacks and Chows on stations, Chows as gardeners, storekeepers, laundry-keepers and contractors'. He concluded with the magazine's slogan, 'Australia for the Australians!'

An historian attuned to the differences has observed that when Australia federated in 1901, 'there were two Australias: North and South'. The South had evolved a successful model of a racially homogenous developmental state that nurtured export-oriented farming and urban manufacturing. The North presented more demanding geographies, more limited opportunities for investment and a sparser, diverse population. The South sought to colonise the North by extending its model of economic development and social integration. But when it ended the recruitment of Pacific Island labourers and closed the door to Asians, it was unable to attract investment to the north or to incorporate the remote Aboriginal communities into the market for goods and labour. The Indigenous people thus remained outside the settler nation.

They were absent from the ceremonies that marked the advent of the Commonwealth. And they were eliminated from the art and literature that served the new national sentiment. While earlier landscape painters had frequently incorporated groups of natives to authenticate the natural wilderness, the Heidelberg school removed them to attach the white race to its harsh and elemental patrimony. Aborigines were even deprived of their indigeneity by the members of the Australian Natives Association, who appropriated that term for the locally born Europeans. Yet they remained to discomfort the white conscience. Compassion came more readily to the usurper than acceptance, as fatalism lightened the burden of charity. Earlier humanitarians had been prepared to ease the passing of those they had wronged. In gloomy anticipation they proclaimed a duty to smooth the pillow of the dying race.

Now, as Darwinian science displaced evangelical Christianity and natural law as a source of authority, the scientist provided new confirmation of this forecast. Seen from the perspective of evolutionary biology, Australia had been cut off from the process of continuous improvement brought about by the competition for survival, and constituted a living museum of relic forms. Separated by such a wide gulf from the march of progress, its original people were incapable of adaptation and therefore doomed to extinction.

Census data seemed to support this theory. They presented a downward trend, to just 67,000 Aboriginal natives in 1901. But several of the States failed to enumerate all their Aboriginal inhabitants, and the Commonwealth constitution excluded them from the national census (so that their numbers would not be used for purposes of electoral representation). More than this, the State counts excluded a significant proportion of the Aboriginal population that was incorporated, albeit on the margin of the social and economic arrangements in the south – in effect, the government confirmed the expected disappearance of the indigenous people by defining these ones out of existence.

Again, the process enlisted science to validate coercion. Between 1890 and 1912 every State government took over what remained of the mission settlements by making Aborigines wards of the state. New agencies, usually called protection boards, were empowered to prescribe their residence, determine conditions of employment, control marriage and cohabitation, and assume custody of children. The actual use of these powers varied – Queensland and Western Australia, with the largest Aboriginal populations, had the most extensive reserves and settlements and the most authoritarian regimes – and many Aborigines minimised their exposure to them. The forcible separation of children from parents ensured that.

In this horrifying practice the government drew on the doctrine of race as a genetic category. While Aborigines were held incapable of supporting themselves, those born of Aboriginal and European parents were believed to possess a greater capacity. If denied assistance and removed from the reserves, they might be expected to support themselves and within a couple of generations even produce progeny no longer recognisably Aboriginal. It would thus be possible to reduce or close down the reserves as the residual numbers held there declined. In making these judgements the protectors employed a vocabulary of 'full-blood', half-caste', 'quadroon' and 'octoroon'; more often they worked by estimations of degrees of 'whiteness', which was taken as synonymous with capacity and acceptability. They did not encourage miscegenation, and several of the protectors insisted that their staff must be married men, but once it occurred they believed it would 'breed out' the Aboriginal blood.

Such a programme was beset by contradictions. Ostensibly protective, the settlements and missions were premised on the demise of their residents. Others, on the other hand, were forcibly evicted and expected to interact and intermarry with non-Aboriginals. In sharp contrast to other white-supremacist settler societies, there was no uncrossable barrier between black and white, for Australia's policy inverted the logic of racial separation that operated in the United States. All of this was premised on the elimination of Aboriginality, the abandonment of language, custom and ritual, and the severing of kinship ties so that absorption could be complete.

It was an impossible condition, and for many present-day Aborigines it constitutes a policy of genocide. So it was in the literal sense, except that the genes were to be diluted rather than eliminated by mass execution in the manner made infamous by the Holocaust. The more common accusation is of cultural genocide, meaning the destruction of a distinctive way of life, and that undoubtedly was intended; though it is a further irony that the scientists who justified this objective were also the collectors and recorders of Aboriginal culture who made it possible for some of the Aboriginal survivors to reclaim that culture as their own.

The proclamation of the Commonwealth on the first day of the new century fused national and imperial ceremony. In a competition to design a national flag that drew 32,000 entries, five people shared the prize by imposing the British one on the corner of a Southern Cross; though the Union Jack remained the official flag until 1950. A coat of arms, supported by a kangaroo and emu, also had to wait until 1908, backed after 1912 by two sprays of wattle. First the Test cricket team and then other sporting representatives adopted the green and gold of the gum tree and the wattle as the national colours.

Australian flora and fauna were popular decorative motifs in the Federation period, with the wattle to the fore as an Australian equivalent of the Canadian maple. The golden wattle went with golden fleece, golden grain, golden ore and the gold in the hearts of the people. According to the Wattle Day League, it stood for 'home, country, kindred, sunshine and love'. But Empire Day had been introduced some years earlier as part of a conscious strengthening of imperial links. Nationalism and imperialism were no longer rivals. You could, as Alfred Deakin described himself, be an 'independent Australian Briton'.

Britain provided this continental nation-state with a portion of its own imperial responsibilities when it handed over its portion of New Guinea as the Commonwealth territory of Papua in 1902. South Australia did the same with the Northern Territory in 1911 and Australians were already active in Antarctic exploration, paving the basis for its subsequent claim to two-thirds of the southern land of ice. Meanwhile federal parliamentarians selected a site for a national capital on a grassy plain in the high country between Sydney and Melbourne and the members of the Cabinet considered various names for it: Wattle City, Empire City, Aryan City, Utopia. In the end they settled on a local Aboriginal word, Canberra.

An American architect, Walter Burley Griffin, won the competition to design the capital. He conceived a garden city with grand avenues linking its governmental and civic centres, and concentric patterns of residential suburbs set in forest reserves and parks. But bureaucrats hampered the execution of his design, which was still incomplete in 1920 when responsibility was transferred to a committee. Melbourne, a monument to nineteenth-century mercantile imperialism, remained the temporary national capital for the first quarter of the twentieth century.

The Australian nation was shaped by the fear of invasion and concern for the purity of the race. These anxieties converged on the female body as nationalist men returned obsessively to the safety of their women from alien molestation, while doctrines of racial purity, no matter how scientific, rested ultimately on feminine chastity. Women participated in this preoccupation with their own maternalist conception of citizenship, which took emancipation from masculine tyranny as a necessary condition of their vital contribution to the nation-state. A woman's personal and bodily integrity thus served as a further condition of her admission to civic status, as

6.4   These trademarks for soap, wine, poison, sporting goods and baking powder were all devised in the early years of the twentieth century when the new nation fashioned native symbols. (Mimmo Cozzolino and G. Fysh Rutherford, *Symbols of Australia*, Ringwood, Vic.: Penguin, 1980)

in the Commonwealth legislation in 1902 that gave all white women the vote. But the same legislation disenfranchised Aborigines, who were deemed to lack both the autonomy and the capacity to make such a contribution.

Some feminists regretted this Faustian compact, just as they criticised the treatment of Aboriginal women who were subjected to sex slavery of a particularly clear and offensive nature. The vulnerability of Aboriginal women to white predators and the denial of their children, the very devices that were expected to bring about a White Australia, were for these white women intolerable iniquities against the institution of motherhood. Here again maternalist citizenship was at odds with the masculine nationalism proclaimed by the *Bulletin* when in 1906 it changed its slogan 'Australia for the Australians' to 'Australia for the White Man'.

***

White Australia, Alfred Deakin stated in 1903, 'is not a surface, but a reasoned policy which goes to the roots of national life, and by which the whole of our social, industrial and political organisation is governed'. He spoke as leader of the Protectionist Party, which held government with the support of the Labor Party. There were three parties in the national parliament until 1909 – Protectionist, Free Trade and Labor – and none commanded a majority. Except for a brief interval, the Protectionists and Labor alternated in office with the qualified support of the other and a sufficient measure of agreement on policy to cause the Free Traders to rename themselves the Anti-Socialists for the 1906 election, though with no greater success. The social, industrial and political forms of the new Commonwealth were therefore worked out by a consensus that spanned the manufacturing interests and progressive middle-class followers of protectionist liberalism with the collectivism of the organised working class.

The task undertaken by these political forces was to restore the prosperity lost in depression and drought, heal the divisions opened by strikes and lockouts, and reconstruct a settler society to meet the external and internal dangers to which it felt itself vulnerable. The external threats – strategic, racial and economic – were also internal, foreshadowing loss of sovereignty, degradation, poverty and conflict. The search for security and harmony produced a coherent programme of nation-building.

Some of the elements of this programme have already been described. The threat of invasion was met by military preparations within the framework of imperial protection. While Australia felt it necessary to assert its own interests in imperial forums, the intention was always to ensure that London was conscious of the needs of its distant Dominion: the independence of 'independent Australian Britons' was premised on the maintenance of the Empire. Australia relied on the Royal Navy not just to defend its shores but to keep open the sea routes for trade. Three-fifths of its imports came from Britain, half its exports went there. British finance underwrote the resumption of growth in the early years of the new century as the pastoral industry was reconstructed and the agricultural frontier expanded.

The fear of racial mixing was met with the White Australia policy, which closed Australia to Asian immigration. But the regime of migration control was more than simply exclusionary. Overseas labour recruitment, along with foreign investment in public projects and private enterprises, was a motor of growth. Immigration resumed in the times of prosperity that returned by the end of the first decade. Forty thousand British settlers were assisted to come to Australia between 1906 and 1910; 150,000 more between 1911 and 1914, when the population passed 4.5 million. Conversely, migrants were discouraged when unemployment was rife and new entrants had a depressive effect on the labour market: there were fewer than 4000 assisted settlers between 1901 and 1905. The counter-cyclical pattern of government migration activity helped secure the labour movement's acceptance of this aspect of nation-building.

Jobs were also safeguarded by tariff duties on imports that competed with Australian products. This arrangement secured the alliance of the Protectionist and Labor parties, representing the manufacturers and their workers. By the time that alliance lapsed and the Protectionist and Free Trade parties merged in 1909 to create the Liberal Party in order to combat the growing success of the Labor Party, the tariff (with lower duties on imperial products) was a settled feature of national policy. Protection allowed local producers to expand their output and increase manufacturing employment from less than 200,000 in 1901 to 330,000 by 1914. The Commonwealth's protection of local industry had a novel dimension: it was available only to employers who provided 'fair and reasonable' wages and working conditions. As Deakin explained, 'The "old" Protection contented itself with making good wages possible', but the New Protection made them an explicit condition of the benefits.

The determination of a fair and reasonable wage was the task of the Commonwealth Arbitration Court, which was an additional component of the national programme. The endemic conflict between employers and unions was to be resolved by a legal tribunal with powers to arbitrate disputes and impose settlements. Several States had created such tribunals in the aftermath of the strikes and lockouts of the 1890s, and the federal one was established in 1904 after prolonged parliamentary argument. In 1907 it fell to its president, Henry Bournes Higgins, to ascertain the meaning of a fair and reasonable wage in a case concerning a large manufacturer of agricultural machinery.

Higgins determined that such a wage should be sufficient to maintain a man as a 'human being in a civilized community'; furthermore, since 'marriage is the usual fate of adults', it must provide for the needs of a family. He therefore used household budgets to work out the cost of housing, clothing, food, transport, books, newspapers, amusements, even union dues, for a family of five, and declared this a minimum wage for an unskilled male labourer. It took some years to extend this standard (which became known as the basic wage and was regularly adjusted for changes in the cost of living) across the Australian workforce, but the principles of Higgins' Harvester judgement became a fundamental feature of national life. Wages were to be determined not by bargaining but by an independent arbitrator. They were to be based not on profits or productivity but human need. They were premised on the male breadwinner, with men's wages sufficient to support a family and women restricted to certain occupations and paid only enough to support a single person. Women contested the dual standard for the next sixty years.

Around these arrangements a restricted system of social welfare was created. The great majority of Australians was expected to meet their needs through protected employment and a legally prescribed wage. They were also expected to provide for misfortune through accident or illness: Higgins' basic wage included the cost of subscription to a voluntary society, which offered coverage for medical costs and loss of earnings. It was recognised that some were not so provident – and State governments supported the private charities – but dependence was discouraged and self-sufficiency a hallmark of masculine capacity. That many mothers were denied the benefit of a husband's earnings was recognised only in the restriction of charitable assistance to women and children; for a man to accept a handout was to forfeit his manliness.

To this logic of the male breadwinner special cases were allowed where the state offered direct assistance: the old-age pension, from 1908, and an invalid pension, from 1910, for those outside the workforce, and a maternity benefit, from 1912, to assist mothers with the expense of childbirth. Australia came early to the payment of benefits for welfare purposes, but it stopped short of the general systems of social insurance developed in other countries where the operation of the labour market imperilled social capacity. Rather, Australia provided protection indirectly through manipulation of the labour market in what one commentator has described as a 'wage-earners' welfare state'.

Such were the components of a system that was meant to insulate the domestic economy from external shocks in order to protect the national standard of living. Contemporaries took great pride in its generous and innovatory character. Social investigators came from Britain, France, Germany and the United States to examine the workings of this 'social laboratory' that had apparently solved the problems of insecurity and unrest. Seen from an early-twenty-first-century vantage point, as its institutional forms were dismantled, it was judged more harshly. An economic historian suggests that a system of 'domestic defence' meant to provide protection from risk lost the capacity for 'flexible adjustment' and innovation. A political commentator sees the 'Australian Settlement' as a premature lapse into an illusory certainty that left 'a young nation with geriatric arteries'.

These judgements are anachronistic. The critics construe the national reconstruction as one that sacrificed efficiency to equity and blame it for slowing the country's economic growth. But Australia had already lost more than a decade of growth as the result of depression and drought, so that the tariff, arbitration and the basic wage can hardly be blamed for the slowdown. The makers of the Commonwealth sought to modify the market to create national mastery of material circumstances, to weld a thinly peopled continent with distant centres and regional differences into a secure whole, and to regulate its divergent interests to serve national goals. That was not simply a defensive or protective project; it was an affirmative and dynamic one.

This can be seen in the impressive record of technological innovation. Colonial Australians had cultivated the reputation of improvisers. The rule of thumb prevailed over formal knowledge and the mechanics' institutes and schools of mines were more closely attuned to industrial needs than the fledgling universities. By the end of the century there was an enhanced scientific effort. Miners found improved methods of extracting minerals; the flotation process developed at Broken Hill was copied around the world. Farmers used fertilisers and new wheat varieties to extend into the low rainfall zones beyond the Great Diving Range and out onto Western Australia's inland wheatbelt. The locally produced mechanical harvester that gave rise to the basic wage was as advanced as the ones used on the North American plains. Governments built substantial irrigation works to support more intensive horticulture and diversify the country's rural exports.

Factories, shops and offices were quick to embrace new machines and techniques that increased productivity. Australians took up the pocket watch, the typewriter and the telephone with the enthusiasm they showed later for the personal computer. This, moreover, was a society that was equally innovatory in its leisure: from the 1880s the Saturday half-holiday became common and a biblical division of the week into six days and one gave way to five and two. Australians might not have invented the word 'weekend' but they certainly made good use of it.

They were quick also to adopt the gospel of efficiency. The striving for improvement in every corner of national life accorded with the new understanding of progress, no longer as the fruits that came from planting civilisation in an empty continent but as a conscious task of national survival in an uncertain, harshly competitive world. 'The race is to the swift and strong, and the weakly are knocked out and walked over', warned a leading businessman. Thus employers applied the methods of scientific management to industry through simplification of the labour process, careful measurement of each task and close supervision of its performance.

The domestic market was too small for these techniques to be applied fully to any but the biggest companies, and their impact was probably greater in public enterprises, such as the railways, and major government departments, which dwarfed private sector organisations in scale and complexity. Vast engineering projects were required to construct underground sewerage systems for the principal cities. Both federal and State governments expanded to take on new tasks, administrative, infrastructural, financial, industrial and even commercial. Public transport, communication, gas, electricity, banks, insurance, and coalmines, timberyards, butchers, hotels and tobacconists when the Labor Party held office, provided essential services, checked profiteering and acted as pacesetters for wages and conditions.

Beyond industrial and administrative efficiency lay the goal of social efficiency. This was pursued through a range of reforms aimed at reinvigorating the race and strengthening its capacity to contribute constructively to national goals. The reformers were modernists, seized with the pace of change and the powerful currents that ran through human conduct, and they were experts, confident that they could harness the creative impulse and instil purposeful order. They were concerned with the ills of modernity: the slum, the broken home, social pathology, degeneracy. They worked through professional associations and voluntary bodies, and they embedded their plans in public administration. They styled themselves progressives, after the American progressivist movement on which they drew. Progressivism found application in town planning and national parks, community hygiene, 'scientific motherhood', kindergartens, child welfare and education. The New Education replaced the old rote learning with an emphasis on individual creativity and preparation for the tasks of adulthood: manual skills, nature study, health and civics, to promote an ethic of social responsibility.

The Australian Settlement, then, was not a settlement. The reconstruction of the Australian colonies came in response to challenges that jolted established arrangements and assumptions. In their search for security the colonists adopted the forms of the race and nation, both artefacts of the modern condition of uncertainty and constant change. White Australia bound the country more tightly to Britain. At a time when the United States was taking in the huddled masses of Europe, and Canada too accepted immigrants from east and south Europe, Australia restricted its intake to the old country. It was more monolingual by 1914 than ever before.

With British stock as the basis of a new nation came the problems of dependence and economic vulnerability, the old quarrels over rank and religion, and further ones over class and gender. William Lane had sought to preserve the innocence of the New World with his New Australia, a forlorn endeavour. Alfred Deakin used New Protection to provide a measure of autonomy and harmony. But the New World was tethered to the old and could not escape its effects.

7

Sacrifice, 1914–1945

In the space of thirty years the circumstances of Australian nation-hood changed irrevocably. The country's strategic dependence on Britain drew it into two wars that both originated in European rivalry and together exhausted European supremacy. The first sapped the political stability of the combatants and cut the flows of trade and investment that sustained their prosperity. The second destroyed their empires, leaving an impoverished rump of a continent divided and bound by the two superpowers to its east and west. Britain, a victor in both wars, was perhaps the most diminished by their cumulative effects and Australia, as the largest British outpost in the Pacific, also incurred heavy losses. The fading of imperial certainties created doubt and division. The nation-building project faltered under the weight of debt and increased dependence. Only as the second war spread to the Pacific, and Australia found itself isolated and in danger of inva-sion, came a belated recognition of the need to reconstruct the nation for changed circumstances.

Those who survived the first of these wars knew it as the Great War; they had never experienced such a catastrophe and could not imagine that another would follow so soon. Europe had enjoyed a century of peace since the conclusion of the Napoleonic wars – although European powers waged repeated wars of colonial conquest, at home there were only occasional and limited conflicts that were quickly settled by a decisive encounter of professional troops. The Great War involved mass conscript armies and absorbed the entire resources of the combatants in a prolonged contest of attrition that lasted from 1914 to 1918. It was sparked in the Balkans, a powder-keg of imperial and national rivalry, when a Serb terrorist assassinated a member of the Austrian royal family as he toured an outlying province. Since Germany supported Austria-Hungary in its ultimatum to Serbia, and Britain and France joined with Russia to resist them, the war extended from the Atlantic seaboard to Europe's eastern borderlands. Soon it drew in Turkey and Italy. The United States came late, but the global reach of the combatants made this a world as well as a continental war.

After Germany overran Belgium and repulsed a Russian advance, the initial movement of the combatants bogged down in static trench warfare. On land and sea the application of industrial technology to military conflict gave defenders supremacy over attackers. Mines and submarines paralysed the offensive potential of battleships; massive land fortifications, barbed wire, machine guns, chemical weapons and flame-throwers cut down the waves of advancing soldiers. Although commanders sacrificed millions of troops, the outcome was determined ultimately by the capacity of the two sides to maintain their war effort and sustain their populations. Hunger weakened Russia and allowed revolutionaries to seize power with their slogan of 'peace, bread and land'. Food shortage played a critical role in Germany's final collapse. The merchant ships that carried Canadian and Australian produce contributed as much to the final Allied victory as the troopships that took their young men to the battlefield.

The young men went first. At the outbreak of war a federal election was in progress and party leaders vied in their enthusiasm for Australian participation: Joseph Cook, the Liberal prime minister, declared that 'all our resources in Australia are in the Empire and for the Empire'; Andrew Fisher, the Labor leader, pledged 'our last man and our last shilling'. Labor won and affirmed the outgoing administration's offer to dispatch a force of 20,000 troops. That Australia would participate was not in question – it was still constitutionally bound to follow Britain, and the governor-general passed on the announcement of war to the prime minister. The question at issue was the form that participation would take.

The answer was given by the formation of an expeditionary force. It was raised by recruitment of volunteers and named the Australian Imperial Force. Behind that decision lay a protracted argument in the years leading up to 1914 between those who sought a citizen militia on the Swiss model for purposes of national defence and those who wanted an army under British control that could serve abroad. The dispute was resolved by blending the voluntary principle with the imperial design. The Australian Imperial Force would be commanded by British generals until the last year of the war and consist predominantly of front-line troops reliant for most support functions on the British Army. The Royal Australian Navy, similarly, was placed under control of the Royal Navy from the beginning of the war.

There was first a local task. In 1914 the German Empire in the Pacific stretched along a chain of islands that began close to the Chinese coast and extended to the northeast corner of New Guinea. These territories allowed radio bases to eavesdrop on naval communications and assist German cruisers to intercept Allied shipping. The British Admiralty therefore instructed the Australians to occupy New Guinea and the New Zealanders to capture German Samoa. This they did, and the Australians were preparing to proceed further north when the British told them not to bother: the German territories above the equator had been occupied already by Japan. The Japanese navy was to police the Pacific, thereby freeing British ships to serve closer to home. In exchange, the British government assured Japan that it would retain control of these northern islands, an arrangement initially concealed from Australia because of the alarm it would cause there. The governor-general was instructed to 'prepare the mind' of his ministers for the unwelcome news and urged that no anti-Japanese agitation should 'during the progress of the war be allowed to arise in Australia'. Here already a divergence of imperial strategy and national interests was opening.

A further strain became apparent when the Dominion troops completed their initial training and departed for service at the end of 1914. They joined with their New Zealand counterparts to form the Australian and New Zealand Army Corps: from that cumbrous title the acronym ANZAC soon entered general usage as Anzac, signifying a citizen soldier with the distinctive qualities of the settler societies from which he sprang, resourceful and willing. A more colloquial term, 'digger', was also quickly adopted, harking back to the egalitarian fraternity of the goldfields.

There was no room for the Anzacs in the training camps of England, so they disembarked in Egypt, where the raw turbulence of the Australians quickly impressed the British officers responsible for licking them into shape. Their reluctance to salute was an affront, the roughneck treatment of the Egyptian hosts a scandal. These uncouth colonials were needed, however, to repel the Turkish army from its advance on the Suez Canal, a vital imperial thoroughfare. Subsequently the Light Horse Brigade participated in the Allied advance through Palestine, Lebanon and Syria, where Australians fought some of the last great cavalry battles in military history.

Before then the Anzacs were employed in an attempt to forestall that campaign and knock Turkey out of the war. The idea was to force the straits at the eastern edge of the Mediterranean that opened to the Turkish capital. Once Istanbul was taken, the expeditionary force could enter the Black Sea and link with the Russian forces. It was first necessary to secure the Gallipoli peninsula that guarded the strait. In the early morning of 25 April 1915 British, French and Anzac forces therefore made separate landings on the peninsula. The Australians and New Zealanders scrambled ashore at Anzac Cove and stormed the precipitous slopes before them. Checked in their advance by Turkish defenders, they dug in and defied all attempts to dislodge them, but were unable to capture the heights despite repeated attempts to do so. With the onset of the winter, they abandoned Gallipoli and left behind 8000 dead. The withdrawal, five days before Christmas 1915, was the most impressive operation in the eight-month campaign.

The Australian casualties were a fraction of those incurred during the war and fewer than the British themselves suffered at Gallipoli. Although the Anzacs had performed creditably under fire, the campaign revealed errors of command and execution. Even so, their exploits on the Turkish peninsula quickly gave rise to an enduring legend of martial valour. The Anzac legend began with the reports of the initial landing given by a British war correspondent: 'there has been no finer feat in this war', this journalist assured Australian readers. It was fostered by Australian correspondents, one of whom contrasted the prowess of the Anzacs with the incompetence of their British commanders – his name was Keith Murdoch, and his son Rupert, who entered the British newspaper industry as the 'Dirty Digger', would exact a painful colonial revenge.

The principal Australian correspondent, Charles Bean, did most to establish the legend. A journalist before the war, after it the official war historian and creator of the Australian War Memorial, he attributed the qualities of the Australian soldier to the stimulus of local conditions. 'The Australian is always fighting something', he had written in 1907. 'In the bush it is drought, fires, unbroken horses, wild cattle; and not unfrequently wild men.' Wrestling with man and nature made the Australian 'as fine a fighting man as exists'. Within a few days of the Gallipoli landing Bean was able to confirm that 'the wild independent pastoral life of Australia, if it makes rather wild men, makes superb soldiers'. He quickly produced an anthology of stories, verse and skits collected from the troops at Gallipoli as a popular tribute, *The Anzac Book*. This oral testimony celebrated the individuality of front-line soldiers who collectively affirmed the legend. As the official war historian Bean would expand this technique into a vast encomium to the national character.

The Anzac legend dealt with sacred themes: baptism under fire in the pursuit of an unattainable objective, sacrifice, death and redemption through the living legacy of a nation come of age. It told of courage and stoicism in the ultimate test of mateship and thus converted a military defeat into a moral victory. Within a year the Australian servicemen commemorated the anniversary of the landing and Anzac Day was quickly established as a public holiday, marked by a dawn service when the immortality of the fallen was proclaimed, and then a march by the returned soldiers through the city streets before they repaired to the pubs.

Anzac Day has ever since been Australia's principal anniversary. Attendance began to dwindle as the ranks of the old diggers thinned, and the event came under challenge by the 1960s from those opposed to the celebration of war. But it revived in the closing years of the twentieth century, so that record numbers now attend the dawn service and city march. In its new popularity the ceremony has changed: the marchers include descendants as well as former members of the armed forces; and whereas the veterans traditionally marched in suits, having exchanged their uniforms for civilian clothing on discharge, many have now reverted to military dress.

There is also a new dimension of Anzac commemoration – the pilgrimage to Turkey. Several hundred veterans travelled to Anzac Cove in 1965 for the fiftieth anniversary of the landing and were welcomed by their Turkish counterparts as well as four young travelling Australians. Twenty-five years later, when the prime minister accompanied the last surviving veterans back to Gallipoli, his invocation of the Anzac legend was witnessed by thousands of reverent compatriots and televised nationally. Australians have assembled on the peninsula for the dawn service ever since and a massive parking lot had to be built over the original trenches to accommodate the growing numbers. The significance of this new enthusiasm is keenly debated. A young woman among the 15,000 antipodeans who gathered for the dawn service on 25 April 1995 said it had become 'an important part of the backpacker calendar', but for others it was a spiritual experience that induced pride, sorrow, even anger at the senseless loss. A national ballot was needed to choose from 40,000 Australians seeking to attend the centenary gathering in 2015.

After their withdrawal from Gallipoli, the Australian infantry divisions were reinforced and deployed in the defence of France. Here they participated in mass offensives against the German line during 1916 and 1917 that inflicted many more casualties and called for new qualities of endurance.

> We stumble, cursing, on the slippery duck-boards,
> Goaded like the damned by some invisible wrath,
> A will stronger than weariness, stronger than animal fear,
> Implacable and monotonous.

The horrors of this ordeal exceeded participants' powers of description; the most notable war novels appeared many years later. There was already a sharp disjuncture, however, between the response to war by those on the Western Front and the representations created for domestic consumption. The lurid propaganda posters that showed the bestial Hun violating Australian womanhood contrast with the sombre paintings of the war artists selected by Bean or Will Dyson's battlefield drawings of human extremity. In 1916 the demotic poet C. J. Dennis had a scruffy, undisciplined larrikin from the Melbourne slums answer 'the call of the stoush' and affirm the values of the digger in Turkey, but an Australian serving in the French trenches a year later had no such certainty:

> Adieu, the years are a broken song,
> And the right grows weak in the strife with wrong,
> The lilies of love have a crimson stain,
> And the old days will never come again.

The Western Front was lethal. There were 14,000 Australian deaths in 1916, 22,000 in 1917, and the much greater numbers of nonfatal casualties constantly thinned the ranks. The rate of enlistment rose after Gallipoli, from 52,000 volunteers in 1914 to 166,000 in 1915, but then declined to 140,000 in 1916 and just 45,000 by 1917. The first recruits were predominantly young and single men, many of them attracted by the pay, which was not far short of average earnings and higher than other countries offered their servicemen. As these enthusiasts ran short, it became necessary to appeal to the patriotic duty of older, married men.

Women were excluded from the armed forces (even the 2000 nurses who served abroad were denied official military rank) and, in contrast to other combatant countries, few Australian women were brought into the paid workforce. Their war effort was channelled into voluntary activities and their greatest service was to provide and sustain fighting men. The Red Cross alone recruited as many women as worked in the munitions industries, and Lady Munro Ferguson, the wife of the governor-general, turned the grand ballroom of Melbourne's Government House into a warehouse for the comforts they prepared for dispatch. In the course of the war, it has been estimated, 10 million woman-hours went into knitting 1,354,328 pairs of socks. Poems and prayers were tucked into clothing, gumleaves and sprigs of wattle into packets of tobacco. These patriotic women were also ardent recruiters. The 'One Woman, One Recruit League' urged each of its members to enlist at least one recruit, 'even if he were the poor, unfortunate but eligible tradesman who knocked at the back door each day', and the Universal Service League echoed the women of ancient Sparta with its injunction that their men should 'Return on or with your shield'.

The leadership of the country passed at the end of 1915 from Andrew Fisher, a Labor moderate uncomfortable with the demands of war, to Billy Hughes, his bellicose deputy. Hughes was a union organiser turned politician with an authoritarian streak and a nation at arms provided him with the licence to strengthen the hand of government. Diminutive and deaf, a wizened firebrand with a rasping voice and rancorous manner, he travelled to England to press the British to remedy Australian grievances.

The war also exacted a heavy economic toll. It cut the inflow of labour and capital, and deprived Australia of German, French and Belgian markets that had taken 30 per cent of the country's exports. The economy contracted by 10 per cent in the first year of the war. Price rises ran ahead of wages, and Hughes' abandonment of a referendum to control prices angered the labour movement. He therefore wanted Britain to underwrite the output of wool, wheat, meat and minerals, and in this he eventually prevailed. His was perhaps a pyrrhic victory, for it froze the existing economic structure. Even though heavy industry developed around the country's first major steelworks, which opened in 1915, the opportunity for more substantial diversification was lost.

In pressing his country's needs Hughes called for a renewed war effort, yet the number of Australian volunteers was flagging. He returned to Australia in mid-1916 committed to conscription. Opposition could be expected from a labour movement that was increasingly critical of the slaughter, and the Labor parliamentarians were most unlikely to pass the necessary legislation. Accordingly, the prime minister appealed over the heads of his party to the country with a referendum. He had the support of the press, the Protestant churches, business and professional leaders. The principal opposition came from socialists, radicals and feminists, all of whom challenged the assumption of a unified national interest in war and the supposed equality of sacrifice embodied in military conscription.

These critics were already hampered by draconian restrictions. Under the War Precautions Act passed in 1914, the federal government was empowered to proclaim regulations necessary for public safety and the defence of the Commonwealth. It had interned 7000 enemy aliens with little regard to their circumstances or sympathies: they included eminently respectable German-Australians, migrants from the Balkans who were unwilling subjects of the Hapsburg Empire, even Afghan camel-drivers who had come from well beyond the limits of the Ottoman Empire. Here the government had popular support: an upsurge of anti-foreign behaviour swept the country as the passions released by war hardened the identification of nation with race, and narrowed the boundaries of acceptable difference. It was the same with dissidents. Anti-war meetings were broken up, anti-conscription speakers prosecuted, offices and homes raided. The most forthright opponents of the war, the Industrial Workers of the World, were framed in 1916 on charges of arson and treason.

The government's response to anti-war feminists, who challenged the expectation of maternal sacrifice, was also severe. War accentuated sexual divisions and in separating men from women, it licensed a masculine aggression that spilled over into disturbing irregularity. The marked wartime increase of sexually transmitted diseases (by 1917 one soldier in seven had contracted venereal disease) became a metaphor for national insecurity, which in turn brought closer regulation of women. Such circumstances allowed an intensification of the moral reform movement, though some of its principal achievements – six o'clock closing of pubs, for example – involved regulation *by* women.

The excessive censorship of news from the front and the heavy-handed domestic repression probably rebounded on the Australian government. The British government's military bombardment of Dublin to repress an Irish nationalist uprising in Easter 1916 certainly disturbed the substantial minority of Australians of Irish descent. The men at the front were divided: some were disenchanted, and some who remained ardent believed their volunteer status should not be sullied by compulsion. When the country voted in October 1916 in the referendum, it narrowly rejected a proposal to conscript Australians for overseas military service.

Hughes tried again a year later, and his second referendum campaign was even more divisive. By now the prime minister cast his opponents as traitors. The labour agitators were doing the work of the Bolshevik revolutionaries who had seized power in Russia and taken it out of the war; they were agents of Germany, said Hughes. The workers who turned increasingly to strike action were wreckers. The women who refused to give up their sons were emasculating the nation. The Irish Catholics who criticised the war were adopting the separatist disloyalty of the Sinn Fein movement back in Ireland; Sinn Fein meant 'ourselves alone', but according to Hughes it meant stabbing the home country in the back. The Irish Archbishop of Melbourne, Daniel Mannix, emerged during the second referendum debate as the prime minister's most formidable opponent. So wounding was the churchman's invective that Hughes asked the Vatican to restrain its turbulent priest. King George V also requested that Mannix be transferred to Rome: 'God forbid', replied Cardinal Gasquet.

The prime minister, who carried his own revolver, brooked no opposition. He raided the printing office of the Queensland government to seize copies of an anti-conscription speech by the State premier that had been censored from publication. Pelted with eggs on the return journey, Hughes created his own Commonwealth police force. The second referendum failed by a slightly greater margin than the first. Australia remained one of the few combatants to maintain a volunteer force and the only one to have rejected conscription.

Out of a population of five million the armed forces recruited 417,000 men, more than half of those eligible to serve. Of the 324,000 who served abroad, two out of every three were killed or wounded. The 60,000 war dead represented a higher proportion of enlistments than any other contingent of Britain and its Empire (though other countries with conscript armies lost a higher proportion of their total population). Long before the final victory at the end of 1918, the common enthusiasm for war gave way to grim resignation. Not even the prominence of the Australian Corps in

7.1   Billy Hughes, the bellicose Labor prime minister, split his party during the First World War when he campaigned for military conscription. The 'Little Digger' is shown here on the shoulders of soldiers at the end of the war. (William Morris Hughes collection, National Library of Australia, an23150756)

resisting Germany's last offensive and then leading a decisive advance under the command of its own general, John Monash, could restore the purposeful unity of 1914.

Armistice Day eventually became Remembrance Day, but in memory of what? Sacrifice in the service of empire and the defence of freedom was the best explanation contemporaries could provide. As Australia drifted further away from Britain and Europe, it has become increasingly difficult for later Australians to understand why an earlier generation travelled half-way around the world to fight a distant foe. We forget that many Australians believed Britain was endangered, and rallied to its support out of ethnic loyalty as well as self-interest. There are memorials in almost every Australian township and suburb, but most of these bear mute testimony to those named on them – and it is a distinctive feature of the Australian war memory that they record the names of the survivors as well as the dead. The most common forms are the obelisk and the lone digger on a pedestal, typically a private who stands with head bowed and rifle reversed.

Younger Australians are hard-pressed to distinguish the combatants, much less the passions that animated them. Those passions were still strong at the Paris peace conference where the victors divided the spoils. Hughes joined with France in demanding a Carthaginian peace, a punishment of Germany so severe that it could only imbalance the international economy and poison international relations. He took issue with the United States for wanting to replace the old order of empire with a new system of liberal internationalism that would encompass free trade, national self-determination and settlement of differences through a League of Nations. He affronted the Japanese with his opposition to a declaration of racial equality in the Covenant of the League of Nations. He importuned the British with his insistence that Australia retain control of New Guinea; in the end a special category of mandated territories was created to ensure that the former German colony would be administered as an 'integral portion' of Australia, with full control over trade and immigration.

British support was essential. With it Australia secured New Guinea; without it, Japan could not be denied the northern islands. In his public confrontation with the United States, Hughes could take the high ground of brutal realism. 'I represent sixty thousand dead', he told the idealistic President Wilson. In private arguments with Britain he might well have added that he spoke for a government debt of £350 million, half of it owed in London, but Britain had incurred deaths and debts of much greater magnitude. The overriding purpose of the war, for Hughes, was to maintain the Empire on which Australian security depended. His chief goal at the peace conference was to hold Britain to its Empire. He therefore sought a greater role in imperial affairs through direct access to the British government (so that the practice of communication through the governor-general and the Colonial Office was abandoned) and separate representation at Paris.

Hughes wanted to go further with closer coordination of imperial affairs but the fellow-Dominions of Canada, South Africa and, after

1921, Ireland would not have that. They were loosening their ties with Britain; Hughes with his idiosyncratic methods of aggressive dependence was holding to them. Behind this parapet, moreover, he could be franker in his racial exclusivism, more reckless in his disregard of Japanese sensitivities, than the other English-speaking nations of the Pacific. The United States, Canada and New Zealand also restricted Asian immigration, but none advertised their prejudice as provocatively as the thinly populated island-continent of the south.

At home the prime minister's assertive loyalism drove deep divisions. An immediate political effect of the first conscription referendum was a split in the Labor Party. At the end of 1916 Hughes led his supporters out of a meeting of its federal parliamentarians; in early 1917 he joined with the non-Labor forces to form a new Nationalist Party, which was returned to office in a federal election four months later. Similar splits brought down Labor governments in New South Wales and South Australia. Betrayed by its leaders, vilified for its failure of national duty, the labour movement turned for a period towards the militant class rhetoric of direct action. Even when moderates reimposed control of the federal Labor Party, they were unable to regain the initiative they had enjoyed before it. For a quarter-century after 1916, Labor remained in opposition in national politics except for two disastrous years during the economic emergency of the Depression.

Those who left the Labor Party called themselves Nationalists, and the nation they upheld was loyal to the Empire. They retained connections to the ancestral homeland in sentiment, recreation and worship. The sectarian animosities fanned during the argument over conscription confirmed the Protestant ascendancy in its religious prejudices, while Catholics were estranged from the new forms of national ceremony: their church did not participate in the post-war commemoration of Anzac Day and it was absent when the foundation stone of the national war memorial was laid in Canberra in 1929. The gendered division of protector and protected also persisted, hardening the aggressive qualities of masculinity, emphasising the vulnerability of femininity. The 60,000 who had fallen in the service of the Empire gave the alignment of loyalty with conservative, Protestant men a sacral force, yet the nation that came of age in war was more resentful, less confident of its capacity for independent experiment.

War is sometimes regarded as a regenerative force, rather like the Australian bushfire that consumes energy, burns away the outmoded accretion of habit and allows new, more vigorous growth to occur. The Great War brought no such national revitalisation. It killed, maimed, and incapacitated. It left an incubus of debt that continued to mount as the payments to veterans and war widows continued; even in the depths of the Depression of the early 1930s there were more Australians on war benefits than in receipt of social welfare. Its public memorials were a constant reminder of loss but provided little solace to those who mourned, for the ethos of national sacrifice discouraged excessive personal grief as selfish. So, far from strengthening a common purpose, it weakened the attachment to duty: to live for the moment was a common response to the protracted ordeal.

***

Capitalising on his exploits at the Paris peace conference, Hughes presented himself to the electorate at the end of 1919 as the 'Little Digger' and renewed the Nationalist majority. At the next election three years later, he faced greater opposition. A Country Party had formed to represent the disgruntled farmers, and city businessmen were growing restless under Hughes' erratic regimen of state control. The Nationalists lost their parliamentary majority and in early 1923 overthrew Hughes to form a coalition with the Country Party.

The new Nationalist prime minister, Stanley Bruce, and his Country Party deputy, Earle Page, held office till the end of the decade. They were an unlikely pair – the one a patrician Melbourne business leader who completed his education in England, the other an excitable doctor from rural New South Wales – and their administration made little use of the new broom that its supporters hoped would sweep away the excesses of the little imp they had ejected. The lines of national policy were too firmly established, the problems too persistent.

Hughes had sought to rebuild national capacity within the imperial fold. He looked to Britain for the sale of primary products, import replacement for the expansion of secondary industries, state activity to augment population and state regulation to maintain living standards. Without some corresponding gains in productivity, however, these protective devices would increase the cost structure of producers. A substantial increase of tariff protection at the end of the war gave impetus to the newly formed Country Party, while urban business interests expected Bruce to curtail the profligacy of government expenditure and regulation. These expectations were dashed. Rather than reducing the tariff, the Bruce–Page government extended assistance to the primary producers. Instead of curtailing public expenditure, it increased it. The new administration was locked into a policy of 'protection all round', and within this framework the economy was marked by collusion between the large companies that dominated key sectors of manufacturing and retailing. Australia was a late industrialiser, its industrialists confined to a fragmented domestic market, heavily dependent on imported technology and unable to generate the scale or scope to compete in foreign markets.

Bruce is the only businessman to have made a successful transition to national politics. Displaying a politician's grasp of the need for striking phrases, he explained the elements of that policy to an Imperial Conference in 1923 with an alliterative jingle: 'Empire development is dependent upon three things, men, money and markets.' Men from Britain were needed, along with women and children to fill up the empty spaces, but most of all to make the land productive – the British government helped finance a new wave of more than 200,000 assisted migrants during the decade. Money was required from British investors so the Australian government could undertake the necessary development projects and Australian producers could expand their capacity – the Commonwealth and the States, now coordinating their borrowing, returned to the city of London in the 1920s and borrowed an additional £230 million. Markets had to be found for the increased primary production – Britain remained the principal customer for Australian wool and wheat, along with shipments of dairy produce, meat, fruit and sugar.

The policy was premised on expanding rural exports. When officials selected British emigrants, they looked for those who would go onto the land. When treasurers raised loans, they spoke of extending railways to the new farm districts, of irrigation projects, and of the schools, hospitals and other facilities associated with land settlement. The principal form of assistance to returned servicemen was soldier settlement, a scheme whereby the government set up 37,000 diggers on their own farms. The Commonwealth's Council for Scientific and Industrial Research, founded in 1926, concentrated its efforts on the eradication of pests and the improvement of stock. The popular phrase 'Australia Unlimited' denoted an abundant resource, land, which needed only capital and labour to blossom; the very word development was synonymous in the 1920s with land settlement and its associated public works.

Closer settlement revived the yeoman ideal of self-sufficiency. Some of the new farms were established at the limits of settlement, consolidating the wheat belt in the hinterland of Western Australia and carving dairy holdings out of the dense forests in the southwest of that State, while on the other side of the continent large pastoral runs were cut up into agricultural blocks. The family farm was consolidated as the operational unit of primary industry and rural life.

These farmers were largely self-sufficient in labour (though the assisted migrants included 20,000 'farmboys') but otherwise tied to the operation of the market, for they were engaged in commercial enterprises with substantial entry costs and dependent on machinery, fertiliser and other inputs. Many of the entrants incurred heavy debts as they struggled to clear their land and bring it into production. It was their misfortune to do so just as European farmers recovered from the war, along with other New World producers who competed for export sales. When prices stalled after the middle of the decade, the mounting dissatisfaction of the farmers strengthened the Country Party.

Rural development failed to halt the drift to the cities. They grew rapidly (Sydney passed the million mark in 1922, Melbourne in 1928, when together they held more than one-third of the country's inhabitants) and absorbed much of the new investment. Residential construction accounted for nearly half of private capital formation during the decade, while provision of roads, power lines, water and waste disposal to the spreading suburbs drew heavily on public funds. These investments in turn supported a wide range of industries. Real estate transactions boosted the finance sector. Building, servicing and fitting out the new homes stimulated brickyards, timber mills, pipemakers, paintmakers, textile mills and furniture manufacturers.

The highways and city streets carried motor traffic – by 1929 Australia's rate of car ownership was surpassed only by the United States, Canada and New Zealand. The new electricity grids encouraged Australian factories to turn out novel domestic products: while few homes yet boasted an electric stove, refrigerator or washing-machine, most had an electric kettle, iron and vacuum cleaner. With labour-saving devices came greater opportunities for leisure and a move in domestic design towards the modern and the convenient. The cigarette replaced the pipe, the beard gave way to the cleans-haven chin, the long skirt to the light frock. New forms of packaging and advertising promoted a wider range of consumer goods – soap, toothpaste and toothpowder, cosmetics, processed food and branded confectionary.

Australians were already avid readers. 'We'd sit round the fire', one reader recalled of her early-twentieth-century childhood, 'no radio, no TV, but reading, all the family, round the fire, with these books. And we read and read, every night'. In the inter-war era Australians also became intense listeners. The phonograph displaced the piano in home entertainment. The radio began as a handsome piece of furniture in the front room, and the first broadcasts had the formality of a public performance, but as the medium spread, it acquired intimacy. The addition of sound made the imaginary world of the picture palace come alive, so that by 1927 there were 1250 cinema theatres that sold 110 million tickets in the course of the year. From flickering images of modernity and the syncopated strains of pleasure the idea took hold of the 1920s as a time of growth and renewal, a release from wartime hardship.

That most striking symbol of modern science, the aeroplane, attracted public attention with epic flights from England and the United States. A Queenslander and former war pilot, Bert Hinkler, completed the first solo flight between England and Australia in 1928. In the same year a merchant prince, Sidney Myer, supplemented a government grant to allow Charles Kingsford Smith and Charles Ulm to make the first flight across the Pacific. Myer had arrived in Australia from a Russian shtetl; Kingsford Smith was born in Canada, Ulm's father was French; their plane was designed by a Dutchman, built in the United States and christened the *Southern Cross* – aerial flight joined Australia to the world. A Yorkshire lass, Amy Johnson, failed narrowly to eclipse Hinkler's record when she landed at Darwin on Empire Day, 1930, but her reception was even more acclamatory: 'not only has she spanned the distance between England and Australia; she has cleared the Sahara which still lay between the sexes'. The aeroplane found its apotheosis in the Flying Doctor Service, formed in 1928 to take medicine to the Australian inland.

Not all shared in the progress. When the soldiers returned, jobs were scarce. The labour market improved in the early 1920s but increased mechanisation shrank the demand for unskilled workers. With no job security and no public assistance when laid off, casual labourers were excluded from the new forms of consumption. The larger, more cohesive groups of manual workers in vital industries such as mining and maritime transport were best able to express their dissatisfaction: a wave of post-war industrial disputes paralysed the economy for lengthy periods. The demand that ex-servicemen be given preference over unionists added a further strain: all too often the volunteer for military service became a volunteer to jump a queue or even to break a strike. In a series of further confrontations at this time former members of the AIF attacked radical demonstrators: the title of their organisation, the Returned Soldiers and Sailors Imperial League of Australia, testified to their traditional loyalty.

The most common cause of dispute was the red flag, a familiar symbol of the labour movement now associated with communism and revolution. The Bolshevik seizure of power in Russia at the end of 1917 had been followed by further uprisings elsewhere, and then by the formation of the Communist International, which appealed to workers around the world to make common cause against the capitalist ruling class and urged colonial peoples to rise up against their imperial masters. Although the newly formed Communist Party of Australia remained tiny, its very existence was an affront to conservatives. It conjured up the threat of a foreign conspiracy led by rootless malcontents to impose an alien despotism on Australia.

Although the Australian Labor Party rebuffed the Communist Party's attempt to affiliate, the Nationalists used trade union links to make the 1925 election an anti-communist crusade, and followed their victory with new criminal sanctions against militant unions. During the 1920s the Red Menace displaced the Yellow Peril as the source of imminent danger. More than this, Russia's abandonment of the war against Germany revived memories of the domestic electorate's failure of national duty during the conscription plebiscites. Could the fickle voters be trusted? It seemed to conservatives that democracy itself might have to be qualified in the defence of God, King and Empire. Former officers of the AIF formed secret armies to be ready in the hour of need.

An influenza epidemic that struck Europe at the end of the war encouraged the idea that Australia was threatened by foreign evils. Despite attempts to quarantine those returning to Australia who were infected, the disease carried off 12,000 Australians in 1919. As with the influenza virus, so with other pathogens. Seditious and obscene publications were censored, degenerate art condemned, undesirable aliens deported. In procedures for both immigration and naturalisation of immigrants, Australia developed an exhaustive system of classification of different races and nationalities. Entry quotas were introduced for southern Europeans and other undesirable immigrants, naturalisation procedures made contingent on a test of political loyalty administered by the Commonwealth security agency, which was another product of the war.

The policy of exclusion was both vainglorious and timorous. Protection of local manufacturers had been extended through the New Protection to wage-earners before the war, after it by marketing and assistance schemes to farmers. Protection of racial purity had spread to keep Australia free of all foreign dangers to civic and moral virtue. Australia was not alone in this stance. After championing internationalism at the Paris peace conference, the United States turned its back on the League of Nations, but it did so from a position of strength. In a report to Washington in 1925 an

American diplomat was struck by how his country's isolationism was affirmative and confident, the Australian version cramped and defensive. 'Selfishness would seem to be the dominating motive in most people's lives.' They showed no capacity for initiative, lived for the moment and acted only when there was no alternative. More people went to the races on 25 April than attended the Anzac Day ceremony. 'There is little spirit in the people ... there is nothing in their past that really stirs them nationally.' Despite the higher duties on non-imperial products, American goods increased to more than a quarter of all Australian imports. American films, comics and jazz were avidly consumed. By comparison, British culture seemed stilted, local work provincial. Life appeared more vital and glamorous on the other side of the Pacific.

As a small, strategically vulnerable and export-dependent country, an Australia that retreated into isolation became more reliant on Britain, but Britain's own capacity was weakened, its willingness to sustain the old imperial arrangements uncertain. Britain represented Australia at an international conference in Washington where it was agreed in 1921 that the major Pacific powers would maintain a ratio of naval strength: five British and five American for every three Japanese vessels. Australia welcomed the agreement, which replaced the much-resented Anglo-Japanese treaty, but overlooked the fact that the British and American navies would operate outside the Pacific. Much would depend on the new British naval base to be constructed at Singapore.

Meanwhile at a 1926 imperial conference Britain devised a new formula for its Dominions. They were to be autonomous, equal, united by common allegiance to the Crown, and freely associated as members of what was now called 'the British Commonwealth'. The formula was a concession to Canada and South Africa, a rebuff to Australia which wanted no part of the new status and did not ratify the measure that enacted it until a new world war forced acceptance of an established fact. Even the economic links were straining now that Britain was no longer the world's financial centre; its attempt to regain that status by returning to the gold standard in 1925 added to its trading difficulties. Australia was more than ever committed to the production of raw materials and food – 95 per cent of its exports were primary products – but Britain was no longer the workshop of the world.

That left the financial links, and Australia was the principal public borrower from the City of London in the 1920s, but most of those funds went not to building rural export industries but to the further growth of swollen cities. The imbalance caused unease, for the city was the site of social problems and its pleasures seemed to sap the national character, but there was no alternative. The bush could not absorb a population growth of one million persons during the decade, for it no longer provided sufficient jobs: at the turn of the century one in three was employed in farming and mining; by 1929 fewer than one in four worked in those occupations. Since maintenance of the standard of living was an established condition of national policy, the Commonwealth protected the workers in city factories with tariffs on competing imports and the States provided additional jobs in government enterprises and public works. Wage regulation through industrial arbitration allowed modest increases in earnings, and the employer's additional costs were passed on to the consumer through an adjustment of the tariff.

It was a fortuitous arrangement that permitted investment without saving. As Australians responded to the new forms of household credit, they discarded habits of thrift learned in the depression of the 1890s. As the country increased its foreign borrowing, it was able to pursue growth without having to stint on consumption. Lenders provided these funds, however, in the expectation of returns. As export prices slipped, they began to question the profligacy of the borrower. The tariff, the arbitration system, and the application of loans to urban construction all came under criticism. Among these construction works was the Sydney Harbour Bridge, an heroic project to link the city to the north shore of the harbour that was awarded to an English firm using Australian materials and Australian labour. Work began in 1925, and by 1929 the two halves of the 500-metre arch were creeping across the harbour when Australia's credit collapsed. Before the span was completed, a toll was introduced to pay for its cost.

Even before the Wall Street crash in October 1929 made further borrowing impossible, the government attempted to stem a mounting imbalance of payments by reducing the cost of Australian exports. Having stacked the Arbitration Court with new appointments and introduced new laws against strikes, it welcomed a series of industrial awards designed to get more work for less pay. Three groups of workers resisted their new awards, and each one was bludgeoned into submission after long, violent disputes. The first were the waterside workers, who from August 1928 to the winter of 1929 tried in vain to prevent strikebreakers from taking their livelihood. Next were the timber workers, who picketed the sawmills and lumberyards for most of 1929. Last and most bloody was the dispute in the coal district of New South Wales, which began in February 1929 when the owners locked out the miners for refusing to accept wage reductions. Armed police occupied the Hunter Valley, broke up all assemblies, bashed protestors, fired on pickets and killed one of the protestors.

The miners held out until 1930, but by then the wave of industrial conflict had brought down the federal government after Bruce, the prime minister, decided to go the whole hog and abandon the field of arbitration. Billy Hughes, the man he had supplanted, gathered together a group of parliamentary malcontents to combine with the Labor members and defeat the measure late in 1929. Bruce called an election. Labor won an overwhelming victory. During the 1920s, then, Australia embarked on a dash for growth that relied heavily on favourable external circumstances and increased the country's vulnerability. It was the misfortune of the labour movement, excluded from most of its benefits and vilified for criticising its inequalities, to assume responsibility just as the growth stalled.

***

Labor took office in the week the New York stock exchange on Wall Street crashed. The prices of wool and wheat were already falling and in the following year they would plunge. This meant that more than half the country's exports were needed just to meet the payments due on foreign loans. After the collapse of the international financial system, there could be no new borrowing. On the contrary, the Bank of England sent a senior official to Australia in 1930 to prescribe the economies that would be necessary to restore Australia's credit. The Commonwealth and

State governments would have to balance their budgets by reducing outlays on both public works and welfare payments. Wages would also have to come down, and in January 1931 the Arbitration Court cut them by 10 per cent. In the same month the currency was devalued by 25 per cent.

With the sharp reduction of export income and foreign funds, the Australian economy contracted. The new government resorted to the conventional methods of economic protection, an increase in tariffs and a halt in immigration, but without money for consumers to spend these devices brought no relief. Unemployment increased, from 13 per cent at the end of 1929 to 23 per cent a year later and 28 per cent at the end of 1931. The Labor ministry could not even force the owners to re-employ the miners they had illegally dismissed. The new prime minister, James Scullin, was a decent man overwhelmed by forces beyond his grasp. He pleaded that the government was hamstrung by the absence of a majority in the Senate and the refusal of the head of the Commonwealth Bank to accept its economic measures. In fact it was paralysed by its own irresolution, hopelessly divided between those who could see no alternative but to follow the bankers' demands and those who demanded that human needs come before obligations to foreign lenders.

As a debtor and a commodity exporter, Australia was hit hard by the Depression. Its unemployment level was higher than that of Britain and most other industrial economies; the level of distress was closer to Canada or Argentina. Yet unlike Argentina, and despite the urging of Labor radicals, Australia did not repudiate its debts. Instead the Commonwealth and six States (three of them also with Labor governments) agreed in 1931 to implement the economies needed to meet the bankers' insistence on balanced budgets: higher taxes, reduced spending. Conversion of domestic public loans to lower interest rates and a voluntary conversion of private borrowings were the sole concessions to the principle of 'equality of sacrifice'. The agreement estranged the unions and aggravated divisions within the Labor Party.

Joseph Lyons, a former premier of Tasmania and from 1930 the acting federal treasurer, emerged as the champion of financial orthodoxy. Assiduously courted by an influential group of Melbourne businessmen, he quit the Labor Party in early 1931 and was installed as leader of the opposition, now reconstituted as the United Australia Party. Jack Lang, the premier of New South Wales, spoke for the Labor left. A former auctioneer with a rasping voice and snarling mouth, he catalysed public resentment against the economic measures when he proposed that interest payments to British bondholders should be cut before Australian living standards. While the federal Labor Party rejected the Lang Plan, his own State branch insisted on it and the defection of New South Wales parliamentarians from the federal caucus brought down the Scullin government at the end of 1931. The United Australia Party easily won the ensuing election.

Labor had failed both to protect jobs and to protect the jobless. The calamity of mass unemployment overwhelmed the existing charities. State governments resorted to distribution of rations, some compelling breadwinners to work for their meagre allowance, and some dispatching single men to work camps in the country where they were less of a threat. Many city dwellers who could not keep up rent payments took to the bush in any case to search for casual jobs or handouts, hitching a ride or jumping a train but always moving on. Shantytowns sprang up on waste land and river banks, with a constant turnover of inhabitants. The gulf between the employed and unemployed was a striking feature of the 1933 census, which revealed that unemployed men had on average been out of work for two years. The Depression widened inequalities of wealth and income. There was compassion for those in need, and there was rejection. They were objects of pity and fear.

The Depression gave rise to literature and art that responded to human extremity with a grim realism; it depicted men and women tossed about by inexorable forces, stripped of dignity by constant humiliation and reduced by hunger to passive stupor. Yet some victims responded with defiance rather than despair, and an Unemployed Workers Movement, formed by the Communist Party in 1930, provided them with leadership. Initially it organised demonstrations at suburban ration depots and led marches on government offices in the State capitals, but these protests were broken up and the leaders gaoled; the party's national conference had to be postponed at the end of the year because most of the delegates were behind bars.

7.2   As victims of the inter-war Depression lost their homes, shanty towns sprang up on waste land. This improvised dwelling in the docklands of Melbourne uses a water tank as a chimney and bedsteads for a front fence. (Department of Health and Human Services, Victoria)

The Unemployed Workers Movement turned next to campaign against eviction. By assembling local residents it sought to prevent landlords from putting tenants onto the street. The activists also channelled the discontent of the itinerant unemployed as they gathered seasonally, and brought communal purpose to the shanty-towns. These activities were episodic in character and difficult to sustain; the 30,000 nominal members of the Unemployed Workers Movement were far in excess of the 2000 members of a Communist Party characterised by doctrinal excess and repeated expulsions. But as one of them put it, 'we've got to make a stand. Do something! Don't cop it passively'.

The economic and social emergency of the early 1930s was also a political emergency that strained the country's democratic institutions. Both left and right believed that representative government had failed. For communists, the state was an instrument of class rule, and the capitalist crisis forced Labor politicians to abandon their pretence to represent the workers and reveal themselves for the traitors they were. The followers of Jack Lang joined a similar resentment of wealth and privilege to an aggressive nationalism that blamed British bondholders and international financiers. 'Lang is greater than Lenin', the former communist secretary of the New South Wales Labor Council proclaimed, and his followers looked to 'the Big Fella' to defy the bankers. Conservatives, on the other hand, saw parliament as a talking-shop of self-serving parasites, Labor as irresolute and unfit to govern, Lang as a dangerous demagogue.

The Scullin government's reluctance to impose cuts, the talk of repudiation and its failure to quell communist agitation among the unemployed prompted a right-wing mobilisation. It began during 1930 when prominent citizens appealed over the heads of the political parties for a programme of unity that would set the country's affairs in order. Their solution to the emergency – sound finance and self-sacrifice – presented a conservative course of action as uncontentious common sense, the fulfilment of debt obligations a matter of national honour. The rejection of politics was a recurrent feature of political life in a country where voting was compulsory and there were three levels of government.

Part of this resentment came from the growing power of the federal government at the expense of the States. The move of the national parliament to remote Canberra in 1927 symbolised the distance that separated legislators from their constituents. Western Australia, which felt itself particularly neglected by the federal administration situated on the other side of the continent, voted to secede from the Commonwealth in 1933. Some felt the same about the concentration of State activities in the capital cities, and separatist New State movements sprang up in outlying regions. The principal national organisation with 100,000 members, the All for Australia League, used an anti-political politics to promote a spurious consensus. Ostensibly non-partisan, it joined with the Nationalist Party to form the United Australia Party and shared in the spoils of office when that reinvigorated force won the election at the end of 1931.

Behind this electoral strategy lay more forceful preparations. The secret armies of the right, formed after the war, took the activity of the Unemployed Workers Movement as their cue for action. In country centres they broke up unemployed camps and ran troublemakers out of town. In cities they closed down meetings and assaulted public speakers. The old hands increased their readiness for the expected revolutionary insurrection, but it was a New Guard, formed in New South Wales following Jack Lang's return to power at the end of 1930, that took the offensive. Motorised detachments of the New Guard descended on working-class neighbourhoods of Sydney to do battle for control of the streets. 'Nothing more lethal than a pick handle' was their commander's instruction, though he 'noted with amusement many a bulge on the hip'.

The New Guard's most celebrated success came in early 1932 when one of its officers, mounted on a horse, slashed the red ribbon with his sabre to open the Sydney Harbour Bridge before Lang, the premier, could cut it with scissors. The incident was theatrical, but it came as the demagogic Lang was defying legislation passed by the new federal government to bring him to heel and street violence was building an atmosphere of public hysteria. There was a huge protest meeting in May 1932 when the State governor dismissed Lang, but he went quietly: 'I must be going, I am no longer premier but a free man.' A coalition of the United Australia Party and the Country Party took office in that State, leaving Lang Labor as the official opposition and the official Labor Party without a single seat in the New South Wales parliament.

Economic recovery began with improved export sales and a recovery of manufacturing, both assisted by the cheaper currency. An imperial trade conference in Canada in 1932 increased the preferential tariff for British imports in return for greater access to British markets for Australian farmers. The public foreign debt stabilised, private investment flowed back into the industrial sector, and there was substantial construction around iron and steel centres in New South Wales and South Australia. Local firms thrust forward in car components and assembly, petroleum products, electrical equipment, general engineering, rubber, fertilizers, textiles and food processing Employment lagged behind the increased production, however, and even in the late 1930s 10 per cent of the workforce remained without jobs. Wage increases were also resisted, and it was only as the unions rebuilt their membership that they were able to press their demands for improvement.

In this process the unemployed activists turned into industrial militants. Mostly young men, they found positions in manual occupations such as mining, transport, construction and heavy industry, and applied their organisational zeal to the improvement of pay, conditions and job security. Their earlier experience was formative. They were class warriors, linking the bread-and-butter issues of working life to the iniquity of capitalist exploitation and its generation of imperialism, fascism and war. By the end of the decade communists held leading positions among the miners, waterside workers, seamen, railway workers, ironworkers, and a host of smaller occupational groupings. The radicalisation of the unions was a lasting effect of the Depression.

Recovery from the physical and social effects of the Depression was more protracted. The birth-rate dropped to a new low, immigration did not resume until the end of the decade, and population growth slowed. On the other hand, infant mortality also fell and public health improved. Fewer children, more widely spaced, more carefully nurtured, marked the extension of government and medical influence over the family, as well as the increasing attention of the housewife to nutrition, hygiene and domestic management.

In the aftermath of the Great War, Australian feminists had sought to expand citizenship. They pressed for increased participation in public life and equality in the workplace. Instead of providing that all adult males be paid a family wage, a device that one Labor woman said treated women and children as mere 'appendages of men', it would be better to distinguish the different needs of households and supplement workplace earnings with direct state support for families. While feminists stressed the maternal contribution to the nation, they also participated in international forums that affirmed a common sisterhood – and were prominent critics of the barbarous treatment of Aboriginal women and children.

Their endeavour to expand social welfare foundered on the conservative aversion to higher taxes and the trade union attachment to the basic wage. Only in New South Wales was a limited system of child endowment introduced in 1927. The Depression turned attention back to safeguarding men's employment and disqualification of married women from more occupations. In response, feminists concentrated on the demand for equal pay with a campaign that gathered momentum among left-wing unions. Even so, women's wage rates remained pegged at little over half those of men.

The existing lines of public policy remained intact. As other countries responded to the failure of the market to maintain living standards with new forms of welfare provision, Australia held fast to the threadbare protective devices of the wage-earners' welfare state. The inter-war difficulties seemed to have smothered an earlier talent for innovation. Or perhaps the resumption of established patterns of sport and recreation suggested the under-lying resilience of popular habits. Cricket, football, horseracing and cinema held attention in the Depression and soon rebuilt attendances. Sporting champions came to occupy an exalted place for their affirmation of grace and fortitude, but the most celebrated heroes were those betrayed by unscrupulous foes. Thus Les Darcy, the boy boxer forced to leave Australia in 1916 because he would not volunteer for the AIF, dead within six months; or the chestnut colt Phar Lap who won the Melbourne Cup in 1930 but also died in America, 'poisoned by the Yanks'; or Don Bradman, the wonder batsman, against whose incomparable skills the English had to bend the rules of cricket during the 'Bodyline Tour' of 1932–3.

There was a vacuum of national leadership. The new prime minister, Joseph Lyons, was a homely, avuncular man who shied from controversy; his United Australia Party ministry anything but united as its senior members jostled for influence. One of the younger and more principled ministers resigned within a year from what he described as 'a sort of government of the feeble for the greedy'. The admission of the Country Party back into coalition after the 1934 election only aggravated divisions, while the inclusion of new talent accentuated leadership rivalries. The ablest and most impatient was Robert Menzies, a Melbourne barrister; among his many qualities a seemly modesty was conspicuously absent.

A series of resignations traced the dissatisfaction with policy. In 1935 Hughes was forced to resign when he published a book critical of the government's foreign policy. As the fascist regimes in Germany and Italy embarked on a policy of military belligerence, and the Australian government clung tightly to Britain in its initial reliance on collective security through the League of Nations, Hughes demanded military readiness. Restored to office in 1937 as minister for external affairs, he continued to attack Hitler and Mussolini: to yield to their territorial claims, he said, would be 'like giving a snack of sandwiches to a hungry tiger'.

But this was precisely what the Lyons government did. From the Italian invasion of Ethiopia in 1935 to the German seizure of Czechoslovakia in 1939, Australia's appeasement of the dictators was as abject as Britain's, partly because it was desperate to avoid another war and partly out of admiration, if not sympathy, for the aggressors' achievements. 'There is a good deal of really spiritual quality', Menzies declared on his return from Germany in 1938, 'in the willingness of young Germans to devote themselves to the service and well-being of the State'.

In 1937 another minister resigned in protest against the government's trade policy. Concerned that a decline in Australian purchases of British manufactured goods might imperil the privileged access of primary producers to the British market, the government had imposed new restrictions on non-British imports. In doing so, it singled out textiles from Japan, a country with which Australia had a substantial trade surplus. The Japanese retaliated with damaging sanctions against Australian woolgrowers. Apart from the loss of export income, the trade diversion dispute set back earlier attempts to build closer relations in the region. A growing body of Australian diplomats, commentators and business leaders recognised the signs of an emergent nationalism in Asia. If Australia still offered few concessions in its immigration policy, they hoped that trade links would promote regional co-operation. Now Australia affronted the most powerful and belligerent of the Asian countries.

Finally, in early 1939, Menzies resigned in protest against the government's retreat from a scheme for social insurance. This was scarcely a radical or comprehensive measure, for it covered just medical benefits and pensions, but it offended the doctors and insurance societies. The irresolute prime minister died in the following month, and Menzies quickly succeeded him, but by now a decade of conservative supremacy was drawing to a close. The inability to proceed with social insurance was a signal demonstration of the paralysing grip of sectional interests.

The government was more resolute in dealing with dissidents. The Labor Party, still suffering from the divisions created in the Depression and hopelessly split on foreign policy between isolationism and anti-fascism, offered ineffective opposition. Communist unions took the lead in resisting appeasement and imposed a boycott on Japan following its invasion of China. After waterside workers refused to load a shipment of iron, that trade was curtailed, but in the course of the dispute the government shut down a critical radio station. Isolationism and appeasement extended from foreign policy to immigration and cultural life. The Lyons government censored criticism of the foreign dictators, and allowed a limited number of Jewish refugees to enter Australia only on the payment of a substantial fee. The most celebrated critic of the fascist regimes was Egon Kisch, a Czech journalist. Denied entry to speak at a conference of the Movement Against War and Fascism in 1934, he jumped ship and appealed to the High Court so that he could tour the country.

Despite the government's endeavours to shut it out, the ferment and strife of the outside world pressed in on Australia. During Kisch's visit a Writers League was formed to affirm an alternative, experimental literature, a literature of commitment in the service of humanity. It merged in 1938 with the Fellowship of Australian Writers, concerned to validate the national experience. From a Book Censorship Abolition League, formed in 1935 to reduce the long index of prohibited literature, there came a Council for Civil Liberties, contesting other infringements on freedom. Against the attempt in 1937 to establish a traditional Academy of Art with a royal charter, the Contemporary Art Society embraced modern styles. The Australian Broadcasting Commission, established in 1932, supported orchestral music and provided a forum for discussion of current affairs. The six dilapidated universities, still teaching just 12,000 undergraduates in 1938, were flickering with fresh energy. Across these various sites of creative endeavour there was a mood of progressive engagement and dissatisfaction with

7.3 A large blackboard advertised the meeting of Aborigines in Sydney on the 150th anniversary of white settlement as a Day of Mourning. (*Man*, March 1938)

established orthodoxies. The gulf between these intellectuals and the mistrustful, practical men who exercised authority had never been wider.

The two groups came together, however, to lay down the policies that regulated how others lived. The inter-war years were the heyday of the expert as the determining intelligence of official policy, still unencumbered by considerations of consultation or consent. In urban planning, public administration, health, education, industry and finance, these experts prevailed, and at the end of the 1930s they were extending their reach to native policy. By this time the earlier forms of knowledge that defined Aboriginal Australians as a primitive race were losing their authority; the regime of protection was demonstrably failing.

The Aboriginal communities of southeast Australia had formed their own organisations, which reworked the terms protection and advancement to demand the abolition of the protection system and seek new ways of advancement. As Sydney staged a re-enactment of Governor Phillip's landing on 26 January 1938 to commemorate the 150th anniversary of European occupation, the Aborigines' Progressive Association observed a Day of Mourning

for 'the White-man's seizure of our country' and enslavement of
their people. It called for a 'new policy which will raise our people
to full citizen status and equality'.

A week later these activists met with the prime minister and a
new minister for the interior, who turned for advice from the
administrators to the anthropologists. A national meeting of
administrators in 1937 affirmed the policy of biological assimilation; the anthropologists offered an alternative expertise that
replaced biology with culture. Culture was both universal
and particular: it was an organising principle of all peoples but
distinctive to each one of them. Accordingly, any attempt to assist
Aborigines should be based not on the imposition of alien practices but rather on what A. P. Elkin, the professor of anthropology
at the University of Sydney and chief adviser to the minister,
described as 'helping them to develop further along their own
cultural lines'.

Elkin therefore called for an Aboriginal administration informed
by anthropological expertise. He saw such a regime operating in
Papua, where benevolent paternalism protected the Indigenous people from expatriate exploitation, in contrast to the mandate territory
of New Guinea, where the plantation *mastas* enforced the obedience
of indentured native labour. These two territories, however, were
exotic places of exile and adventure for a thin sprinkling of white
men and women; the indigenous Australians were an occupied
minority, aliens in their own land.

Elkin's recognition of cultural difference was qualified. While
softening the rigid definitions of racial capacity that distinguished
the savage from the civilised, he still discerned a hierarchy of
racial development: the role of the anthropologist was to guide
administrators with insights that would assist in 'raising primitive races in the cultural scale'. While expounding the rich
complexity of Aboriginal culture, he believed that it was fragile
and unlikely to withstand exposure to European culture. He
thought that those in the settled districts and towns had already
lost much of their cultural identity. Other anthropologists in
northern Australia were more concerned still by the threat of
white contact, believing that the very survival of the Aboriginal
population was at stake.

Even so, Elkin saw no alternative but further development. In the paper he drafted for the minister, which was released in early 1939 as a 'New Deal for Aborigines', assimilation became government policy. The official objective was now 'raising of their status' to 'the ordinary rights of citizenship', but this in turn was to be achieved by extending the practice of forcible removal of Aboriginal children from their families. By a twisted logic that now horrifies all Australians as it then tormented its victims, the popular association of Aboriginality with dirt, disease and neglect allowed whites to deny the civic rights of the Stolen Generations and deprive them of their own culture. One of the participants in the 1937 conference on Aboriginal administration, and a leading advocate of child removal, was A. O. Neville, the Chief Protector of Aborigines in Western Australia. He appears as a character in the 2002 film *Rabbit-Proof Fence*, which follows three young Aboriginal girls taken from their families in 1931 and transported more than 1500 kilometres before they escaped and made their way home. Based on a written account of the journey by the daughter of one of the girls, the film's veracity has been hotly disputed, not least because of its depiction of Neville's implacable pursuit.

***

Australia entered a second world war in September as instinctively as it had entered the first. As soon as he was informed that Britain had declared war on Germany, Menzies declared it his melancholy duty to announce that 'as result, Australia is also at war'. This time, however, there was no rush to enlist: just 20,000 volunteered for the Second Australian Imperial Force in the three months after the outbreak of war in September 1939. Neither the United Australia Party nor the Labor Party welcomed the hostilities. The prime minister, who used the unfortunate phrase 'business as usual', had to be pressured by London to dispatch an army division in November.

Britain and France went to war because, after unsuccessfully appeasing the fascist dictators in repeated acts of belligerence, they felt bound to honour their guarantee to Poland when Germany invaded it. But, as Menzies observed, 'nobody really cares a damn about Poland'; it was already lost. Italy stayed out; so did the Soviet Union, which had cynically entered an agreement with Germany to divide up Poland and other East European territories. As the combatants faced each other on the Western Front during the 'phoney war', Menzies still hoped that full hostilities might be avoided. Apart from his lingering preference for appeasement, he had a particular concern for Australia's safety. In 1914 Japan had been an ally; in 1939 it was a potential enemy. Between the wars Australia had run down its defence capacity in the belief that the Royal Navy was the key to its security. The British naval base at Singapore was thus vital, and Menzies insisted on assurances that it would be reinforced before he allowed Australian troops to depart along with naval forces and aircrews.

In the northern spring of 1940 Germany launched its western offensive and quickly overran France. By the middle of the year Britain stood alone and was under air attack from an enemy-occupied Europe. Australian enlistments increased rapidly and two additional divisions went to North Africa, where the Anzacs were once again defending Egypt and the Suez Canal, this time from Italian forces in the Western Desert following Mussolini's decision to enter the war in June 1940. They were successful, but the defeat of the Italians in Africa and Greece brought German reinforcement. The decision in early 1941 by Winston Churchill, the British prime minister, to send Anzac forces to defend Greece from German invasion proved disastrous; the expeditionary force was quickly driven out and suffered further losses in the subsequent fall of Crete. By the middle of 1941 the German advance across the Western Desert forced a desperate defence of Tobruk. Meanwhile Hitler launched an attack on the Soviet Union and rapidly advanced east.

The entry of Japan into the war with the raid on Pearl Harbor at the end of 1941 realised Australia's worst fears. The enemy descended on South-East Asia and soon overran Malaya. The British undertaking to defend the base at Singapore could not be fulfilled: Churchill was able to spare just a battleship and a cruiser, and enemy aircraft soon sank both of them. Without air support, the defence of Singapore crumbled and in February 1942 the

British commander surrendered. Among those captured were 16,000 Australian infantry. By this time the Japanese were moving rapidly down the chain of islands to Australia's northern approaches, and bombing Darwin.

Australians then and now interpret their initial experience of the Second World War as a betrayal. The valour of the 'rats of Tobruk' (as they were dubbed by an enemy propagandist) joined the heroism on the heights of Gallipoli, but whereas the first sacrifice in the service of empire was glorious the second was ignominious.

> Say Crete, and there is little more to tell
> Of muddle tall as treachery, despair
> And black defeat resounding like a bell

wrote the disenchanted son of a pastoral dynasty in remembrance of a friend who died there. Mary Gilmore, whose self-appointed role as the conscience of her nation found expression in the inspirational 'No Foe Shall Gather Our Harvest', expressed outrage in the principal women's magazine at the fall of Singapore:

> And black was the wrath in each hot heart
> And savage oaths they swore
> As they thought of how they had all been ditched
> By 'Impregnable' Singapore.

The bitterness was all the greater for Australian self-deception. The Dominion had provided for its external security with an imperial insurance policy in which the premium was paid in lives rather than military expenditure – a lethal form of defence on the cheap – and now found the coverage had expired. There was an acerbity in relations between Australian and British leaders during the early years of the Second World War unprecedented in the First. The Anglophile Menzies was openly critical of Churchill's lack of consultation, while the head of the British Foreign Office was contemptuous of antipodean concerns: 'what irresponsible rubbish these Antipodeans talk'. If the Australians had known that the United States agreed with Britain it was necessary to beat Hitler first and then worry about the Pacific, their anger would have been even greater.

The backbiting affected the armed forces, with constant feuding among the generals, and strengthened a reluctance in the domestic population to accept the need for sacrifice. The Menzies government imposed some financial controls but did little to mobilise the country's resources. It declared the Communist Party illegal for opposing the war and denounced the coalminers for striking in 1940, but failed to curtail the usual round of domestic pleasures. Menzies came under increasing criticism. He 'couldn't lead a flock of homing pigeons', declared the ageing warhorse, Billy Hughes. The government fell in August 1941.

A month later the Labor Party took office under John Curtin. When Japan commenced hostilities in December, the country made its own declaration of war. At the end of the year the prime minister published a message that 'Australia looks to America, free of any pangs as to our traditional links or kinship with the United Kingdom'. In early 1942 the government informed Churchill that a failure to defend Singapore would be regarded as an 'inexcusable betrayal' and insisted that the Australian troops in North Africa return to defend the homeland rather than join in the defence of Burma. The Australian Broadcasting Commission stopped playing 'The British Grenadiers' before its news bulletin in favour of 'Advance Australia Fair'. With the adoption of the Statute of Westminster later in 1942, Australia consummated its constitutional independence.

These moves, under dire emergency, to end the subordination to Britain and perhaps create a new dependence on the United States, constitute a powerful national legend, one that has found expression since 2008 in official commemoration of a supposed 'Battle for Australia'. Japanese air raids on Darwin, shipping losses in Australian waters and even a midget submarine attack on Sydney Harbour certainly reinforced the fear of invasion, but that was not Japan's intention. The main thrust was further north and it sought to occupy the islands of the southwest Pacific to isolate but not overrun Australia. The Americans fell back on Australia as their principal base, but in their conduct of operations in the region they consulted Australia no more than the British had done. There was no special relationship. Even the adoption of the Statute of Westminster was prompted by the need to exercise certain government powers rather than any impulse for independence.

Curtin welcomed the arrival in March 1942 of General Douglas MacArthur as Supreme Commander of the South-West Pacific, and accepted the division of labour that the theatrical American proposed: 'You take care of the rear, and I will handle the front'. MacArthur in turn ensured that Australian troops did not detract from his glory or impede his country's post-war plans to impose military and economic control of the region. Even though two epic naval battles between the United States and Japan – the first in the Coral Sea in May 1942 and the second at the Midway Atoll in the Pacific a month later – ensured that there would be no enemy landing in Australia, there remained cause for Australian concern. A large Japanese force landed on the northern coast of Papua New Guinea and advanced south, until by September 1942 it was only 50 kilometres from the capital, Port Moresby, on the Torres Strait. Along a rough track that traversed precipitous ranges and in appalling conditions that spread malaria and dysentery, Australian infantry fought with Papuan support to turn the Japanese advance. This battle along the Kokoda Track cost 12,000 Japanese, 2000 Australian and perhaps 500 Papuan lives. It was here that Australians first fought in jungle green uniforms rather than khaki.

7.4 Douglas MacArthur, the United States general and commander of the Allied forces in the Pacific, confers with the Australian prime minister, John Curtin. (National Archives of Australia, A1200, L36449)

The jungle was at first a strange and menacing environment, recalled by another descendant of a pastoral dynasty from the dry grasslands to the south:

> And I think still of men in green
> On the Soputa track,
> With fifteen spitting tommy-guns
> To keep the jungle back.

A communist infantryman who became the most successful of the war novelists wrote of the tropical undergrowth as a malign presence, no less alien and menacing than the fascist enemy: 'a poisonous, material thing, heavy with foul scents; a huge, infested womb, swallowing us, mingling us in its corruption'. There had been contempt for the Italian enemy, grudging respect for the Germans, but there was visceral hatred for the Japanese. The commanding officer of the Australians told Australian troops at Port Moresby in 1942 that the enemy was a 'subhuman beast'. The Department of Information issued a poster showing a gigantic Japanese soldier astride the globe, machine gun at the ready, his foot poised to descend on the Australian mainland. 'We've always despised them', it exhorted, 'now we must smash them'. The publicity campaign ended in April 1942 following complaints from religious leaders and Curtin felt it necessary to point out that this was not a racial conflict but a 'war of ideas and ideals'.

After leading the defence of Papua New Guinea, the Australians were relegated to an auxiliary role in the Pacific war effort. The Americans led the advance on Japan, leaving the Australians to mop up. The operations they conducted during 1943 and 1944 were substantial but overshadowed by battles further north; formerly a site of heroic resistance, New Guinea had become a 'green hole'. Australia played no part in the meetings of the three principal Allies – the United States, the Soviet Union and Britain – which thrashed out the allocation of responsibilities and spoils. Nor was Australia consulted on the terms of the Japanese surrender, though it did insist on signing the instrument in its own right and subsequently led the Commonwealth occupation force.

The exclusion of Australia from the determination of Allied strategy only intensified its determination to exert a greater influence

7.5 The Kokoda Track was a route of strategic importance as Australian troops defended the capital of New Guinea against Japanese forces advancing from the north. (Australian War Memorial)

in international affairs. It was the threat of a Pacific war that caused Menzies to establish the first Australian diplomatic missions, to Japan, China and the United States, in 1940. The Labor government built up the Department of External Affairs and Herbert Evatt, its thrusting minister, harangued the senior Allies. He was as omnipresent at the founding conference of the United Nations in San Francisco in 1945 as Hughes had been in Paris in 1919 and as uncompromising – the head of the British Foreign Office judged him 'the most frightful man in the world'. But unlike Hughes, Evatt affirmed the principles of liberal internationalism. He fought in vain to limit the veto power of superpowers in the Security Council, had some success in enlarging the role of the General Assembly and campaigned to have colonies placed under the supervision of the world body. The final meeting of the steering committee adopted by acclamation a tribute to 'the greatest champion of the smaller powers'.

Australia's fatalities in the Second World War were lighter than in the First: 37,000 deaths out of a population of seven million and a total enlistment of one million, of whom 560,000 served overseas. Improved medical treatment allowed more casualties to survive, though the 10,000 aircrew (most of whom died in Europe) emphasised the lethal nature of the war in the skies. Perhaps the most disturbing losses were the prisoners of war; of the 22,000 captured by the Japanese, only 14,000 lived to return to Australia in 1945. Some were executed, but most died of malnutrition and disease. The men put to work on the construction of a railway from Burma to Thailand were treated appallingly, while women army nurses suffered equal brutality. A ship evacuating army nurses from Singapore was sunk in February 1942. Of fifty-three who made it to land, twenty-one were executed and eight more died in captivity.

The stories the survivors told were shocking. Hatred of Japanese brutality was kept alive after the war in memoirs and fiction, notably Nevil Shute's unforgiving novel, *A Town Like Alice* (1950), which became a film. Eventually the hatred softened into an affirmation of human endurance and even a partial reconciliation, especially through the efforts of Edward 'Weary' Dunlop, an army surgeon who showed extraordinary courage and ingenuity in defending his men in prisoner-of-war camps and improvising treatment for cholera, malaria, typhoid and tropical ulcers. The publication in 1986 of his war diaries, which record the daily struggle with disease, cruelty and hopelessness, consolidated his status as a national hero.

Dunlop, a sporting champion and a man's man, represented the older military qualities of loyalty, endurance, egalitarianism and valour with the newer values of healing, compassion and forgiveness.

Although the Second World War killed fewer Australians than the first, it reached more deeply into national life. It was fought with weapons of advanced design, requiring a long lead-time for design and production as well as elaborate supply systems and a complex machinery of industrial planning and coordination. While manufacturing had diversified between the wars, the country was still unable to produce a motor car in 1939 yet by 1945 it was manufacturing the most advanced four-engine aircraft. The task of building facilities for the American forces required a construction workforce of 50,000. The responsibility of feeding and supplying them required the full use of the country's resources. Through national security regulations issued under the Commonwealth's defence power, wages, prices and rents were fixed, capital issues controlled, bank credit tightly regulated and inessential industries prohibited. The Commonwealth acquired control of income tax. A Manpower Directorate used a national register to direct labour to where it was most needed. Women were drawn into the armed forces and directed to essential industries, with a special tribunal created to increase their pay. From the middle of 1942 there was rationing of clothing, and soon tea, sugar, butter and meat were also rationed. By holding down consumption, deferring maintenance and mobilising all available resources, this war economy increased output by 40 per cent over the pre-war level.

Rapid strides in metal fabrication, engineering and food processing were assisted by equipment the United States provided. Almost a million United States servicemen passed through Australia on their way to the front, and even though the numbers in Australia at any one time were seldom more than 100,000, this was a foreign presence of unprecedented significance. One in ten of the GIs was African-American, in contrast to the restriction on Aboriginal enlistment to those with a European parent (there were probably 4000 Aboriginal soldiers, with a further 3000 working as labourers in the north), and forced Australia to confront its own segregationist practices.

The Australian soldiers envied the Americans' higher pay, superior conditions and access to luxury goods. There was particular resentment of their attractiveness to local women, and the image of rampant sexuality was explicit in wartime fiction and art. In occupied Australia the fickle female was the fifth columnist; the war brides who left for the United States were regarded as defectors. Brawls between American and Australian soldiers attested to local sensitivity to the friendly invasion.

Australia's acceptance of the sacrifice required in this second war without the deep divisions of the first was assisted by the quality of its leadership. Hughes, the firebrand, had polarised the country. John Curtin, an austere and self-doubting man, unified it. He demanded much of the people to meet the unprecedented emergency. 'The enemy thunders at our very gates', he declared, 'and your every waking hour must be an hour devoted to Australia'. In calling on civilians to 'strip every selfish, comfortable habit, every luxurious impulse, every act, word or deed that retards the victory march', he coupled the shared sacrifice to a new spirit of mutual purpose: 'You must not moan. You have to glorify the nation.' At the end of 1942 he overcame the opposition of his own party to introduce conscription for military service beyond Australia's borders.

In return for the self-denial he demanded, the government undertook far-reaching reform. As early as December 1942 it established a Department of Post-War Reconstruction to plan the new order. The enhanced powers of the wartime Commonwealth would carry over to peacetime with regulation of the economy for industrial expansion, population growth, maintenance of full employment, housing, health, education and social welfare. Post-war reconstruction was in fact anticipated during the war as post-Depression reconstruction in a series of measures that mobilised the country's neglected resources. Statutory authorities brought unions into the conduct of strategic industries, and replaced the inefficiencies of the casual labour market with stable employment. Graduates were recruited for an expanded and far more active bureaucracy. Pensions were improved, unemployment and sickness benefits introduced.

There were setbacks. After winning a sweeping victory in the 1943 national election, the government failed to carry a 1944 referendum to enshrine its wartime powers after the war. Powerful business interests chafed against controls, newspaper magnates challenged censorship. 'Nothing would come to the men and women of the working class as a gift from the gods', Curtin warned. 'Everything they gained had to be fought for.' He did not live to see the final victory, for he suffered a heart attack at the end of 1944 and died at the Lodge in July 1945, widely mourned for his dedication to the country's survival. Curtin had turned the ordeal into a people's war, a war to abolish the injustice and insecurity that had undermined democracy and nurtured fascism, a war that would finally end the thirty-year crisis. From the tragic sacrifice of the First World War, and rancorous discontent that followed, a sufficient unity was created in the Second World War to make the sacrifice seem worthwhile.

8

Golden age, 1946–1975

The end of the war released a pent-up demand for goods and services that had long been unavailable, yet the task converting a war economy back to peace conditions called for continuing restraint. In asking voters for patience during the 1946 election, Ben Chifley assured them of the benefits that would flow. 'Australia was entering a golden age', he said. With so many chafing at the shortage of housing and household goods, the opposition derided the prime minister's claim, but he was vindicated. The third quarter of the twentieth century was an era of growth unmatched since the second half of the nineteenth century. The population almost doubled, economic activity increased more than threefold. There were jobs for all men who wanted them. People lived longer, in greater comfort. They expended less effort to earn a living, had more money for discretionary expenditure, greater choice and increased leisure.

Sustained growth brought plenty to Australians and habituated them to further improvement: a belief in the capacity of science to turn scarcity into abundance was matched by the confidence that planners could guide prosperity and experts use it to solve social problems. The facilities of intellectual life and the possibilities for artistic creativity expanded. The country became less isolated from the rest of the world and less beleaguered in its domestic arrangements. But as the ancients discerned a cyclical pattern of history, which saw the purposeful vigour of an ascendant civilisation soften into indulgence, disunity and eventual collapse, so post-war

Australia followed a worrying trajectory. The iron age of austerity occupied the 1940s; the 1950s were the silver years of growing confidence and comfort; by the golden 1960s indulgence and decay had set in, and the regime could not withstand the discordant forces it had released.

This might be too parochial a perspective. The long boom of the 1950s and 1960s was an international phenomenon, the fruits of prosperity shared by all advanced economies. As a trading country, Australia benefited from the revival of world trade and investment, shared in the new technologies, followed the same techniques of management and administration. As a junior partner of the Western alliance it was also caught up in the Cold War with the Communist bloc and drawn into military commitments that ended by the 1970s in overextension and humiliation just as the golden age of plenty ran out. Decision-makers would never again enjoy such luxury of choice or feel the same confidence. Some looked back on the post-war period as an era of strong leadership and responsive endeavour; others lamented the lost opportunities and timorous complacency.

***

The iron age spanned the production of weapons of war and the beating of swords into ploughshares. The wartime Labor government had assumed unprecedented controls over investment, employment, production, consumption and practically every aspect of national life. Planning for peace began at the end of 1942 with the appointment of a young economist, H. C. ('Nugget') Coombs, to direct the Department of Post-war Reconstruction. A railwayman's son with a strong social conscience and a doctorate from the London School of Economics, Coombs was emblematic of the enhanced role of the planner.

His minister until 1945 was Ben Chifley, who was also the Treasurer and Curtin's closest confidant. An engine-driver who had been victimised for his part in a strike during the First World War, Chifley was one of an older generation of stalwarts determined that after this war there would be no return to hardship and humiliation. He frequently recalled the degrading treatment of the working class during the Depression, when men were thrown on the streets and left to starve, forced to beg for jobs at factory gates, treated worse than pit-ponies in the mines. 'I was not one of those who suffered want in those years', he told parliament in 1944, 'but it left a bitterness in my heart that time cannot eradicate'.

An austere man of simple dignity with a voice damaged by too many open-air addresses, and possibly his pipe, Chifley did not often venture on flights of rhetoric. Speaking to a Labor Party conference in 1949, however, he conjured a phrase for the goal that sustained him through half a century of service in the cause. It was not simply a matter of putting an extra sixpence in workers' pockets, or elevating individuals to high office. Labor strove to bring 'something better to the people, better standards of living, greater happiness to the mass of the people'. Without that larger purpose, that 'light on the hill', then 'the labour movement would not be worth fighting for'.

His government's plans required the demobilisation of the armed forces and the return of workers from war production to peacetime employment. The munitions industries were to revert to domestic manufacture behind the traditional tariff wall, but with an enhanced scope and capacity. The government therefore gave the American General Motors Corporation generous concessions to establish a local car industry and the first Holden sedans rolled off the assembly line in 1948. The rural industries, badly run down after the pre-war decade of low prices and then the sudden demand for increased output, were to be modernised. Tractors replaced horses, and 9000 new soldier settlers were placed on the land. The shortage of skills was to be met by retraining ex-servicemen in technical schools and universities: the country's lecture theatres were packed and an Australian National University was established as a centre of research. The backlog of demand for housing was to be filled with federal funding for State authorities: 200,000 homes were constructed between 1945 and 1949.

This spurt of state-sponsored development had a social as well as an economic aspect, for the war had augmented the call to 'populate or perish', and the Labor government embarked on the first major migration programme for two decades. In 1945 Arthur Calwell became Australia's first minister for immigration. He set a target of 2 per cent annual increase in the current population of 7.5 million, half of which was to be contributed by new arrivals. The minister sought them in Britain but that country was no longer encouraging emigration, so Calwell turned of necessity to continental Europe, where millions of refugees had been uprooted by the abrupt shifts of national and political boundaries. In 1947 he toured the refugee camps and confirmed that they offered 'splendid human material', which moreover could be shipped to Australia at international expense and required to work for two years under government direction. Over the following four years 170,000 of these 'Displaced Persons' were brought to Australia, chiefly from the nations transferred from German to Soviet control in the corridor of eastern Europe that ran from the Baltic down to Aegean Sea.

Calwell also negotiated agreements with European governments to recruit additional migrants. His successor extended these arrangements in the early 1950s from northwest to south and east European countries. In that decade Australia received another million permanent settlers and most of them were non-British, with the largest contingents from Italy, the Netherlands, Greece and Germany. In 1947 the number of locally born Australians was at an all-time high of 90 per cent (with another 8 per cent from Britain or New Zealand). By 1961 the locally born dropped to 83 per cent. This decisive break with previous practice was confirmed by the creation of a separate citizenship in 1948 with provisions for those who were not British subjects to acquire the status of Australian citizen.

The migration programme, while maintained and expanded by the non-Labor government that took office at the end of 1949, was Labor's. Calwell, a former trade union official deeply embedded in the lore of the labour movement, shared its national prejudices and occupational concerns. 'Two "Wongs" do not make a White', he declared in defence of his decision to deport Chinese refugees in 1947. Yet it was Calwell who coined the term 'new Australian' to encourage the assimilation of unfamiliar newcomers. The pressure on them to give up their ethnic identities in order to conform to 'the Australian way of life', another new locution, was insistent; equally striking was the assumption that so many people from such diverse origins could do so.

8.1　The magnitude of the post-war migration programme required special accommodation for new arrivals, and the government sought to promote acceptance of non-English-speaking migrants with favourable publicity. Happy families are shown here at the Bonegilla Reception Centre in rural Victoria, 1949. (Department of Immigration and Multicultural Affairs)

The acceptance of new Australians was also premised on reassuring the host population that they would not swamp the labour market and threaten local living standards. The system of wage determination by industrial tribunals ensured that migrants enjoyed the same wages as other workers and, by emphasising its new commitment to the maintenance of full employment, the Labor government won the support of the unions for this large influx of new ones. Full employment was the centrepiece of Labor's post-war planning, the indispensable condition of the light on the hill. In the negotiations at Bretton Woods in 1944 that brought the International Monetary Fund and the World Bank as instruments of trade liberalisation for the new economic order, Australia's most distinctive contribution was the demand that there be a guarantee of full employment.

In its landmark 1945 White Paper on Full Employment the government outlined a Keynesian approach to management of the economy by control of aggregate demand. Fatalist acceptance of market forces yielded to a close and continuous intervention to ensure the national interest was served. For good measure, the government prepared a raft of public works schemes to soak up any labour surplus that might emerge once the pent-up demand from the war was satisfied. The widely anticipated slump did not occur; rather, the post-war boom continued and gathered force, but the Commonwealth did proceed in 1949 with the most ambitious of these schemes: a diversion of the Snowy River into the inland river system with major hydroelectric generation plants and irrigation works. Accompanying full employment was an expanded social security system, in which cash benefits for the unemployed accompanied increased public provision of housing, health and education.

In all this the Chifley government had to juggle with formidable constraints. A shortage of basic materials meant that rationing continued. An aversion to external debt was one of the legacies of the Depression and this, with support for the British currency and trading bloc, meant that foreign exchange was strictly rationed. Even though the government won national elections in 1943 and 1946, it failed in a 1944 referendum to persuade the electorate to extend its wartime powers into peace, and, in a series of decisions the High Court struck down some of its more innovative measures.

As wartime consensus faded, the omnipresent hand of officialdom became irksome. The frank explanation of a federal minister of the penalties he imposed on State authorities that sold public housing indicated a growing line of division: 'The Commonwealth is concerned to provide adequate and good houses for the workers; it is not concerned with making workers into little capitalists.' Yet it was the workers who were expected to show the greatest restraint.

The greatest fear of the government as it grappled with shortages at a time of full employment was inflation. Instinctively frugal, Chifley was determined to hold down wages. His delay in allowing the Arbitration Court to consider the unions' case for a forty-hour week, which was finally conceded in 1948, and his even greater reluctance to allow wage increases imposed a heavy strain on the loyalty of moderate union officials. Communists were prominent in a wave of strikes in the transport, metal and mining industries,

8.2 With pipe in hand, Ben Chifley, the Australian prime minister, stands with his British counterpart, Clement Attlee. On his left, the assertive minister for external affairs, H. V. Evatt, is temporarily silent. (National Library of Australia)

but they were by no means alone in their impatience. Chifley nevertheless interpreted a national stoppage by the coalminers in 1949 as a direct communist challenge and responded with confiscation of the union's assets, imprisonment of its leaders, raids on the offices of the Communist Party, and the introduction of soldiers into the pits. Three months after the defeated miners returned to work as victims of the iron discipline of Labor austerity, the government was defeated at the polls.

The silver age opened with the election of a coalition government of the Liberal and Country parties under the leadership of the revitalised Robert Menzies. His recovery from humiliating rejection in 1941 began with the formation of a new and more broad-based political movement – the Liberal Party – and the construction of a new political constituency that Menzies characterised as 'the forgotten people': those salaried and self-employed Australians who identified neither with the company boardrooms nor the tribal solidarity of the manual workers. In extolling the value of his forgotten people, Menzies laid primary emphasis on their 'stake in the country' through 'responsibility for homes – homes material, homes human, homes spiritual'. He solicited the support of wives and mothers whose domestic wellbeing was threatened by the impersonal regimen of bureaucracy and the militant masculinity of striking unionists; yet he also tapped the youthful vigour of the returned servicemen impatient with the regulatory stolidity of Labor politicians still exorcising the ghosts of the Depression.

The new government came to power with an anti-socialist crusade aimed at an electorate weary of controls and shortages. It undertook to reduce taxation and cut red tape. Restrictions on foreign investment were lifted, private enterprise encouraged, wage increases allowed. Yet the continued emphasis on migration and national development ensured the continuation of economic management. During the 1949 election the new Treasurer had singled out Coombs as a meddling socialist; on the day after the poll he phoned Coombs and said: 'That you, Nugget? You don't want to take any notice of all that bullshit I was talking during the election. We'll be needing you, you know.' As governor of the Commonwealth Bank, which Labor had given the powers of a central bank, Coombs continued to hold the financial levers.

Exporters benefited from the outbreak of war in Korea in 1950, which caused leading industrial countries to stockpile essential commodities. The price of wool increased sevenfold during 1951 to reach record levels, and other primary producers also prospered as new markets emerged. A trade treaty with Japan in 1957 signalled a shift in orientation from Europe to East Asia as the former enemy began to rebuild and industrialise. Domestic industry expanded rapidly with the advantage of tariffs and import quotas. The service sector grew even faster as mechanisation released blue-collar workers to join the white-collar salariat and office blocks rose up over the city streetscape.

An annual growth rate of over 4.2 per cent was maintained in the 1950s and 5.1 per cent in the 1960s. There was full employment, higher productivity, improved earnings, a pattern of sustained improvement that no-one could recall. The chief problem that exercised the economic managers was not insufficient but excessive demand: outbreaks of inflation required credit squeezes in the early 1950s and again in 1960. It was a measure of the new mood that when unemployment rose to 3 per cent, it almost cost the Menzies government the 1961 election.

This was the era in which an economist could characterise Australia as a 'small, rich, industrial country', the point at which the ambitions of a settler society to outgrow the confines of dependence reached their zenith. The industrial base broadened as improvements in transport allowed manufacturers to develop a national market and family-owned companies floated on the stock exchange to expand their scale of operations. When he opened a new stage of the Snowy Mountains project in 1958, Robert Menzies declared that 'this scheme is teaching us and everybody in Australia to think in a big way, to be thankful for big things, to be proud of big enterprises'. A committee of inquiry took economic success as the essential dynamic of national life: 'growth endows the community with a sense of vigour and social purpose'.

For all its homage to private enterprise, the Menzies government was firmly committed to a strong public sector. The prime minister, who had made his name at the bar in a constitutional case over the powers of the Commonwealth, augmented the national government. When he took up residence in the prime minister's lodge, Canberra had a population of only 20,000: it was the smallest capital city in the world. A number of his ministers still based themselves in their electorates, visitors to their departments. Although the parliament had shifted from Melbourne a quarter-century before, there were more Commonwealth public servants in the southern city during the mid-1950s than in the national capital. The urbane Menzies embarked on a programme to consolidate administration in Canberra. He, more than anyone else, turned the Australian Capital Territory into a genuine seat of government. By 1965, when the first traffic lights were introduced, it had a population of 100,000.

The augmentation of the Commonwealth increased the rivalry of the States, which competed for investment in the new industries. Tom Playford, who held office in South Australia from 1938–65 with the assistance of a notorious gerrymander, built up steel and motor vehicle production in his State by offering cheap land, infrastructure, and utilities along with quiescent unions. Henry

Bolte achieved a similar supremacy in Victoria from 1955–72, and used similar methods to consolidate the manufacturing sector in his State. Among the fruits of his trips to overseas boardrooms was a large petro-chemical complex on the shores of Port Phillip. Others were built at Kwinana, south of Perth, and at Botany Bay, on the southern outskirts of Sydney; in 1971 the novelist David Ireland would make the last of these the site for his dark novel of economic servitude, *The Unknown Industrial Prisoner*.

That was not how such projects were seen in the 1950s, but they did mark a new phase of development, away from public borrowing and public works to direct foreign investment in business ventures. The new mode of development was more capital-intensive, less concerned with job creation than with profitable enterprise, and it was orchestrated by Liberal rather than Labor premiers. Playford and Bolte were farmers and they exhibited an earthy parochialism as they did their deals and brushed aside critics. 'They can strike till they're black in the face', was Bolte's response to one group of recalcitrant public employees. Both men joined an insistent cult of development to moral conservatism: strict censorship, six o'clock closing of hotels, and capital punishment were among their hallmarks. Both blamed Canberra for their parsimony.

Each year the revenue of the Commonwealth increased and each year it made grants to the States, which retained primary responsibility for health, education, public transport and other services, though the federal support was never enough to satisfy the rising demand. In its own expenditure the Menzies government encouraged citizens to help themselves. There was assistance to home-buyers, a tax rebate for dependent spouses, subsidies for private medical insurance. Old-age pensions were maintained, other forms of social welfare neglected. The maxim of the silver age was individual initiative.

***

The transition from the iron to the silver age occurred under the shadow of the Cold War. An intense bipolar contest between communism and capitalism dominated world politics from the late 1940s and forced Australia to bind itself more tightly to the

Western alliance. The inability of the Labor government to resist the demands of the international Cold War contributed to its fall in 1949 and kept it out of office over the next two decades. At home the Cold War gripped the country and divided the labour movement. A fear of communism permeated almost every aspect of public life, at once impelling the government to improve the welfare of citizens and inhibiting the opportunities for dissent.

At the end of the Second World War the Labor government was both grateful to the United States for leadership of the war in the Pacific and wary of its plans for the post-war settlement. Roosevelt, Stalin and Churchill had already allocated the territorial spoils, and the United States was proceeding with plans that would give it unrestricted economic access to the non-communist sphere. Liberal internationalism through the United Nations seemed the best chance for lesser countries such as Australia to safeguard their interests. Revival of the British Commonwealth as an economic and military alliance provided the best chance of a counterweight to American dominance.

Britain was clinging to the white Commonwealth as it struggled to maintain its status as a world power. The loss of India, Pakistan, Sri Lanka and Burma, intractable conflict in Palestine, and a communist uprising in Malaya brought home the need to reduce the imperial role. After communists won power in China and Indonesian nationalists overthrew Dutch rule in 1949, the independence movement in East Asia was irresistible. In Africa the same impulses forced a less speedy, more contested decolonisation, while the island peoples in what the British high commissioner described as the 'peaceful backwater' of the Pacific proceeded subsequently along the same path to self-government.

Other European countries either accepted the loss of their colonies or fought costly rearguard actions to delay the inevitable transfer of sovereignty. Formal empires based on direct rule and displayed in colour-coded maps of the world gave way to an informal imperialism based on trade and investment, aid and armaments, these devices creating shifting spheres of influence and a far less stable world order. Under Labor, Australia accepted claims in the region for national independence (and assisted the formation of the

Indonesian republic) while holding fast to its own colonial regime in
Papua New Guinea.

The mercurial minister for external affairs, H. V. Evatt, made this
a period of intense busyness in Australian foreign policy. In both
international forums and direct dealings with Britain and the United
States, Evatt sought to play a prominent role, capped by his election
as president of the General Assembly of the United Nations in 1948.
So it was that as luxury cars drew up at the entrance of a palace
in Paris to disgorge pinstriped and homburg-hatted diplomats
for the opening ceremony, a late-model Ford appeared with 'a
tousle-headed man in a baggy suit, tie askew, sitting beside the
driver'. A gendarme instructed to admit dignitaries only who barred
his entry was flabbergasted to learn the man he delayed was the new
president. On the other hand, a translator at the Conference remembered him years later because he was so rude.

What role could a remote and thinly populated outpost of the
white diaspora play? The Americans had no intention of altering
their global strategy to accommodate this abrasive representative of
a socialist government; they would not share military technology
and in 1948 suspended Australia's access to intelligence information. The British Labour government was also relegated to second-
rank status by the United States, and Australia provided important
support for its residual economic and strategic interests in the
region. The two countries thus embarked on a plan to develop
their own atomic weapons with test sites in Australia. It was this
project that brought the Cold War security regimen to Australia as
British intelligence supervised the formation of the Australian
Security and Intelligence Organisation in early 1949 to safeguard
defence secrets.

Labor had sought to avert such harsh dictates of the Cold War.
While opposed to communist expansion, it could see that the polarisation of world politics into two armed camps would subordinate it
to American foreign policy and impose an extreme anti-communism
inimical to its own foreign and domestic aspirations. By 1949,
however, the Cold War divisions had hardened. Stalinist regimes
were installed in Eastern Europe, Germany was divided and the
American airlift to Berlin to break a Soviet blockade signalled the
heightened confrontation across the Iron Curtain.

The Liberals won office at the end of the year on a platform of resolute anti-communism; it was implemented with military assistance to help Britain defeat the communist insurgency in Malaya, and the dispatch of troops to Korea in 1950 when fighting broke out there between communists and American-led forces. The new minister for external relations discerned a global pattern of communist aggression, now projected south from China to threaten the entire South-East Asian region. In 1951 Robert Menzies warned against the 'imminent danger of war'.

'With our vast territory and our small population', he added later, 'we cannot survive a surging Communist challenge from abroad except by the cooperation of powerful friends'. The first and indisputably the most powerful of those friends was the United States, and this friendship was formalised in 1951 with the negotiation of a security treaty between Australia, New Zealand and the United States (commonly abbreviated to ANZUS). For the Australian government this treaty cemented a special relationship with its protector, but there were many claimants to such a status and in truth the agreement obliged the United States to provide only as much assistance to Australia against an external aggressor as it judged expedient. ANZUS was essentially a corollary to its system of alliances in the Asia–Pacific region, and served to reconcile Australia to America's far more important relationship with the former enemy, Japan. Australia was also included in the South-East Asian Treaty Organisation (SEATO), arranged by the United States in 1954 after communist forces defeated France in Vietnam, but that too guaranteed no more than Washington determined.

Britain was a member of SEATO and Australia continued to encourage Britain's development of nuclear weapons and assist its military presence in Malaya. This was a special relationship of a different kind and in 1956, when Britain defied the United States to join with France in war on Egypt over the administration of the Suez Canal, Menzies unhesitatingly threw his efforts behind the mother country. On returning to office he had announced that 'the British Empire must remain our chief international occupation' and he now derided the troublesome 'Gyppos' as 'a dangerous lot of backward adolescents, mouthing the slogans of democracy, full of self-importance and basic ignorance'. He was never reconciled to Britain's reduced dominion.

A romantic monarchist and fervent admirer of an idealised ancestral homeland, Menzies in his own words was 'British to his bootstraps'. His gallantry during the Royal Tour of 1954 was attuned to the immense popularity of the young Queen Elizabeth, the first reigning monarch to visit Australia, but his hyperbole during her subsequent visit a decade later, when he recited the

8.3   At a state reception in Parliament House, Canberra, on 18 February 1963, Robert Menzies pays fulsome tribute to Queen Elizabeth. (© News Limited)

verse of a seventeenth-century court composer, 'I did but see her passing by / And yet I love her till I die', made listeners squirm and the Queen blush. His final gesture on the eve of retirement, a suggestion that the country's new unit of decimal currency should be named the 'royal', was mocked into oblivion.

If the delayed but inevitable withdrawal of the British military presence was regretted, the reluctant but equally inescapable turn by Britain away from its Commonwealth trading relationships in order to enter Europe dealt a much heavier blow. It left Menzies' regular trips to London for Commonwealth meetings and Test cricket as a nostalgic anachronism. His discomfort with the multiracial composition of the Commonwealth, as former colonies became new members, and his defence of the apartheid regime in South Africa made Australia seem another outpost of an obsolete white man's club.

While Menzies' foreign ministers displayed greater interest in Asia, they regarded it always through the distorting prism of the Cold War. Even the Colombo Plan, a scheme for co-operative economic development among the Commonwealth countries of South and South-East Asia that brought 10,000 Asian students to study in Australia, was justified as a prophylactic against communist infection. It also brought the beneficiaries into direct experience of a still obdurately White Australia. Australians were present in Asia as advisers, technicians, teachers, diplomats and journalists, but most of all as soldiers. They engaged with their neighbours through travel, study, art and literature, yet Asia remained a zone of contest and danger that required the presence in force of their powerful friends. That need in turn required the Australian government during the 1950s and 1960s to play up the communist danger, to reduce the complexities of history, culture and nationality to the Cold War choice: are you ours or theirs?

It also meant that Australia had to follow the United States even when it was ahead. Fearful of the communist threat from the north, the Australian government exerted all of its limited influence to interpose American forces between China and the South-East Asian countries. From 1962 it provided military instructors to assist the anti-communist government of South Vietnam prevent unification with the communist north. Even before this country became directly involved in Indochina, it reintroduced military conscription, and as soon as President Johnson made the fateful decision to introduce ground troops, in 1965, Australia responded immediately to the request for assistance it had solicited. South Vietnam itself played little part in the decision; it was regarded by the minister for external affairs simply as 'our present frontier'. Harold Holt, who succeeded Menzies as prime minister in 1966, told his host at the White House that Australia would 'go all the way with LBJ'. By then, all the way fell some distance short of American expectations: in late 1968, when the American force had grown to 500,000, Australia contributed just 8000. As before with Britain, so now with the United States – obeisance to a powerful protector was payment in kind for defence on the cheap.

A preoccupation with the communist threat from without was linked always to the danger within. During the 1949 election campaign Menzies had undertaken to ban the Australian Communist Party. It was not a legitimate political movement, he insisted, but an 'alien and destructive pest' that threatened civilised government and national security. Once elected, he proceeded with the passage of the Communist Party Dissolution Bill, which was enacted in 1950 but immediately challenged by the Communist Party itself as well as ten trade unions. Evatt, the deputy leader of the federal Labor Party and a former High Court judge, appeared before the court on behalf of the Waterside Workers Federation. He persuaded all but one of the current judges that the legislation, which relied upon the Commonwealth's defence powers, was unconstitutional since the country was not at war.

Menzies persisted with an attempt to obtain the constitutional power by referendum. Evatt, who became leader of the Labor Party following the death of Chifley in mid-1951, carried his party into opposing the proposal. The campaign was intense and the outcome close. While the government failed narrowly to obtain the necessary majority of votes and a majority of States, if just 30,000 voters in South Australia or Victoria had voted Yes rather than No, the proposal would have succeeded. Public opinion polls both before and after the referendum showed a clear majority favoured banning the Communist Party – and it has been suggested that it was the proposal to reverse the onus of proof that defeated the referendum.

Even so, it is difficult to imagine that a similar plebiscite in the United States, Britain or elsewhere would have failed to produce a majority in favour of suppressing communism. The affirmation of a basic freedom, the presumption of innocence, even for adherents to a small and vilified cause in the fevered atmosphere of the early 1950s did the country credit.

This was Evatt's finest hour. He was in no sense a communist sympathiser but alarmed by the sweeping powers the government proposed to employ. Its legislation would have allowed citizens to be declared as communists; upon such a declaration the person named could be dismissed from the public service and disqualified from trade union office; failure to cease activity in a banned organisation would be a crime punishable by up to five years imprisonment. That in proposing these provisions Menzies had falsely identified some trade union officials as communists, and even warned a Labor critic that he might be caught up in their operation, seemed to Evatt and others to threaten essential liberties. The Australian Security and Intelligence Organisation had increased its surveillance over a wide range of non-communists – scientists, academics and writers – and was at this time preparing for the internment of 7000 of them should war be declared. For Evatt to forestall the implementation of this repressive plan was a considerable achievement.

His referendum victory brought him no further success. There was a substantial and growing anti-communist element within the labour movement that condemned Evatt's appearance before the High Court and was angered by his decision to fight the referendum. It had its origins in a lay religious organisation, the Catholic Social Studies Movement, led by a masterful zealot, B. A. Santamaria, who conducted his crusade against atheistic materialism with the assistance of powerful members of the church's hierarchy. Through its leadership of Industrial Groups, the Movement had weakened communist influence in trade unions. Since the unions were affiliated to the Labor Party, the Groupers began to capture leading positions in that organisation also. 'Mad buggers', Chifley called them shortly before he died, when they defied him to welcome Menzies' anti-communist measures.

Evatt lost the 1951 election called by Menzies to capitalise on the division in the Labor ranks over the banning of the Communist

Party, and the following election in 1954, which was dominated by allegations of communist espionage. The second defeat enraged Evatt, who denounced the Movement and prevailed on the federal executive of the party to replace the hostile leadership of the Victorian branch. A federal conference of the party in 1955 narrowly affirmed the executive's action. The dissidents broke away to form their own Anti-Communist Labor Party, later renamed the Democratic Labor Party, and they brought down Labor governments in Victoria and Queensland.

Through the preferential system of voting, which allowed those who followed the Democratic Labor Party to direct their support to the coalition, this split ensured conservative dominance in national politics for more than a decade. At the end of the war there were Labor governments in the Commonwealth and five of the six States, but by 1960 just New South Wales and Tasmania, where Labor moderates cared more for power than ideological purity, remained in the party's hands. The split divided workmates and neighbours, poisoned the labour movement, and left a Labor leadership clinging to past glories with policies that were increasingly remote from the interests and sympathies of younger voters. As affluence and education eroded its manual working-class base, one commentator wondered if it was not doomed to *Labor in Vain?*

The very failure of Menzies to carry his referendum proposal to ban the Communist Party enabled him to take maximum advantage of the red scare. On the eve of the 1954 election the prime minister announced the defection of a Soviet diplomat, Vladimir Petrov. His wife, Evdokia, was rescued at the Darwin airport from two thugs escorting her back to Moscow. Petrov claimed to have gathered information from a communist spy ring in Australia that included diplomats, journalists, academics and even members of the staff of the leader of the Labor Party. The government established a royal commission to investigate these allegations, before which Evatt appeared until his intemperate response to its partial conduct led to his being barred from the hearings. In the Cold War atmosphere of the 1950s, the Petrov inquiry strengthened Menzies' claim that the Labor Party was contaminated by communism, its leader's 'guise of defending justice and civil liberties' merely a cloak for shielding traitors.

8.4   Soviet officials escort Evdokia Petrova, the wife of a
Russian diplomat, onto an aircraft at Sydney after her husband
asked for political asylum. Petrova was released from their
custody and taken off the flight at Darwin. (© News Limited,
19 April 1954)

The royal commission found no evidence that would justify the
laying of charges against any Australian, but it blackened the names
of many Australians who were denied any right of reply, their
careers blighted, their children bullied at school. The Communist
Party itself was a declining force, the revelations made in 1956 by
Khrushchev about the Stalinist terror and then the Soviet repression
of Hungarian liberalisation destroying its credibility and reducing
the membership to fewer than 6000. Nevertheless, the domestic
Cold War continued to excoriate dissent. Apart from the Petrov
inquiry and an earlier State royal commission into communism,
the domestic Cold War did not produce any Australian equivalent
to the American system of loyalty oaths, Congressional inquisi-
tions and systematic purges. Rather, it operated at two levels, the
clandestine surveillance of the Australian Security and Intelligence
Organisation and the mobilisation of public opinion to secure
acceptance of security measures.

The process was advanced in a campaign launched on the national
radio network two months after the defeat of the referendum to ban
communism. Advised of an announcement of the gravest national

importance, listeners heard the chairman of the Australian Broadcasting Commission deliver the warning that 'Australia is in danger . . . We are in danger from moral and intellectual apathy, from the mortal enemies of mankind which sap the will and darken the understanding and breed evil dissensions.' This 'Call to Australia' was encouraged by Menzies, headed by the chief justice of the Victorian supreme court, endorsed by all but one of his interstate counterparts and the leaders of the four principal churches, financed by business magnates, and organised by a Movement associate of Santamaria.

It set the tone for much of the subsequent campaign with its language of chiliasm. In an unusual departure from his usual separation of church and state, Menzies talked of the Cold War as a battle between 'Christ and Anti-Christ'. Tactical Cold War initiatives included the creation of the Australian arm of the American-sponsored Congress for Cultural Freedom to fight the war against communism among the intellectuals. The editor of its magazine, *Quadrant*, was James McAuley, a poet converted from anarchism to Catholicism of so conservative a temper that he railed against the liberal humanism his organisation was ostensibly defending.

The Cold War was prosecuted in the government's scientific organisation, the universities, literary associations and almost every corner of civic life. The mother of a well-known communist was expelled from her local branch of the Country Women's Association for refusing its loyalty oath; since she could no longer play the piano at its meetings, the members had to endure an inferior rendering of 'God Save the Queen'. Not even sport escaped. During the 1952 season of the Australian Rules football competition in Victoria, ministers gave half-time addresses on the Call for Australia. A prominent Methodist preacher found the audience at the Lakeside Oval in South Melbourne unreceptive and appealed to common ground with the claim that 'After all, we are all Christians.' 'What about the bloody umpire?' came a reply from the outer.

***

The communist threat operated as a powerful inducement for capitalist democracies to inoculate their peoples with generous doses of improvement. The rivalry between the Eastern and Western blocs was conducted both as an arms race and a competition for economic growth and living standards. Freedom from hardship and insecurity would deprive the agitator of his audience; regular earnings, increased social provision and improved opportunity would attach beneficiaries to their civic duties. But improvement brought its own dangers. In the Call to Australia there was a concern that a prosperous mass society was vulnerable to a loss of vigour and purpose; hence its admonition against moral and intellectual apathy. As early as 1951 Menzies warned that 'If material prosperity is to induce in us greed or laziness, then we will lose our prosperity.' Between 1945 and 1965 average weekly earnings increased by more than 50 per cent, and the five-day working week became the norm along with three weeks of paid annual leave. The transformation of social life this prosperity effected was accompanied by a cluster of moral anxieties.

In the course of the long boom the mainland cities spread rapidly beyond their earlier limits. The population of Sydney passed 2 million in the late 1950s, Melbourne in the early 1960s, while Adelaide and Brisbane were approaching 1 million and Perth had grown to more than half a million. The city centres were rebuilt in concrete and glass to provide for their expanded administrative and commercial activities, but the most significant movement was out of the inner suburbs to new ones on the peripheries. At the end of the war an acute housing shortage forced families to share dilapidated terraces. By the beginning of the 1960s a modern, detached home on a quarter-acre block had become the norm. While some of the new housing was publicly constructed, most of it was built by private developers or the occupiers themselves. The first object of most married couples was to purchase a lot, then save till they could build. A 1957 'portrait of a new community' on the outskirts of Sydney described 'nights and weekends ... alive with the constant beat of the hammer, the whirr of the saw, the odorous skid of the plane'. After this initial occupation came the erection of fences, the making of gardens and the weekend whine of the motor mower; then the working-bee on the school playground and the church hall.

Religious participation increased during the 1950s to a high point of 51 per cent of women and 39 per cent of men by the end of decade. The growth was particularly marked in the new suburbs, where the church provided a range of community activities for young families: Sunday schools, youth clubs, choirs, discussion groups, tennis, football and cricket. It was an era of religious zeal sustained by missions, campaigns and crusades to claim converts and heighten commitment. An Irish-American priest brought the World Family Rosary Crusade to Australia in 1953 with his slogan 'The family that prays together stays together', and drew huge rallies. The American evangelist Billy Graham attracted record crowds during his Crusade in 1959. Christianity flourished as a protector of family life and moral guardian of youth.

The rate of home ownership increased from 53 per cent in 1947, which was the historic norm, to an unprecedented 70 per cent by 1961, among the highest in the world. Along with the residences went the factories. The older workshops and warehouses that threaded the inner-city streets were abandoned for new purpose-built plants further out. The sound of the hooter, the bustle of movement, the discharge of waste and the din of industry yielded to the hum of the generator and the orderly motion of the assembly line on free-standing industrial estates.

Joining home to work was the motor car. In the early 1950s one Australian household in three owned a car; by the 1960s, two in three. Cars and trucks freed industry from the constraints of location on rail-lines. They enabled the cities to sprawl, filled the wedges of country between the radial transport routes with commuter suburbs. Public transport languished, trams were removed to make way for the rush-hour stream of motor traffic, and by the 1960s freeways were slicing through inner suburbs. Cars created new forms of leisure, such as the drive-in theatre; new ways of holidaying with the caravan or motel replacing the guest-house; new forms of shopping at suburban supermarkets; new rituals such as the Sunday drive, customs in common but now performed with greater privacy. Even courtship was mobilised as young men borrowed the family car on a Saturday night. In 1950 the majority of engaged couples in the city of Melbourne lived in the same or adjoining suburb, but by 1970 most came from suburbs well beyond walking or cycling

8.5 The convenience and abundance of the supermarket proclaimed the triumph of modernity. This early example combines the technology of the space age with national and imperial flags. (Coles-Myer Archives)

distance. A 1956 advertisement for General Motors-Holden exploited the new possibilities:

> Holdin' you in my Holden,
> You were meant to be mine
> We will have a wedding, no regretting,
> Baby ain't that fine.

The move to the suburbs and the accumulation of possessions within the suburban home redefined the role of the housewife. Her contribution as a domestic provider was shrinking, her role as a consumer growing. She shopped less frequently now that she had a refrigerator, and home deliveries of ice, bread, meat, vegetables and groceries from local traders were giving way to shopping by car at 'cash-and-carry stores', and soon the supermarket.

Visitors to Australia were struck by the segregation of the sexes; local experts took it as an amenity of the growing affluence. 'Whenever they can, Australian women mostly revert to their favoured roles of full-time wives and mothers', one wrote in 1957. Whether through choice or need, an increasing proportion did not. Between 1947 and 1961 the number of married women in the workforce increased fourfold, and in 1950 the Arbitration Court increased women's pay to 75 per cent of the male basic wage. Yet women's employment remained subsidiary to their responsibilities in the home. The new commuter suburbs on the edges of the cities were places where men commuted and women stayed.

The cities themselves became far more conscious of their images. When Melbourne won the right to stage the 1956 Olympic Games, its image-makers worried that the licensing restrictions, the lackadaisical taxi drivers and even the bare linoleum on hotel floors might hold it up to international ridicule. Friendliness became the motif, the dominant theme a mix of graceful parks and gardens with 'rising tiers and spreading flats of steel and concrete, bronze and glass, in great buildings, modern in conception, at once functional and imaginative in execution'. The year 1956 also brought television, a potent medium to extend familiarity with the plenitude of idealised American family shows and to enlist viewers of the commercial channels in the drama of consumer desire. Advertising became a major business, divining and shaping those desires.

The first television consoles took pride of place in the family living room. Along with the advertising industry, programmers distinguished the male breadwinner from the housewife and the children but took longer to disaggregate its audience into markets with distinct styles and tastes. The post-war family was widely regarded as the basic unit of society, undifferentiated in structure and function if not in circumstance. It was a 'nuclear family', that term denoting the absence of additional members in the self-sufficient suburban setting, but also suggesting that this arrangement animated social life. The post-war demographic bulge, with marriages deferred until after the war and then several children coming in rapid succession, encouraged the belief. A higher marriage rate at younger ages increased the birthrate. The 'baby-boomers' swamped the maternity hospitals and infant welfare centres after the war, then during the 1950s burst the capacity of primary schools. By the 1960s they forced a crash programme to build and staff secondary schools for the increasing numbers that stayed on beyond the school-leaving age and even continued to university.

The Commonwealth government welcomed the trend as an investment in social capital and an enhancement of national capacity. A nuclear research laboratory was the first major building to go up at the post-war Australian National University, its school of physics the most ambitious and expensive section of the institute of advanced studies. After Menzies initiated a review in 1956 that led to Commonwealth funding of universities, a nuclear physicist conducted a second major inquiry in 1961–64 that guided the expansion of higher education. The boost to science education following the success of the Soviet Sputnik led in 1963 to the first government support of private schools with Commonwealth provision of their science laboratories. Never before had the custodians of scientific knowledge commanded such authority or flaunted it so confidently. The chairman of the country's Atomic Energy Commission explained that 'technological civilisation' presented a stream of complex problems that 'only a small proportion of the population is capable of understanding'. To submit such issues to the voter or the politician could 'only lead to trouble and possible disaster': 'the experts must in the end be trusted'.

Yet the nuclear family was beset by dangers. It was menaced by sexual irregularity, the repression of homosexuality gathering force from its Cold War associations with disloyalty. It was vulnerable to breakdown, the sharp increase in divorce after the war of intense concern to churches that, despite their revival, seemed to be losing their moral authority to materialism and secularism. It was preoccupied with youth, the discovery by psychologists of the adolescent and the cultivation by consumer industries of the teenager helping to mark out a disturbing additional figure: the juvenile delinquent.

Two contrary tendencies operated here. On the one hand, young people were readily able to find work, had greater disposable income and were presented with an array of products – clothes, records, concerts, comics, dances, cinema, even motorbikes and cars – on which to spend it. On the other, the demands of suburban domesticity and the extended dependence associated with further education enclosed teenagers within heightened expectations. The moral panic generated by the 'bodgie' and 'widgie' in the rock-and-roll era of the 1950s, and variant identities associated

8.6   Sydney teenagers gather to see the film *Rock Around the Clock* in 1956. The presence of the photographer encourages their self-display. (Sydney *Daily Telegraph*, 16 September 1956)

with later musical styles, each with its distinctive dress, dialect and ritual, was also a class phenomenon. The teenager from a working-class home was least likely to defer entry to the workforce, most likely to become the 'social misfit' who resisted the suburban dream.

At the same time as conservatives denounced this juvenile delinquent, however, radicals lamented the disappearance of the working-class rebel. Cold War inroads into the trade unions, coupled with new powers of the Menzies government to penalise strikes, reduced industrial conflict. The decline of the older occupational neighbourhoods, with their dense overlay of work and leisure, family and friendship, seemed to such critics to weaken class solidarity. They saw the increased social and geographical mobility, the new patterns of consumption and recreation, as attaching suburban Australians to the pleasures of the home and family at the expense of work-based loyalties.

As before when confronted with the failure of millennial expectations, the left retreated into a nostalgic idealisation of national traditions. Its writers, artists and historians turned from the stultifying conformity of the suburban wilderness to the memories of an older Australia that was less affluent and more generous, less gullible and more vigilant of its liberties, less conformist and more independent. In works such as *The Australian Tradition* (1958), *The Australian Legend* (1958) and *The Legend of the Nineties* (1954) the radical nationalists reworked the past (passing over the militarism and xenophobia in the national experience) to assist them in their present struggles. Try as they might to revive these traditions, the elegiac note was clear. The radical nationalists codified the legend of democratic and defiant mateship just as modernising forces of change were erasing the circumstances that had given rise to that legend.

As the radical romance faded, the conservative courtship of national sentiment prospered. It was embedded in government policies designed to assimilate a population of increasing ethnic diversity into the customs and values of their adopted country. In the two decades after 1947 more than 2 million migrants settled here, the majority from non-English-speaking countries. With their children they contributed more than half the population increase to more than 12 million by the end of the 1960s. 'Our aim', Arthur Calwell had laid down in 1949, 'is to Australianise all our migrants ... in as short a time as possible'. Although his Liberal successors relaxed the opposition to foreign-language newspapers and ethnic organisations, that aim continued. 'We can only achieve our goal through migration', the new minister declared, 'if our newcomers quickly become Australian in outlook and way of life'. On the ships, in the holding centres and migrant hostels, in English-language classes and naturalisation ceremonies, through 'Good Neighbour' committees and other voluntary bodies, they were taught the Australian Way of Life.

That term allowed a shift from the restrictions of ancestry or the traditions of national legend to the cultivation of life-style. Its depiction of Australia as a sophisticated, urban, industrialised consumer society had clear Cold War implications. An article on 'The Australian Way of Life' written by a refugee for the celebration of the fiftieth anniversary of the Commonwealth spelt them out: 'What the Australian cherishes most is a home of his own, a garden where he can potter and a motor car ... A person who owns a house, a garden, a car and has a fair job is rarely an extremist or a revolutionary.'

The gap between expectation and reality was there from the beginning. On New Year's Day 1947 two Commonwealth ministers welcomed the first party of post-war British migrants. There were 200 of them, ex-servicemen with trade skills who were to work on building projects in Canberra. Yet within a week they were complaining about living conditions in the barracks in which they were quartered. 'There has been a little too much pandering to these fellows', insisted the minister for works who claimed he had put up with poorer conditions and was adamant 'we are certainly not going to wet nurse them'. A special effort was made to attract British settlers and over 600,000 were assisted to come to Australia over the next two decades, but complaints persisted. The term 'whingeing pom' entered contemporary usage in the early 1960s. It might well have been that British migrants were more ready to express dissatisfaction than their non-English-speaking counterparts; but it also indicated that the Australian way of life was becoming less British.

More modest expectations governed Aboriginal policy. In 1951 the Commonwealth minister for territories confirmed the official objective of assimilation: 'Assimilation means, in practical terms, that, in the course of time, it is expected that all persons of Aboriginal blood or mixed-blood in Australia will live like white Australians do.' That would require 'many years of slow, patient endeavour' and 'to be accepted as a full member of Australian society, he has to cease to be a primitive Aboriginal'. The States began to close down their reserves, pushing them into country towns where they experienced pervasive discrimination. Migrant Australians responded to broken promises with protest but their ultimate recourse was to return home. Indigenous Australians had no such opportunity, though they too sought their homelands.

Aboriginal pastoral workers in the Pilbara region of Western Australia went on strike for better pay in 1946 and, despite official harassment, they secured improvements; but not all of them returned to work, for they had established their own co-operative settlement. Again in 1966, 200 Gurindji walked off a pastoral

8.7 Aboriginal children form up in military ranks at the Bungalow, Northern Territory, during the Second World War. They were subsequently removed from the Territory for the duration of the war. (Australian War Memorial, 6746381)

station in Central Australia and a claim for equal pay turned into a demand for their own land. Between these two most celebrated actions were numerous lesser ones, fiercely resisted by pastoralists and governments and commonly blamed on communist agitators. There were communists involved on both occasions, and communist-led unions were most active in their support. In Darwin the communist officials of the North Australian Workers Union backed post-war Aboriginal claims for equal pay, while their successors abandoned the campaign. The Federal Council for the Advancement of Aborigines, formed in 1957 by the left, assisted a new generation of Aboriginal activists.

There was growing unrest on the reserves. Palm Island, an Aboriginal settlement off the coast of Queensland used for the confinement of recalcitrants on similar lines to the convict settlements more than a century earlier, saw an uprising against a tyrannical superintendent in 1957. The victimisation of the Aboriginal artist Albert Namatjira, denied permission to build a house in Alice Springs a year after he was presented to Queen Elizabeth, and gaoled for six months in 1958 for supplying alcohol to a relative who was not a citizen, drew attention to the absence of assimilation.

That policy was proclaimed in government publications showing Aboriginal children in the classroom, the boys in shorts and white socks, the girls in cotton tunics, novitiates to the Australian way of life. It was practised in the removal of children from their families so that they could better be trained in 'white ways', an activity that continued through the 1950s and into the 1960s. Not until the early 1980s was there a belated recognition by government of the trauma of separation with the establishment of the first Link-Up agencies.

The casualties of the Australian way of life were seldom acknowledged in the celebration of post-war achievement. It was a golden age of sport, with Australian triumphs on the cricket field against England after the war heralding an era of success in athletics, swimming, tennis and golf. The 'golden girls' dominated the track at the Melbourne Olympics, when Australia won thirty-five medals, and both men and women continued their supremacy in the pool. In the post-war decades Australian men won half the major tennis titles and achieved fifteen Davis Cup victories in twenty years. These keenly followed contests with the United States became a surrogate for the relationship between the two countries, mediating dependence as Test cricket had done for the imperial relationship.

Australians liked to think that their egalitarian ethos, favourable climate and broad participation (there were more tennis courts in relation to population than any other country in the 1950s) prevailed over the grim professionalism of the Yanks. In truth, tennis in America was restricted to the wealthy amateur, whereas the Australians bent the rules with sponsorship, coaching and other forms of 'shamateur' assistance. It was an American professional who remarked that the Australians had 'short arms and deep pockets'.

The amateur ideal was expressed better at the beach, where surf lifesaving clubs patrolled the breakers to rescue over-adventurous swimmers from the treacherous rip. With their combination of voluntarism, masculinity (women were initially excluded) and competition, the lifesaving clubs blended the hedonism of the beach with the militarised discipline of belt drill and march past. As one club historian put it, they were 'truly Australian in spirit', their free association in 'humanitarian mateship' without barriers of creed, class or colour an example of democracy 'as it was meant to be'.

***

The golden age lasted through the 1960s until the early 1970s, but before then Australia was caught up in mounting problems. The retirement of Robert Menzies at the beginning of 1966 might be taken as a turning-point in the government's fortunes. The last prime minister to choose his moment of departure, he was at the age of seventy-one a man out of sympathy with the times. At a recent

8.8   Surf life-saving clubs patrolled Australian beaches to rescue swimmers from being swept out to sea. A formal march was a feature of their competitive carnivals. Here a stylised flag-bearer leads the way. (*History of Bondi Surf Bathers Life Saving Club 1956*, Bondi, NSW)

meeting of Commonwealth prime ministers in London he had been 'sad and depressed', for 'people like me are too deeply royalist at heart to live comfortably in a nest of republics'. His minister for immigration wanted to ease the White Australia policy on the grounds that its restrictions were discriminatory, but Menzies was adamant: 'Good thing too – right sort of discrimination'. His departure released the brake on these aspects of national policy so that in 1966 Australia signed the international convention on the elimination of racial discrimination, and in the same year began to admit larger numbers of non-European immigrants. The discriminatory provisions against Aborigines in the Commonwealth Constitution were repealed in 1967.

Yet so complete was Menzies' political mastery that the task of succession proved beyond the conservatives. The remaining six years of the 'Ming dynasty' saw three prime ministers, Harold Holt, John Gorton and William McMahon, pass in rapid succession. Holt was a genial, easygoing man who drowned while swimming at an unpatrolled beach as discontent mounted – a pillar of the Melbourne establishment remarked later that he was out of his depth. Gorton struck out more boldly with a larrikin style of assertive nationalism that offended traditionalists, and fell to a palace revolt. McMahon was the feeblest and he was routed in a general election that drove the Liberal and Country Party coalition from office. Some of the difficulties the coalition faced were beyond its control, some of its own making; such were the expectations after two decades of rule that it was blamed for most of them.

The Vietnam War proved the heaviest millstone round the conservatives' neck. At first it was popular and used by them to renew the coalition's electoral mandate in 1966 and 1969. Visits by the American president as well as the leader of South Vietnam boosted the government's stocks, as much because of as despite the noisy protests these visits occasioned. 'Ride over them', the Liberal premier of New South Wales responded when informed that demonstrators were blocking the motorcade of President Johnson in 1966, and then improved on that by telling a United States Chamber of Commerce luncheon that he had instructed a police superintendent to 'run over the bastards'. But the Tet Offensive of 1968 punctured the illusion of American superiority and drove Johnson out of office. His successor resorted to mass bombing and invasion of Cambodia, then Laos, in a forlorn endeavour to stave off inevitable defeat. Meanwhile the Australian casualties mounted. Of 50,000 who had served in Vietnam by 1972, 500 were killed and they included nearly 200 conscripts.

Conscription for an unjust war was the primary issue for a peace movement that began with the lonely vigils of the women's group, Save Our Sons, and swelled into noisy protest by radical students until by 1970 it filled city streets with a demonstration, the Moratorium, in numbers not seen for decades Horrifying images of children with napalm burns, television footage of street executions and reports of village massacres combined with the bizarre ritual whereby young Australian men were required to register for national service and then face selection by drawing birthdates from a barrel in a 'lottery of death'. A generational divide widened between government ministers who sought to justify the war and those they sent to fight it.

8.9 In 1966 the prime minister Harold Holt visited the United States to proclaim that Australia would go 'all the way' with its ally in Vietnam. Four months later President Johnson returned the visit. He is shown here speaking at the Canberra airport with Holt in submissive deference. (David Moore Photography)

We are the young they drafted out
To wars their folly brought about.
Go tell those old men, safe in bed,
We took their orders and are dead.

By 1970 the government began withdrawing Australian forces and scarcely bothered to pursue the growing numbers of draft resisters.

The war came to an end with the fall of Saigon in 1975, but the Australian involvement ceased in 1972 when it was clear that its strategy of forward defence lay in tatters. President Nixon had signalled the withdrawal of the United States from the Cold War alliance in South-East Asia; his visit to China in 1972, exploiting the breach between that country and the Soviet Union, undermined the insistent logic of Australian foreign policy since 1950, which was built on the assumption of a monolithic communist threat. Australia had eagerly followed its powerful friend into Indochina, only to discover 'how military decisions are being made for political ends', as one minister lamented. More than this, he was astonished to discover 'that public opinion can be mobilised to interfere with public policy', an intrusion he likened to the actions of the London mob on the eighteenth-century British parliament. An egregious colleague attempted a more modern comparison when he described the Moratorium demonstrators as 'political bikies who pack-rape democracy'. This was a government badly out of touch.

The Korean War had stimulated the world economy; the Vietnam War overtaxed it. The United States met the huge cost by printing dollars, which as the reserve currency for international trade washed into the financial system and increased inflationary pressures. By the end of the 1960s there were clear signs of strain in the Australian economy. Farmers continued to increase production but faced a steady decline in returns; caught in a cost-price squeeze, they had to form larger holdings. The new technologies were eroding rural life. Small towns that served locals during the horse-and-buggy days dwindled as farmers drove to larger centres; the local telephone exchange no longer employed rural girls once it was automated; the railway station where their brothers worked lost out to the bus stop, and the bush school closed now that the bus could take children to a larger one. By 1971 there was an absolute drop in the rural population to less than 2 million, just 14 per cent of the national total.

It was fortunate that new mining discoveries allowed the sale of bauxite and iron ore to Japan. There had been a ban on the export of iron ore until the discovery of rich reserves in Western Australia enabled the premier to persuade Canberra to lift it in 1960, and soon new mines in Queensland and the Northern Territory increased the production of bauxite. The bulk shipping of base metals contributed a quarter of the country's exports by the end of the decade and discovery of a major oil field in Bass Strait in 1966 brought Australia closer to self-sufficiency in fossil fuels.

While the mineral boom excited a speculative flurry on the stock exchanges, the national economy remained heavily dependent on foreign capital and imported technology. Large companies dominated major industries, with protection restricting competition, and a high level of foreign ownership in key sectors such as the car industry. Full employment allowed unions to become more aggressive in demands for wage increases. Twenty years of industrialisation and urban growth created new dissatisfactions. The inner suburbs were pocked with decay and pollution. The outer suburbs lacked basic services; many remained unsewered. Provision of health and education lagged behind demand. A pattern of private affluence and public neglect was clear.

The beneficiaries of affluence began to reject their inheritance. As the Australian way of life was established in the new suburbs, its chief critics were intellectuals who used the weapons of irony and parody. In his stringent condemnation of *Australia's Home* (1952), the architect Robin Boyd condemned the 'aesthetic calamity' of a suburbia that carried bad taste to the 'blind end of the road'. He inveighed against the 'wild scramble of outrageous featurism' that disfigured the wealthier neighbourhoods, just as another architect deprecated the 'sterile little boxes tinged with an anaemic echo of wrought iron and a carport' in the mortgage belt. In satirical monologues first developed for a university revue in 1955, the entertainer Barry Humphries, who had grown up in the heart of Melbourne's middle-class suburbia in a house designed by his father, created a range of characters addicted to mediocrity: the upwardly mobile Edna Everage and her hen-pecked husband, Norm; the invincibly platitudinous Sandy Stone. 'I always wanted more', is the opening sentence of Humphries' memoirs.

He and tertiary-educated contemporaries such as Germaine Greer, Robert Hughes and Clive James would abandon Australia to achieve international success. Unable to reconcile themselves to the dullness, the conformity and the philistinism of their youthful homeland, as 'expats' they would remain trapped in the role of gadflies. Other malcontents fled suburbia for the refuge of the inner--city surrounds, where European migrants were beginning to create a more metropolitan ambience with wine, food and street life – only to assist in the gentrification of their sanctuary.

Before that occurred there was a flurry of rebuilding as houses were replaced by flats – not the high-rise monoliths of bleak uniformity erected for public tenants, as their heyday was the 1950s, but smaller constructions of six or eight units that private developers squeezed onto suburban blocks. More than 200,000 were built during the 1960s, mostly in Sydney and Melbourne, either for sale to retirees or rent to young Australians wanting their own self-contained accommodation. Here was a further challenge to the conventional family home as the flat offered independence from parental supervision and 'flatting' became shorthand for sexually active young men and women living alone or with friends of either sex. The flat provided a refuge from the norms of heterosexual monogamy at a time when the baby-boomers were experimenting with alternative lifestyles, and the counter-culture was demanding liberation from laws against obscenity, abortion, homosexuality and hallucinogenic substances. In 1967 the editor of Sydney University's student newspaper, Keith Windschuttle, proclaimed a demonstration in Hyde Park 'where groovers would turn on in public with LSD' to defy new State legislation declaring it a drug of addiction.

All three of Menzies' successors sensed the mood for change but struggled to satisfy it. Harold Holt seized on the International Exhibition at Montreal in 1967 as an opportunity to present Australia as a modern and sophisticated country. Robin Boyd designed a 'luxurious and civilised' pavilion, yet it was stocked with kangaroos, wallabies and sheep. The official guide celebrated artists such as Sidney Nolan, writers such as Patrick White (who would win the Nobel prize for literature in 1973) and singers such as Joan Sutherland, yet the entertainers at Montreal featured Rolf Harris singing 'Tie Me Kangaroo Down, Sport'. Rupert Murdoch's new national broadsheet, *The Australian*, lamented that 'the Aussie flavour of the whole performance was one of dedicated provincialism'.

John Gorton endorsed the establishment in 1968 of an Australian Council for the Arts to nurture creativity, and in 1969 created the Australian Film Development Corporation. Its first feature film was *The Adventures of Barry McKenzie*, based on a cartoon series in the satirical London weekly, *Private Eye*. Barry Humphries was its author, and drew on a mixture of schoolboy and service slang, as well as his own imagination, for the dialogue. A New Zealander was the artist and he invented the character of Barry McKenzie as a colonial innocent in post-imperial London, taking his first name from Humphries, his surname from a strong-bodied Australian cricketer, his suit and wide-brimmed hat from middle-aged Anzacs he had seen marching down Whitehall on Remembrance Day, and his jutting chin from the comic-strip character Desperate Dan. The comic strip was censured in Australia but its English readers delighted in Barry McKenzie's colloquialisms and adopted them as their own, so that they too were soon pointing Percy at the porcelain. Humphries used the film to mock the Australian government's cultural patronage: he has Bazza visiting an expatriate mate in Paris and telling him: 'Don't let this clapped out culture grab you, mate. I mean back in Oz now we've got culture up to our arseholes.'

McMahon, the last of the Liberal lineage, was the least comfortable with the forces of change. He inherited the Council for Aboriginal Affairs, established by Holt in the aftermath of the 1967 constitutional referendum to improve the circumstances of Indigenous Australians and chaired by H. C. Coombs, the former governor of the Reserve Bank. McMahon was anxious to capitalise on this prestigious association but found himself caught between the expectations of Aboriginal progress and the intransigence of his ministers who were responsible for its implementation.

Earlier reforms – in 1962 the franchise was extended to Aboriginals, in 1965 the Arbitration Court awarded equal pay to Aboriginal pastoral workers – were designed to remove the formal disadvantages that prevented Aborigines from becoming free and equal citizens of Australia. The constitutional changes introduced in 1967, while commonly regarded as conferring citizenship, singled out Aboriginal Australians as a special category of people for whom the Commonwealth could legislate over the discriminatory arrangements of more conservative States. The Coalition government failed to do so. Rather, it resisted the growing demands of Aborigines for self-determination. Just as the Commonwealth had rejected the land claim of the Gurindji in Central Australia in 1967, so it opposed a court action brought in 1968 by the Yolngu people of Arnhem Land who opposed mining of bauxite on their land. Back in 1963 the Commonwealth parliament had dismissed their bark petition against the excision of this land. Now it condemned the legal claim as 'frivolous and vexatious'.

These disappointments in areas of traditional occupation were accompanied by an upsurge of Aboriginal protest in the towns and cities of the south. Young activists no longer worked through white organisations for equality; rather, they celebrated their distinctiveness, their 'black pride' and their 'black power'. 'Black is more than a colour, it is also a state of mind', said Bobbi Sykes. These ideas drew on overseas precedents. Just as a Freedom Ride by student radicals through rural New South Wales in 1965 echoed a tactic of the civil rights movement in the United States, so the more forceful assertion of a separate identity followed a similar turn there.

The most spectacular display of black power in Australia came after McMahon used an Australia Day speech to reject land rights. Aboriginal protestors responded by occupying the lawns in front of Parliament House in Canberra. Erected on Australia Day, 1972, this tent embassy symbolised the changed objective – no longer acceptance but recognition. For months it remained until a rattled prime minister created a new ordinance to have it removed. Television screens showed the ensuing struggle between the police and its custodians. 'Everybody knows', the leader of the Labor Party proclaimed, 'that if it were not the young and the black involved in this matter the Government would not have dared to proceed'. He was in fact performing the obsequies for a government that was voted out of office a few weeks later.

***

The Labor leader was Gough Whitlam, elected to that position in 1967 after a long struggle with Arthur Calwell, the gnarled centurion of the old guard. Calwell was steeped in Labor tradition, hamstrung by its rules – a newspaper photograph of the parliamentary leader waiting outside a meeting of the federal executive in 1963 allowed the Liberals to claim that Labor was directed by thirty-six 'faceless men'. Whitlam, a large man of magisterial self-regard, was a moderniser who directed his initial energies into modernising his own party. He sought to discard its socialist shibboleths, the preoccupation with trade union concerns and Cold War recriminations, so that it could attract the suburban middle class. Accordingly, he developed policies designed to make good the failures of twenty years of coalition rule. In modern conditions, he argued, the capacity to exercise citizenship was determined not by an individual's income 'but the availability and accessibility of the services which the community alone can provide and ensure'.

Through an enlargement of government activity, he would apply the national wealth to projects of urban renewal, improved education and health, and an expanded range of public amenities. He would sweep away the accretion of restrictions and special interests to augment the nation's capacity and enlarge the life of its citizens. Whitlam was the first 'silvertail' to lead the federal Labor Party (in South Australia another defector from the establishment, Don Dunstan, anticipated his success with similar policies at the State level) and the first to abandon labourism for social democracy. Tellingly, when asked to give an example of how he understood equality, he replied that 'I want every kid to have a desk, with a lamp, and his own room to study'. The light on the desk replaced the light on the hill.

The renovated Labor Party won office in 1972 with the election slogan 'It's Time', and commenced to implement its programme at a gallop. In the first month the government withdrew the last troops from Vietnam, ended military conscription, established diplomatic relations with China, announced independence for Papua New Guinea and the ratification of international conventions on nuclear weapons, labour conditions and racial discrimination. Over the past two decades, the new leader proclaimed, Australia had conducted itself as 'insignificant, racist, militaristic, sycophantic, a timid and unworthy creature of the great powers to whom it had surrendered its identity'. One of his initial decisions was to abandon the award of imperial honours.

Whitlam cultivated a nationalism that allowed for internationalism. Expansion of support for the arts, increased Australian content requirements for television and preservation of historic sites were among the initiatives designed to promote greater national awareness. With the revival of local publishing, theatre and film, his government encouraged a cultural renaissance that made it possible to see life in this country as possessing a depth of meaning and richness of possibility. The completion in 1973 of the Sydney Opera House and the acquisition by the new National Gallery of *Blue Poles*, the large, dribbling creation of Jackson Pollock, caught the mood of expansive engagement. For Manning Clark, whose vast and prophetic *A History of Australia* caught the new mood (the third volume, with its emphasis on the struggle for and against an independent Australia, appeared in 1973), this was the end of the Ice Age.

The Whitlam government recast nationhood to remove official discrimination against non-British migrants and prohibit all forms of discriminatory treatment on the basis of race or gender. Assimilation was abandoned as incompatible with an increasing diversity that was now celebrated for its enrichment of national life. As monoculture yielded to multiculture, so the recognition of difference became an aid to the removal of disadvantage. Ethnic groups were accorded their own services to ensure that their particular needs were met. The designation 'multiculturalism' came from Canada, where it signified the contribution made by immigrant groups who were neither British nor French in origin. Australian multiculturalism paid little attention to this provenance and it was less influenced by the usage in the United States to signify the rights of minorities. Here it was defined by language as a marker of ethnicity (so that 'non-English-speaking background' became a synonym for an 'ethnic', someone not of British descent) and closely associated with migrant settlement.

Women finally achieved the full adult minimum wage as the result of an Arbitration Court decision in 1974, and more was promised to give practical effect to that formal equality: maternity leave and child-care centres for working women along with women's health centres and refuges, and simplification of divorce. The prime minister's appointment of an adviser on women's issues, Elizabeth Reid, brought a new conjunction of feminism and public policy, and soon a new Australianism, 'femocrat', to capture the novel role of those who sought to reconcile their duties as public servants with their loyalties to the women's movement in regulatory affirmative action.

Similar strains were apparent in the new Department of Aboriginal Affairs where Aboriginal administrators answered to white superiors as they introduced a range of activities, including a medical service and a legal service tailored to the particular needs of their people. The simultaneous creation of an elected national council to represent Aboriginal interests did not defuse the tension since it was restricted to an advisory role. The government introduced its social policies through major national inquiries and implemented them by the creation of new authorities. A Schools Commission provided the charter for Commonwealth support of private as well as government schools on the basis of need; there was increased university funding and the abolition of tuition fees. A health inquiry created a scheme of universal medical insurance. A commission of inquiry into poverty expanded the welfare system. Another commissioner prepared recommendations for the legal recognition of Aboriginal land rights in the federal territories, though the government fell before they could be implemented. A Department of Urban and Regional Development assisted State and local government to improve urban amenities and funded the acquisition and development of land for housing.

Whitlam extended the ambit of national government further than any peacetime leader before or since. The son of a senior public servant, he created many new departments – though he also expanded the role of advisers from outside the public service who saw themselves as making it more amenable to Labor's policy objectives. His fiercest critic was Joh Bjelke-Petersen, who had been premier of Queensland since 1968 and would remain so with the help of a gerrymander (he never won more than 39 per cent of the vote) until 1987. Like those earlier long-serving, populist premiers whom he admired – Playford and Bolte – Bjelke-Petersen was a farmer; unlike them, he was a devout Lutheran and a member of the Country Party, which he would enlarge into the National Party in 1974 as his aggressive leadership ate into the urban constituency of the Liberal Party.

Bjelke-Petersen had come to national attention during a 1971 tour of Australia by the South African rugby union team, which attracted anti-apartheid protest. He declared a state of emergency and encouraged police to attack the demonstrators; later he banned street marches altogether. The premier rode roughshod over all sensitivities, dismissing media scrutiny with his trademark phrase 'don't you worry about that'. Described by an exasperated Whitlam as a 'bible-bashing bastard', he condemned the prime minister's environmentalism, Aboriginal land rights, feminism and much else. He was joined in 1974 by Charles Court, previously the minister for industrial development in Western Australia and now the leader of its coalition government. Court was less rambling in style but no less steely. 'You know, young Charles', he recalled Tom Playford advising him early in his career, 'this country, and especially the individual states, are still at a stage when they need benevolent despots'. These two men governed the large, outlying states with rich mineral resources and an expanding frontier. They spoke for the ethos of development, State rights and conservative rectitude.

Whitlam's catchphrase, 'crash through or crash', indicated the government's way of dealing with constitutional and political obstacles. He was less attentive to the economic constraints, even though his government doubled public expenditure in its three years of office. In keeping with its modernising ambitions, the government made a 25-per-cent across-the-board cut in the tariff in 1973. With upward revaluation of the currency, many local manufacturers went to the wall. At the same time prices and wages were both rising, at an annual rate of more than 10 per cent by the end of 1973.

Then came the oil embargo imposed on the West by the Arab states in retaliation for the Yom Kippur War at the end of 1973, and a fourfold increase in the cost of oil. The direct effect on Australia was limited, for it was able to meet most of its energy needs. The indirect effects were catastrophic – with Japan hard hit by the energy crisis, its demand for Australian minerals collapsed. The inflationary effects of the oil crisis sent a shock wave across the entire world economy that fractured the networks of trade and investment. In the years following 1974 the advanced industrial nations experienced the novel malaise of 'stagflation' – stagnant output with high inflation. The Keynesian techniques of economic management that had guided the post-war long boom provided no remedy for such a combination, since one was meant to be the obverse of the other. For a brief period the Whitlam government ignored Treasury advice and kept the throttle open, but unemployment still rose to levels not seen since the 1930s. In 1975 it tackled inflation with a contractionary budget, and unemployment passed 250,000. The golden age was over.

By this time the government was beset by crisis. Several senior ministers had resigned or were sacked following scandals. One of them had been negotiating with shady international financiers for an unauthorised $4 billion loan to keep national control over Australian oil, gas and uranium processing. The Opposition, which controlled the Senate, used the 'loans affair' as a reason to refuse supply; by starving the government of funds it hoped to force it to an election.

In this strategy it had many allies. Business leaders had lost confidence in the government; the press was baying for blood. Sir John Kerr, the governor-general, resented his prime minister's imperious manner. Sir Garfield Barwick, a former conservative minister turned chief justice, was advising the governor-general that he had the power as head of state to dismiss the government, and encouraging him to do his duty. Both the United States ambassador and officers of its Central Intelligence Agency were highly critical of the Labor government, especially its desire to exercise some control over the American military communications facilities that had been built at the North-West Cape and Pine Gap during the 1960s.

The government had its loyal defenders – it was remarkable how many libertarian activists accommodated themselves to Whitlam's expansion of state activity – but doubted it would prevail in an election. It therefore determined to hold out in the expectation that coalition members of the Senate would lose their nerve. Some were close to allowing supply after a deadlock of twenty-seven days, but the governor-general acted first. In the early afternoon of 11 November 1975 he dismissed the government and commissioned the Liberal leader, Malcolm Fraser, as a caretaker prime minister to obtain supply and call an election. Fraser did so and won the election by a record majority.

The Dismissal was the most serious constitutional crisis in Australian history. As news of the governor-general's actions spread, a crowd gathered at the national parliament in Canberra. When the governor-general's secretary stood on the steps of the parliament to read the proclamation that dissolved both its chambers, a minatory Gough Whitlam glared over his shoulder to denounce Fraser as 'Kerr's cur' and exhort the assembly to 'maintain your rage'. In the nation's principal cities work stopped for impromptu demonstrations that canvassed direct action. Yet Whitlam acceded to his dismissal, and the leader of the Australian Council of Trade Unions quelled all talk of a general strike.

The events of 1975 certainly strained the system of government. The heated atmosphere fomented a conspiratorial interpretation of political activity; the willingness of men in high office to bend the rules inflicted severe damage on constitutional propriety. Whitlam himself remains a highly controversial figure. For some he was a hero, cut down in his prime; for others he was a dangerous incompetent. The last national leader to follow his convictions regardless of consequence, he rose and fell as the possibilities for a confident and expansive national government ended.

9

Rectification, 1976–1996

After the chronic political instability that marked the conservative collapse and then the feverish pace of the truncated Whitlam regime, the ensuing years present an outward appearance of equilibrium. Between 1975 and 1991 there was just one change of government, and two prime ministers held office for roughly equal terms. Both in their own ways were striving for the security the electorate desired, and both held to the middle ground. Yet in the circumstances that now prevailed there could be no security without upsetting the ingrained habits of the past. One prime minister preferred confrontation and the other consensus as the way to bring change, but the changes they secured were never sufficient. There was always a need to go further, to abandon yet another outmoded practice and make additional improvements. Both leaders employed their considerable personal authority to force the process and both were condemned as soon as they lost office for excessive timidity and insufficient leadership.

Australians were subjected in the closing decades of the last century to an unending pursuit of the constantly receding goal of a competitive edge. Those who directed this quest talked of reform, a process of change that was painful but necessary to bring greater equity and efficiency. Each instalment of reform was followed by another, for the process was never complete. It is not unusual for zealots to explain the failure of their creed by its incomplete adoption, but with their emphasis on doctrinal purity these reformers followed in the spirit of those Protestant theologians who proclaimed of the Reformation that the reformed church is always to be reformed. Their drive to set the country to rights was conducted as a mission of unflagging rectification.

The first of the leaders was Malcolm Fraser, who headed a Liberal–National Country Party coalition from 1975–83. The tall, lean scion of a pastoral dynasty from the Liberal heartland of Victoria, he was educated at private schools and Oxford

9.1 During the constitutional crisis that culminated with the Dismissal of the Labor government in 1975, the caretaker government organised mass rallies. Malcolm Fraser, leader of the Liberal Party, acknowledges a throng of supporters in Melbourne. (*The Age,* 1975)

University. A shy, awkward manner was commonly interpreted as patrician aloofness. The grim determination with which Fraser had pursued power carried over into his exercise of it: he was constantly driving his colleagues, involved in every aspect of policy, impulsive yet deliberate. 'Life isn't meant to be easy' was a provocative pronouncement from one who seemingly inherited the privileges of a ruling class, but it was the genuine credo of a man who drove himself to the limit. Fraser believed that Australians had been coddled into softness and complacency, that they needed to be weaned from dependence on public provision to embrace the stern rigours of competition. Try as he might to reduce government, however, he intervened habitually to right wrongs. A rugged individualism warred with instinctive Tory paternalism.

Fraser won elections in 1977 and 1980 over a discredited Labor Party. In 1983 the voters rejected him for a new Labor leader, Bob Hawke. Apart from also studying at Oxford, though as a Rhodes Scholar, Hawke differed from Fraser in almost every respect. One was tall, the other short; one was clipped in speech, the other cultivated a stridently vernacular accent. Fraser was angular, Hawke a conciliator; Fraser prim, Hawke a reformed drinker and womaniser; Fraser exercised power as a duty, Hawke wooed popularity with an almost biblical conviction of personal destiny.

The new prime minister was a child of a Congregational manse who worked for the Australian Council of Trade Unions and in 1970 became its first president to have bypassed the factory floor. Others would follow, but none as skilful in interposing himself between his members and their employers to conjure a settlement of differences. After he entered parliament and laid siege to the leadership, Hawke gave up most of his indulgences. A flash larrikin now appeared in power dress, behind an imposing desk and before a fake bookcase, peevishly insisting on the need for national reconciliation.

Both leaders searched for solutions. There were strategic difficulties abroad, symptoms of domestic strain such as environmental degradation, family breakdown, homelessness and crime. In the absence of older certainties, governments sought to restore national cohesion and purpose. Most of all, they tried to repair an economy that no longer provided reliable growth and regular employment.

With the end of the long boom the world economy was dogged by weak, unreliable rates of growth and persistent unemployment. Australia confronted particular problems: its reliance on commodity exports made it increasingly uncompetitive in a global economy dominated by advanced manufacturing and service industries. Its own manufacturing sector was based on import substitution and heavily reliant on tariff protection that left it lagging behind more innovative competitors.

Out of the turmoil in the world economy during the 1970s a new economic order would emerge. It involved the growth of finance markets, liberalisation of trade, an increased mobility of capital and the emergence of new participants as Asian countries embarked on industrialisation. For the advanced economies, this brought a shift from labour-intensive factory production to high-technology manufacturing and service industries. The digital revolution augmented information flows, linked capital markets and allowed supply chains that crossed national boundaries, placing additional pressure on a closed and inward-looking economy.

The needs of business came to dominate national life as never before, and economists claimed an unprecedented authority. Stock exchange indices and currency rates became the staple fare of news bulletins. The vocabulary of the market served as the language of public policy and entered into almost every aspect of social life: the market would promote competition and reward effort; it would discipline and punish any failure to ensure a level playing field. A new orthodoxy arose – neoliberalism – and a distinctive Australian term for it: here it was called economic rationalism. It was remarkable not so much for devotees' capacity to incorporate almost every form of human behaviour into its syllogisms as for the assumption that there could be no other way of reasoning than by the logic of the market.

***

The Fraser government sought a remedy to the country's economic difficulties by tackling the problem of inflation. If prices and wage costs could be reduced and profits restored, then a resumption of business activity would follow. Cuts in government expenditure would close the budget deficit, reduce the public sector's demands on savings and ease interest rates to stimulate increased private investment. Public revenue and expenditure had grown incrementally with the national product for thirty years; now a Cabinet committee was created, which became known as the 'razor gang', to slash government programmes and pare back spending.

Inflation did decline, but by 1978 the number of unemployed passed 400,000. At the same time restrictions on foreign investment were lifted to finance an expansion of export industries. Wool gave way to meat and wheat as the chief farm exports, but the largest foreign earnings came from energy and minerals. The rapid increase in the price of energy allowed Australia to become the principal supplier of coal, along with increased sales of oil, gas and uranium. New mines were developed in Western Australia and Queensland for the sale of minerals to Asian markets.

The promotion of Australia as a quarry at a time when the world economy had stalled was a risky strategy. Commodities other than energy made up a declining share of world trade, and their prices continued to fall. The new resource projects created relatively few jobs, not least because they depended upon labour-saving technology, and the effect of the mineral boom on the exchange rate only increased pressure on other industries. As the export growth ended with a new recession in 1982 and drought ravaged the agricultural sector, the government relaxed its tight control over public spending and the monetary supply. Renewed inflation, a breakout of wages and a further jump in unemployment ensured its defeat in the 1983 election.

Labor came to power with an alternative strategy based on its special relationship with the unions. Under the terms of an Accord negotiated with the Australian Council of Trade Unions, workers would forgo wage increases in return for job creation and co-operation would replace conflict in a concerted effort to put Australia back to work. The National Economic Summit held in Canberra within a month of the election legitimated the arrangements in a theatrical break from conventional practice. Opening it, the new prime minister likened the economic crisis to the wartime emergency of 1942, and claimed that it called again for 'the united efforts of a united people working together to achieve agreed goals and common objectives'. The country's elected representatives were therefore banished from Parliament House to make room for business and union leaders to pledge their agreement; the unions accepted wage restraint, the employers a return to the system of centralised wage fixation. There were offsets to compensate wage-earners for their forbearance – restoration of public medical insurance and other improvements in the social wage – and there were government programmes to ensure that key industries such as steel and car production remained viable.

As an employment strategy, the Accord worked. One and a half million new jobs were created during the remainder of the decade and the jobless rate fell back from over 10 per cent in 1983 to just over 6 per cent by 1989. But in the search for greater competitiveness the Labor government made other changes. At the end of 1983 it abandoned the defence of the currency and allowed the value of the dollar to be set by the market. Foreign exchange controls were lifted, controls on domestic banks were reduced, and in 1985 foreign banks were licensed to compete with them. If the Accord was the carrot that secured the co-operation of industry for the reconstruction of the Australian economy, financial deregulation was the stick that impelled it forward. Paul Keating, who as Treasurer drove these changes, boasted that 'We are the first generation of post-war politicians and economic managers to foster a genuinely open Australian economy.'

With financial deregulation, Australia's economic performance was subjected to the fickle judgement of international currency traders. With the rapid increase of overseas borrowing and a persistent trade deficit, the dollar lost 40 per cent of its value by 1986. By this time the net foreign debt, about half of it public borrowing and half private, represented 30 per cent of the national product, and every new drop in the exchange rate increased its cost. In May 1986 Keating declared that 'We must let Australians know truthfully, honestly, earnestly, just what sort of international hole Australia is in.' Without a reduction of costs and an improvement of trade performance, he warned, 'we will just end up being a third-rate economy ... a banana republic'.

The epithet sent shock waves through the country, for it seemed that Australia was in danger of following other white settler societies on the path to ruin. Like them it had built its amenities and advanced living standards on export staples for which there was no longer a reliable demand. Like them it imitated European civilisation, but two economic historians now judged that 'The modern Australian economy is not really very "European".' They saw it rather as a less efficient Canada, importing most of its advanced technology to support a small population that depended for its comfort on the exploitation of natural resources. 'Of the three classical factors of production, the land was stolen, the capital is borrowed, the labour productivity is low.'

Keating's banana republic speech prepared his audience for shock therapy: cuts in public spending, further wage restraint, greater exposure of Australian business to international competition. After the earlier financial deregulation came plans for the progressive dismantling of the tariffs that protected local industry and the first talk of relaxing the centralised system of wage fixation. With these further instalments of liberalisation, the essential features that had sustained the Commonwealth since its inception would disappear. The central principle of that original national compact, a strong state to protect living standards, would yield to the operation of the market – and this at the hand of Labor.

The campaign to dismantle the regulatory edifice of the Australian state drew heavily on overseas precedents. After the end of the long boom and the failure of Keynesian techniques of economic management to restore prosperity, there was a general movement to the right. The election of a Conservative government in Britain and a Republican president in the United States at the end of the 1970s heralded an assault on unions, social welfare, and the mixed economy. The apostles of the New Right spoke not of market failure but government failure, not of freedom from insecurity but the freedom of the market as the very foundation of liberty. Their supporters used that designation – the New Right – to distinguish themselves from the older, more pragmatic conservatives.

The ideas of the New Right were taken up in Australia by policy institutes and think tanks, promoted by media commentators, and quickly assimilated into public policy. They appealed to export producers and other enemies of protectionism: a newly formed National Farmers Federation, along with prominent mining magnates, demanded that the crippling burden of tariffs and fixed wages be swept away. They were embraced by opponents of public welfare, who suggested that such assistance merely kept recipients in a state of dependence while sustaining an unproductive bureaucracy. They were used by enemies of the unions, who alleged that the system of arbitration and centralised wage determination fostered an incestuous 'industrial relations club'. Some employer organisations were at first resistant to the call for its abolition but as Australian business felt the chill wind of international competition, they too embraced labour market deregulation.

Conservative politicians were more wary of the electoral implications of New Right policies: outflanked by Labor's financial deregulation, they lost an early election in 1984; a populist crusade to install the authoritarian premier of Queensland, Joh Bjelke-Petersen, as national leader ruined their chances in 1987. His march on Canberra was a forlorn enterprise, but it forced the leaders of the federal National Party (who had followed his lead and adopted that identity for the Country Party in 1982) to tear up the coalition agreement and support him. Shut out of government, the Liberal Party was already succumbing to chronic instability and would change the leader five times during its exile from office.

Both major parties supported the turn to neoliberalism, as did senior bureaucrats, the press gallery, and other opinion setters. To them it was obvious that the established methods of regulation were not working and had to be dismantled. Ordinary Australians were by no means convinced of the need for such a radical break with the past and their exclusion from decision-making (symbolised by the absence of those without organisational clout from the National Economic Summit) weakened confidence in the political process. Both parties were suffering a long-term decline in membership and loyalty, though Labor's electoral success allowed its leaders to ride roughshod over that party's decision-making procedures.

The predicament of the Liberal Party was more deep-seated. The liberalism of the Menzies era, with its unifying symbols of the Crown and British race patriotism, was obsolete. So too the civic virtues that Menzies upheld – individualism accompanied by the acceptance of responsibility, initiative tempered by sobriety and thrift – were challenged by the understanding of human nature associated with neoliberalism – public choice theory – which reconfigured citizens as consumers and saw no interest that was not vested. Labor's embrace of the market pushed the Liberal Party to the right, so that the sterner 'dries' won control of the party at the expense of the 'wets', who still believed in government intervention in the national interest.

There was good cause for popular resistance to the neoliberal consensus. Financial deregulation allowed the major Australian banks to relax their prudential limits, and the entry of fifteen foreign banks in 1985, eager to gain a foothold, brought a frenzy of business lending. That, in turn, allowed highly geared speculators to acquire successful companies with debt-financed takeovers and plunder their assets. In this heady phase of wealth acquisition the overseas borrowing that might have gone to investment in research, development and improved productivity went instead into the war chests of corporate buccaneers who tested the limits of business practice. As a financial journalist observed, 'never before in Australian history had so much money been channelled by so many incompetent to lend it into the hands of so many people incompetent to manage it'. The adventurers created paper empires and built grandiose mansions, acquired private jets and art collections, entertained lavishly and were generous with political donations. The golden age had become a gilded age of rampant excess.

Labor politicians found the freewheeling tycoons far more congenial than the old wealth of the clubs and boardrooms. They admired the entrepreneurial zest of the newcomers and welcomed their acquisition of overseas assets at absurdly overvalued prices as evidence of a more outward-looking Australian business. The surge in credit and asset prices was exacerbated by the decision to allow landlords to deduct interest and other property expenses from their taxable income. Keating had abolished such negative gearing provisions in 1985, describing them as an 'outrageous rort' that directed capital away from the productive sector. His restoration of the concession in 1987 brought a 60 per cent increase in house prices over the following two years, which exacerbated inflation.

The government, having removed the instruments to control the economy, could slow it only by repeated increases of the official interest rate, which reached 18 per cent by 1989. It was impossible to bring about a soft landing from such dizzy heights and the recession that followed brought down the high-flying entrepreneurs, along with two State banks, several merchant banks and a number of building societies, while two of the big four banks had to be recapitalised. The damage was not confined to the financial sector as thousands of small businesses went to the wall. 'This', the defiant Treasurer insisted, 'is a recession that Australia had to have'.

Unemployment was again on the rise and passed 11 per cent in 1992. The effort to realign the Australian economy to new patterns of trade and investment had brought improvements in productivity, and the fall in the value of the Australian dollar assisted a growth in the export of agricultural products, manufactures and services, but still left a persistent trade deficit and a large external debt. The debt was private but it was used even less productively than the public foreign debt had been in the 1880s and 1920s. Australia remained dependent on international capital, and vulnerable to cycles of boom and bust. The exposure to market forces yielded not higher but lower growth rates than were achieved during the post-war era when governments regulated the economy, together with greater inequality and greater vulnerability – as was the case with other countries that embarked on neoliberal economic policies in the 1980s.

Australia's experience of deregulation was moderated, however, by its introduction under a Labor government. Labor combined neoliberal economic policies with a corporatist style of decision-making in an attempt to preserve a social dimension in the operation of the market. The Accord maintained some protection from the consequences experienced in Britain and the United States: there was lower unemployment, a floor under wages, greater assistance to those in need. By conceding the economic arguments of the New Right, Labor still hoped to escape its ruthless repudiation of responsibility for the weak and vulnerable.

Like Margaret Thatcher, Paul Keating insisted that there was no alternative. In 1990 he affirmed the necessity 'of removing the meddling hands of bureaucracy from the operation of markets'. The choice he offered was stark: Australia could continue 'to confront the realities of world markets' or it could 'retreat to the failed policies of the past'. Globalisation, the catchword for these realities, served both as diagnosis and remedy for the rapid changes that were transforming Australia. They were anticipated by the Australian polymath Barry Jones in his book *Sleepers Wake!* (1982), which canvassed the country's future in a post-industrial world with his own prisoner's dilemma. Australia could adapt to the challenges and opportunities of the information age or it could face a future without work. Jones became the minister for science in the Hawke government; he popularised the appellation the 'Clever Country' for the inventive, alert and adaptable Australia he wished to see. But in 1990 Jones was dropped from the ministry.

By this time his dystopian alternative seemed uncomfortably plausible. The occupations that had once provided secure employment were disappearing. The manufacturers of clothing and footwear could no longer compete with cheap imports; white goods were shipped in from low-cost factories in South-East Asia; the city offices that had once been full of typists and clerical workers were refitted with personal computers, designed in Silicon Valley, assembled offshore. Employment in manufacturing fell 17 per cent by the end of the 1980s. Yet the growth of the new high-tech industries that would supposedly take up the slack remained disappointingly fitful. Rather, the service industries were polarised between highly paid jobs and ones that paid low rates and used part-time and casual arrangements to increase flexibility. Employers were no longer prepared to maintain a large permanent workforce. The expectation of a career, of committing oneself to a lifelong vocation that valued experience and allowed workers to retire with dignity, now seemed antediluvian. Among managers and professionals, to remain in the same position for more than a few years was a confession of failure.

There was a similar change in the public sector as the Labor ministry embarked on reforms to make it more responsive to the government's objectives. Legislation in 1984 scrapped established methods of public administration for private sector procedures that were meant to improve efficiency: corporate planning, programme budgeting, performance evaluation and benchmarking for 'best practice'. The government subsequently moved to a contractual model of service provision in which companies tendered for the delivery of services and in 1995 a national competition policy required all public agencies – federal, State and local government – to compete on equal terms with the private sector in their business activities.

By then the Commonwealth public service had shed 76,000 employees over a decade. The contractual model, as well as claiming greater efficiency, postulated members of the public as clients or customers who would be offered greater choice by a range of providers – though their capacity to choose the provider or question the quality of the services was limited. The new public management conceived of government as 'steering rather than rowing', designing services rather than administering them, and preferring generic management skills to specialist expertise. With the changes in employment conditions and the new emphasis on results, the professionalism, impartiality and ethical standards of the older model of public service were at a discount.

The new order was apparent in the national parliament. When it moved in 1927 from Melbourne to Canberra, the members occupied a temporary building of simple elegance that provided chambers for the Representatives and Senators along with meeting rooms, a library, bar and dining room and a small number of offices. First the prime minister and then other ministers moved their principal office into this building, which had to be extended to accommodate the growing number of parliamentarians and their staff, but all continued to share the principal entrance and mingle with the public in the central hall. The new Parliament House that was opened in 1988 dispensed with such accessibility by separating the public section from that of the members, and locating a separate ministerial wing symbolically in the centre of a vast edifice. Occupying 32 hectares and containing more than 4500 rooms, it took seven years to build and was the largest construction project since the Snowy Mountains Scheme. From their opulent bunker the ministers of state, together with a large retinue of advisers, conducted the country's affairs.

Government enterprises, meanwhile, were required to corporatise their operations and maximise commercial outcomes. From 1991 the Commonwealth began the sale of large undertakings, including the Commonwealth Bank and Qantas, and States began selling utilities such as water, gas and electricity, along with their transport, banks and insurance operations. Since the proceeds were generally used to reduce public sector debt but the income stream was no longer available to government, some privatisations increased the net worth of the public sector and others reduced it. The experience of consumers was also mixed. Executive salaries, share options and other incentives enriched the managers of these enterprises, but many of them achieved their bonuses by cutting costs and shedding labour.

The chief burden of the changes fell on those least able to carry it. The loss of process work particularly affected middle-aged migrant men and women who had settled close to the factories in the principal cities. The decline of heavy industry struck industrial centres such as Newcastle and Wollongong in New South Wales, Whyalla and Elizabeth in South Australia. The closure of processing plants in smaller towns placed further strain on rural dwellers, who saw schools, hospitals, shops and banks close as farming populations declined. Large companies that once cross-subsidised their less profitable operations abandoned them, while public agencies that accepted a service obligation no longer provided that service. The reconfiguration of staffing practices that combed out the less skilled and replaced permanent full-time employees with part-time and casual ones bore particularly on the young. With fewer jobs for school-leavers, the rate of youth unemployment was persistently high.

Workforce participation increased during the 1980s: a movement of women into paid employment, which had gathered force in the 1960s and 1970s, was assisted by the growth of part-time employment. The discriminatory practices associated with the protection of the male breadwinner were disappearing, yet many families now found that two incomes were needed to make ends meet while the pressures on family life were increasing. Particularly vulnerable to poverty were families consisting of a single parent with dependent children. Between 1974 and 1987 the number of these families doubled to comprise one in six of all families.

The Hawke government was uncomfortable with its inability to restore full employment or stem the clear signs of distress; the prime minister's rash election promise in 1987 that 'by 1990 no Australian child will be living in poverty' came back to haunt him. Labor maintained a commitment to social welfare but directed assistance far more closely to those in need with stringent asset and income tests on most benefits. The primary emphasis was on job creation and training, which brought a rapid increase of school retention rates and corresponding expansion of post-secondary education. This in turn was aligned more closely with vocational outcomes through changes in the school curriculum that redefined education as training.

The government took longer to extend its reform project to higher education. There had been a rapid expansion of universities in the post-war years, when the Commonwealth government assumed financial responsibility for the sector. With more school-leavers seeking to continue their studies and a growing demand for professional expertise, enrolments increased ninefold between 1955 and 1975. Universities were not spared the cuts in public expenditure that ensued, and doubts were raised about their overly academic orientation, but no one seemed to know what to do with them. For more than a decade they stagnated.

Then in 1987 a new minister took charge: John Dawkins, who had previously initiated the public sector reforms, headed an enlarged Department of Employment, Education and Training. At breakneck speed, Dawkins raised teachers' colleges and other training institutions to university status in an enlarged Unified National System. To restore growth he introduced a student charge that was paid after graduation on an income-contingent basis. He set in train a process of mergers that created large, multi-campus universities; imposed greater accountability through new funding arrangements; required universities to replace older collegial practices with line management; and expected them to reorient their teaching and research to the task of rebuilding international competitiveness.

All of this was accompanied by scathing criticism of academics as pampered and privileged, and universities as unworldly, 'ossified bodies incapable of adaptation'. Dawkins disdained consultation with the vice-chancellors and was scornful of their resistance. 'The universities are very, very cross', warned the head of their national body, 'and if they think we're a mob of wimps, they'd better have another think'. In fact the vice-chancellors were readily reconciled to their enhanced authority, opportunities and rewards – one complaisant university council was even happy to provide a new residence, limousine and chauffer, baulking only at the request for a helicopter and pilot to facilitate visits to the outlying provinces.

The chief casualty of the new order was the pursuit of equality. For thirty years after 1945, social-democratic governments had sought to reduce the inequalities of income and wealth generated by the capitalist market while workers took advantage of full employment to improve their lot. That endeavour broke down with the end of the long boom so that the 1980s brought increased polarisation of the rich and poor around the world. Australia, with its residual system of public welfare, continued to ease the plight of the vulnerable. While it spent less, more of what it spent went to the needy. But this limited redistribution to the needy failed utterly to curb the growing inequality at the other end of the income scale.

With wages pegged, the profit share increased. The rich became richer. They paid themselves higher executive salaries, and realised windfall gains on property and financial markets. They also became less willing to share their bounty, using tax shelters to minimise their contribution to public revenue, and more ostentatious in flaunting it. Deregulation removed not just the institutional framework that bound individuals into relations of mutual obligation but the sentiments that sustained social solidarity. A meanness of spirit was apparent in the periodic vilification of the victims of unemployment as work-shy 'dole bludgers'. The weakening of mutuality, the rampant individuality that spurned the virtues of love, duty and sacrifice, allowed a cult of selfishness to flourish.

The 1980s were punctuated by political scandals that eroded confidence in government. In Queensland, where Bjelke-Petersen was a law unto himself, graft and corruption went unchecked until his failed bid for national office brought him undone. A commission of inquiry spent almost two years uncovering the systematic abuse of office. The premier escaped due to ill health, and his particularly venal deputy died before charges could be laid, but three ministers and the police commissioner were convicted and gaoled. Brian Burke, the Labor premier of Western Australia from 1983 to 1988, established such close links with entrepreneurs that that the State became known as in the media as WA Inc. He resigned as the deals turned sour following the stock exchange crash of 1987 but was called back from his post as Ambassador to Ireland and the Holy See in 1992 to appear before a royal commission, which found that leading businessmen had made substantial contributions to party funds under his control. Burke and his deputy both served gaol terms. In New South Wales special deals for mates were a way of life and embroiled the chief magistrate, the minister for prisons and even a High Court judge.

Australia was marked by a high concentration of media ownership, and it increased during the 1980s as all three of the commercial television networks changed hands. Alan Bond paid the largest price, $1 billion, to Kerry Packer for Channel 9 in 1987, who then bought a controlling share for $200 million three years later; 'you only get one Alan Bond in your lifetime', Packer remarked. With his acquisition in 1987 of the newspaper chain once controlled by his father, Rupert Murdoch controlled the majority of the country's metropolitan dailies. These media moguls were the two richest Australians by the end of the 1980s (though Murdoch was an absentee owner who took out American citizenship as a condition of his expansion there), and it was a rash politician who defied them. When the Hawke government was determining new rules on media ownership, a member of the Cabinet asked the prime minister, 'Why don't you just tell us what your mates want?' The role of the media was supposedly to invigilate the actions of government so that citizens could hold their elected representatives to account. Now media tycoons had a direct interest in government policy across the full range of their business interests.

Sport itself became a form of big business. In 1977 Kerry Packer's television network bought the services of the country's leading cricketers, put them into coloured clothing and reworked a leisurely game into a frenetic performance. Other sporting codes succumbed afterwards to the same commercial pressures, forming national competitions for a national audience. Games provided media product, clubs became corporations, sporting heroes turned into celebrities. The distinction between the amateur and the professional had once affirmed a preference for the voluntary participant over the mercenary, enjoyment over reward. Professionalism was now synonymous with success, and sporting idols became prey to allegations of drug enhancement, match-fixing and sexual misconduct.

Alan Bond was the most audacious of the corporate pirates who flourished in the 1980s. An English migrant, he began working life as a signwriter in Perth, moved into property development and achieved celebrity in 1983 when he financed the syndicate that won the America's Cup, thus ending more than a century of American supremacy. The Australian team yacht sported a boxing kangaroo and took as its anthem a boastful pop-song inspired by *The Adventures of Barry McKenzie*. Upon their return from this triumph, Bond and his wife were accorded a parade through the main streets of Perth, lined with cheering crowds. 'These people are our royalty', one local remarked.

In preparation for the defence of the America's Cup four years later, there was substantial redevelopment of the port city of Fremantle. So too the waterfronts of Sydney, Melbourne and Brisbane were turned into places of pleasure. Darling Harbour, alongside the central business district of Sydney, was upgraded first, in the mid-1980s. A historian noted how hotels and bars, cinemas and a fun park, a shopping precinct and a casino, 'every modern commercial cliché', were crammed around the foreshores of what had been a vital artery of the city's older trading economy. Soon an enormous casino rose up along the south bank of the Yarra River in Melbourne, a city that had steadfastly resisted gambling venues.

9.2 Bob Hawke basked in the success of Alan Bond's yacht, which won the America's Cup in the same year he came to office. (West Australian Newspapers Ltd © News Limited)

Bond's defence of the America's Cup in 1987 proved unsuccessful, and the stock market crash in that year left him overexposed, so that by 1990 receivers were picking over the wreckage in an effort to track down shareholders' assets. Bond himself was gaoled, unlike some other entrepreneurs who fled overseas, but in 1989, as the financial journalists who had puffed up his business acumen began to question his solvency, he spoke defiantly at the National Gallery where part of his art collection was on display. He had an affinity, he said, with the French impressionist painters who were bold and creative men subjected to 'criticism and mockery'. They too had been victims of that impulse to cut down tall poppies, which continued unabated in his own country.

As he appropriated the paintings, so he embezzled the phrase. Egalitarian Australians had once used the term 'tall poppies' to decry those who got above themselves, and such healthy irreverence was celebrated as a national virtue. Then, in the last year of the Whitlam government when the impulse for greater equality was faltering, a senior Liberal sounded a new note: 'tall poppies, more and more tall poppies, are what this country needs'. By the 1980s the term had lost all pejorative connotations. Tall poppies were now national treasures, celebrated in lavish encomia across almost every field of endeavour – a tribute to successful Australian women appeared in 1984 as *Tall Poppies*. As inequalities of prestige, wealth and power were a necessary correlate of enterprise and achievement, so Australians were urged to cast off their unseemly modesty in order to achieve. Knocking had become a vice in a country that had forgotten that 'achieve' is a transitive verb.

During the 1980s, then, Australia dismantled most of the national institutions that had provided a small, trading economy with a measure of protection from vulnerability to external shocks. Few lamented their demise. Critics blamed them for entrenching sectional interests, sheltering inefficiency and stifling initiative. Most of all, they argued that protection was simply unsustainable because globalisation was sweeping away the capacity of national governments to resist market forces. Some in the Labor government wanted to graft a reform process onto egalitarian traditions and maintain a capacity to protect living standards. That aspiration weakened as deregulation proceeded and the capacity to control its effects diminished. By the end of the decade Australia had cut itself loose from the past and was drifting on the choppy waters of the global market, more exposed, more vulnerable.

***

The turn to the right in domestic politics coincided with a revival of the international Cold War. In the United States, after the country's defeat in Vietnam, partial détente with the Soviet

Union and a reduction of military expenditure, a series of humiliating reversals in the late 1970s brought a new president, Ronald
Reagan, and a fresh determination to confront the communist
Evil Empire. With the encouragement of Margaret Thatcher, the
United States resumed the arms race. Australia was an early and
vociferous supporter of the second Cold War. Malcolm Fraser
warned repeatedly against the Soviet naval presence in the Indian
Ocean; he encouraged the expansion of American communication
facilities in Australia and responded to the Soviet intervention in
Afghanistan with an attempt to prevent Australian participation
in the 1980 Moscow Olympics.

Fraser therefore welcomed the advent of Reagan and supported the reassertion of American strength. His relations with
Thatcher were much cooler, partly because of arguments within
Commonwealth forums over the white supremacist regimes of
southern Africa. He was a courageous critic of apartheid, and
human rights became an important element of his foreign policy.
There was also a strong regional element. Fraser saw China as
an ally against the Soviet Union. He visited Beijing before
Washington, supported China's 1979 invasion of Vietnam, and
encouraged a loose coalition of China and Japan with the
Association of South-East Asian Nations (ASEAN) to contain
the Soviet threat. This in turn guided Australia's closer relations
with ASEAN as the principal regional forum, and highlighted the
problematic relationship with Indonesia.

Australia's nearest and most populous neighbour had emerged in
the second half of the twentieth century as its most proximate threat.
Under the presidency of the aggressively anti-imperial Achmad
Sukarno, Indonesia's incorporation of the western half of New
Guinea in 1962 and then its confrontation with the Malaysian
confederation in 1963 aroused fears of further anti-Western belligerence. The suppression by General Suharto in 1965 of the
Indonesian Communist Party in an action that slaughtered hundreds
of thousands eased that anxiety, but Suharto's corrupt and author-
itarian regime proved no less assertive. In 1975 it invaded the former
Portuguese colony of East Timor, and in the following years brutally
repressed local resistance both there and in its province of New
Guinea. The Whitlam and Fraser governments acceded abjectly to

these acts of aggression. The Hawke government continued to extenuate them as it negotiated with Indonesia for a division of the rich oil deposits that lay under the bed of the Timor Sea.

The primacy of the economy reshaped foreign as well as domestic policy: in 1987 the Departments of Foreign Affairs and Trade were amalgamated. Trade patterns increased the regional orientation as the balance of world economic power shifted towards the Pacific: by 1984 the volume of trans-Pacific trade exceeded that of trans-Atlantic trade. While European economies stagnated in the 1980s, those of Japan and the 'four tigers' – South Korea, Taiwan, Hong Kong and Singapore – achieved rapid growth. Indonesia and Malaysia followed on the same path of industrial development, and China cast off the shackles of its command economy and rumbled into motion.

Australia increased trade with Asia (which took half of Australia's exports and provided half of its imports by the end of the 1980s), but the Australian market share was falling. With European and North American trading blocs pressing for greater access to Asian markets, there was a grave danger that Australia would be excluded. Shut out of Asia, it would see the newly industrialised countries of the region surpass its living standards, leaving Australians as the 'poor white trash' of the South Pacific. The government showed ingenuity in establishing the Cairns group of agricultural producers in preparation for a new round of international trade negotiations in 1986, but it proved far more difficult to make the United States comply with free trade in agriculture. Closer economic ties with New Zealand followed an agreement in 1983.

The desire to fashion an independent role saw Australian initiatives both in the region and beyond it. The foreign minister after 1987, Gareth Evans, was as active in international forums as Evatt, his predecessor forty years earlier. He promoted a settlement in Cambodia, sent peace-keeping forces there and to other local conflicts, pushed for nuclear disarmament and generally played the reforming role of an international good citizen. Defence policy shifted to a regional orientation, and foreign policy invoked the idea of Australia as a 'middle power' that could join in coalitions and exert influence in international forums – in these areas of national endeavour, as in others, the phrase 'punching above its weight' quickly became a national cliché. The aspiration was always constrained by the Hawke government's absolute commitment to the Western alliance, which in the last phase of the Cold War meant support of the United States as it exerted its augmented dominance. The American communication bases in Australia, more important than ever for a new generation of strategic weapons, were therefore sacred. The right of American warships to enter local ports, regardless of whether they were carrying nuclear weapons, was inviolable.

When the New Zealand Labour government refused to allow such visits in 1986 and the Reagan administration suspended its obligations under ANZUS to the impudent outpost, Australia stuck firmly with its more powerful ally. ANZUS remained vital, not as a guarantee of Australian security (for it had been made clear during the Timor crisis that Indonesia was more important to the United States than Australia) but because it provided membership of the western alliance and thus afforded access to American technology and intelligence. Such were the burdens of a middle power.

Then, at the end of the 1980s, the second Cold War ended in communist collapse. The Soviet economy, with its emphasis on heavy industry, was unable to adapt to the challenge of the new information industries. The need to divert increasing resources from an ailing economy to match the increased military expenditure of the United States squeezed the living standards of its people, who were no longer sustained by faith nor as easily cowed into submission. The rigid system of centralised control, the imposition of conformity to a bankrupt ideology, the endemic corruption and cynicism, ended in a chain reaction of peaceful revolutions in eastern Europe and the overthrow of Gorbachev by Yeltsin in Russia. The great twentieth-century contest between capitalism and socialism was over. Socialism was vanquished, and not just the dead-end command socialism of the communist countries but the more moderate collectivism pursued by labour movements in the West.

***

With that triumph came renewed declarations of an end of ideology, even the end of history. As this claim was made, however, there was a sharpening of ideological differences in Australian politics. The coalition parties, which lost a further election in 1990, turned to a bone-dry economist, John Hewson, who quickly developed a thoroughgoing New Right policy that included a regressive tax system, further reduction of the public sector, speedier removal of tariff protection and labour market deregulation. Bob Hawke had lost interest in pursuing further change; the very occupation of office exhausted his energies, and he was overthrown at the end of 1991 by Keating.

While the prime minister had orchestrated the national consensus, it was the treasurer who drove the far-reaching reforms of the 1980s. In his impatience for change, sartorial tastes and passion for French antique clocks, if not in his savage polemics, Paul Keating was an unlikely product of Australia's nearest equivalent to Tammany Hall: the New South Wales branch of the Labor Party. He was born in a working-class suburb of Sydney, the son of a boilermaker, and left school at the age of fifteen to pursue a political apprenticeship in the Labor machine; a friendship with the aged warhorse Jack Lang deepened his appreciation of Labor's tribal traditions. Keating secured election to parliament in 1969 at the age of twenty-five, and his factional seniority ensured him the treasurer's post in 1983. He was a quick learner who rapidly mastered his Treasury briefings and soon went beyond them; one of his first announcements was that his predecessor in the former Fraser government had concealed the size of the budget deficit.

This was John Howard, five years older, who had grown up in a modestly comfortable neighbourhood just a few kilometres distant from Keating and pursued a similar path through the Liberal Party that brought him also to Canberra five years after the Labor prodigy. Howard made up for lost time and was dubbed the 'boy treasurer' when promoted by Fraser to the post in 1977. The son of a service-station owner, he too sat at the feet of party elders and absorbed their antipathy to trade unions and preference for free enterprise. He wanted to reduce the role of government but could not see how to do so without treading on the toes of business and in any case deferred to Fraser in framing the pre-election budget. As leader of the opposition from 1985 he moved closer to the New Right, but the Liberal and National Parties remained divided over deregulation,

9.3   Paul Keating on the hustings in 1996, counting the
achievements of his administration. (Andrew Chapman)

and Howard's ill-judged conservatism on social issues contributed
to his loss of the leadership in 1989. An intense, awkward man, his
dogged pursuit of the ultimate prize seemed to have failed. Many
wrote him off; Keating didn't.

The new prime minister feared that he too had been kept waiting
too long. The sharp recession threatened an electoral backlash that
would allow the Coalition to reap the benefits of the changes he had
implemented. The international economy was entering a period of
sustained prosperity. With inflation finally tamed, fiscal policy under
control, a free exchange rate and reduced protection, Australian
producers were poised to benefit from strong demand. Keating
pressed ahead after 1991 with further instalments of reform, including the strengthening of competition laws, the relaxation of centralised wage fixation and the introduction of a universal system of
superannuation.

At the same time Keating used the opportunities of his prime
ministerial office, and the spectre of Hewson's more doctrinaire
embrace of the New Right, to reinvent himself. He was no longer
the combative economic rationalist, now he was the competent
manager who appreciated that government had a larger responsibility. 'When Australia opted for an open economy', he maintained,
'the nation committed itself to succeed in an endless race', but the

capacity to endure relentless change depended on the resilience of what Keating now recognised as the 'social fabric'. Those countries that would prosper were 'social democracies where government is involved in making the societies tick, where there is a happy mix between efficient economics and a comprehensive social policy in this post-monetarist, post-communist era'. In marking these discontinuities Keating increasingly cast back to national traditions of fortitude and achievement; he invoked the instinctive loyalty of the labour movement to vouchsafe his concern for the underdog. 'This was a victory for the true believers', he proclaimed when he defeated Hewson in the 1993 election.

He cast back in order to look forward. As the collapse of old industries ate into Labor's working-class constituency, as the membership and the capacity of the unions declined, the Labor Party was increasingly dependent on a coalition of social movements. Multiculturalism, environmentalism and the Aboriginal movement became vital to the electoral fortunes of the government.

When Labor took office in 1983 it was by means apparent it would forge a close relationship with migrant communities. Whitlam had championed multiculturalism, but he also cut the migrant intake and was unsympathetic to refugees. Fraser, on the other hand, oversaw an expansion of new arrivals and extended multicultural services. Moreover, he welcomed refugees who fled Vietnam following the fall of Saigon in 1975 against charges by Bob Hawke, then president the Australian Council of Trade Unions, that they were jumping the immigration queue. The Vietnamese settlers, 150,000 of them by 1983, were part of a substantial realignment of migrant policy that saw the Asian intake increase to 38 per cent of all settlers in that year.

The Hawke government maintained the same policy as part of its endeavour to develop closer ties with Asia, and defended it when the historian Geoffrey Blainey claimed in 1984 that the level of Asian immigration was straining public acceptance. Stung by accusations of racism, Blainey responded with his own allegation that the government was arrogant and insensitive to the feelings of ordinary Australians who were uncomfortable with the invasion of their suburbs, and soon he was warning of race riots. His further claim that multiculturalism had become 'rabid' and 'divisive' opened a divide with other ethnic groups. At first the Liberal Party maintained bipartisan support for multiculturalism, but in 1988, when Blainey repeated his warning that it was turning Australia into 'a cluster of tribes', he found support from John Howard, who as leader of the opposition suggested the influx of Asian immigrants should be slowed to preserve social cohesion.

That Labor should develop such a close relationship with the environmental movement was even more unlikely. The movement emerged from the late 1960s in campaigns to protect wilderness sites from being swallowed up by development projects such as mining, logging and damming – projects that provided jobs for union members. It had extended into the cities as young professionals mobilised to protect their inner-city neighbourhoods from redevelopment, and it found an ally in New South Wales from the Builders Labourers Federation, which assisted a group of women in the fashionable Sydney suburb of Hunters Hill to save the last remaining piece of open land in that area. But the Builders Labourers Federation was led by communists, and Keating was a product of the brutally pragmatic school of right-wing Labor politics who in 1981 derided the left as standing for 'wider nature strips, more trees and let's go back to making wicker baskets in Balmain'.

The end of the long boom coincided with an enhanced appreciation of the costs of development as the great triumphs of the post-war period turned out to be illusory. The Snowy Mountains Authority had turned back the rivers from the southeast coast to water the inland plains, and poisoned the soil with salt; the Ord River on the northwest coast had been dammed for irrigation, but infestations of insects killed most of the crops. The government's scientific organisation waged biological warfare against the rabbit, but the survivors returned to compete for pasture. A loss of confidence in the capacity to direct economic growth was accompanied by similar doubts about the ability of science to control nature.

A campaign to save a Tasmanian river system of great natural beauty from a proposed project to generate hydro-electricity became the turning-point. Protestors occupied the Franklin dam site in 1982 and Labor undertook during the federal election of 1983 to prevent

9.4   The campaign in the early 1980s to save the Franklin
River from damming by the Tasmanian Hydro-Electric
Commission marked the triumph of environmental over devel-
opmental values. Photographic images of pristine wilderness
catalysed Green sentiment. (Peter Dombrovskis, West Wind
Press)

its construction, a promise kept by the passage of legislation to
confer World Heritage status on the region. The same method was
used subsequently to protect the Daintree rainforest in northern
Queensland and other wilderness areas. As membership of environmental groups grew to dwarf that of the Labor Party, Graham
Richardson, the numbers man for the New South Wales right,
took the environment portfolio and emerged as a fervent conserva-
tionist. His green strategy secured the support of the Australian
Conservation Foundation and the preference votes of smaller parties
that brought Labor victory in the 1990 election.

The course of Aboriginal policy proved more tortuous.
Malcolm Fraser found racial discrimination as repugnant as
Gough Whitlam had, and the 1975 legislation that prohibited it
used the Commonwealth's external affairs power to override any
inconsistent State measure. Fraser's enactment in the following year
of the Northern Territory land rights legislation initiated by Gough
Whitlam, along with his creation of an Aboriginal Development

Commission to fund land purchase, housing development and Indigenous enterprises, suggested a bipartisan consensus in favour of Aboriginal self-determination. The difficulty in this liberal consensus was that legal equality stood alongside land rights legislation that posited Indigenous Australians as a people with special needs and entitlements.

Indigenous numbers were growing – from 156,000 in 1976 to 352,000 by 1996 – in part because more Australians identified themselves as Aboriginal and Torres Strait Islanders. Some were assisted to do so when an upsurge of interest in Aboriginal history increased knowledge of the Stolen Generations; others needed no prompting and shared their life stories in a stream of publications. Sally Morgan, an artist and writer who had grown up in suburban Perth, related a journey from childhood silence and evasion to recovery of family links that culminated in a return to *My Place* (1987). Her book became a bestseller that reworked a stigma into a celebration: 'What had begun as a tentative search for knowledge had grown into a spiritual and emotional pilgrimage. We had an Aboriginal consciousness now and were proud of it.'

Such proclamation of Aboriginal identity was accompanied by a cultural renaissance in music, cinema, theatre, dance, art and literature that reached a wide commercial audience. Aboriginal artists in Central Australia used acrylic paints to put traditional knowledge onto boards and canvas, and others revived the use of bark in art and craft. Among the most powerful voices were those of Jack Davis, the playwright; Jimmy Chi, the composer of *Bran Nue Day* (1990); and Ruby Langford Ginibi, who wrote *Don't Take Your Love to Town* (1988). Yothu Yindi, an Aboriginal band from Arnhem Land, found an international audience for songs both in English and their own language. Indigenous Australians created powerful symbols. The Aboriginal flag, a striking arrangement of black, gold and ochre, was one of them. It became increasingly common in the 1990s for public meetings to begin with an Aboriginal elder giving a 'welcome to country' and a non-Aboriginal Australian to respond with an acknowledgement of the original inhabitants of the country on which they were meeting. There was a revival of Aboriginal languages, a return to Aboriginal names.

9.5   The adoption of Aboriginal decoration by Qantas, the Australian airline, attested to popular acceptance of indigeneity as a distinctive national marker. (Qantas Boeing 747-400 'Wunala Dreaming', Qantas Airways Limited)

Despite this growing popular interest and sympathy, it proved difficult to overcome the entrenched disadvantages of Indigenous Australians. They had lower income levels than the rest of the population and higher rates of ill health and mortality. More of them were arrested and imprisoned. A royal commission into Aboriginal deaths in custody was just one of the initiatives taken at this time in an effort to remedy these inequalities.

The pursuit of self-determination proved more contentious. There was government support for a range of national, regional and local Indigenous organisations that provided employment and delivered services, but such self-management ran up against government expectations of accountability for the public funds spent on the Indigenous sector. Charlie Perkins, a former footballer and organiser of the 1965 Freedom Ride who became the first Aboriginal secretary of the Department of Aboriginal Affairs, had to walk 'with one foot on either side of a barbed wire fence'. The campaign for land rights clashed with the rapid expansion of mining in northern Australia. In 1980 the Western Australian premier Charles Court sent a large police escort to accompany a road convoy of drilling rigs on a journey of 2500 kilometres to a pastoral station, Noonkanbah, to drill for oil over the objections of the Yungngora community to the disturbance of their sacred sites. In Queensland Bjelke-Petersen maintained an obdurate resistance to land rights and even abolished Aboriginal reserves: 'We don't want them set aside in some country that becomes black man's country', he explained.

After Fraser refused to override these actions, the Labor Party undertook during the 1983 election to legislate for national land rights. In preparing to do so it encountered fierce opposition from Western Australia to the proposal that these rights should include a veto on mining. The mining industry embarked on a publicity campaign to discredit Aboriginal entitlement; one executive even claimed that capitalism and mining were 'part of the divine order', though he threatened the churches with legal action for their criticism of the industry. The government's capitulation to this campaign led to condemnation from Aboriginal people and then abandonment of the measure.

The prospect of Aboriginal protest disrupting the Bicentenary of white settlement in 1988 caused Hawke to propose a new approach through a compact or even a treaty, and in June of that year he gave an undertaking to Indigenous leaders at the Barunga cultural festival in central Australia to begin work on such an agreement. It too encountered resistance, so that in 1991 the government established a Council for Aboriginal Reconciliation to work towards an agreement by the end of the century. The replacement in 1989 of the Department of Aboriginal Affairs and the Aboriginal Development Commission by a new and elective Aboriginal and Torres Strait Islander Commission also raised hopes only to dash them. While this met a longstanding desire for a representative body, it remained under ministerial control and supervision by white administrators.

It was the High Court that broke the impasse. In June 1992 it ruled in favour of a claim brought by Eddie Mabo seeking native title for his people of the Mer islands in the Torres Strait.

In doing so the court rejected the doctrine of *terra nullius*. It found that native title was not extinguished with the establishment of British sovereignty over Australia and that it continued to operate unless valid title had been granted over Crown land. The language the judges used to describe the consequences of British settlement – 'the conflagration of oppression and conflict' that 'spread across the continent to dispossess, degrade and devastate the Aboriginal people and leave a legacy of unutterable shame' – challenged Australians. Since the decision required legislative clarification of how far native title ran, and how it might be claimed and exercised, it also presented the government with an explosive issue as it prepared for the 1993 election.

Keating accepted the challenge. 'Mabo was the hand history dealt me, and I was never going to walk away from it', he stated later. State and territory governments demanded the Commonwealth reduce their exposure to native title claims; Indigenous leaders, who came together at Ern Valley in the Northern Territory in the largest such assembly in Australian history, insisted that their rights be upheld. The campaign waged by mining and pastoral interests was vitriolic, with claims that ordinary Australians would lose their homes, and the coalition parties fanned such fears. After long and difficult negotiation, legislation validated the extinguishment of native title on areas in dispute, set up a Native Title Tribunal for establishing it elsewhere, and created a land corporation to buy land for the descendants of those who would be able to make such claims.

The Mabo judgement gave rise to Keating's most celebrated speech, delivered late in 1992 before an Aboriginal audience in the inner-Sydney suburb of Redfern. The crowd was sceptical, the prime minister initially speaking over catcalls. But when he proceeded to the frank declaration of responsibility quoted in chapter 1, those present fell silent:

We took the traditional lands and smashed the traditional way of life. We brought the diseases. The alcohol. We committed the murders. We took the children from their mothers. We practiced discrimination and exclusion. It was our ignorance and prejudice.

With each of these statements, the applause grew louder. In acknowledging the responsibility of 'non-Aboriginal Australians' for the plight of the Indigenous population, the prime minister also reminded them that Australia had 'reached out to us'. It had taken in the poor of Britain, provided a new start for the dispossessed Irish, given shelter from war and persecution in Europe and Asia. If it was possible to build 'a prosperous and remarkably harmonious multicultural society in Australia, surely we can find just solutions to the problems which beset the first Australians'.

This was just one of the speeches delivered by Keating that attained an eloquence rare in Australian public life. Assisted by his speechwriter, Don Watson, a historian with the gift of whimsy to complement the prime minister's earthy vernacular, they renewed national legends by enlarging them. His frequent evocations of sacrifice in overseas wars were more controversial; they affirmed national heroism at the expense of imperial folly to serve his call for a final break with Britain through the reconstitution of Australia as a republic. The republican cause, in turn, served to differentiate the forward-looking Labor Party from the backward-looking Liberals, to engage the creative energies of the cultural sector and to use the diversity of a multicultural society as a national strength.

Keating's nationalism was expansive. He wanted to make Australia 'competitive, outward looking, phobia-free', to equip Australians with the confidence to operate in the globalised economy and attach them to their Asian destiny. A major achievement was to expand the Asia-Pacific Economic Cooperation (APEC) group into a major regional forum. It had been established by his predecessor in 1989 as an opportunity for economic ministers to meet, but Keating converted it into a regular gathering of national leaders and persuaded President Clinton that the United States should become a member. Engagement with Asia was a recurrent theme of his leadership – he even suggested that mateship could be understood as an Asian value.

Some Asian leaders were not so sure. Indonesia's rulers found criticism by the Australian press a sign of disrespect, the preoccupation with human rights an indication that the white outpost was still wedded to Western values. Australia was denied membership of ASEAN, the other major regional forum, and opposed by Malaysia's prime minister, Mahathir, in its attempt to promote APEC as a broader regional bloc. Keating's frustrated description of his counterpart as recalcitrant did not assist his cause.

***

After his electoral victory in 1993 Keating became more preoccupied with his 'big picture', more petulant with commentators who suggested that he was no longer attentive to economic reform. The Liberal Party, meanwhile, had turned back to its former leader, John Howard. This time he avoided the hectoring stridency that had brought him undone in the 1980s and learned from the forthright naivety of Hewson, who had helpfully laid out a comprehensive New Right programme for Keating to demonstrate its unpalatable implications. Capitalising on the growing dissatisfaction of electors with a tired government, Howard offered as small a target as possible.

He took advantage also of the cumulative results of a difficult economic transition, and especially its divisive effects on incomes. Between 1982 and 1994 the top 10 per cent of income earners enjoyed an increase of $100 a week, and the bottom 10 per cent (assisted by Labor's welfare spending) gained $11 a week, but many of those in between struggled. It was to this amorphous statistical construct that the coalition parties had appealed with the equally fuzzy appellation of 'Middle Australia'. This was a far cry from Menzies' forgotten people: he had divined that expressive term in a substantial renovation of the conservative tradition; the geographically implausible Middle Australia was suggested by a firm of consultants.

During his first period as Liberal leader in the 1980s, Howard had issued a policy document with a cover picture that showed an idealised family – the husband in a suit, a decorous wife and two neat, clean children – standing in front of their substantial dwelling with its leafy front garden and white picket fence. The image of suburban security harked back to the way that Menzies had made the family the consensual symbol of domestic life, but by the 1980s only one in five households consisted of a male breadwinner with a full-time housewife and children. Howard's clumsy evocation ignored the homes that now consisted of partners who both pursued careers but might not be married; it excluded the gay couples, single parents and parents still support-ing children of working age, and the blended families with children from earlier marriages. Keating mocked Howard as a man living in the past, wanting to take Australia back to the stifling conformity of the 1950s.

Many Australians, however, did not share the prime minister's views on the merits of change. These included the victims of economic reform, for Labor's emphasis on growth did not dent the structural unemployment that persisted in older industrial regions, and the severe recession at the beginning of the 1990s undid much of its job creation. This recession, moreover, was caused by the government's reliance on interest rates in a largely deregulated financial system, and the steep rise of mortgage pay-ments caused widespread distress among homebuyers. It damaged the authority of the government as an economic manager. The consensus it had secured at the 1983 Summit, and maintained by subsequent renewal of the Accord with the trade union leadership and the incorporation of peak bodies of the social movements, was breaking up – the problem with summits is that the view becomes Olympian.

Howard capitalised on this discontent to portray Keating as aloof and out of touch. He translated the construct of Middle Australia into an appeal to the 'men and women of mainstream Australia' whose interests had been disregarded by the 'noisy minority groups' of feminists, environmentalists, the ethnic lobby, the Aboriginal industry and the intellectuals who held the government captive to their special interests. He did better than this: he found a term in the Australian lexicon for those who were doing it tough – the 'battlers'.

The word had popular currency among earlier generations, acknowledging the fortitude of the underdog who battled on regardless of the odds. The original battler was a stoic who defied misfortune, unlike John Howard's enlargement of the description to encompass an aggrieved majority, but his appropriation caught the mood. Juxtaposing the practical concerns of his battlers to the indulgences of Labor's pampered 'élites', the revitalised Liberal leader emphasised the national interest: the Coalition would govern 'For All of Us'. That slogan appealed to many in the Labor heartland in the 1996 election, and the voters gave the Coalition a decisive victory.

10

Outcomes, 1997–2015

'The times will suit me', John Howard proclaimed some months after he won the leadership of the Liberal Party in 1985. The first leader of that party to embrace neoliberalism, he believed Labor's attempt to reconstruct the economy through an agreement with the unions was doomed to failure and expected that a mounting crisis of national solvency would turn voters to a statesman prepared, like Reagan or Thatcher, to apply the same reforming vigour to the labour market. On regaining the leadership a decade later, Howard played on the hardship inflicted by the recent recession: 'The Australian people cannot understand why they should have to suffer the indignity, the denial and disappointment of a bare five minutes of economic sunlight.'

The economy was in fact already on an upward trajectory that would last for a quarter-century. The painful transformation of the 1980s yielded a marked improvement in productivity in the following decade, while the recession of 1990–91 finally cured the problem of inflation. Then, in the new century, Australia caught the tailwind of China's seemingly insatiable demand for energy and metals. With surging exports, record investment and high levels of immigration, the country's living standards rose to surpass those of the United States and Europe.

This extraordinary prosperity rested heavily on a fortuitous combination of circumstances – high terms of trade and record investment attracted by the country's bounteous resources – but the windfall lifted expectations. Beneficiaries spent lavishly, and the governments used their additional revenue to reduce the tax paid by the well-to-do and subsidise their access to private education and health care. A leading economist worried that what he called the 'Great Australian Complacency' was sapping the appetite for reform, making public policy once more the captive of interest groups and preventing the further changes needed to keep it competitive when the mining bonanza ran its course. He and others pressed for action to deal with problems of affluence such as urban congestion, rising health costs, social exclusion, welfare dependency and global warming.

Howard espoused economic liberalism and social conservatism. The first Liberal leader to break with that party's commitment to protection and a mixed economy, he was also the first to identify himself as a conservative. He did so initially by championing the battlers against the hectoring and privileged elites, and in doing so upheld the traditional values of the family and the nation. To this end, on taking office he dismantled the government agencies that served feminism and multiculturalism, rejected Aboriginal claims on the grounds that they were divisive, and waged a war against the cosmopolitan intellectuals who would tear down the symbols of national identity.

Howard's querulous carping against academics, teachers, artists, the Australian Broadcasting Corporation and even the judiciary gave this initial offensive an aggrieved tone, more populist than conservative. The prime minister displayed courage early in his first term when he imposed tighter gun control following a massacre at the tourist centre of Port Arthur in Tasmania, but he was still searching for the language and imagery that would project his own inheritance of hard work and self-reliance, stable family values, Christian morality, respect for the monarchy, and pride in one's country onto the discordant patterns of twenty-first century Australia. An early prop was the Australian tracksuit he wore for his early-morning walk, a daily exercise adopted when he first set himself for the Lodge. A dogged and disciplined man free of the hubris of his predecessor and the cupidity of some of his colleagues, his every waking hour was devoted to politics.

Howard held office for eleven years, a term exceeded only by Menzies. Lacking that prime minister's natural authority and without the popular touch of the long-serving Hawke, it was a remarkable achievement. He had learned lessons of political management from his humiliating failure as opposition leader in the 1980s: he exercised authority dexterously, knew how to delegate, controlled the Cabinet and was given little trouble by the Liberals' dwindling coalition partner, the National Party. Mistrustful of the press gallery, he adapted himself to the accelerated news cycle of the electronic media with a special aptitude for talkback radio, which enabled him to speak directly to his battlers. But while Howard won four elections and saw off five opposition leaders, it took some time before his position was secure. The early years were contentious.

The new regime began with the sacking of a third of the public service heads and installation of a corporate executive to head the Prime Minister's Department. Hand-picked operatives in his own office invigilated the administration, which was ruthless in appointing its own to the boards of public agencies. There was a reduction of the public service, additional sale of government assets, and more contracting out of services. An adversarial relationship with Canberra was compounded by Howard's decision to live in the prime ministerial residence on the north shore of Sydney Harbour, Kirribilli, which had been acquired when Melbourne was still the seat of government but now symbolised Sydney's status as the place where decisions were made. On the first day of the new parliament, Howard announced a new code to ensure higher ministerial standards. It soon cost him five ministers as well as a trusted adviser and was unceremoniously abandoned; henceforth the convention that a minister was responsible for the actions of his department, never robust in Australian practice, was defunct.

The underlying problem was how to convince a reform-weary electorate of the need for yet more of it. Before the election Howard declared that his goal was to see an Australian nation feeling 'comfortable and relaxed'. His would not be 'a government of ideology' but one committed to 'practical outcomes'. After the election he wielded the knife. Substantial cuts in public expenditure inflicted in the first 1996 budget fell heavily on welfare recipients, Aboriginals, universities and the arts. They were justified by the new treasurer's serendipitous discovery of a 'black hole' in the accounts, but the prime minister's credibility was damaged by his attempt to distinguish between 'core' and 'non-core' promises.

Thereafter the government maintained a budget surplus and made debt reduction a priority, along with greater autonomy for the Reserve Bank in determination of monetary policy. The collapse of stock exchanges in South-East Asia at the end of 1997 and the serious recession that followed in the region provided justification for these policies. A fall in demand from Asian customers for Australian exports was partially offset by new markets, where the falling value of the Australian dollar gave a competitive advantage. Peter Costello, the Treasurer, even boasted that he had 'fireproofed' the Australian economy.

The Howard government scrapped most of its predecessor's training programmes for the unemployed and replaced them with a new scheme of 'work for the dole' that required young unemployed to undertake community projects. It subsequently extended the principle of 'mutual obligation' to other welfare recipients, though the number in receipt of benefits continued to increase. At the beginning of the 1990s, 1.5 million Australians of working age were receiving income support; by the end of the decade, the number had risen to 2.6 million, or 20 per cent of the workforce.

There were more working poor because of changes to the labour market. The Labor government had begun the process in the early 1990s when it encouraged wage bargaining at the workplace or enterprise level as an alternative to the centralised system of national awards. The coalition government went further in its Workplace Relations Act of 1996 by encouraging individual contracts in addition to the enterprise agreements and restricting the scope of the Industrial Relations Commission's awards. The commission no longer determined national wage levels; rather, it provided 'safety net' adjustments for those lower-paid workers who were unable to bargain for a better deal.

The coalition would have liked to go further in industrial relations, but it lacked a majority in the Senate and had to negotiate a compromise with the small parties that held the balance of legislative power. In particular, it wanted to break the grip of trade unions. Union membership had declined to just 31 per cent of the workforce by 1996, but remained strong in key industries such as maritime transport. The transformation of the Australian economy relied on the giant tankers that carried iron ore, bauxite and coal to furnaces in Japan, South Korea, Taiwan and China, and the vast container vessels that brought steel boxes – several thousand at a time – full of manufactured goods. Where hundreds of men had once loaded and unloaded cargo, now a crane-operator sufficed and each of the containers was tracked on a computer and directed to its ultimate destination without recourse to storemen and packers. The Maritime Union of Australia (MUA) demanded a share of the productivity gains won by standardisation, automation and barcode logistics.

In 1997 the government put together a plan with the National Farmers Federation and one of the principal stevedoring companies to destroy the MUA. New workers were recruited from the army and flown to Dubai for training. On the evening of 7 April 1998 security guards, wearing balaclavas and with dogs on leashes, moved into the nation's ports to dismiss all members of the union who worked for the company. The minister for workplace relations, who had previously denied all knowledge of the scheme he had initiated, was jubilant: 'today the government has acted decisively

10.1　A private security guard sits in an improvised shelter inside the cargo terminal at the port of Fremantle during the maritime dispute in 1998. The union publicised this disturbing image of industrial relations by intimidation. (Tony McDonough)

to fix the waterfront once and for all'. He spoke too soon. Mass pickets prevented the movement of cargo, and the courts ordered the reinstatement of the workers. The MUA agreed to a smaller workforce and gave up many of its practices, while the men who had volunteered to replace the unionists were simply abandoned.

Indigenous Australians took the brunt of the government's insistence on broad community values in place of 'the noisy, self-interested clamour of powerful vested interests with scant regard for the national interest'. In 1996 the High Court handed down a second landmark decision on land rights when it found in the *Wik* decision that the granting of pastoral leases had not automatically extinguished native title. 'I think this decision has just about ended Aboriginal reconciliation', warned the president of the National Farmers Federation, and the leader of the National Party promised 'bucketloads of extinguishment'. The government's legislation to circumscribe the judgement was held up in the Senate but finally enacted in 1998.

Howard had already adopted a phrase of the historian Geoffrey Blainey to repudiate the 'black armband' view of the national past and condemn those engaged in 'endless and agonised navel-gazing', who had made Australian history 'a basis for obsessive and consuming national guilt and shame'. His own national story was tested when an inquiry into the removal of Aboriginal children commissioned by the previous government issued its report, *Bringing Them Home*, in May 1997. The inquiry heard the testimony of hundreds of Aboriginal witnesses, and found that from 1910–70 between one and three in ten Aboriginal children had been removed, most by force or under duress. The minister for Aboriginal affairs refused the call for a parliamentary apology to the Stolen Generations on the grounds that this could imply present-day Australians were responsible for actions that earlier ones had 'believed to be in the best interests of the children concerned'.

The prime minister still insisted that these 'blemishes' in the national record should not detract from patriotic pride. In the same month that *Bringing Them Home* was tabled, he told a Reconciliation Convention that while he felt a deep personal sorrow for those Aborigines who had suffered past injustices, there was nothing to be gained by 'symbolic gestures and overblown promises'. A section of the audience responded by standing and turning their backs on the prime minister, but this only made him more adamant that Australia was 'one of the fairest, most egalitarian and tolerant societies in the world'.

John Howard was not alone in his campaign to liberate the battlers from political correctness. Shortly before the 1996 election the Liberal Party had selected a small-business owner to contest an electorate based on the Queensland industrial town of Ipswich; the party withdrew endorsement when she published a letter in the local newspaper alleging discrimination in favour of Aborigines. 'Governments shower them with money, facilities and opportunities', she claimed, at the expense of hard-working, white Australians. Her lack of polish, unabashed ignorance of national politics and defiance of its rules made her irresistibly attractive to the media and voters, who sent her to the House of Representatives with the largest swing in the federal election. Her name was Pauline Hanson.

Hanson's maiden speech played to her strengths as an interloper: 'I come here not as a polished politician but as a woman who has had a fair share of life's knocks', as an 'ordinary Australian who wants to keep this country strong and independent'. Her principal message was 'equality for all Australians', which meant ending the 'reverse racism' of multiculturalism, Asian migration ('we are in danger of being swamped by Asians', she claimed) and 'the Aboriginal industry'. Her speech was widely criticised for inflaming prejudice, but the prime minister refused to condemn her. On the contrary, he told one of the talkback radio hosts who set the new rancorous tone that he thought 'some of the things she said were an accurate reflection of what people feel'.

Hanson had captured a traditional Labor electorate with her condemnation of the policies of the former Labor government. Her rapid rise to prominence drove a wedge into Labor's support base: she affronted its tertiary-educated, cosmopolitan, city progressives while she appealed to older, less mobile, blue-collar workers. The very disdain she attracted only increased her credentials as an underdog. 'Please explain', her response to a current affairs presenter who asked whether she was xenophobic, expressed both puzzlement and defiance. In April 1997 Hanson formed her own One Nation Party, and within a year it attracted 25,000 members. One Nation was a franchise operation trading as a political party that capitalised on its founder's aura to purvey antagonism to politics and politicians, including those in the coalition. It drew much of its impetus from the convergent economic policies of the major parties.

Those who felt cheated by the open economy and who bore the scars of the recent recession felt disenfranchised but the political system provided little opportunity for them to voice their discontent. The major parties had shrunk in membership and vitality; local branches were largely excluded from the determination of policy or choice of parliamentary candidates, who were now drawn from the ranks of publicly funded operatives working inside politicians' offices. As older loyalties faded, the Liberal and Labor parties relied increasingly on the professional expertise of pollsters and media consultants to compete for the middle ground. They appealed to the voters as consumers rather than citizens. With her hurt and angry defiance of neoliberal orthodoxy, Pauline Hanson challenged this cartel.

Her sway became apparent in elections for the State of Queensland in June 1998. One Nation candidates won 23 per cent of the vote, pushing the Liberals into third place and allowing Labor to gain office. Fear of a similar result in the imminent federal election opened divisions in the coalition. Although John Howard had begun criticising Hanson's views, he resisted Labor's proposal that the major parties direct their preferences away from the One Nation Party until the disastrous outcome for the coalition in the Queensland election forced his hand. In the event, Hanson ran a poor federal campaign and attracted just 10 per cent of the national vote. Even so, nearly one million Australians endorsed her views.

Howard was therefore under pressure during the election in October 1998. It was a mark of his leadership that he made tax reform the centrepiece of his campaign with an undertaking to introduce a consumption tax. Labor's new leader was Kim Beazley, a large and amiable man widely admired for his decency at a time when the voters appeared weary of confrontation. Howard again took the front foot by suggesting that his opponent lacked the 'ticker' to make tough decisions. The contest was tight and a narrow majority of voters indicated a preference for Labor, but the distribution of electorates favoured the coalition and it was returned with a safe parliamentary majority.

The prime minister was also painting out his predecessor's 'big picture'. A prominent motif in Keating's canvas was a fully independent Australian republic. Howard tried to neutralise the issue at the 1996 election with an undertaking that he would provide an opportunity for the country to decide. Even though he took office as a monarchist, a significant section of his party and even his ministry favoured a republic. The momentum seemed unstoppable and would require all of his political skills to halt.

He was able to work on two weaknesses in the republican cause. The first was the composition of the organisation that promoted it, which was dominated by celebrities – their enthusiastic advocacy could be dismissed as an example of the estrangement of the élites from the practical concerns of the battlers. The second weakness was the decision of this organisation to campaign for a minimal republic – to simply replace the monarch by a president and tidy up some consequential sections of the existing constitution. To do more than this, to rethink the principles of responsible government or challenge the aggrandisement of the executive branch at the expense of the legislature, would in their judgement risk scaring the citizenry. Their chief argument was no more than an appeal to national prejudice: Australia should not have a foreigner as its head of state. Since an Australian governor-general already exercised those functions, this allowed monarchists to divert the republican debate into an arcane argument over constitutional law.

Howard redeemed his undertaking by creating a Constitutional Convention. Half its delegates were elected and half appointed, a remarkable retreat from the elected Federal Convention that had devised the Commonwealth a hundred years earlier. Howard welcomed them all to Canberra in the new year as 'a wonderfully diverse group of Australians', and after two weeks of wrangling they narrowly adopted the republican movement's proposal for a president elected by a two-thirds majority of a joint sitting of the Federal parliament. The prime minister had not finished: he announced that he would draft a new preamble to the Constitution to be considered along with the new procedure for choosing the head of state. Drawing on the assistance of a like-minded poet, he produced a platitudinous statement that invoked mateship, refused to recognise Aboriginal Australians' prior occupancy of the land and took a gratuitous swipe at political correctness. Both the preamble and the minimal model were put to a referendum in November 1999, and both were rejected.

There was a further twist in this failure to change the system of government. On coming to office in 1996, Howard inherited a governor-general, who had been appointed in the previous year after service on the High Court, Sir William Deane. A mild man of compassion and integrity, Deane gave presence to public ceremonies and outback gatherings. He also gave offence to conservatives with the speeches he delivered on such occasions expressing concern and sympathy for the homeless, the unemployed, and the outcast. 'The ultimate test of our worth as a truly democratic nation', he declared, 'is how we treat the most disadvantaged and vulnerable of our citizens'.

Following the expiry of Deane's term of office in 2001, the prime minister took care to appoint more amenable successors. The first was an Anglican archbishop, a choice that strained the Australian separation of church and state and led to the governor-general's resignation after criticism of his earlier handling of sex-abuse cases in the church. The next was a retired military officer, who kept out of trouble but also seemed conspicuously absent from the ceremonial occasions where the governor-general would once have represented the nation. On visits of foreign dignitaries, at commemorations of national events and even at state funerals, it was the prime minister who performed this role. That an avowed monarchist should take on the trappings of a president only emphasised the failure of the republicans.

***

During its first term in office the Howard government sought to expunge Keating's legacy at home and abroad. It was particularly critical of Labor's attempt to forge closer relations in the region and decried the suggestion that Australia's destiny lay in Asia, preferring to emphasise the distinctive character of Australian culture and traditions. The storm surrounding Pauline Hanson threatened to blow this realignment of foreign policy off course, for her strident denunciation of Asian immigrants made front-page news in their countries of origin and seemed to revive the spectre of White Australia. The government was forced to despatch the minister for foreign affairs on a tour of Asia to reassure Australia's neighbours that she did not speak for her compatriots.

The government took little interest in other regional groupings – Howard attended just half the meetings of the South Pacific Forum – and was insensitive to the growing difficulties of Papua New Guinea and smaller Pacific Island states. It eschewed the idea of Australia as a 'good international citizen', reiterating instead a 'hard-headed' pursuit of the national interest. While supportive of continued trade liberalisation through the new World Trade Organization, Australia refused to accept the greenhouse gas emission targets set at the Kyoto conference on global warming in 1997, and was critical of United Nations forums. Where Labor had taken a multilateral approach to international affairs, the coalition stressed bilateralism and national sovereignty.

The Asian economic crisis of 1997 forced a more active engagement. Australia was drawn into the rescue packages organised by the International Monetary Fund and supported the strict conditions the IMF attached to financial assistance. For Indonesia, those conditions included the removal of food subsidies and price controls. In 1995 just 11 per cent of its population had been living in poverty; by 1998 nearly half were suffering hardship and mounting unrest forced the resignation of President Suharto in May of that year. His successor was powerless to halt communal violence and the brutal repression of separatist movements by the armed forces, including in East Timor. The western half of this island had been a Dutch possession and was incorporated into Indonesia when the republic was formed at the end of the Second World War, but the eastern half had been Portuguese until acquired by force in 1975. Greater autonomy for the province was a condition of IMF aid, but the prospect of independence intensified the intimidation of the population by local militias armed by the Indonesian military. In September 1999 an international force of 10,000 under the authority of the United Nations landed to restore order; Australia provided the commander and the majority of the force.

There was widespread support for the action, and many Australians volunteered to help rebuild the shattered new state. The government was criticised for not acting sooner, but had been fearful of the consequences of pressing the beleaguered Indonesian government harder, and the Labor Party could hardly claim a position of moral superiority after its earlier handling of the issue. Howard was disappointed that the United States did not lend greater assistance, but blundered badly when he allowed himself to be cast as the region's 'deputy sheriff'. Dr Mahathir of Malaysia seized on that description to bolt the door that shut Australia out of ASEAN, now enlarged to include the northern Asian powers, China, Japan and South Korea. Howard insisted after Timor that 'we have stopped worrying about whether we are Asian, in Asia, enmeshed in Asia or part of a mythical East-Asian hemisphere', and simply 'got on with the job of being ourselves in the region'.

The lingering Indonesian resentment had a further consequence. Its network of islands lay across the sea-route that led from the Asian mainland to the north coast of Australia, and, in the closing decades of the twentieth century, new groups were tracing the journey made by the original Australians down the archipelago. Violent conflict in the Middle East and Afghanistan brought a wave of asylum-seekers in the late 1990s, and Indonesia would not help. Rather than deterring their movement, it allowed entrepreneurs to load them on to dilapidated boats and take them on to Australian territory. The numbers were small – 3300 in 1999, 2900 in 2000 – but the government regarded them as 'queue-jumpers' and treated 'people-smuggling' as a threat to Australian sovereignty and security. A solution required international co-operation, but Australia was increasingly at loggerheads with the agencies of the United Nations over domestic human rights as well as refugees. In 2000 the government announced that it would adopt 'a more economical and selective approach' to requests for information from the United Nations and 'a more robust and strategic approach to Australia's interaction with the treaty system'.

The Howard government pressed on during its second term with the economic measures it had foreshadowed: tax reform, full sale of Telstra, further deregulation of industrial relations, and further conditions on welfare beneficiaries. The government's lack of a majority in the Senate necessitated lengthy negotiations with the small parties and independent senators, leading to substantial compromises. The tax on goods and services went ahead, with exemptions and compensation. The sale of Telstra was restricted to just a further slice, leaving half in public hands. Tony Abbott, the belligerent new minister for employment services, made little progress in his attempt to change legislation that gave protection against unfair dismissal but did tighten eligibility for unemployment benefits, admonishing job-seekers not to be 'snobbish'.

The implementation of the new Goods and Services tax in 2000 coincided with a fall in the value of the Australian dollar (it dropped below 50 US cents early in the following year). Both were blamed for a rise in the cost of petrol, which ignited a more general dissatisfaction. Australia was still running a large deficit in the current account, still accumulating foreign debt. It still relied on commodity exports, lagged in the new technology industries and, in the absence of any internationally recognised brands, its producers were restricted to the lower levels of the global supply chain. When the two leading mining companies, BHP and Conzinc Riotinto, merged with international companies and Rio Tinto shifted its headquarters to London, there was renewed talk of Australia becoming a branch-office economy. With an election due at the end of 2001, the president of the Liberal Party warned his colleagues that the government was perceived as 'mean, tricky, out of touch and not listening'.

Labor still struggled to present a persuasive alternative, and then found itself fighting a khaki election. The destruction of the World Trade Center on 11 September 2001 brought Bush's war on terror, and Howard's immediate support for the invasion of Afghanistan. A fortnight earlier Australia had been caught up in its own military drama when a Norwegian container vessel, the *Tampa*, came to the rescue of a drifting Indonesian fishing vessel loaded with 433 passengers, mostly Afghans. The captain of the *Tampa* made for Christmas Island, an Australian territory to the south of Java, but the Australian government ordered him not to land. With the distressed passengers outnumbering his crew by sixteen to one, the captain dropped anchor offshore. A detachment of Australia's élite SAS force seized control of the *Tampa*. Some of the asylum-seekers were taken by New Zealand, most were dispatched to a specially constructed internment centre on the tiny island of Nauru, and some went later to another camp on the Papua New Guinean territory of Manus Island. This was the Pacific Solution, a chilling title that the prime minister apparently devised without any awareness that Hitler had proclaimed a solution to his own problem of unwanted people.

The *Tampa* crisis made headlines around the world. It brought forthright criticism from Norway, argument with the secretary-general of the United Nations, and refusal by the Indonesian president to accept the prime minister's phone calls. The Pacific Solution was directed from his office, facilitated by special legislation that excised Christmas Island from Australia's immigration zone and left Canberra to operate with almost complete freedom from scrutiny by the courts. These asylum-seekers were held in strict seclusion. The press secretary to the minister for defence issued an instruction to the department that no 'personalising or humanising images' of them were to be permitted.

The crisis also turned the election into a debate on border control. Labor initially refused to support the special legislation, then capitulated and lost both ways. The government capitalised on its advantage with claims that another boatload of illegal immigrants had thrown children overboard when approached by a naval vessel. After the claim was challenged, the minister for defence insisted it was an 'absolute fact' and a photograph was released showing men, women and children struggling in the water. The photograph, it emerged following the election, had been taken after an Australian naval vessel towed the crippled boat until it sank.

The fears and uncertainties created by the events of 11 September fed into the issue of border control. The prime minister was in Washington for the fiftieth anniversary of the ANZUS treaty when two airliners crashed into New York's World Trade Center, and he was due to visit the Pentagon on the same day it came under attack. He was quick to affirm Australia's support for the war on terror and ready to link it to illegal immigration. 'You don't know whether they do have terrorist links or not', the prime minister said of the asylum-seekers shortly before polling day. Full-page newspaper advertisements appeared on the morning of the election showing John Howard with his fists clenched and the declaration 'We decide who comes to this country'. He was returned to office with a slightly increased majority.

The war on terror began with a strike on Afghanistan and broadened after President Bush denounced the 'axis of evil' in his State of the Union address at the beginning of 2002. Howard supported the new American doctrine of pre-emptive defence, and ignored regional sensitivities when he announced at the end of the year that Australia also would consider sending troops to a neighbouring country to strike at terrorist cells if they threatened homeland security. By then a terrorist cell bombed tourists in a nightclub on the Indonesian island of Bali, and eighty-eight Australians were among the 200 casualties.

10.2 'The fact is the children were thrown in the water', insisted the minister for defence on the eve of the 2001 election. The photograph shows men, women and children struggling in the water but it was taken more than a day after the Australian navy vessel *HMAS Adelaide* identified SIEV (Suspected Illegal Entry Vessel) 04, and the photograph makes it clear that the boat was already sinking. (Australian Government Department of Defence)

Australia joined the United States and Britain in the operation to disarm Iraq, and a contingent of Australian forces participated in the three-week war that toppled Saddam Hussein in March 2003. 'America has no better friend anywhere in the world than Australia', Howard declared when he addressed the United States Congress in the previous year. The public was by no means persuaded that this 'coalition of the willing' should override the United Nations, but anti-war protest dropped away after the conquest of Iraq. The subsequent inability to justify the *casus belli* with discovery of weapons of mass destruction was far less contentious in Australia than in the United States and Britain because it was apparent that this country had followed behind them. The violent resistance to the military occupation of Iraq was less damaging to the Australian government because Howard resisted American pressure to make a greater contribution.

***

The war on terror reinforced the prime minister's standing as the custodian of national security and gave him a patriotic platform to farewell military contingents leaving for overseas service, then express the country's gratitude on their return. With Australians once more bearing arms in the Middle East, he put renewed emphasis on the country's baptism in blood there ninety years earlier. Howard's father and grandfather had both served in the First World War – though on the Western front rather than at Gallipoli – and he had a strong attachment to the Anzac legend. In public addresses he placed particular emphasis on the qualities that Australians who volunteered for service evinced, their independence, self-reliance and loyalty to mates. His patriotism gained a deeper foothold.

After a third electoral victory he was also less troubled by ministerial mishaps, more adept in repairing problems in troublesome policy areas. In contrast to his more reckless colleagues, the prime minister gave few hostages to fortune. In statements on the children overboard incident, for example, he was careful to add the qualification that 'he had been informed they were thrown overboard'. The lines of communication correcting this misinformation led clearly to the prime minister's office, yet seemingly did not reach him. One

10.3   John Howard at the National Press Club on the eve of the 2001 election, adamant that 'We decide who comes to this country'. (Loui Seselja, National Library of Australia, an23381704)

political commentator noted Howard's skill in using the political 'dog whistle', pitching a message to one group of voters that other voters could not hear.

Howard was not the only political leader to flourish in an era of political disenchantment. Those State premiers who revived the robust style of a Henry Bolte or a Charles Court seldom lasted long. Jeffrey Kennett swept into office in 1992 with the announcement that he was 'reopening Victoria for business' and embarked on sweeping changes, but the electors tired of his ebullience after two terms. Bob Carr, the Labor premier of New South Wales from 1995 to 2005, was a leader in the new mould, cautious, reflective, assiduous in his attention to the middle ground. Facing a media backlash on law and order in 2001, he replaced his police minister and police commissioner, and introduced mandatory sentencing. 'Howls from the left (civil libertarians) and the right (an aggrieved State Opposition)', he noted with satisfaction in his diary. Carr retired as dissatisfaction mounted with his government's management of health, education and transport services. So too Peter Beattie, his Queensland counterpart from 1998 to 2007, rode out repeated failures by pre-empting critics in condemnation of the scapegoats.

By the early years of the new century Labor governed all the States and territories, and this political alignment placed further strain on the unwieldy federal system. The Commonwealth government, which held the purse-strings, sought greater control over the way the States conducted their affairs. It was impatient with the slow pace of change achieved by negotiation in the Council of Australian Governments established by Labor in 1992, and prepared to act unilaterally in health, education and other areas of State responsibility. The result was an inefficient pattern of duplication and blame shifting.

Social commentators warned of a 'growing distrust of and disillusionment with governments and governance' that threatened a 'crisis of cynicism'. They discerned a retreat from commitment to the public good and suggested that the widening gulf between the people and their representatives threatened the legitimacy of political institutions. Sceptical academics have noted that political disengagement is not new, nor is it peculiar to this country. They point out that the fall in trust of politicians is matched by a decline of confidence in lawyers, doctors and other professions. But the role of government is so omnipresent in Australian history that the loss is felt keenly.

No one tapped the mood of resentment more profitably than Alan Jones, a prominent radio broadcaster. The large audience of this self-declared champion of 'struggle street' gave him remarkable influence. Howard was happy to appear on Jones's breakfast programme, as it allowed him to put forward his views unfiltered by journalists, though such was the volume of unsolicited advice the prime minister received from his host that a member of his office was assigned to keep up with Jones' demands. 'Get John Howard on the phone', Jones would instruct his own staff, 'and remind him who voted for him'. Other less compliant politicians fell victim to his crusades.

In 1999 Jones was accused of receiving payments from companies in return for making favourable comments about their products, and the Australian Broadcasting Authority ordered him to disclose these arrangements. The head of the authority had to stand down after appearing on radio to promote the monarchist cause in the lead-up to the 1999 referendum on the republic. It was subsequently revealed that he had sent a stream of admiring letters to Jones, and he publicly defended Jones when the broadcaster publicised violent confrontations in the summer of 2005 between youths of Lebanese origins and opponents flying the Australian flag.

These affrays at the seaside suburb of Cronulla were as much a product of the younger generation's mobile phones as the older one's talk-back radio programmes: more than 270,000 text messages were sent calling for a show of strength on the beach, and Jones achieved his purpose by simply reading one of them on air. With a quarter of the Australian population now foreign-born, the Cronulla riot seemed to bear out the earlier warnings of racial conflict. In fact Cronulla was a one-off. Hostility between local lifesavers and visitors from the western suburbs was inflamed by religious tensions (there was a strong Islamic concentration in western Sydney) and sexual assaults. It was Jones who cast the brawls in racial terms with his statement that 'we don't have Anglo-Saxon kids out there raping women in Western Sydney'. The prime minister insisted it was simply mob violence. He had dropped his earlier rejection of multiculturalism as immigration rose once more, reaching a new high of 180,000 arrivals in 2007. Asked why he had changed, he replied simply, 'You have to go with the flow'.

By this time John Howard had the measure of senior Labor figures. The party therefore turned at the end of 2003 to a new leader from a younger generation. Mark Latham was a representative of Sydney's west, attuned to the concerns of those juggling work and family responsibilities in the mortgage belt. He was forceful, articulate and above all he brought refreshing novelty to an electorate weary of the choices on offer – that he was also headstrong and volatile took longer to become apparent. Latham assumed an immediate lead in opinion polls, and Howard spent much of the following year cutting it and him down. Assisted by the buoyant economy and surge in revenue, the government spent freely: new family payments and grants to home-buyers, along with the existing subsidies for private health insurance and assistance to private schools, swelled the expenditure on middle-class welfare. Even so, Howard made much of his government's credentials as an economic manager and claimed Labor could not be trusted to keep the interest rate low. Finally, he pounced on Latham's undertaking that a Labor government would return Australian troops from Iraq. This tactic was effective not so much because voters felt confidence in that military commitment, but because Latham's manifest inability to back his pledge with a plausible foreign policy weakened his credibility.

Howard won the election in October 2004, his fourth and probably most convincing victory. Labor suffered a decline in its vote, while the Coalition improved its majority in the House of Representatives and for the first time in more than two decades achieved a majority in the Senate. When the new senators took their seats in the middle of the next year, the government controlled both houses of the parliament and was able to secure passage of legislation that had been blocked or amended in the upper house.

He whom the gods wish to destroy they first give a Senate majority. John Howard probably sensed the danger of tempting fate when he warned his exultant colleagues against hubris. Either they lacked familiarity with the classics or else weren't listening, for senior ministers were quick to flaunt their supremacy. Holding absolute legislative power, they no longer needed to negotiate more contentious measures and soon forgot how to justify them. Howard himself was ill-served by flattery of his political skills and more inclined to indulge himself in flights of triumphalism. During his third term he had rejoiced in Australia's liberation from a surfeit of critical introspection: 'As a nation we're over that sort of identity stuff'. In his fourth term he set about prescribing the national identity in a needlessly provocative fashion.

In 1999 the government had tilted school funding to the private sector; now it intensified an ideological assault on the public sector by accusing government schools of pursuing educational progressivism and neglecting values. In 2004 the Commonwealth made its support for government schools conditional on a flag-raising ceremony, and in 2006 it introduced school chaplains. In addition, the government provided financial support to fundamentalists offering religious instruction in these public schools.

This intrusion would have confounded earlier generations of Australians, for whom the separation of church and state was a necessary consequence of denominational division. The Catholic minority, which had established its own faith-based schools, sought government assistance. The Protestant majority, which opposed it, insisted that public schools must be secular. Now the older Protestant churches were dwindling, giving way to the charismatic faith of Pentecostalism, with an emphasis on conversion, witness and empowerment, while the conservative Cardinal Pell was imposing his authority on the Catholic Church. An unlikely ecumenism asserted the demands of a religious minority against the secular conventions of the non-observant majority. Unlike the United States, however, fundamentalism had shallow roots in Australia and the Howard government's conflation of educational values with religious doctrine was a provocation.

Howard also imposed another doctrinal creed when he initiated a school curriculum in Australian history that would again be forced on the State-run government schools by a threat to withhold Commonwealth assistance. With similar intent he introduced a test for those migrants seeking citizenship, one designed to inculcate patriotic values by ensuring familiarity with such essential knowledge as the batting feats of the country's most successful cricketer, Sir Donald Bradman. All these indulgences ignored voters who expected the government to attend to their practical needs and Howard's long-serving deputy, Peter Costello (who attended meetings of a Pentecostal megachurch) displayed increasing impatience for the prime minister to fulfil an undertaking to pass over the leadership. By the time the Coalition realised its ideological zeal had estranged the electorate, it was too late.

The government used its parliamentary majority to complete the privatisation of Telstra, strengthen anti-terrorism measures, impose further conditions on welfare recipients and undertake a comprehensive reform of industrial relations. The last of these measures was by far the most contentious. The power to determine a minimum wage was removed from the independent Industrial Relations Commission, along with its role of amending awards and approving agreements, which were now circumscribed by restrictions on collective bargaining. Preference was given to individual contracts that dispensed with all but the most basic award conditions, while protection against unfair dismissal was abolished for companies employing fewer than 100 workers. All this was encompassed in an elaborate statute of 762 pages entitled *WorkChoices* and hailed as a final deregulation of the labour market, even though it was replete with prohibitions and penalties.

The government claimed that the new regime would encourage employers to take on new workers, but some immediately took the opportunity to dismiss existing ones and invite them to apply for reinstatement at lower pay. The new law was aimed particularly at an old adversary, the trade unions, and in an odd inversion of class terminology the government directed its criticism at 'union bosses'. Union coverage of the workforce was down to 22 per cent, but the prime minister was clearly unprepared for the determined response of the Australian Council of Trade Unions. Using marches and rallies, it launched a campaign for 'Your Rights at Work'. In television advertisements it dramatised the predicament of casual and part-time workers stripped of protection, and of breadwinners made to forego their entitlements. Howard had won four elections on the basis of economic security and now seemed to remove it. *WorkChoices* was a time-bomb ticking in the electorate.

The expanded security powers also proved troublesome. For some time the government had warned of the threat of home-grown terrorism and it made a particular example of an Australian held by the United States. David Hicks was a troubled youth who converted to Islam and was captured in Afghanistan at the end of 2001. After interrogation he was transported to Guantanamo Bay, where he was held in solitary confinement and subjected again to what the White House described as enhanced interrogation techniques. As public opinion turned against this denial of justice, David Hicks was persuaded to plead guilty to lesser charges and repatriated in May 2007 to serve out a prison sentence on condition that he not speak to the media until after the imminent federal election. Two months later the Australian Federal Police arrested an Indian doctor, Mohamed Haneef, who worked in a Queensland hospital. He was erroneously accused of assisting a terrorist cell that had bombed the Glasgow airport, and when released on bail was taken back into detention by the minister for immigration.

The prosecution quickly collapsed, and a court ordered the restoration of Haneef's visa.

Even more embarrassing was the revelation that Australia had rendered substantial assistance to Saddam Hussein. As the occupying forces searched in vain for evidence of weapons of mass destruction after the fall of Baghdad in 2003, they found documents showing that the Australian Wheat Board had violated the sanctions imposed by the United Nations to prevent Iraq from rearming. The board had legitimately sold large quantities of wheat to Iraq between 1999 and 2003 under the 'oil-for-food' programme, but the contracts were loaded with additional charges that were then funnelled back to the Iraqi government. The Wheat Board was a fiefdom of the National Party, and its culpability was apparent, but what about the government that approved these contracts? A documentary trail led to senior ministers, but apparently stopped short of them. In his testimony to the commission the trade minister, who was leader of the National Party, took refuge in ignorance and amnesia: more than twenty times he pleaded 'I don't know' or 'I have no recollection'. The prime minister and the minister for foreign affairs were even less forthcoming.

Throughout the deliberations of the commission, the shadow minister for foreign affairs provided a constant commentary on the failure of accountability. This was Kevin Rudd, a former diplomat and head of the public service in his home State of Queensland who entered federal politics in 1998. Rudd's self-promotion did not endear him to colleagues in the Labor Party, but he was articulate, urbane and relentless in his use of the media. At the end of 2006 Rudd joined forces with an equally formidable member of the Labor left, Julia Gillard, to capture the leadership.

The times no longer suited John Howard. Economic liberalism and social conservatism, never a stable combination, were tugging in different directions. As Hanson had demonstrated, many social conservatives were opposed to an open economy: those doing it hard in rural Australia or as retirees expected government support. Many who relied on such essential human services as health, education and aged care found them less accessible as they were turned over to commercial providers. Conversely, those professionals who flourished in the burgeoning service industries, especially finance,

were comfortable with change. Their skills gave them the opportunity to work abroad, their incomes allowed foreign travel and
a cosmopolitan lifestyle. They were untroubled by displays of
difference – so that Sydney's annual Gay and Lesbian Mardi
Gras was the largest festival of its kind in the world – and attuned
to progressive social movements.

One such movement, environmentalism, gained fresh impetus in
the early years of the new century as the result of climate change.
Australia had sided with the United States in refusing to ratify the
Kyoto Protocol on greenhouse gas emissions, but American voters
turned away from the likeminded Republican administration in
the Congressional elections of 2006, and Al Gore's documentary
An Inconvenient Truth caught the growing concern with global
warming. Howard scoffed at its criticism of the two environmental
pariah countries – 'I don't take policy advice from films' – but it was
a different matter when Rupert Murdoch announced he too believed
in climate change. The prime minister did take policy advice from
the Murdoch press, so he conceded the threat was real and began to
search for a middle way that would bring greenhouse gas reduction
while protecting the resource sector. Most Australians needed no
persuasion that the climate was changing, in part because of a
common confusion of global warming with the long-lasting drought
that by this time imposed severe restrictions on water use. Hence
in January 2007 the federal government sought to assume control
of the river-system in southeast Australia, but State resistance
frustrated this initiative.

Howard again tried to gain momentum following the release
in June 2007 of a report into abuse of Aboriginal children in the
Northern Territory. Declaring this to be a national emergency,
the government sent in soldiers, police and medical teams to inspect
all children for signs of abuse. Few questioned the need to protect
the health and welfare of Indigenous families, but the intervention
was accompanied by far-reaching changes that overrode self-
management, banned the consumption of alcohol and withheld
half of welfare payments to ensure they were spent on the needs of
children. After eleven years of 'practical reconciliation', this was a
remarkable confession of failure, as the prime minister belatedly
admitted when he said he had found Aboriginal issues 'a challenge'

and finally committed himself to constitutional recognition of Indigenous Australians as 'the first inhabitants of this country'.

The pre-election budget provided no relief for the government. That federal taxation had risen from 22.8 per cent of gross domestic product when Howard took office to 24.6 per cent by 2007 undermined his claims to be an economic liberal. Once again the government used the surplus created by the commodities boom to direct new benefits to electorally sensitive interest groups. There was a conspicuous failure to deal with capacity constraints in transport and communication that clogged the roads, left long lines of ships waiting at the congested ports and slowed the adoption of digital technology. The under-investment in health, education and research at a time of unprecedented prosperity was striking.

Characteristically, Kevin Rudd undertook to match the tax cuts while improving infrastructure and services. By this time he had found a phrase to appeal to voters – 'working families'. It had emerged from research that found most Australians thought the economy was prospering but personally felt no better off, and was used by the Australian Council of Trade Unions during its campaign against *WorkChoices*. Rudd adopted the term and used it so often that journalists who covered the election campaign at the end of 2007 kept tallies to keep from falling asleep.

***

Howard lost the 2007 election as comprehensively as Keating had done in 1996. A substantial swing brought heavy losses to the Coalition and a substantial majority to the Labor Party. The prime minister suffered the rare indignity of losing his own seat, and several of his senior colleagues, including Costello, indicated they would retire from politics. Kevin Rudd confirmed the change of national mood upon taking office by ratifying the Kyoto Protocol, closing the overseas internment camps to end the Pacific Solution, and making an official apology to the Stolen Generations.

These signals were received with relief and a strong measure of support. In contrast to the previous prime minister who had run out of ideas, the new one was full of them. An outsider who was closer to the universities than the unions and married to a rich business-woman, he bypassed the Labor caucus to choose his own ministry. Adept in the new media and attuned to the concerns of younger voters, he was 'a brand in his own right'. The new times also seemed to suit him; the rapid onset of a global financial crisis that Australia, with its low level of public debt, was able to ride out with a stimulus programme of public spending allowed him to pronounce the obsequies for neoliberalism.

Australia was less exposed to the financial crisis than the United States. Its regulatory authority kept a closer watch on the banks, and its housing sector was not so vulnerable because borrowers could not abandon their mortgages. Even so, a wave of overseas bank failures and the freezing of international liquidity threatened to drag Australia into recession. The advice of the Treasury was to ward off that threat by stimulating consumer confidence, and to 'go early, go hard and go households'. This the government did by injecting $60 billion into the economy in cash payments along with major projects of school buildings, public housing and home insulation. The stimulus succeeded: Australia suffered a slight contraction in the last quarter of 2008 before growth resumed, while the unemployment rose to 5.8 per cent before falling back. The cost was a substantial and persistent budget deficit that left little room for new initiatives, especially after the government commenced construction of a national broadband network in 2009 at a public cost estimated to be $30 billion.

Both Rudd and his minister for education, Gillard, were determined to restore support for schools and universities (where Australia's public expenditure lagged most advanced countries) and improve educational outcomes (where international comparisons again showed the country falling behind). They increased university provision and established a new authority to prepare a better school curriculum. But Gillard, a scholarship girl, was wedded to rote testing of numeracy and literacy as a form of evaluation that estranged many teachers. Many Australians felt that if just a fraction of the $15 billion that went to school buildings had gone to lifting the teaching profession, it would have been better spent. Moreover, the rushed nature of the construction projects brought complaints, while the home insulation programme compromised occupational safety standards and led to several deaths.

10.4   Kevin Rudd won the leadership of the Australian Labor Party in 2006, with Julia Gillard as his deputy. They appear here at their first press conference and a year later they turned the Howard government out of office with a decisive electoral victory. (Wikimedia Commons, Adam Carr, 2006)

In all three of the areas where it undertook to do better than the previous government – Indigenous policy, refugees and climate change – the Rudd government struggled. As was now the habit in Indigenous affairs, it deplored the failure of previous attempts and proclaimed a new solution that would be practical, one based on evidence rather than ideology. It therefore reviewed the Northern Territory 'emergency response', noted the mixed results and determined to continue intervention in a non-discriminatory manner. It restored a representative Indigenous body but withheld control over service provision. That was undertaken by Commonwealth departments in conjunction with their State counterparts by using a set of performance indicators for health, education, employment and other measures under a rubric of 'Closing the Gap'. The assumption here was that Indigenous Australians constituted a population whose disadvantages were to be remedied by making good the deficiencies in their economic and social condition, rather than as peoples with a distinctive identity, heritage and entitlements.

The ground was shifting as a new spokesman challenged an older generation of Indigenous leaders. Noel Pearson, who grew up on the Lutheran mission of Hope Vale in the Cape York Peninsula of Far North Queensland, emerged in the 1990s as a remarkably eloquent advocate for his people. He revered Gough Whitlam, admired Paul Keating and was a vitriolic critic of the conservative campaign against land rights. But by 2007 he had come to despair at the impasse in Indigenous affairs and reached out to Howard in the belief that only a conservative could resolve it. Pearson supported the intervention in the Northern Territory, for he judged that 'passive welfare' was destroying Aboriginal communities in a cycle of alcohol-fuelled violence and family breakdown. He believed that 'white guilt' resulted in Aboriginal victimhood and called for 'rational incentives' that would allow Aboriginals to accept responsibility for their lives and participate in the 'real economy'. These arguments, and Pearson's criticism of progressives as false friends of Indigenous interests, were taken up by Rupert Murdoch's national broadsheet and exerted a growing influence.

In dealing with asylum-seekers the Rudd government sought a more humane approach. It ended offshore processing at Nauru and Manus Island, undertook to expedite the process of determining refugee status and improved the conditions of detention. The goal was to end the punitive character of the previous regime, but as the number of new arrivals rose sharply from 2009 they were confined on an overcrowded facility on the Australian territory of Christmas Island. Rudd insisted they would not be allowed on the mainland.

His handling of climate change was even more ignominious. This, he insisted, was 'the great moral challenge of our generation'. After receiving a comprehensive report from the economist Ross Garnaut, Rudd committed the government at the end of 2008 to reduce greenhouse emissions by means of a trading scheme in carbon permits. The plan fell short of the reductions Garnaut recommended and offered substantial compensation to large emitters. It thus fell between two stools, satisfying neither the Greens nor business, and by this time the Murdoch press had reverted to climate change denial. With support faltering, Rudd delayed implementation and, when the climate change conference at Copenhagen at the end of 2009 failed to agree on binding reductions, lost his nerve.

By then he was under siege from the mining industry. Following a similarly comprehensive review of tax reform, this one undertaken by the head of Treasury, the government plucked out a scheme to levy a new tax on the mineral and energy sector. Announced abruptly in 2010 as the resource boom drove up the revenue of the sector to unprecedented heights, the measure was intended in part to ease the strains on a two-speed economy.

The price of iron ore, under US$30 per ton in 2005, climbed above US$150 during the first half of 2010. In the Pilbara region of Western Australia mechanised shovels with a capacity of more than 200 tons were filling gigantic trucks with red dirt that was passed through crushers and screeners, then loaded onto trains of 2.5 kilometres in length and hauled to ports where it was poured into ships of more than 100,000 tons in capacity. While the highly mechanised mining sector employed fewer than 200,000 workers and imported much of the machinery, its rapid growth and high earnings drove up wages and the Australian dollar, placing strain on

10.5   This open pit of the Sunrise Dam Gold Mine, 220 kilometres from Kalgoorlie, began operations in 1997 and reached a depth of 440 metres. Most of the miners fly in and fly out of the isolated mine village located in harsh and arid conditions. With underground operations the mine has produced 6 million ounces of gold. (David Dare Parker)

other export sectors such as agriculture, tourism and education, and threatening the viability of trade-exposed industries such as manufacturing.

The announcement of the new tax brought an advertising blitz by BHP and Rio Tinto. It excited a frenzy of protest from two rival magnates, Andrew Forrest and Gina Rinehart, who were both building their operations on borrowed funds. Forrest, who shared Noel Pearson's views on welfare dependency, enjoyed the support of the Rudd government for his efforts to promote Aboriginal employment. Rinehart, who inherited substantial mineral tenements from her father, Lang Hancock, also inherited his political views. The two richest Australians, they came together in a rally on the Perth esplanade, Rinehart wearing pearls and leading the crowd in a chant of 'Axe the tax'.

Rudd's mishandling of the carbon-trading scheme brought down the opposition leader. Malcolm Turnbull, who had previously led the republican movement and was a Liberal moderate, accepted the need for action on climate change. In the closing months of 2009, as coalition members hardened their opposition, his senior colleague Tony Abbott declared that the science was 'crap', and in December this former leader of the monarchist cause won the Liberal leadership from Turnbull.

The resource tax cost Kevin Rudd his own job. Stories of the unreasonable demands he placed on his staff were already circulating, but it came as a surprise to the Labor ministry that someone who had worked as a senior administrator could fail miserably in implementing the decisions in which he invested such moment. Despite his demands for 'detailed programmatic specificity', Cabinet ministers and departmental heads would be summoned to an early-morning crisis meeting and then left waiting outside his office while he attended to some other, more pressing concern. He took credit for appointing the country's first female Governor-General, Quentin Bryce, yet issued her with peremptory instructions. As the campaign by the miners reduced his public standing, Rudd seemed to shut down. When Julia Gillard announced a challenge in June 2010, he tested caucus numbers and resigned.

Hers was a poisoned chalice. Even though as deputy she had covered for his failures, she cut him down with no prior warning, and the fact that she had been so closely associated with every major decision of the Rudd ministry made it impossible to explain why she had done so. 'I believed that a good government was losing its way', was the best she could manage, but that did not stop an embittered Rudd from plotting revenge. Seeking legitimacy, she brought on an immediate election. A campaign slogan of startling banality, 'Moving Forward', did not help her cause, and persistent leaks to the press from Rudd robbed it of any momentum. Labor's vote fell to 38 per cent and even with preferences from the Greens party, which won 12 per cent, it fell short of a parliamentary majority. The undertakings Gillard gave to the Greens and independent members of the House of Representatives to form a minority government hobbled her policy options.

She had already negotiated modifications to the resource tax with the large mining companies, making concessions that sharply reduced its yield. This loss of revenue, together with new expenditure commitments on health, education and welfare, meant that undertakings to restore the budget to surplus receded into forward estimates. She had also ruled out a carbon tax, but her post-election agreement with the Greens bound the government to action on climate change. Hence the adoption of a carbon-pricing scheme that began with a fixed price on emissions and was to transition into a trading scheme. No amount of semantic distinction between taxing, pricing and trading could rebut the accusations of dishonesty. And the retreat on refugee policy brought similar recriminations. As the number of new arrivals mounted and the opposition bayed for stronger measures, the government established new Australian detention centres and soon it was seeking a return to offshore processing. After East Timor declined to co-operate and the High Court ruled out an agreement with Malaysia, asylum-seekers were once more incarcerated on Nauru and Manus Island.

Australia's first female leader, Julia Gillard was subjected to unprecedented personal abuse. Her clothing and body shape, her childlessness and lack of domesticity – all were grist to the mill. Alan Jones referred to her as 'Ju-liar' and following the death of her father said he had died of shame. 'Women are destroying the joint', Jones stated, and proposed that she should be shoved into a chaff bag and dumped at sea. Tony Abbott appeared at a rally outside Parliament House against the carbon tax and stood before a placard that read 'Ditch the Witch'. After two years of such treatment, she let fly when Abbott accused her of ignoring a sexist email sent by a Liberal parliamentarian who defected to support the government. Her rejoinder, beginning with the line 'I will not be lectured about sexism and misogyny by this man', was electrifying, but it was a rare departure from the gratingly demotic deliberation of her prepared speeches.

With a hostile press and obstinately low opinion polls, there was unrest in the Labor ranks. Rudd launched a premature challenge in February 2012 and was soundly defeated, but he continued to plot. Abbott as leader of the opposition was relentlessly negative. A university boxing champion who still drove himself in endurance events, he gave no quarter. A former seminarian, he framed his criticism in terms of moral absolutes: hence the repeated claim that Gillard's was a bad government and his widely reported statement that the prime minister 'should make an honest woman of herself'. It was a measure of Labor's desperation that in June 2013 it decided, by a narrow majority, to turn back to Rudd. He made many new promises but was powerless to stem the tide. A general election in September of that year brought a substantial swing to the Coalition, while Labor's support fell to just a third of the electorate. The new government thus had a large majority in the House of Representatives, but it would rely on the votes of at least six of the eight cross-bench senators to secure the passage of legislation.

Three of these senators were elected as members of the Palmer United Party, an offshoot of a business magnate's extensive interests. Clive Palmer was one of the Queensland 'white-shoe brigade' who had backed Bjelke-Petersen and benefitted from his regime. A large, grandiloquent man (among the stories he told was how as a boy he sat on Chairman Mao's knee), he was used to getting his way. From real estate, Palmer moved into tourist resorts (the Australian golf association had to move its tournament when Palmer installed animatromic dinosaurs on the Coolum resort's course) and acquired extensive mining tenements. Prominent in the merged Liberal National Party of Queensland, he formed his own party after the

10.6   The Leader of the Opposition from 2009, Tony Abbott
was an ostentatious exerciser. Active in a local surf life saving
club, he instituted an annual 'Pollie Pedal' to raise funds for
charity and participated often in fun runs and triathlons. Many
noticed the contrast with the sedentary Kevin Rudd, but during
the 2013 election Abbott declared the campaign would be a
'budgie-smuggler free zone' and was duly elected to become
Australia's twenty-eighth prime minister. (*Herald Sun* © News
Limited)

premier of that State backed development of Gina Rinehart's coal
deposits at the expense of his own. There were other operators
who took advantage of the electoral system for upper houses to
set up their pitch – shooters and fishers, motoring enthusiasts and

Christian fundamentalists among them – but none with the effrontery and resources of Palmer.

Seldom has a new government so quickly lost its way. Abbott, a polarising figure, found it hard to make the transition from opposition to office and established royal commissions into the misdeeds of Gillard and the previous government. Australia was 'under new management', he declared, and 'once more open for business', but the business leader he appointed to conduct a commission of audit suggested that drastic changes were necessary. The Treasurer padded the budget deficit to justify his warning that the 'age of entitlement' was over, and that Australians must become lifters rather than leaners.

Abbott had given an emphatic assurance during the election that there would be no cuts to health, education or pensions. The government's first budget in May 2014 proposed a charge on medical consultations, a sharp reduction in government support for universities along with deregulation of student fees, early termination of the school funding the Gillard government had introduced, indexation of pensions and restrictions on unemployment benefits. There was a token levy on high income-earners, but a reduction of company tax and a generous scheme of parental leave that gave the greatest benefit to those earning the most. This was a budget that failed the fairness test, and many of the measures were blocked in the Senate.

The budget also made cuts to Indigenous programmes. Abbott was close to Noel Pearson and on taking office he transferred Indigenous affairs to his own department. He also replaced the representative body with an unrepresentative one headed by Warren Mundine, an Indigenous consultant who had previously worked for Andrew Forrest. The government persisted with Closing the Gap, and when the indicators showed no sign of doing so, Mundine said the task should be handed over to the private sector. Forrest, who had reviewed Indigenous policy for the Abbott government, called for 'seismic change' in place of the 'itsy bitsy approach' of the public sector.

The government did manage to abolish the carbon and mining taxes, and had greater success in its draconian changes to asylum policy. On coming to office the deputy chief of the army was appointed to take control of Operation Sovereign Borders. Henceforth the boats were turned back or, if necessary, their passengers were transferred to orange fibre-glass capsules and sent back. Incursions into Indonesian waters by Australian naval vessels caused diplomatic difficulties and protests by those interned on Manus Island brought heavy-handed response by Papua New Guinean police and troops. While the minister ceased regular briefings of the press, he was able to declare the country's borders were now secure.

By this time the investment phase of the mining boom was coming to an end, and a sharp fall in the price of minerals and energy slowed the economy. During 2014 the exchange rate of the Australian dollar also fell, but before that the high cost of local production terminated the car industry. Ford announced it would cease operations in May 2013; General Motors and Toyota were rebuffed in their requests for government support and announced their departure in December 2013 and February 2014. With these and other closures, unemployment rose and confidence faltered.

The government trailed badly in opinion polls and such was Abbott's personal unpopularity that he was asked not to appear during State elections in Victoria in November 2014 and Queensland in January 2015. Even so, first-term coalition governments were defeated in both States. The prime minister's habit of making what he described as 'captain's calls' brought coalition discontent to a head: he had reinstituted knighthood and damehood in 2014 and chose Australia Day 2015 to announce that Prince Philip, the ageing royal consort, was to be invested as a knight of Australia. Backbenchers brought on a challenge to his leadership, and in February 2015 a majority of them voted in favour of declaring the prime minister's position vacant. Since his ministers were required to support him, he survived this spill motion but with diminished authority.

Abbott was not alone in his sudden fall from grace. Over recent decades Australia has seen a merry-go-round of political leaders. They over-promise and under-deliver, comport themselves as celebrities and rapidly wear out their appeal. Some commentators see them as victims of the dark arts they employ: the trite slogans and sound-bytes that feed the voracious news cycle. They are no longer able to frame their message on newsprint, talkback radio and television, for the digital media conduct different conversations, and online social networks make every malcontent a pundit. It is also suggested that a binary party system can no longer accommodate the different concerns of a more diverse society; in the absence of popular support, they rely on public funding and private donations to compete for the spoils of office. Public policy is turned over to consultants who justify the demands of the interest groups that employ them, along with institutes of applied research endowed by magnates in a manner similar to medieval rulers' founding of monasteries. Politics has ceased to be a vocation; it is a career path that takes its practitioners into parliament and out to the corporate world as lobbyists for government favours. The disregard for politics and politicians is neither new nor unique to this country, but it is marked – there has been no successful change of policy on a contested issue of major import since the turn of the century.

***

Economists are not given to exuberance and Australian economists have habitually regarded the conduct of public policy with gloomy foreboding. Yet in 2013 one of them looked back on the country's remarkable success. His explanation of *Why Australia Prospered* was that it had made good decisions. The country's abundance of natural resources was not a sufficient reason – resource abundance elsewhere has often led to misallocation of resources and resource booms created a tension between population increase and improvement of per capita income. Australia prospered because of institutions that enabled it to capture the opportunities. There had been mistakes that reduced living standards, but there was a willingness to adopt new arrangements or adapt new ones to restore prosperity.

Between 1997 and 2015 the Australian population grew from 18.5 million to 23.7 million. Half the growth came from natural increase and half from migration, so that more than a quarter of all Australians were born overseas. Britain and New Zealand remain the principal countries of origin, but they are now followed by China and India, with Vietnam, the Philippines and Malaysia also contributing significant numbers. Three-quarters of the migrants who speak a language other than English live in New South Wales and Victoria, for Sydney and Melbourne are the magnets for these newcomers. Sydney's population approaches 5 million, Melbourne's 4.5 million. The resource boom has brought some reduction of the concentration in the southeast: Queensland now has one-fifth of the country's population and Western Australia one-tenth. The Indigenous population has reached 700,000, and more than half live in cities or nearby regional centres.

With 70 per cent of its population in the capital cities, Australia remains one of the most highly urbanised countries and 85 per cent live within 50 kilometres of the coast. As the cities have grown, they have also been reconfigured. Some people shut out of the housing market by rising city costs have moved to cheaper regional towns, while some economically secure retirees and families looking for a 'sea change' have decamped for picturesque coastal locations. Within the cities those on lower incomes are displaced by the rising living costs associated with gentrification to the outer suburbs, where housing is more affordable but a lack of services and the cost of commuting reduces options. Others have chosen to move out to a larger, more luxurious 'McMansion', built on the outskirts of cities. The average floor area of a new house has reached 243 square metres, an increase of 40 per cent since 1990, and these trophy homes are much larger with luxury kitchens, games and theatre rooms, and a bathroom for every bedroom.

The terrace-houses and cottages of the inner suburbs have also been enlarged by extensions that rise up behind their modest street facades. These are the habitat of urban professionals, with cafés and coffee shops on every corner of narrow streets that have become a maze of traffic restrictions and bicycle lanes. With urban consolidation comes high-rise apartments, which now make up half of residential construction. They have transformed the city centres and waterfront precincts into places of outdoor eating and drinking where nightfall only increases activity.

People live longer in more fluid relationships. An earlier way of life organised around the family home changed as a couple with

10.7   The city of Wyndham, on the western outskirts of
Melbourne, has doubled in size over the last decade to more
than 200,000 residents, yet the average household size is just
three. As the large garage suggests, most residents commute by
car, with public transport and other facilities lagging behind
the population growth. (*The Age*)

dependent children became the exception rather than the norm.
Children no longer walk to school; now they are driven and often
some distance in pursuit of an educational advantage. They no
longer play in the backyard or street since the one has shrunk and
the other is too hazardous; they spend after-school hours online and

those with more prosperous parents are more likely to be at a music lesson or hockey practice than making up a game. Time is scarce in such families since a successful career requires long hours at work and keeping the iPhone switched on at home.

The neighbourhood community has given way to communities of interest and lifestyle. Women's workforce participation is approaching parity with men's, and they have less time for local voluntary organisations. The extension of shopping and leisure activities into Sundays has displaced the church as a centre of activity. But just as the car increased mobility, so the internet enables people to come together across longer distances spanned by shared interests. Volunteering has benefitted from the growing number of active retirees and also from younger people, some wanting to serve and some to embellish their curriculum vitae in the transition from education to employment. Three-quarters of school-leavers now complete a secondary education, and more than a third have a degree, so the competition to get a start is fierce.

With affluence has come consumption. Television shows such as *My Kitchen Rules* and *The Biggest Loser* testify to Australians' love affair with food: 35 per cent of them are overweight and another 28 per cent obese. They have stopped smoking, cut back on drinking, are more cautious with drugs but are addicted to calories and caffeine. A television comedy series that ran from 2002, *Kath and Kim*, parodied the consequences of 'effluence'. Kath is an upwardly mobile single mother living in a waterfront townhouse in the outer suburbs of Melbourne and Kim her endlessly self-indulgent daughter. Both are addicted to shopping, kitsch and malapropisms. Kath's love interest is Kel, a gourmet butcher and metrosexual, and Kim's estranged husband strives for success at Computa City but ends up working in a doughnut shop.

Kath and Kim reworked an old theme, the ignorance and crassness of the parvenu, one that had particular resonance in a country where so many made good. In their own way, they followed the example of the richest Australians who flaunt success with mansions, luxury yachts and private aircraft. It was in this period that the super-rich climbed into world ranks, so that in 2012 Gina Rinehart was named as the world's richest woman, and a sharp rise in income inequality placed Australia seventh of the twenty-two

OECD countries. Inequality had fallen during the twentieth century, but increased from the mid-1970s. Full-time wages for the lowest paid rose by only 15 per cent over the following four decades as the decline of trade unions reduced their bargaining power. Those at the mid-point of the income table enjoyed a 35 per cent increase and at nine-tenths of the way up the table there was a 59 per cent gain. The top 1 per cent did best: excluding capital gains – and most senior executives had lucrative share options – their share of total income doubled.

Taken together with the devices that enabled the wealthy to accumulate and consolidate their assets, this polarisation had profound effects on a society that had taken pride in its egalitarian ethos. Across a range of services that in the mid-twentieth century were considered to be part of inclusive citizenship – health care and education, access to the legislature and the courts, shared public space and parity of esteem – the rich were able to buy preferential treatment. A further consequence was the way that the transmission of these advantages from one generation to the next reduced social mobility.

There are many international measures that suggest why Australia remains so attractive to newcomers: it is near the top of the United Nations Human Development and Gender Development indices. It scores highly for freedom, personal safety and life expectancy, and its cities are regularly judged to be among the most liveable. It remains a place of space, light and an easy informality. Social analysts have found that Australians are more optimistic than the citizens of most other advanced countries, for they adapt to change and retain a belief in future possibilities, but the same analysts also detect a widespread nostalgia for a simpler, more easygoing past. Theirs is a selective history, some parts heavily accented and others lightly worn but with possibilities still to be realised.

SOURCES OF QUOTATIONS

I BEGINNINGS

Barron Field wrote in *First Fruits of Australian Poetry* (Sydney, 1819), p. 5; the naval officer who imagined a second Rome was J. H. Tuckey, *Account of a Voyage to Establish a Colony at Port Phillip* (London: Longman, 1805), pp. 185–90. Justice Brennan's judgement in the Mabo case is quoted in Tony Blackshield et al. (eds), *The Oxford Companion to the High Court of Australia* (Melbourne: Oxford University Press, 2001), p. 446; Keating's speech to the Aboriginal audience is reproduced in Mark Ryan (ed.), *Advancing Australia: The Speeches of Paul Keating, Prime Minister* (Sydney: Big Picture Publications, 1995), p. 228; Keith Windschuttle's views on European settlement are in *The Fabrication of Aboriginal History*, vol. 1: *Van Diemen's Land, 1803–1847* (Sydney: Macleay Press, 2002), p. 3; Rudd's statement appears in the *Sydney Morning Herald*, 13 February 2008.

Wandjuk Marika tells the Djankawa story in Jennifer Isaacs (ed.), *Australian Dreaming: 40,000 Years of Aboriginal History* (Sydney: Ure Smith, 1980), p. 76; Paddy Japaljarri Stewart's 'Dreamings' are in David Horton (ed.), *The Encyclopaedia of Aboriginal Australia* (Canberra: Aboriginal Studies Press, 1994), vol. 1, pp. 305–6. James Bonwick wrote in *Daily Life and Origins of the Tasmanians* (London: Sampson, Low, 1870), pp. 1–2; Claude Lévi-Strauss is quoted in Josephine Flood, *Archaeology of the Dreamtime: The Story of Prehistoric Australia and its People* (rev. edn, Sydney: Angus & Robertson, 1994), p. 15.

2 NEWCOMERS

The eminent historian who wrote of 'indescribable hopelessness' was C. M. H. Clark, *A History of Australia*, vol. 1: *From the Earliest Times to the Age of Macquarie* (Melbourne: Melbourne University Press, 1962), p. 77, quoted by Alan Frost, *Botany Bay Mirages: Illusions of Australia's Convict Beginnings* (Melbourne: Melbourne University Press, 1994), p. 110.

The prime minister was Robert Menzies, quoted in R. G. Neale (ed.), *Documents on Australian Foreign Policy, 1937–49*, vol. 2 (Canberra: Australian Government Publishing Service, 1976), p. 96; the national broadcast of his successor, John Curtin, appears in *Digest of Decisions and Announcements*, no. 39 (30 August – 3 September 1942), p. 17. The Spanish and Dutch disappointment is quoted in Glyndwr Williams and Alan Frost (eds), *Terra Australis to Australia* (Melbourne: Oxford University Press, 1988), pp. 9, 103; Swift in P. J. Marshall (ed.), *The Oxford History of the British Empire*, vol. II: *The Eighteenth Century* (Oxford: Oxford University Press, 1998), p. 554. Cook and Banks are quoted by J. C. Beaglehole, *The Life of Captain James Cook* (London: A. and C. Black, 1974), pp. 148, 251–2, and J. C. Beaglehole (ed.), *The Endeavour Journal of Joseph Banks, 1768–1771* (Sydney: Angus & Robertson, 1962), vol. 2, p. 51. The instructions are in Maria Nugent, *Captain Cook Was Here* (Cambridge: Cambridge University Press, 2009), p. 73, and their meaning is elaborated by Alecia Simmonds, 'Friendship, Imperial Violence and the Law of Nations: The Case of Late-Eighteenth Century British Oceania', *Journal of Imperial and Commonwealth History*, vol. 42, no. 4 (2014), pp. 645–67.

Frost quotes the colonial surgeon in *Botany Bay Mirages*, pp. 91–2; Francis Grose, the commanding officer, appears in Alan Frost, *Arthur Phillip, 1738–1814: His Voyaging* (Melbourne: Oxford University Press, 1987), p. 192; the instructions to Phillip are in Russel Ward, *Concise History of Australia* (Brisbane: University of Queensland Press, 1992), p. 55. The interpretation of dancing is that of Inga Clendinnen, *Dancing with Strangers* (Melbourne: Text Publishing, 2003), pp. 92, 295; the rejoinder comes from Grace Karskens, *The Colony: A History of Early Sydney* (Sydney: Allen & Unwin, 2009), p. 50. Watkin Tench, the marine officer, wrote on Aborigines in *A Complete Account of the Settlement at Port Jackson in New South Wales* (London: G. Nicol and J. Sewell, 1793), p. 135; his colleague is quoted in David Day, *Claiming a Continent: A History of Australia* (Sydney: Angus & Robertson, 1996), pp. 65–6. Banks' testimony to the parliamentary committee is quoted by David Andrew Roberts, '"They Would Speedily Abandon the Country to the New Comers": The Denial of Aboriginal Rights', in Martin Crotty and David Andrew Roberts (eds), *The Great Mistakes of Australian History* (Sydney: UNSW Press, 2006), p. 15.

3   COERCION

The Tasmanian historian is James Boyce, *Van Diemen's Land* (Melbourne: Black Inc., 2009), pp. 45, 76. Arthur Phillip's description of Sydney Harbour is in *The Voyage of Governor Phillip to Botany Bay* (London: John Stockdale, 1789), p. 47. Elizabeth Macarthur is quoted in Hazel King, *Elizabeth Macarthur and Her World* (Sydney: Sydney

University Press, 1980), pp. 21–2. Phillip's views on homosexuality are in Gary Wotherspoon, 'A Sodom in the South Pacific: Male Homosexuality in Sydney, 1788–1809', in Graeme Aplin (ed.), *A Difficult Infant: Sydney Before Macquarie* (Sydney: UNSW Press, 1988), p. 94; descriptions of Aboriginal women are provided by Ann McGrath, 'Aboriginal–Colonial Gender Relations at Port Jackson', *Australian Historical Studies*, vol. 24, no. 95 (1990), p. 199.

Sydney Smith is quoted in A. G. L. Shaw, *Convicts and the Colonies* (London: Faber, 1966), p. 77; Samuel Marsden in A. T. Yarwood, *Samuel Marsden: The Great Survivor* (Melbourne: Melbourne University Press, 1977), p. 54; Hunter in Russel Ward, *Concise History of Australia* (Brisbane: University of Queensland Press, 1992), p. 81. Blackstone is quoted by David Neal, *The Rule of Law in a Penal Colony: Law and Power in Early New South Wales* (Cambridge: Cambridge University Press, 1991), p. 6. The convicts making for China are discussed by Paul Carter, *The Road to Botany Bay* (London: Faber, 1987), p. 298.

King's description of Macarthur appears in Stephen Murray-Smith (ed.), *The Dictionary of Australian Quotations* (Melbourne: Heinemann, 1984), p. 137. Macquarie is quoted in Shaw, *Convicts and the Colonies*, p. 88, and Brian Fletcher, *Landed Enterprise and Penal Society: A History of Farming and Grazing in New South Wales Before 1821* (Sydney: Sydney University Press, 1976), pp. 128–9. The treasury official is quoted by Shaw, *Convicts and the Colonies*, p. 93, and the Spanish priest by K. S. Inglis, *The Australian Colonists: An Exploration of Social History, 1788–1870* (Melbourne: Melbourne University Press, 1974), p. 74. Marsden's views on Maoris appear in Yarwood, *Samuel Marsden*, p. 164; Macquarie on Aborigines is quoted by D. J. Mulvaney, *Encounters in Place: Outsiders and Aboriginal Australians, 1606–1985* (Brisbane: University of Queensland Press, 1989), and Inglis, *The Australian Colonists*, p. 160.

Flinders' suggestion of the name Australia appears in *A Voyage to Terra Australis* (London: G. and W. Nicol, 1814), vol. 1, p. iii; D. W. Meinig is the American geographer, quoted in Tom Griffiths and Libby Robin (eds), *Ecology and Empire: Environmental History of Settler Societies* (Melbourne: Melbourne University Press, 1997), p. 9; Palmer is quoted in Alan Atkinson, *The Europeans in Australia*, vol. 1: *The Beginning* (Melbourne: Oxford University Press, 1997), p. 295.

4   CONQUEST

Macquarie's views on New South Wales are in *Australian Dictionary of Biography*, vol. 2, p. 194; those of Bigge are in *Australian Dictionary of Biography*, vol. 1, p. 99.

Mitchell is quoted by R. H. W. Reece, *Aborigines and Colonists: Aborigines and Colonial Society in New South Wales in the 1830s and 1840s* (Sydney: Sydney University Press, 1974), p. 120. Events at Slaughterhouse Creek are described in Reece, *Aborigines and Colonists*, p. 33; those at Bells Falls by David Roberts, 'Bells Falls Massacre and Bathurst's History of Violence', *Australian Historical Studies*, vol. 26, no. 105 (1995), p. 615; the Rufus River exchange was narrated in J. W. Bull, *Early Experiences of Colonial Life in South Australia* (Adelaide: Advertiser, 1878), pp. 140–1, quoted in J. J. Healy, *Literature and the Aborigine in Australia* (2nd edn, Brisbane: University of Queensland Press, 1989), p. 12. Hobbles Danaiyairi's saga of Captain Cook is presented by Deborah Bird Rose in *Aboriginal Studies*, vol. 2 (1984), pp. 24–39. Henry Reynolds suggested the pantheon of national heroes in *The Other Side of the Frontier: An Interpretation of the Aboriginal Response to the Invasion and Settlement of Australia* (Townsville: James Cook University, 1981), p. 201. The fear of Aborigines is quoted by Henry Reynolds, *Frontier: Aborigines, Settlers and Land* (Sydney: Allen & Unwin, 1987), p. 10; the Aboriginal rejoinder is in L. L. Robson, *A History of Tasmania*, vol. 1: *Van Diemen's Land from the Earliest Times to 1855* (Melbourne: Oxford University Press, 1983), p. 212; the spot of blood appears in Henry Reynolds, *This Whispering in Our Hearts* (Sydney: Allen & Unwin, 1998), p. 43; the report of the select committee is quoted by Henry Reynolds, *The Law of the Land* (Melbourne: Penguin Books, 1987), p. 85 and Elizabeth Elbourne, 'The Sin of the Settler: The 1835–36 Select Committee on Aborigines...', *Journal of Colonialism and Colonial History*, vol. 4, no. 3 (2003), p. 19. The secretary of state and the 'settlement' of Myall Creek are quoted in Reece, *Aborigines and Colonists*, pp. 41, 135, who also quotes the secretary of state on the Port Phillip Association agreement, p. 123; Bourke's justification of pastoral leases appears in the *Australian Dictionary of Biography*, vol. 1, p. 132; the consequences of his acceptance of settlement of the Port Phillip District are treated by James Boyce, *1835: The Founding of Melbourne and the Conquest of Australia* (Melbourne: Black Inc., 2011), p. xiii. The Colonial Office's views on South Australia are in Reynolds, *The Law of the Land*, p. 106; the Governor's proclamation and subsequent testimony appear in Robert Foster, Rick Hosking and Amanda Nettelbeck, *Fatal Collisions: The South Australian Frontier and the Violence of Memory* (Adelaide: Wakefield Press, 2001), pp. 3, 5. Mahroot's lamentation is in J. P. Townsend, *Rambles and Observations in New South Wales* (London, 1849), p. 120, quoted in Reece, *Aborigines and Colonists*, p. 12; the account of Eliza Fraser is given in Kay Schaffer, *In the Wake of First Contact: The Eliza Fraser Stories* (Cambridge: Cambridge University Press, 1995), p. 5.

Arthur is quoted by A. G. L. Shaw, *Sir George Arthur, Bart, 1784–1854* (Melbourne: Melbourne University Press, 1980), p. 71; 'A Convict's Lament on the Death of Captain Logan' is reproduced in Russel Ward (ed.), *The Penguin Book of Australian Ballads* (Melbourne: Penguin Books, 1964), p. 37; 'ferocious severity' is quoted in Shirley Hazzard, *Punishment Short of Death: A History of the Penal Settlement at Norfolk Island* (Melbourne:

Hyland House, 1984), p. 223. The ethnic diversity is documented by Kristyn Harman, *Aboriginal Convicts: Australian Khoisan and Maori Exiles* (Sydney: UNSW Press, 2012), pp. 1–2. Mary Sawer's experience is discussed by Kay Daniels, *Convict Women* (Sydney: Allen & Unwin, 1998), p. 195. Robinson is quoted in C. M. H. Clark, *A History of Australia*, vol. II: *New South Wales and Van Diemen's Land, 1822–1838* (Melbourne: Melbourne University Press, 1968), p. 55; Darling on Wentworth is quoted in K. S. Inglis, *The Australian Colonists: An Exploration of Social History, 1788–1870* (Melbourne: Melbourne University Press, 1974), p. 42; the secretary of state's views on the end of transportation appear in A. G. L. Shaw, *Convicts and the Colonies* (London: Faber, 1966), pp. 288–9; The hapless Governor Gipps' comment on the squatters is in *Historical Records of Australia*, ser. 3, vol. 21, p. 127; the report of the select committee on transportation is quoted by Amanda Laugesen, *Convict Words: Language in Early Colonial Australia* (Melbourne: Oxford University Press, 2002), p. xiv.

The description of Thomas Peel is in Geoffrey Bolton and Heather Vose (eds), *The Wollaston Journals*, vol. 1: *1840–1842* (Perth: University of Western Australia Press, 1991), p. 185; Wakefield wrote *A Letter from Sydney and Other Writings* (London: J. M. Dent, 1929). Chisholm is quoted in Margaret Kiddle, *Caroline Chisholm* (Melbourne: Melbourne University Press, 1950), p. 83; 'No Sunday beyond the Mountains' is in H. R. Jackson, *Churches and People in Australia and New Zealand, 1860–1930* (Sydney: Allen & Unwin, 1987), p. 24. Frank the Poet, 'Farewell to V. D. Land', is quoted by Noel McLachlan, *Waiting for the Revolution! A History of Australian Nationalism* (Melbourne: Penguin Books, 1989), p. 73. Robinson's and Wentworth's verses are in Robert Dixon, *The Course of Empire: Neo-Classical Culture in New South Wales, 1788–1860* (Melbourne: Oxford University Press, 1986), pp. 43, 135; St Patrick's day is described by Patrick O'Farrell, *The Irish in Australia* (Sydney: UNSW Press, 1986), p. 44.

5 PROGRESS

Hargraves and Clarke on gold are quoted by Geoffrey Blainey, *The Rush that Never Ended* (3rd edn, Melbourne: Melbourne University Press, 1978), pp. 8, 13; Spence, *Clara Morison*, is quoted in David Goodman, *Goldseeking: Victoria and California in the 1850s* (Sydney: Allen & Unwin, 1994), p. 37. Kennedy and the Eureka oath are quoted in Noel McLachlan, *Waiting for the Revolution: A History of Australian Nationalism* (Melbourne: Penguin Books, 1989), pp. 79, 96; the declaration of popular sovereignty comes from David Goodman, 'The Gold Rushes of the 1850s', in Alison Bashford and Stuart Macintyre (eds), *The Cambridge History of Australia* (Cambridge: Cambridge University Press, 2013), vol. 1, p. 178; the conservative historian was Henry Gyles Turner, *Our Own Little*

Rebellion (Melbourne: Whitcombe and Tombs, 1912); Lawson is quoted in Goodman, *Goldseeking*, pp. 7–8.

The British secretary of state's announcement is given by C. C. Eldridge, *Victorian Imperialism* (Atlantic Highlands, NJ: Humanities Press, 1978), p. 39; Deniehy's satire appears in E. A. Martin, *The Life and Speeches of Daniel Henry Deniehy* (Sydney: George Robertson, 1884), pp. 53–4; Higinbotham is quoted in Stuart Macintyre, *A Colonial Liberalism: The Lost World of Three Victorian Visionaries* (Melbourne: Oxford University Press, 1991), p. 57.

The Land Convention notice is recorded in Macintyre, *A Colonial Liberalism*, p. 32; Charles Thatcher, 'Hurrah for Australia', in *Thatcher's Colonial Minstrel* (Melbourne: Charlwood, 1859), is quoted in Stuart Macintyre, *Winners and Losers: The Pursuit of Social Justice in Australian History* (Sydney: Allen & Unwin, 1985), p. 30; *Argus*, 21 April 1856, on patriarchy is quoted in Patricia Grimshaw, Marilyn Lake, Ann McGrath and Marian Quartly, *Creating a Nation* (Melbourne: McPhee Gribble, 1994), p. 104. Henry Lawson was first published in the *Bulletin* in 1892, and quoted by Richard Waterhouse, 'Australian Legends: Representations of the Bush', *Australian Historical Studies*, vol. 31, no. 115 (2000), p. 219; Barcroft Boake was first published in the *Bulletin* in 1891, quoted in Geoffrey Blainey, *A Land Half Won* (Melbourne: Macmillan, 1980), p. 188. The anti-Chinese editorial is in Andrew Markus, *Australian Race Relations, 1788–1993* (Sydney: Allen & Unwin, 1994), p. 68; Governor George Bowen, writing in 1860, is quoted in Dane Kennedy, *The Last Blank Spaces: Exploring Africa and Australia* (Cambridge, MA.: Harvard University Press, 2013), p. 102. The phrase 'workin' longa tucker' is a chapter title in Ann McGrath, *'Born in the Cattle': Aborigines in Cattle Country* (Sydney: Allen & Unwin, 1987); the Victorian Board of Aborigines is reported by D. J. Mulvaney, *Encounters in Place: Outsiders and Aboriginal Australians, 1606–1985* (Brisbane: University of Queensland Press, 1989), p. 148; Curr is quoted by J. J. Healy, *Literature and the Aborigine in Australia* (2nd edn, Brisbane: University of Queensland Press, 1989), p. 17.

The English Scot was J. M. Barrie, *The Oxford Dictionary of Quotations* (3rd edn, Oxford: Oxford University Press, 1979), p. 34; Marcus Clarke, *The Future Australian Race* (Melbourne: A. H. Massina, 1877), p. 22, appears in *Australian Dictionary of Quotations*; p. 50; Fergus Hume is quoted in Robert Dixon, *Writing the Colonial Adventure: Race, Gender and Nation in Anglo-Australian Popular Fiction, 1875–1914* (Cambridge: Cambridge University Press, 1995), p. 161. The examples of Australian speech are given by Bruce Moore, 'Towards a History of the Australian Accent', in Joy Damousi and Desley Deacon (eds), *Talking and Listening in the Age of Modernity* (Canberra: ANU E Press, 2007), p. 100; and the derivation of Cooee comes from Graham Seal, *The Lingo: Listening to*

Australian English (Sydney: UNSW Press, 1999), p. 14. Trollope is quoted in Alan Atkinson, *The Europeans in Australia,* vol. 2: *Democracy* (Melbourne: Oxford University Press, 2004), p. 290; Harpur and Higinbotham by H. R. Jackson, *Churches and People in Australia and New Zealand, 1860–1930* (Sydney: Allen & Unwin, 1987), p. 126. Higinbotham on education appears in Denis Grundy, *Secular, Compulsory and Free: The Education Act of 1872* (Melbourne: Melbourne University Press, 1972), p. 91; Archbishop Polding is quoted in Patrick O'Farrell, *The Catholic Church and Community in Australia: A History* (Melbourne: Thomas Nelson, 1977), p. 151; *The Age,* 15 February 1908, on Syme, is quoted by Macintyre, *A Colonial Liberalism,* p. 83; Parkes and the Centennial cantata are in Graeme Davison, J. W. McCarty and Ailsa McLeary (eds), *Australians 1888* (Sydney: Fairfax, Syme and Weldon Associates, 1987), pp. 7, 24; the critic of the national pantheon is in K. S. Inglis, *Sacred Places: War Memorials in the National Landscape* (Melbourne: Melbourne University Press, 1998), p. 32.

6 RECONSTRUCTION

The shearer was Julian Stuart, *Part of the Glory: Reminiscences of the Shearers' Strike, Queensland, 1891* (Sydney: Australasian Book Society, 1967), p. 99, quoted in Jan Walker, *Jondaryan Station: The Relationship Between Pastoral Capital and Pastoral Labour, 1840–1890* (Brisbane: University of Queensland Press, 1988), p. 175. The president of Sydney Chamber of Commerce is quoted in John Rickard, *Class and Politics: New South Wales, Victoria and the Early Commonwealth, 1890–1910* (Canberra: Australian National University Press, 1976), p. 13; Deakin in *Victorian Parliamentary Debates,* vol. 64, p. 1368 (2 September 1890); the military commander is quoted in Stuart Svensen, *The Sinews of War: Hard Cash and the 1890 Maritime Strike* (Sydney: UNSW Press, 1995), p. 191. Henry Lawson's lament is in *Poems* (Sydney: John Ferguson, 1979), p. 51; John Barnes quotes Louisa Lawson's motto in 'Louisa Lawson', in Graeme Davison, John Hirst and Stuart Macintyre (eds), *The Oxford Companion to Australian History* (rev. edn, Melbourne: Oxford University Press, 2001), p. 383. Lane is quoted in Philip Bell and Roger Bell, *Implicated: The United States in Australia* (Melbourne: Oxford University Press, 1993), p. 29; Gilmore in W. H. Wilde, *Courage a Grace: A Biography of Dame Mary Gilmore* (Melbourne: Melbourne University Press, 1988), p. 51. W. G. Spence wrote in *Australia's Awakening: Thirty Years in the Life of an Australian Agitator* (Sydney: The Workers Trustees, 1909), pp. 78, 220; Ryan's criticism of parliament is in *Dictionary of Australian Quotations*; p. 232; Deakin is quoted in J. A. La Nauze, *Alfred Deakin: A Biography* (Melbourne: Melbourne University Press, 1965), p. 144.

The unique national type was described by Francis Adams, *The Australians: A Social Sketch* (London: Fisher Unwin, 1893), p. 165; Miles Franklin opened *My Brilliant Career* (Edinburgh: Blackwood, 1901), p. 2; Joseph Furphy *Such Is Life* (Sydney: Bulletin, 1903), p. 1; Lawson's 'The Shearers' is in *Poems*, p. 178, and his letter to Emma Brooks, 16 January 1893, in Henry Lawson, *Letters, 1890–1922*, ed. Colin Roderick (Sydney: Angus and Robertson, 1970), p. 53. Mary Gilmore's poem is quoted by Jennifer Strauss, 'Stubborn Singers of their Full Song: Mary Gilmore and Lesbia Harford', in Kay Ferres (ed.), *The Time to Write: Australian Women Writers, 1890–1930* (Melbourne: Penguin Books, 1993), p. 114; the Labor leader was George Black, quoted in *Dictionary of Australian Quotations*, p. 18. The Salvation Army's *War Cry* is quoted by Simon Sleight, *Young People and the Shaping of Public Space in Melbourne 1870–1914* (Farnham: Ashgate, 2013), p. 147; comments on the Mount Rennie rape case come from David Walker, 'Youth on Trial: The Mt Rennie Case', *Labour History*, no. 50 (1986), p. 32, and Susan Magarey, *Passions of the First Wave Feminists* (Sydney: UNSW Press, 2001), p. 92; the WCTU is quoted in Patricia Grimshaw, Marilyn Lake, Ann McGrath and Marian Quartly, *Creating a Nation* (Melbourne: McPhee Gribble, 1994), p. 182.

Parkes is quoted by J. A. La Nauze, *The Making of the Australian Commonwealth* (Melbourne: Melbourne University Press, 1972), p. 11; Deakin wrote of Federation as miraculous in *'And Be One People': Alfred Deakin's Federal Story*, introd. Stuart Macintyre (Melbourne: Melbourne University Press, 1995), p. 173; Barton is quoted in *Australian Dictionary of Biography*, vol. 7, p. 197, and John Hirst, *The Sentimental Nation: The Making of the Australian Commonwealth* (Melbourne: Oxford University Press, 2000), p. 5. The celebrant is John Hirst, *A Republican Manifesto* (Melbourne: Oxford University Press, 1994), p. 35; 'the greatest miracle' appears in *Official Report of the Federation Conference held in the Courthouse Corowa on Monday 31 July and Tuesday 1 August* (Corowa: James C. Leslie, 1893), p. 25. Deakin on racial purity is in *Creating a Nation*, p. 192; Charles Pearson's warnings are in *National Life and Character: A Forecast* (London: Macmillan 1893), p. 16, discussed by Marilyn Lake and Henry Reynolds, *Drawing the Global Colour Line: White Men's Countries and the Question of Racial Equality* (Melbourne: Melbourne University Press, 2008), p. 78; and Deakin's additional observations are in Noel McLachlan, *Waiting for the Revolution! A History of Australian Nationalism* (Melbourne: Penguin Books, 1989), pp. 172, 185. Deakin's parliamentary speech is reported in *Commonwealth Parliamentary Debates*, vol. 4, p. 4807 (12 September 1901). The Labor platform is reproduced in L. F. Crisp, *The Australian Federal Labor Party, 1901–1951* (London: Longman, 1955), p. 271. The racist responses to northern Australia are quoted in Henry Reynolds, *North of the*

Capricorn: The Untold Story of Australia's North (Sydney: Allen & Unwin, 2003), pp. 145, 149; and the two Australias are analysed by Tim Rowse, 'Indigenous Heterogeneity', *Australian Historical Studies*, vol. 45, no. 3 (2014), p. 303. Richard White quotes the Wattle Day League in *Inventing Australia: Images and Identity, 1688–1980* (Sydney: Allen & Unwin, 1981); Deakin's term, 'independent Australian Britons', appears in La Nauze, *Alfred Deakin*, vol. 2, p. 483.

Deakin on White Australia is quoted by Robert Birrell, *A Nation of Our Own: Citizenship and Nation-Building in Federation Australia* (Melbourne: Longman, 1995), p. 172; his views on New Protection are taken from Stuart Macintyre, *The Oxford History of Australia*, vol. 1: *1901–1942, The Succeeding Age* (Melbourne: Oxford University Press, 1986), pp. 102–3; and Higgins is quoted in Stuart Macintyre, *Winners and Losers: The Pursuit of Social Justice in Australian History* (Sydney: Allen & Unwin, 1985), pp. 55, 57. The commentator is Francis Castles, *The Working Class and Welfare: Reflections on the Political Development of the Welfare State in Australia and New Zealand, 1891–1980* (Sydney: Allen & Unwin, 1985); the critical assessments are from Colin White, *Mastering Risk: Environment, Markets and Politics in Australian Economic History* (Melbourne: Oxford University Press, 1992), pp. 231, 223; and Paul Kelly, *The End of Certainty: The Story of the 1980s* (Sydney: Allen & Unwin, 1992), pp. 1, 13; the businessman is quoted in Ken Buckley and Kris Klugman, *The History of Burns Philp: The Australian Company in the South Pacific* (Sydney: Burns Philp, 1981), p. 259.

7 SACRIFICE

Cook and Fisher are quoted in Joan Beaumont, *Broken Nation: Australians in the Great War* (Sydney: Allen & Unwin, 2013), p. 16; the instructions to the governor-general are in E. M. Andrews, *The Anzac Illusion: Anglo-Australian Relations During World War I* (Cambridge: Cambridge University Press, 1993), p. 130. The British war correspondent and C. E. W. Bean are quoted in John F. Williams, *Quarantined Culture: Australian Reactions to Modernism, 1913–1939* (Cambridge: Cambridge University Press, 1995), p. 235; and Alastair Thomson, *Anzac Memories: Living with the Legend* (Melbourne: Oxford University Press, 1994), pp. 53, 54. The testimony from those at Gallipoli in 1995 comes from Bruce Scates, 'In Gallipoli's Shadow: Pilgrimage, Memory, Mourning and Loss in the Great War', *Australian Historical Studies*, vol. 33, no. 119 (2002), p. 8. The verse from the Western Front is by Frederic Manning, 'The Trenches', and the diary of an anonymous soldier is in Les Murray (ed.), *The New Oxford Book of Australian Verse* (Melbourne: Oxford University Press, 1986), pp. 109, 110–11; the exhortations of patriotic women are quoted in Carmel Shute, 'Heroines and Heroes: Sexual Mythology in Australia, 1914–1918', in Joy Damousi and Marilyn Lake (eds), *Gender and War: Australians at War in the Twentieth Century* (Cambridge: Cambridge University Press, 1995), pp. 23–42. Mannix is quoted in *Australian Dictionary of Biography*, vol. 10, p. 400; the formula for mandate territories is in Neville Meaney (ed.), *Australia and the World: A Documentary History from the 1870s to the 1970s* (Melbourne: Longman Cheshire, 1985), p. 272; Hughes is quoted by L. F. Fitzhardinge, *The Little Digger, 1914–1952: William Morris Hughes, A Political Biography* (Sydney: Angus & Robertson, 1979), p. 396.

Bruce is quoted by Barrie Dyster and David Meredith, *Australia in the Global Economy: Continuity and Change* (2nd edn, Cambridge: Cambridge University Press, 1999), p. 115. The recollection of reading appears in Martyn Lyons and Lucy Taksa, *Australian Readers Remember: An Oral History of Reading* (Melbourne: Oxford University Press, 1992), p. 34, and the tribute to Amy Johnson, in the Adelaide *Advertiser*, is quoted by Julian Thomas, 'Amy Johnson's Triumph, Australia, 1930', *Australian Historical Studies*, vol. 23, no. 90 (1988), p. 79; the Australian artist is quoted in Williams, *Quarantined Culture*, p. 175, the American State Department official in Meaney (ed.), *Australia and the World*, p. 367.

Wendy Lowenstein reports the unemployed activist in *Weevils in the Flour: An Oral Record of the 1930s Depression in Australia* (rev. edn, Melbourne: Scribe Publications, 1981), p. 177; the New Guard methods are in Eric Campbell, *The Rallying Point: My Story of the New Guard* (Melbourne: Melbourne University Press, 1965), pp. 70, 107–8; Lang and his supporter are quoted in *Australian Dictionary of Biography*, vol. 9, p. 665. The feminist critic of the family wage was Lena Lynch, quoted in Marilyn Lake, 'A Revolution in the Family: The Challenge and Contradictions of Maternal Citizenship in Australia', in Seth Koven and Sonya Michel (eds), *Mothers of a New World: Maternalist Policies and the Origin of Welfare States* (New York: Routledge, 1993), p. 387. Charles Hawker, the minister who resigned from the government in 1932, is quoted in Macintyre, *The Oxford History of Australia*, vol. 4, p. 299; Hughes is quoted in *Australian Dictionary of Biography*, vol. 9, p. 399, Menzies in Cameron Hazlehurst, *Menzies Observed* (Sydney: Allen & Unwin, 1979), p. 138. The Day of Mourning resolution appears in Bain Attwood, *Rights for Aborigines* (Sydney: Allen & Unwin, 2003), p. 54; the anthropological advice came from A. P. Elkin, quoted in Russell McGregor, *Imagined Destinies: Aboriginal Australians and the Doomed Race Theory, 1880–1939* (Melbourne: Melbourne University Press, 1997), p. 196; and Geoffrey Gray, 'From Nomadism to Citizenship: A. P. Elkin and Aboriginal Advancement', in Nicolas Petersen and Will Sanders (eds), *Citizenship and Indigenous Australians: Changing Conceptions and Possibilities* (Cambridge: Cambridge University Press, 1998), p. 59; the ministerial statement appears in John Chesterman and Brian Galligan, *Citizens Without Rights: Aborigines and Australian Citizenship* (Cambridge: Cambridge University Press, 1997), p. 148.

Menzies' views on war are recorded in R. G. Neale (ed.), *Documents on Australian Foreign Policy, 1937–49*, vol. 2 (Canberra: Australian Government Publishing Service, 1976), pp. 221, 256; and A. W. Martin, *Robert Menzies: A Life*, vol. 1: *1894–1943* (Melbourne: Melbourne University Press, 1993), p. 295. John Manifold, 'The Tomb of Lt John Learmonth, AIF' is in Chris Wallace-Crabbe and Peter Pierce (eds), *The Clubbing of the Gunfire: 101 Australian War Poems* (Melbourne: Melbourne University Press, 1984), p. 119; Mary Gilmore is quoted in Denis O'Brien, *The Weekly* (Melbourne: Penguin Books, 1982), p. 75. The head of the British Foreign Office's criticism appears in David Dilks (ed.), *The Diaries of Sir Alexander Cadogan* (London: Cassell, 1971), p. 358. Hughes is quoted in Donald Horne, *In Search of Billy Hughes* (Melbourne: Macmillan, 1979), p. 123; Curtin's new year message appeared in *Digest of Decisions and Announcements*, no. 13 (24 December 1941–3 January 1942), pp. 11–13; the protest against an 'inexcusable betrayal' appears in David Horner, *High Command: Australia and Allied Strategy, 1939–1945* (Sydney: Allen & Unwin, 1992), p. 152; MacArthur's division of labour is related in his *Reminiscences* (New York: McGraw Hill, 1964), p. 157. David Campbell, 'Men in Green', appears in Pierce and Wallace-Crabbe (eds), *The Clubbing of the Gunfire*, p. 130; Eric Lambert, *The Veterans* (London: Shakespeare Head, 1954), p. 137, is quoted by David Walker, 'The Writers' War', in Joan Beaumont (ed.), *Australia's War, 1939–45* (Sydney: Allen & Unwin, 1996), p. 149; Thomas Blamey, the commanding officer, is quoted in Mark Johnston, *Fighting the Enemy: Australian Soldiers and their Adversaries in World War II* (Cambridge: Cambridge University Press, 2000), p. 86. The hate campaign is described by Lynnette Finch, 'Knowing the Enemy: Australian Psychological Warfare and the Business of Influencing Minds in the Second World War', *War & Society*, 16, 2 (1998), pp. 71–91; and Curtin distanced himself from it in *Commonwealth Parliamentary Debates*, vol. 170, p. 521 (27 March 1942). Curtin's exhortations are in *Digest of Decisions and Announcements*, no. 16 (19–28 January 1942), p. 13, no. 25 (5–22 April), pp. 15–16; no. 20 (30 August–3 September 1942), p. 20 and no. 45 (6–13 November 1942), p. 41. Peter Stanley coined the phrase 'green hole' and discusses it in Peter Dennis and Jeffrey Grey (eds), *The Pacific War 1943–1944* (Canberra: Army History Unit, 2004), pp. 202–11. The description of Evatt is in Dilks (ed.), *The Diaries of Sir Alexander Cadogan*, p. 745, and the acclamation is reported in Paul Hasluck, *Diplomatic Witness: Australian Foreign Affairs, 1941–1947* (Melbourne: Melbourne University Press, 1980), p. 207. Curtin is quoted in *The Oxford Companion to Australian History* (rev. edn, Melbourne: Oxford University Press, 2001), p. 169.

8 GOLDEN AGE

Chifley's golden age and Depression memories are quoted in Stuart Macintyre, *Australia's Boldest Experiment: War and Reconstruction in the 1940s* (Sydney: NewSouth, 2015), pp. 201, 382.

The light on the hill is in A. W. Stargadt (ed.), *Things Worth Fighting For: Speeches by Joseph Benedict Chifley* (Melbourne: Australian Labor Party, 1952), pp. 61, 65. The population statistics come from Simon Ville and Glenn Withers (eds), *The Cambridge Economic History of Australia* (Cambridge: Cambridge University Press, 2015), p. 353. Calwell is quoted in Andrew Markus, 'Labour and Immigration: The Displaced Persons Program', *Labour History*, no. 47 (1984), p. 78, and in *Australian Dictionary of Quotations*, p. 36; the ministerial statement on public housing is in Andrew Spaull, *John Dedman: A Most Unexpected Labor Man* (Melbourne: Hyland House, 1998), p. 97. Menzies' invocation of 'the forgotten people' is quoted in Judith Brett, *Robert Menzies' Forgotten People* (Sydney: Macmillan, 1992), p. 7; the Treasurer, Arthur Fadden, is quoted in Russel Ward, *A Nation for a Continent: The History of Australia, 1901–1975* (rev. edn, Melbourne: Heinemann, 1988), p. 300. The economist was Heinz Arndt, quoted with the committee of economic inquiry in Nicholas Brown, *Governing Prosperity: Social Change and Analysis in Australia in the 1950s* (Cambridge: Cambridge University Press, 1995), p. 123; Menzies' eulogy to bigness is in George Seddon, *Landprints: Reflections on Place and Landscape* (Cambridge: Cambridge University Press, 1998), p. 57. Bolte is quoted by Peter Blazey, *Bolte: A Political Biography* (Brisbane: Jacaranda Press, 1972), p. 239.

The British high commissioner is in Roger C. Thompson, 'Winds of Change in the South Pacific', in David Lowe (ed.), *Australia and the End of Empires: The Impact of Decolonisation on Australia's Near North, 1945–65* (Geelong: Deakin University Press, 1996), p. 161. Carl Bridge provides the description of Evatt in Leonie Kramer et al. (eds), *The Greats: The 50 Men and Women Who Most Helped to Shape Modern Australia* (Sydney: Angus & Robertson, Sydney, 1986), p. 242. Menzies' warning of war appears in Neville Meaney (ed.), *Australia and the World: A Documentary History from the 1870s to the 1970s* (Melbourne: Longman Cheshire, 1985), pp. 598, 616; and Ann Curthoys, A. W. Martin and Tim Rowse (eds), *Australians from 1939* (Sydney: Fairfax, Syme and Weldon Associates, 1987), p. 32; his speech on the British Empire and 1950 diary entry on Egyptian nationalists are quoted in Allan Martin, *Robert Menzies: A Life*, vol. 2: *1944–1978* (Melbourne: Melbourne University Press, 1999), pp. 152, 336; the verse appears in Glen St J. Barclay, *Friends in High Places: Australian–American Diplomatic Relations Since 1945* (Melbourne: Oxford University Press, 1985), p. 128. Garfield Barwick, the minister for external affairs, is quoted by Peter Edwards with Gregory Pemberton, *Crises and Commitments: The Politics and*

Diplomacy of Australia's Involvement in Southeast Asian Conflicts, 1848–1965 (Sydney: Allen & Unwin, 1992), p. 246; Holt is quoted in Barclay, *Friends in High Places*, p. 154; Menzies on communism by Frank Cain and Frank Farrell, 'Menzies' War on the Communist Party, 1949–1951', in Ann Curthoys and John Merritt (eds), *Australia's First Cold War, 1945–1953*, vol. 1: *Society, Communism and Culture* (Sydney: Allen & Unwin, 1984), p. 115. Chifley's views of the Movement are reported by L. F. Crisp, *Ben Chifley: A Political Biography* (London: Longmans, 1961), p. 394; the commentator on the predicament of the Labor Party was D. W. Rawson, *Labor in Vain? A Survey of the Australian Labor Party* (Melbourne: Longmans, 1966). Menzies' view of Evatt is in Meaney (ed.), *Australia and the World*, p. 605; the Call to Australia is quoted in David Lowe, *Menzies and the 'Great World Struggle': Australia's Cold War, 1948–1954* (Sydney: UNSW Press, 1999), p. 115; Menzies' Cold War rhetoric is in Meaney (ed.), *Australia and the World*, p. 605; the episode at the Lakeside Oval was recounted to me by Barney Cooney.

Menzies on prosperity is quoted by John Murphy, 'Shaping the Cold War Family', *Australian Historical Studies*, vol. 26, no. 105 (1995), p. 550; the description of house building is in Peter Spearritt, *Sydney's Century: A History* (Sydney: UNSW Press, 2000), p. 98. The American evangelist's slogan is quoted by David Hilliard, 'Popular Religion in Australia in the 1950s: A Study of Adelaide and Brisbane', *Journal of Religious History*, vol. 16, no. 2 (1988), p. 224; statistics for engagement patterns and the advertising jingle are in Graeme Davison, *The Car Wars: How the Car Won Our Hearts and Conquered Our Cities* (Sydney: Allen & Unwin, 2004), pp. 52–3. The Australian expert on the family is quoted in Stella Lees and June Senyard, *The 1950s* (Melbourne: Hyland House, 1987), p. 83; the Olympic programme is in Graeme Davison, 'Welcoming the World: The 1956 Olympic Games and Re-presentation of Melbourne', *Australian Historical Studies*, vol. 28, no. 109 (1997), p. 74. The chairman of the Atomic Energy Commission was Philip Baxter, quoted in Patrick O'Farrell, *UNSW, a Portrait: The University of New South Wales, 1949–1999* (Sydney: UNSW Press, 1999), p. 76. The radical nationalist works cited are A. A. Phillips, *The Australian Tradition* (Melbourne: Cheshire, 1958), Russel Ward, *The Australian Legend* (Melbourne: Oxford University Press, 1958) and Vance Palmer, *The Legend of the Nineties* (Melbourne: Melbourne University Press, 1954). Calwell is quoted by Gwenda Tavan, '"Good Neighbours": Community Organisations, Migrant Assimilation and Australian Society and Culture, 1950–1961', *Australian Historical Studies*, vol. 28, no. 109 (1997), p. 78; and his successor, Harold Holt, in Sara Wills, 'Passengers of Memory: Constructions of British Immigrants in Post-Imperial Australia', *Australian Journal of Politics and History*, vol. 51, no. 1 (2005), p. 99;

article on 'The Australian Way of Life' is quoted in Richard White, *Inventing Australia: Images and Identity, 1688–1980* (Sydney: Allen & Unwin, 1981), p. 163. The minister for works was Nelson Lemmon, quoted in Andrew Hassam, 'From Heroes to Whingers: Changing Attitudes to British Migrants', *Australian Journal of Politics and History*, vol. 51, no. 1 (2005), p. 79. The minister for territories, Paul Hasluck, is quoted in Tim Rowse, 'Assimilation and After', in Curthoys, Martin and Rowse (eds), *Australians from 1939*, p. 135; and John Murphy, *Imagining the Fifties: Private Sentiment and Political Culture in Menzies' Australia* (Sydney: UNSW Press, 2000), p. 170. The American tennis player was Jack Kramer, quoted in Kevin Fewster, 'Advantage Australia: Davis Cup Tennis, 1950–1959', *Sporting Traditions*, vol. 2, no. 1 (1985), p. 59; the surf life-saving club statement is in White, *Inventing Australia*, p. 155.

Menzies is quoted by Stuart Ward, *Australia and the British Embrace: The Demise of the Imperial Ideal* (Melbourne: Melbourne University Press, 2001), p. 155; and Frank Bongiorno, "The Price of Nostalgia: Menzies, the "Liberal" Tradition and Australian Foreign Policy', *Australian Journal of Politics and History*, vol. 51, no. 3 (2005), p. 415. The Liberal premier was Robin Askin, reported by Ian Hancock in David Clune and Ken Turner (eds), *The Premiers of New South Wales. Volume 2, 1901–1925* (Sydney: Federation Press, 2006), p. 356; the Vietnam poem by A. D. Hope is in Chris Wallace-Crabbe and Peter Pierce (eds), *The Clubbing of the Gunfire: 101 Australian War Poems* (Melbourne: Melbourne University Press, 1984), p. 197; the minister who drew the comparison with the London mob was Peter Howson, quoted in Greg Pemberton, *All the Way: Australia's Road to Vietnam* (Sydney: Allen & Unwin, 1987), p. 325; and recorded in his diaries edited by Don Aitkin as *The Life of Politics* (Melbourne: Penguin Books, 1994), p. 631; his colleague who spoke of 'political bikies' was Billie Snedden, quoted in Peter Edwards, *A Nation at War: Australian Politics, Society and Diplomacy during the Vietnam War, 1965–1975* (Sydney: Allen & Unwin, 1997), p. 266. Robin Boyd and John Freeland are quoted in Brown, *Governing Prosperity*, p. 159; and Alastair Greig, *The Stuff Dreams Are Made Of: Housing Provision in Australia, 1945–1960* (Melbourne: Melbourne University Press, 1995), pp. 149–50; Barry Humphries' memoir is *More Please* (Melbourne: Penguin Books, 1992), p. xiii. The connotations of 'flatting' are discussed in Seamus O'Hanlon, '"The Reign of the Six-Pack"; Flats and Flat-Life in Australia in the 1960s', in Shirleene Robinson and Julie Ustinoff (eds), *The 1960s in Australia: People, Power and Politics* (Newcastle upon Tyne: Cambridge Scholars, 2012), p. 41; and Windschuttle is quoted by Shirleene Robinson, 'The 1960s Counter-Culture in Australia: The Search for Personal Freedom', in *The 1960s in Australia*, p. 131. Robin Boyd's views on the Australian pavilion are in James Curran, '"Australia Should Be There": Expo 67 and the Search for a New National Image', *Australian*

Historical Studies, vol. 39, no. 1 (2008), pp. 81, 88; and Barry McKenzie is dissected in Anne Pender, '"Culture Up To Our Arseholes": Projecting Post-Imperial Australia', *Australian Journal of Politics and History*, vol. 51, no. 1 (2005), p. 65. The government's response to the Yolngu claim is given in Bain Attwood, *Rights for Aborigines* (Sydney: Allen & Unwin, 2003), p. 304; Bobbi Sykes and Gough Whitlam are quoted in Rowse, 'Assimilation and After', p. 142, 144.

The 'faceless men' allegation appears in Allan Martin, *Robert Menzies: A Life*, p. 460; Whitlam's explanation of social citizenship was recorded in Gough Whitlam, *The Whitlam Government, 1972–1975* (Melbourne: Penguin Books, 1985), pp. 182–3; his call for a light on every desk is in Graham Freudenberg, *A Certain Grandeur: Gough Whitlam in Politics* (Melbourne: Macmillan, 1977), p. 82; the assertion of national identity is in James Curran, *The Power of Speech: Australian Prime Ministers Defining the National Image* (Melbourne: Melbourne University Press, 2004), p.79. Multiculturalism and ethnicity are disentangled by James Jupp, *From White Australia to Woomera: The Story of Australian Immigration* (Cambridge: Cambridge University Press, 2002), pp. 2–3, 83–5. Bjelke-Petersen's trademark phrase provides the title of his memoirs, *Don't You Worry About That!* (Sydney: Angus & Robertson, 1990); and Whitlam's response is quoted by Ross Fitzgerald, *From 1915 to the Early 1980s: A History of Queensland* (Brisbane: University of Queensland Press, 1984), p. 255; Charles Court recalled Playford's advice in the preface to Stewart Cockburn, *Playford: Benevolent Despot* (Adelaide: Axiom, 1991); the prime minister's phrase is used by Laurie Oakes, *Crash Through or Crash: The Unmaking of a Prime Minister* (Melbourne: Drummond, 1976); Whitlam's response to the dismissal is in *Dictionary of Australian Quotations*, p. 280.

9   RECTIFICATION

Malcolm Fraser is quoted in Frank Crowley, *Tough Times: Australia in the Seventies* (Melbourne: Heinemann, 1986), p. 309.

Hawke is quoted in James Curran, *The Power of Speech: Australian Prime Ministers Defining the National Image* (Melbourne: Melbourne University Press, 2004), p. 171; Keating by Kevin Davis, 'Managing the Economy', in Brian W. Head and Allan Patience (eds), *From Fraser to Hawke* (Melbourne: Longman Cheshire, 1989), p. 67; and in Paul Kelly, *The End of Certainty: The Story of the 1980s* (Sydney: Allen & Unwin, 1992), p. 212. The two economic historians were Eric Jones and Geoffrey Raby, 'Establishing a European Economy', in John Hardy and Alan Frost (eds), *Studies from Terra Australis to Australia* (Canberra: Australian Academy of the Humanities, 1989), p. 155. The 'wets' and 'dries' are discussed by Judith Brett, *Australian Liberals and the Moral Middle Class: From Alfred Deakin to John Howard* (Cambridge:

Cambridge University Press, 2003), pp. 172–7. The financial journalist, Trevor Sykes, is quoted in Ian Macfarlane, *The Search for Stability* (Sydney: ABC Books, 2006), p. 52; and Keating on negative gearing in George Megalogenis, *The Australian Moment: How We Were Made for These Times* (Melbourne: Viking, 2012), p.191; his comment on the recession is quoted in Kelly, *The End of Certainty*, p. 504. Keating posed the stark choice in John Wiseman, *Global Nation? Australia and the Politics of Globalisation* (Cambridge: Cambridge University Press), pp. 43–4. The terminology of the new public sector management is drawn from Owen Hughes, 'Public Management', and Glyn Davis, 'Public Sector Reform', in Brian Galligan and Winsome Roberts (eds), *The Oxford Companion to Australian Politics* (Melbourne: Oxford University Press, 2007), pp. 477–80. Hawke is quoted in Kelly, *The End of Certainty*, p. 350. Dawkins and the head of the Australian Vice-Chancellors' Committee are quoted in Stuart Macintyre, 'Making the Unified National System', in Gwilym Croucher et al. (eds), *The Dawkins Revolution 12 Years On* (Melbourne: Melbourne University Press, 2013), p. 25. Kerry Packer and the Cabinet minister, John Button, are reported in Paul Barry, *The Rise and Rise of Kerry Packer* (Sydney: Bantam, 1993), pp. 310, 322. The comment on Bond appears in Geoffrey Bolton, *Land of Vision and Mirage: Western Australia since 1826* (Perth: University of Western Australia, 2008), p. 181; and Bond's lament is in Stuart Macintyre, 'Tall Poppies', *Australian Society*, September 1989. Beverley Kingston describes the transformation of Darling Harbour in *A History of New South Wales* (Cambridge: Cambridge University Press, 2006), p. 226. The defender of tall poppies was John Gorton, quoted in G. A. Wilkes, *A Dictionary of Australian Colloquialisms* (Sydney: Collins Books, 1980), p. 260.

Gareth Evans described middle power diplomacy in the account he wrote with Bruce Grant, *Australia's Foreign Relations in the World of the 1990s* (Melbourne: Melbourne University Press, 1995), p. 344, quoted by Carl Ungerer, 'The "Middle Power" Concept in Australian Foreign Policy', *Australian Journal of Politics and History*, vol. 53, no. 4 (December 2007), p. 547; the endless race was declared in a 1994 government white paper on employment, quoted in Wiseman, *Global Nation?*, p. 40, and Keating's glosses on it appear in Kelly, *The End of Certainty*, p. 664, and Stuart Macintyre, 'Who Are the True Believers?', *Labour History*, no. 68 (May 1995), p. 155. Blainey's statements are in Stuart Macintyre and Anna Clark, *The History Wars* (Melbourne: Melbourne University Press, 2004), pp. 86, 122; and the immigration statistics come from Eric Richards, *Destination Australia: Migration to Australia since 1901* (Sydney: UNSW Press, 2008), pp. 280, 282. Keating's ridicule of basket-weavers was reported in *The Age*, 7 December 1981. Sally Morgan is quoted in Bain Attwood, 'Portrait of an Aboriginal as an Artist: Sally Morgan and the Construction of Aboriginality', *Australian*

Historical Studies, vol. 25, no. 99 (1992), pp. 305–6; the predicament of Charlie Perkins and the statement by Joh Bjelke-Petersen are in Peter Read, *Charles Perkins: A Biography* (Melbourne: Viking, 1990), pp. 212, 234. The mining executive was Hugh Morgan, quoted in Mark Davis, *The Land of Plenty: Australia in the 2000s* (Melbourne: Melbourne University Press, 2008), p. 48. The passages of the Mabo judgement comes from Garth Nettheim, 'Mabo', in Tony Blackshield et al. (eds), *The Oxford Companion to the High Court* (Melbourne: Oxford University Press, 2001), p. 448; and Keating's response from Paul Kelly, *The March of Patriots: The Struggle for Modern Australia* (Melbourne: Melbourne University Press, 2009), p. 198. The Redfern Park speech and the call for an outward-looking Australia are in Mark Ryan (ed.), *Advancing Australia: The Speeches of Paul Keating, Prime Minister* (Sydney: Big Picture Publications, 1995), pp. 32–3, 228.

Howard's electoral rhetoric is discussed by Judith Brett, *Australian Liberals and the Moral Middle Class: From Alfred Deakin to John Howard* (Cambridge: Cambridge University Press, 2003), pp. 187–8.

10 OUTCOMES

Howard is quoted in Wayne Errington and Peter Van Onselen, *John Winston Howard* (Melbourne: Melbourne University Press, 2007), pp. 137, 211. Ross Garnaut coined the term 'Great Australian Complacency' 2004 and explained it in *Dog Days: Australia After the Boom* (Melbourne: Redback, 2013), p. 82. Howard's pre-election statements are in Stuart Macintyre and Anna Clark, *The History Wars* (Melbourne: Melbourne University Press, 2003), p. 136; the distinction between 'core' and 'non-core promises' is in George Megalogenis, *The Longest Decade* (rev. edn, Melbourne: Scribe, 2008), p. 277; and the Commonwealth Treasurer is quoted by Richard Leaver and Maryanne Kelton, 'Issues in Australian Foreign Policy', *Australian Journal of Politics and History*, vol. 45, no. 2 (June 1999), p. 242. 'Mutual obligation' and its outcomes are noted by John Roskam, 'Liberalism and Social Welfare', in J. R. Nethercote (ed.), *Liberalism and the Australian Federation* (Sydney: Federation Press, 2001), p. 285. Peter Reith, the minister for workplace relations, is quoted in Helen Trinca and Anne Davies, *Waterfront: The Battle that Changed Australia* (Sydney: Doubleday, 2000), p. 171. The responses to the High Court judgement appear in Paul Kelly, *The March of Patriots: The Struggle for Modern Australia* (Melbourne: Melbourne University Press, 2009), p. 393; and Mark Davis, *The Land of Plenty: Australia in the 2000s* (Melbourne: Melbourne University Press, 208), p. 63. Howard's views of national history are quoted in Macintyre and Clark, *The History Wars*, pp. 132, 201; and the minister's response to the report on the Stolen Generations is quoted in Robert Manne, *In Denial: The Stolen Generations and the Right* (Melbourne: Black Inc.,

2001), p. 75. Howard's address to the Reconciliation Convention is reported by Andrew Markus, *Race: John Howard and the Remaking of Australia* (Sydney: Allen & Unwin, 2001), p. 107. Hanson's maiden speech is reproduced in John Pasquarelli, *The Pauline Hanson Story* (Sydney: New Holland Publishers, 1998), pp. 119–26, who also relates the television incident on p. 182; Howard's response is quoted by Markus, *Race*, p. 101; Howard's claim that Beazley lacked 'ticker' is reported in the 'Political Chronicle' of the *Australian Journal of Politics and History*, vol. 45, no. 2 (June 1999), p. 256; his speech at the Constitutional Convention is quoted by Steve Vizard, *Two Weeks in Lilliput* (Melbourne: Penguin Books, 1998), p. 32; and the Governor-General is quoted in Tony Stephens, *Sir William Deane: The Things That Matter* (Sydney: Hodder Headline, 2002), p. 10.

The hard-headed approach to international affairs is espoused by *In the National Interest: Australia's Foreign and Trade Policy White Paper* (Canberra: Commonwealth of Australia, 1997), p. 111; and the foreign minister, Alexander Downer, is quoted in Ungerer, 'The "Middle Power" Concept in Australian Foreign Policy', p. 549. The interview in which Howard appeared as deputy sheriff is quoted in Henry S. Albinski, 'Issues in Australian Foreign Policy', *Australian Journal of Politics and History*, vol. 46, no. 2 (June 2000), p. 205; his claim to be simply getting on with the job appears on p. 203. The new approach to the United Nations is reported by David Goldsworthy, 'Issues in Australian Foreign Policy', *Australian Journal of Politics and History*, vol. 47, no. 2 (June 2001), p. 241. Tony Abbott's rebuke is quoted in 'Political Chronicle', *Australian Journal of Politics and History*, vol. 46, no. 4 (December 2001), p. 562; and the Liberal Party's president appears in the same journal, vol. 47, no. 4 (December 2002), p. 533. Peter Mares identifies Howard as the author of the Pacific Solution in *Borderline: Australia's Response to Refugees and Asylum Seekers in the Wake of the* Tampa (2nd edn, Sydney: UNSW Press, 2002), p. 127; the imposition of censorship is quoted by David Marr and Marian Wilkinson, *Dark Victory* (Sydney: Allen & Unwin, 2003), p. 277. Peter Reith's statement of 'absolute fact' is quoted by Patrick Weller, *Don't Tell the Prime Minister* (Melbourne: Scribe, 2002), p. 3; the Liberal election advertisements are quoted in Marr and Wilkinson, *Dark Victory*, p. 277; and the prime minister suggestion of terrorist links in Mares, *Borderline*, p. 134. Howard's address to Congress is quoted in Meg Gurry, 'Issues in Australian Foreign Policy', *Australian Journal of Politics and History*, vol. 49, no. 2 (June 2003), p. 228.

Howard's qualification of the report of children overboard appears in Weller, *Don't Tell the Prime Minister*, p. 2; and Laurie Oakes' explanation of the 'political dog whistle' is noted in Marr and Wilkinson, *Dark Victory*, p. 280. Kennett's statement is in Graeme Davison, John Hirst and Stuart Macintyre (eds), *The Oxford Companion to Australian History* (rev. edn, Melbourne: Oxford University Press, 2001), p. 366; and Carr's diary in Marilyn Dodkin, *Bob Carr* (Sydney: UNSW Press, 2003), p. 234. The social commentators are quoted and their claims contested by Murray Goot in David Burchell and Andrew Leigh (eds), *The Prince's New Clothes: Why Do Australians Dislike Their Politicians?* (Sydney: UNSW Press, 2002), pp. 9–46. Alan Jones' instruction appears in Chris Masters, *Jonestown: The Power and the Myth of Alan Jones* (Sydney: Allen & Unwin, 2006), p. 294; and his statement during the Cronulla riots is quoted by David Marr, 'Alan Jones: I'm the Person Who Led This Charge', *The Age*, 23 December 2005; Howard's change is noted in James Jupp, *From White Australia to Woomera: The Story of Australian Immigration* (Cambridge: Cambridge University Press, 2002), p. 130. Howard's declaration of an end to the discussion of national identity is in Errington and Van Onselen, *John Winston Howard*, p. 221. The trade minister's recourse to amnesia is in Caroline Overington, *Kick Back: Inside the Australian Wheat Board Scandal* (Sydney: Allen & Unwin, 2007), p. 278. Barack Obama's response to Howard appears in John Lee, 'Issues in Australian Foreign Policy', *Australian Journal of Politics and History*, vol. 53, no. 4 (December 2007), p. 602; and Howard's response to Al Gore is quoted by George Megalogenis, *The Longest Decade* (rev. edn, Carlton, Vic.: Scribe, 2008), p. 322. His confession on Aboriginal issues is in Judith Brett, 'Exit Right: The Unravelling of John Howard', *Quarterly Essay*, no. 28 (2007), p. 84; and Peter Van Onselen and Philip Senior, *Howard's End: The Unravelling of a Government* (Melbourne: Melbourne University Press, 2008), p. 109. Megalogenis, *The Longest Decade*, pp. 345–6, records the origins and over-use of 'working families'.

Megalogenis provides the description of Rudd's 'brand' and quotes the Treasury secretary in *The Australian Moment*, pp. 322, 340. The review of the 'emergency response' and 'closing the gap' are discussed by Will Sanders and Janet Hunt, 'Sorry, But the Indigenous Affairs Revolution Continues', in Chris Aulich and Mark Evans, *The Rudd Government: Australian Commonwealth Administration 2007–2010* (Canberra: ANU E Press, 2010), pp. 223, 226; Noel Pearson sets out his views in *Up From the Mission: Selected Writings* (Melbourne: Black Inc., 2009), pp. 140, 243. Rudd's statement on climate change is quoted in Murray Goot, 'The New Millennium', in Alison Bashford and Stuart Macintyre (eds), *The Cambridge History of Australia* (Cambridge: Cambridge University Press, 2013), p. 202. The chant of the rally in Perth appears in Malcolm Knox, *Boom: The Underground History of Australia, from Gold Rush to GFC* (Melbourne: Viking, 2013), p. 313; and Abbott's condemnation of climate science in Paul Kelly, *Triumph and Demise: The Broken Promise of a Labor Generation* (Melbourne: Melbourne University Press, 2014), p. 247. Tom Clark reflects on Rudd's jargon in *Stay on Message: Poetry and Truthfulness in Political Speech* (Melbourne: Australian Scholarly Publishing, 2012), p. 100. The abuse of Gillard is documented in Julia Gillard, *My Story* (Sydney: Knopf, 2014), p. 105; and Kelly, *Triumph and Demise*, p. 366; her response is in *Triumph and Demise*, p. 409. Abbott's comments about Gillard's marital status were reported in *The Australian*, 25 January 2011. Abbott's declaration that Australia was under new management appears in Jennifer Rayner and John Wanna, 'An Overview of the 2013 Election Campaign', in Carol Johnson and John Wanna (eds), *Abbott's Gambit: the 2013 Australian Federal Election* (Canberra: ANU E Press, 2015), p. 28; while the end of the age of entitlement is recorded in Kelly, *Triumph and Demise*, p. 488. For Andrew Forrest, 'Forrest Wants "Seismic Change"', *The Australian*, 12 February 2015.

GUIDE TO FURTHER READING

REFERENCE

Jaynie Anderson (ed.), *The Cambridge Companion to Australian Art* (Cambridge: Cambridge University Press, 2011).

Frank Crowley and Peter Spearritt (gen. eds), *Australians: A Historical Library, 5 vols: A Historical Atlas, A Historical Dictionary, Events and Places, Historical Statistics, A Guide to Sources* (Sydney: Fairfax, Syme and Weldon Associates, 1987).

Brian Galligan and Winsome Roberts (eds), *The Oxford Companion to Australian Politics* (Melbourne: Oxford University Press, 2007).

John Hirst, Graeme Davison and Stuart Macintyre (eds), *The Oxford Companion to Australian History* (rev. edn, Melbourne: Oxford University Press, 2001).

David Horton (gen. ed.), *The Encyclopaedia of Aboriginal Australia*, 2 vols (Canberra: Aboriginal Studies Press, 1994).

James Jupp (gen. ed.), *The Australian People: An Encyclopedia of the Nation, Its People and Their Origins* (rev. edn, Cambridge: Cambridge University Press, 2001).

Stephen Murray-Smith (ed.), *The Dictionary of Australian Quotations* (rev. edn, Melbourne: Mandarin, 1992).

Douglas Pike, Bede Nairn, Geoffrey Serle, John Ritchie, Diane Langmore and Melanie Nolan (gen. eds), *Australian Dictionary of Biography*, 18 vols (Melbourne: Melbourne University Press, 1966–2012).

W. S. Ramson, *The Australian National Dictionary: Australian Words and Their Origins* (Melbourne: Oxford University Press, 1988).

GENERAL

Alan Atkinson, *The Europeans in Australia, A History* (Melbourne: Oxford University Press, vol. 1, 1997; vol. 2, 2004; Sydney: UNSW Press, vol. 3, 2014).

Alison Bashford and Stuart Macintyre (eds), *The Cambridge History of Australia*, 2 vols (Cambridge: Cambridge University Press, 2013).

Geoffrey Bolton (ed.), *The Oxford History of Australia* (Melbourne: Oxford University Press, vol. 2, 1992; vol. 3, 1988; vol. 4, 1986; vol. 5, 1990).

Ian Breward, *A History of the Churches in Australasia* (Oxford: Oxford University Press, 2001).

C. M. H. Clark, *A History of Australia*, 6 vols (Melbourne: Melbourne University Press, 1962–87).

Donald Denoon and Philippa Mein-Smith, with Marivic Wyndham, *A History of Australia, New Zealand and the Pacific* (Malden, Mass.: Blackwell, 2000).

Alan D. Gilbert and K. S. Inglis (gen. eds), *Australians: A Historical Library, 5 vols: Australians to 1788, Australians 1838, Australians 1888, Australians 1938, Australians from 1939* (Sydney: Fairfax, Syme and Weldon Associates, 1987).

Jeffrey Grey, *A Military History of Australia* (3rd edn, Cambridge: Cambridge University Press, 2008).

Patricia Grimshaw, Marilyn Lake, Ann McGrath and Marian Quartly, *Creating a Nation* (Melbourne: McPhee Gribble, 1994).

Peter Pierce (ed.), *The Cambridge History of Australian Literature* (Cambridge: Cambridge University Press, 2009).

Simon Ville and Glen Withers (eds), *The Cambridge Economic History of Australia* (Cambridge: Cambridge University Press, 2015).

1   BEGINNINGS

Jim Allen, John Golson and Rhys Jones (eds), *Sunda and Sahul* (London: Academic Press, 1977).

Geoffrey Blainey, *The Triumph of the Nomads* (Melbourne: Macmillan, 1982).

N. G. Butlin, *Economics and the Dreamtime: A Hypothetical History* (Cambridge: Cambridge University Press, 1993).

Josephine Flood, *The Original Australians: Story of the Aboriginal People* (Sydney: Allen & Unwin, 2006).

Peter Hiscock, *Archaeology of Ancient Australia* (New York: Routledge, 2008).

Ian Keen, *Aboriginal Economy and Society: Australia at the Threshold of Colonisation* (Melbourne: Oxford University Press, 2004).

Harry Lourandos, *Continent of Hunter-Gatherers: New Perspectives in Australian Prehistory* (Cambridge: Cambridge University Press, 1997).

D. J. Mulvaney and Johan Kamminga, *The Prehistory of Australia* (Sydney: Allen & Unwin, 1999).

D. J. Mulvaney and J. Peter White (eds), *Australians to 1788* (Sydney: Fairfax, Syme and Weldon Associates, 1987).

Stephen J. Pyne, *Burning Bush: A Fire History of Australia* (Sydney: Allen & Unwin, 1992).

Mike Smith, *The Archaeology of Australia's Deserts* (Cambridge: Cambridge University Press, 2013).

Mary White, *After the Greening: The Browning of Australia* (Sydney: Kangaroo Press, 1994).

2 NEWCOMERS

Alan Atkinson, *The Europeans in Australia, vol. 1: The Beginning* (Melbourne: Oxford University Press, 1997).

J. C. Beaglehole, *The Life of Captain James Cook* (London: A. and C. Black, 1974).

Inga Clendinnen, *Dancing With Strangers* (Melbourne: Text Publishing, 2003).

Alan Frost, *Botany Bay: The Real Story* (Melbourne: Black Inc., 2009).

John Gascoigne, *The Enlightenment and the Origins of European Australia* (Cambridge: Cambridge University Press, 2002).

John Gascoigne, *Encountering the Pacific in the Age of Enlightenment* (Cambridge: Cambridge University Press, 2014).

John Hardy and Alan Frost (eds), *Studies from Terra Australia to Australia* (Canberra: Australian Academy of the Humanities, 1989).

Chris Healy, *From the Ruins of Colonialism: History as Social Memory* (Cambridge: Cambridge University Press, 1997).

E. L. Jones, *The European Miracle: Environments, Economies and Geopolitics in the History of Europe and Asia* (3rd edn, Cambridge: Cambridge University Press, 2003).

Grace Karskens, *The Colony: A History of Early Sydney* (Sydney: Allen & Unwin, 2009).

Shino Konishi, *The Aboriginal Male in the Enlightenment World* (London: Pickering and Chatto, 2012).

P. J. Marshall (ed.), *The Oxford History of the British Empire, vol. II: The Eighteenth Century* (Oxford: Oxford University Press, 1998).

Ged Martin (ed.), *The Founding of Australia: The Argument About Australia's Origins* (Sydney: Hale & Iremonger, 1978).

Maria Nugent, *Captain Cook Was Here* (Cambridge: Cambridge University Press, 2009).

Anthony Pagden, *Lords of All the World: Ideologies of Empire in Spain, Britain and France, c. 1500 to c. 1800* (New Haven, Conn.: Yale University Press, 1995).

Bernard Smith, *European Vision and the South Pacific* (2nd edn, Sydney: Harper and Row, 1985).

Bernard Smith, *Imagining the Pacific: In the Wake of the Cook Voyages* (Melbourne: Melbourne University Press, 1992).

O. H. K. Spate, *The Pacific Since Magellan*, 3 vols (Canberra: ANU Press, 1979–88).

W. E. H. Stanner, *White Man Got No Dreaming: Essays, 1938–1973* (Canberra: ANU Press, 1979).

Glyndwr Williams and Alan Frost (eds), *Terra Australis to Australia* (Melbourne: Oxford University Press, 1988).

3   COERCION

Alison Alexander, *Tasmania's Convicts: How Felons Built a Free Society* (Sydney: Allen & Unwin, 2013).

Graeme Aplin (ed.), *A Difficult Infant: Sydney Before Macquarie* (Sydney: UNSW Press, 1988).

Alan Atkinson, *The Europeans in Australia, vol. 1: The Beginning* (Melbourne: Oxford University Press, 1997).

Tim Bonyhady, *The Colonial Earth* (Melbourne: Miegunyah Press, 2000).

James Boyce, *Van Diemen's Land* (Melbourne: Black, Inc., 2008).

Frank Broeze, *Island Nation: A History of Australians and the Sea* (Sydney: Allen & Unwin, 1997).

C. M. H. Clark, *A History of Australia*, vol. I (Melbourne: Melbourne University Press, 1962).

Joy Damousi, *Depraved and Disorderly: Female Convicts, Sexuality and Gender in Colonial Australia* (Cambridge: Cambridge University Press, 1997).

Kay Daniels, *Convict Women* (Sydney: Allen & Unwin, 1998).

Brian Fletcher, *Landed Enterprise and Penal Society: A History of Farming and Grazing in New South Wales Before 1821* (Sydney: Sydney University Press, 1976).

Lucy Frost and Hamish Maxwell-Stewart, *Chain Letters: Narrating Convict Lives* (Melbourne: Melbourne University Press, 2001).

J. B. Hirst, *Convict Society and Its Enemies: A History of Early New South Wales* (Sydney: Allen & Unwin, 1983).

Robert Hughes, *The Fatal Shore: A History of the Transportation of Convicts to Australia, 1787–1868* (London: Collins Harvill, 1987).

K. S. Inglis, *The Australian Colonists: An Exploration of Social History, 1788–1870* (Melbourne: Melbourne University Press, 1974).

Grace Karskens, *The Colony: A History of Early Sydney* (Sydney: Allen & Unwin, 2009).

Sharon Morgan, *Land Settlement in Early Tasmania: Creating an Antipodean England* (Cambridge: Cambridge University Press, 1992).

David Neal, *The Rule of Law in a Penal Colony: Law and Power in Early New South Wales* (Cambridge: Cambridge University Press, 1991).

Stephen Nicholas (ed.), *Convict Workers: Reinterpreting Australia's Past* (Cambridge: Cambridge University Press, 1988).

Cassandra Pybus, *Black Founders: The Unknown Story of Australia's First Black Settlers* (Sydney: UNSW Press, 2006).

John Ritchie, *Lachlan Macquarie: A Biography* (Melbourne: Melbourne University Press, 1986).

L. L. Robson, *The Convict Settlers of Australia* (Melbourne: Melbourne University Press, 1965).

L. L. Robson, *A History of Tasmania*, vol. 1 (Melbourne: Oxford University Press, 1983).

A. G. L. Shaw, *Convicts and the Colonies: A Study of Penal Transportation from Great Britain and Ireland to Australia and Other Parts of the British Empire* (London: Faber, 1966).

4 CONQUEST

Alan Atkinson, *The Europeans in Australia, vol. 2: Democracy* (Melbourne: Oxford University Press, 2004).

Alan Atkinson and Marian Aveling (eds), *Australians 1838* (Sydney: Fairfax, Syme and Weldon Associates, 1987).

Geoffrey Bolton, *Land of Vision and Mirage: Western Australia since 1826* (Perth: University of Western Australia Press, 2008).

James Boyce, *1835: The Founding of Melbourne & the Conquest of Australia* (Melbourne: Black, Inc., 2011).

Peter Cochrane, *Colonial Ambition: Foundations of Australian Democracy* (Melbourne: Melbourne University Press, 2006).

Jan Critchett, *A 'Distant Field of Murder': Western District Frontiers, 1834–1848* (Melbourne: Melbourne University Press, 1990).

Joy Damousi, *Depraved and Disorderly: Female Convicts, Sexuality and Gender in Colonial Australia* (Cambridge: Cambridge University Press, 1997).

Kay Daniels, *Convict Women* (Sydney: Allen & Unwin, 1998).

David Denholm, *The Colonial Australians* (Melbourne: Allen Lane, 1979).

Robert Dixon, *The Course of Empire: Neo-Classical Culture in New South Wales, 1788–1860* (Melbourne: Oxford University Press, 1986).

Ian Duffield and James Bradley (eds), *Representing Convicts: New Perspectives on Convict Forced Labour Migration* (London: Leicester University Press, 1997).

Lisa Ford, *Settler Sovereignty: Jurisdiction and Indigenous People in America and Australia 1788–1836* (Cambridge, MA: Harvard University Press, 2010).

Robert Foster, Rick Hosking and Amanda Nettelbeck, *Fatal Collisions: The South Australian Frontier and the Violence of Memory* (Adelaide: Wakefield Press, 2001).

John Gascoigne, *The Enlightenment and the Origins of European Australia* (Cambridge: Cambridge University Press, 2002).

J. B. Hirst, *Convict Society and its Enemies: A History of Early New South Wales* (Sydney: Allen & Unwin, 1983).

K. S. Inglis, *The Australian Colonists: An Exploration of Social History, 1788–1870* (Melbourne: Melbourne University Press, 1974).

Terry Irving, *The Southern Tree of Liberty: The Democratic Movement in New South Wales Before 1856* (Sydney: Federation Press, 2006).

Dane Kennedy, *The Last Blank Spaces: Exploring Africa and Australia* (Cambridge, Mass.: Harvard University Press, 2013).

Bruce Kercher, *An Unruly Child: A History of Law in Australia* (Sydney: Allen and Unwin, 1995).

Ann McGrath, *Contested Ground: Australian Aborigines Under the British Crown* (Sydney: Allen & Unwin, 1995).

Roger Milliss, *Waterloo Creek: The Australia Day Massacre of 1838, George Gipps and the British Conquest of New South Wales* (Melbourne: McPhee Gribble, 1992).

Jessie Mitchell, *In Good Faith? Governing Indigenous Australia through God, Charity and Empire* (Canberra: ANU E Press, 2011).

Stephen Nicholas (ed.), *Convict Workers: Reinterpreting Australia's Past* (Cambridge: Cambridge University Press, 1988).

Douglas Pike, *Paradise of Dissent: South Australia, 1829–1857* (2nd edn, Melbourne: Melbourne University Press, 1967).

Geoff Raby, *Making Rural Australia: An Economic History of Technical and Institutional Creativity, 1788–1860* (Oxford: Oxford University Press, 1996).

Henry Reynolds, *Frontier: Aborigines, Settlers and Land* (Sydney: Allen & Unwin, 1987).

Henry Reynolds, *Fate of a Free People* (Melbourne: Penguin Books, 1995).

L. L. Robson, *A History of Tasmania*, vol. 1 (Melbourne: Oxford University Press, 1983).

Michael Roe, *Quest for Authority in Eastern Australia, 1835–1851* (Melbourne: Melbourne University Press, 1965).

Penny Russell, *Savage or Civilised? Manners in Colonial Australia* (Sydney: UNSW Press, 2010).

Lyndall Ryan, *The Aboriginal Tasmanians* (Sydney: Allen & Unwin, 2006).

5   PROGRESS

Alan Atkinson, *The Europeans in Australia, vol. 2: Democracy* (Melbourne: Oxford University Press, 2004).

Geoffrey Blainey, *The Rush that Never Ended* (5th edn, Melbourne: Melbourne University Press, 2003).

Geoffrey Bolton, *A Thousand Miles Away: A History of North Queensland to 1920* (Canberra: Australian National University Press, 1963).

Tim Bonyhady, *The Colonial Earth* (Melbourne: Miegunyah Press, 2000).

Graeme Davison, *The Rise and Fall of Marvellous Melbourne* (Melbourne: Melbourne University Press, 1978).

Graeme Davison, J. W. McCarty and Ailsa McLeary (eds), *Australians 1888* (Sydney: Fairfax, Syme and Weldon Associates, 1987).

Raymond Evans, *A History of Queensland* (Cambridge: Cambridge University Press, 2007).

John Ferry, *Colonial Armidale* (Brisbane: University of Queensland Press, 1999).

John Fitzgerald, *Big White Lie: Chinese Australians in White Australia* (Sydney: UNSW Press, 2007).

Lionel Frost, *The New Urban Frontier: Urbanisation and City Building in Australasia and the American West* (Sydney: UNSW Press, 1991).

Regina Ganter, with Julia Martinez and Gary Lee, *Mixed Relations: Asian-Aboriginal Contact in North Australia* (Perth: University of Western Australia Press, 2006).

David Goodman, *Goldseeking: Victoria and California in the 1850s* (Sydney: Allen & Unwin, 1994).

Andrew Hassam, *Sailing to Australia: Shipboard Diaries by Nineteenth-Century British Emigrants* (Melbourne: Melbourne University Press, 1994).

Roslynn D. Haynes, *Seeking the Centre: The Australian Desert in Literature, Art and Film* (Cambridge: Cambridge University Press, 1998).

John Hirst, *Adelaide and the Country, 1870–1917: Their Social and Political Relationship* (Melbourne: Melbourne University Press, 1973).

John Hirst, *The Strange Birth of Colonial Democracy: New South Wales, 1848–1884* (Sydney: Allen & Unwin, 1988).

H. R. Jackson, *Churches and People in Australia and New Zealand, 1860–1930* (Sydney: Allen & Unwin, 1987).

Beverley Kingston, *The Oxford History of Australia*, vol. 3 (Melbourne: Oxford University Press, 1998).

Stuart Macintyre, *A Colonial Liberalism: The Lost World of Three Victorian Visionaries* (Melbourne: Oxford University Press, 1991).

Ann McGrath, *'Born in the Cattle': Aborigines in Cattle Country* (North Sydney: Allen & Unwin, 1987).

A. W. Martin, *Henry Parkes: A Biography* (Melbourne: Melbourne University Press, 1980).

Alan Powell, *Far Country: A Short History of the Northern Territory* (2nd edn, Melbourne: Melbourne University Press, 1988).

Henry Reynolds, *With the White People* (Melbourne: Penguin Books, 1990).

Andrew Sayers, *Aboriginal Artists of the Nineteenth Century* (Melbourne: Oxford University Press, 1994).

Geoffrey Serle, *The Golden Age: A History of the Colony of Victoria, 1851–1861* (Melbourne: Melbourne University Press, 1963).

Marjorie Theobald, *Knowing Women: Origin of Women's Education in Nineteenth-Century Australia* (Cambridge: Cambridge University Press, 1996).

Duncan Waterson, *Squatter, Selector and Storekeeper: A History of the Darling Downs, 1859–93* (Sydney: Sydney University Press, 1968).

6   RECONSTRUCTION

Judith Allen, *Rose Scott: Vision and Revision in Feminism* (Melbourne: Oxford University Press, 1994).

Alan Atkinson, *The Europeans in Australia, vol 3: Nation* (Sydney: UNSW Press, 2014).

Melissa Bellanta, *Larrikins: A History* (Brisbane: University of Queensland Press, 2012).

Geoffrey Bolton, *Edmund Barton* (Sydney: Allen & Unwin, 2000).

Verity Burgmann, *'In Our Time': Socialism and the Rise of Labor, 1885–1905* (Sydney: Allen & Unwin, 1985).

John Chesterman and Brian Galligan, *Citizens Without Rights: Aborigines and Australian Citizenship* (Cambridge: Cambridge University Press, 1997).

Robin Gollan, *Radical and Working Class Politics: A Study of Eastern Australia, 1850–1910* (Melbourne: Melbourne University Press, 1960).

Anna Haebich, *Broken Circles: Fragmenting Indigenous Families, 1800–2000* (Fremantle: Fremantle Arts Centre Press, 2001).

John Hirst, *The Sentimental Nation: The Making of the Australian Commonwealth* (Melbourne: Oxford University Press, 2000).

Helen Irving, *To Constitute a Nation: A Cultural History of Australia's Constitution* (Cambridge: Cambridge University Press, 1997).

Marilyn Lake and Henry Reynolds, *Drawing the Global Colour Line: White Men's Countries and the Question of Racial Equality* (Melbourne: Melbourne University Press, 2008).

J. A. La Nauze, *Alfred Deakin: A Biography*, 2 vols (Melbourne: Melbourne University Press, 1965).

Russell McGregor, *Imagined Destinies: Aboriginal Australians and the Doomed Race Theory, 1880–1939* (Melbourne: Melbourne University Press, 1997).

Ross McMullin, *The Light on the Hill: The Australian Labor Party, 1891–1991* (Melbourne: Oxford University Press, 1991).

Susan Magarey, *Passions of the First Wave Feminists* (Sydney: UNSW Press, 2001).

John Merritt, *The Making of the AWU* (Melbourne: Oxford University Press, 1986).

Anne O'Brien, *Poverty's Prison: The Poor in New South Wales 1880–1918* (Melbourne: Melbourne University Press, 1988).

John Rickard, *Class and Politics: New South Wales, Victoria and the Early Commonwealth, 1890–1910* (Canberra: Australian National University Press, 1976).

Michael Roe, *Nine Australian Progressives: Vitalism in Bourgeois Social Thought, 1890–1960* (Brisbane: University of Queensland Press, 1984).

Marian Sawer, *The Ethical State: Social Liberalism in Australia* (Melbourne: Melbourne University Press, 2003).

Gavin Souter, *Lion and Kangaroo. Australia: 1901–1919, The Rise of a Nation* (Sydney: William Collins, 1976).

Stuart Svensen, *The Shearers' War: The Story of the 1891 Shearers' Strike* (Brisbane: University of Queensland Press, 1989).

Stuart Svensen, *The Sinews of War: Hard Cash and the 1890 Maritime Strike* (Sydney: UNSW Press, 1995).

Jan Todd, *Colonial Technology: Science and the Transfer of Innovation to Australia* (Cambridge: Cambridge University Press, 1995).

Luke Trainor, *British Imperialism and Australian Nationalism: Manipulation, Conflict and Compromise in the Late Nineteenth Century* (Cambridge: Cambridge University Press, 1994).

David Walker, *Anxious Nation: Australia and the Rise of Asia, 1850–1939* (Brisbane: University of Queensland Press, 1999).

7   SACRIFICE

E. M. Andrews, *The Anzac Illusion: Anglo-Australian Relations During World War I* (Cambridge: Cambridge University Press, 1993).

Bain Attwood, *Rights for Aborigines* (Sydney: Allen & Unwin, 2003).

C. E. W. Bean, *Anzac to Amiens* (Canberra: Australian War Memorial, 1946).

Joan Beaumont, *The Broken Nation: Australians in the Great War* (Sydney: Allen & Unwin, 2013).

Sean Brawley, *The White Peril: Foreign Relations and Asian Immigration to Australasia and North America, 1919–78* (Sydney: UNSW Press, 1995).

Judith Brett, *The Australian Liberals and the Moral Middle Class: From Alfred Deakin to John Howard* (Cambridge: Cambridge University Press, 2003).

Joy Damousi and Marilyn Lake (eds), *Gender and War: Australians at War in the Twentieth Century* (Cambridge: Cambridge University Press, 1995).

L. F. Fitzhardinge, *The Little Digger, 1914–1952: William Morris Hughes, A Political Biography* (Sydney: Angus & Robertson, 1979).

Bill Gammage, *The Broken Years: Australian Soldiers in the Great War* (Melbourne: Penguin, 1975).

Bill Gammage and Peter Spearritt (eds), *Australians 1938* (Sydney: Fairfax, Syme and Weldon Associates, 1987).

Stephen Garton, *The Cost of War: Australians Return* (Melbourne: Oxford University Press, 1996).

Anna Haebich, *Broken Circles: Fragmenting Indigenous Families, 1800–2000* (Fremantle: Fremantle Arts Centre Press, 2001).

Carolyn Holbrook, *Anzac: The Unauthorised Biography* (Sydney: NewSouth, 2014).

David Horner, *High Command: Australia and Allied Strategy, 1939–1945* (Sydney: Allen & Unwin, 1992).

K. S. Inglis, *Sacred Places: War Memorials in the Australian Landscape* (3rd edn, Melbourne: Melbourne University Press, 2008).

Lesley Johnson, *The Unseen Voice: A Cultural Study of Early Australian Radio* (London: Routledge, 1988).

Mark Johnston, *Fighting the Enemy: Australian Soldiers and their Adversaries in World War II* (Cambridge: Cambridge University Press, 2000).

Marilyn Lake, *The Limits of Hope: Soldier Settlement in Victoria, 1915–38* (Melbourne: Oxford University Press, 1987).

Marilyn Lake, *Getting Equal: The History of Australian Feminism* (Sydney: Allen & Unwin, 1999).

David Lee, *Stanley Melbourne Bruce: Australian Internationalist* (London: Continuum, 2010).

Janet McCalman, *Struggletown: Public and Private Life in Richmond, 1900–1965* (Melbourne: Melbourne University Press, 1984).

Janet McCalman, *Journeyings: The Biography of a Middle-Class Generation, 1920–1990* (Melbourne: Melbourne University Press, 1993).

Stuart Macintyre, *The Oxford History of Australia, vol. 4: 1901–1942: The Succeeding Age* (Melbourne: Oxford University Press, 1986).

Stuart Macintyre, *The Reds: The Communist Party of Australia from Origins to Illegality* (Sydney: Allen & Unwin, 1998).

A. W. Martin, *Robert Menzies: A Life, vol. 1: 1894–1943* (Melbourne: Melbourne University Press, 1993).

Barrie Dyster and David Meredith, *Australia in the Global Economy: Continuity and Change*, (2nd edn, Cambridge: Cambridge University Press, 2012).

Andrew Moore, *The Secret Army and the Premier* (Sydney: UNSW Press, 1989).

Hank Nelson, *P.O.W. Prisoners of War: Australians Under Nippon* (Sydney: Australian Broadcasting Commission, 1985).

Fiona Paisley, *Loving Protection: Australian Feminism and Aboriginal Women's Rights, 1919–1939* (Melbourne: Melbourne University Press, 2000).

John Robertson, *1939–1945, Australia Goes to War* (Sydney: Doubleday, 1984).

Michael Roe, *Australia, Britain, and Migration, 1915–1940: A Study of Desperate Hopes* (Cambridge: Cambridge University Press, 1995).

C. B. Schedvin, *Australia and the Great Depression* (Sydney: Sydney University Press, 1970).

Chris Waters, *Australia and Appeasement: Imperial Foreign Policy and the Origins of World War II* (London: I. B. Tauris, 2012).

8   GOLDEN AGE

Michelle Arrow, *Friday on Our Minds: Popular Culture in Australia since 1945* (Sydney: UNSW Press, 2009).

Bain Attwood, *Rights for Aborigines* (Sydney: Allen & Unwin, 2003).

Geoffrey Bolton, *The Oxford History of Australia, vol. 5: 1942–1988: The Middle Way* (2nd edn, Melbourne: Oxford University Press, 1996).

Frank Bongiorno, *The Sex Lives of Australians: A History* (Melbourne: Black Inc., 2012).

Judith Brett, *Robert Menzies' Forgotten People* (Sydney: Macmillan, 1992).

Judith Brett, *Australian Liberals and the Moral Middle Class from Alfred Deakin to John Howard* (Cambridge: Cambridge University Press, 2003).

Nicholas Brown, *Governing Prosperity: Social Change and Analysis in Australia in the 1950s* (Cambridge: Cambridge University Press, 1995).

Nicholas Brown, *A History of Canberra* (Cambridge: Cambridge University Press, 2104).

L. F. Crisp, *Ben Chifley* (Melbourne: Longmans, 1961).

Ann Curthoys, A. W. Martin and Tim Rowse (eds), *Australians from 1939* (Sydney: Fairfax, Syme and Weldon Associates, 1987).

Graeme Davison, *Car Wars: How the Car Won Our Hearts and Conquered Our Cities* (Sydney: Allen & Unwin, 2004).

Barrie Dyster and David Meredith, *Australia in the Global Economy: Continuity and Change,* (2nd edn, Cambridge: Cambridge University Press, 2012).

Ross Fitzgerald, *The Pope's Battalions: Santamaria, Catholicism and the Labor Split* (Brisbane: University of Queensland Press, 2003).

Graham Freudenberg, *A Certain Grandeur: Gough Whitlam in Politics* (Melbourne: Macmillan, 1977).

Anna Haebich, *Spinning the Dream: Assimilation in Australia 1950–1970* (Fremantle: Fremantle Press, 2008).

Ian Hancock, *National and Permanent? The Federal Organisation of the Liberal Party of Australia, 1944–1965* (Melbourne: Melbourne University Press, 2000).

Lesley Johnson, *The Modern Girl: Girlhood and Growing Up* (Sydney: Allen & Unwin, 1993).

Marilyn Lake, *Getting Equal: The History of Australian Feminism* (Sydney: Allen & Unwin, 1999).

David Lowe, *Menzies and the 'Great World Struggle': Australia's Cold War, 1948–1954* (Sydney: UNSW Press, 1999).

Stuart Macintyre, *Australia's Boldest Experiment: War and Reconstruction in the 1940s* (Sydney: NewSouth, 2015).

Allan Martin, *Robert Menzies: A Life, vol. 2: 1944–1978* (Melbourne: Melbourne University Press, 1999).

John Murphy, *Harvest of Fear: A History of Australia's Vietnam War* (Sydney: Allen & Unwin, 1993).

John Murphy, *Imagining the Fifties: Private Sentiment and Political Culture in Menzies' Australia* (Sydney: UNSW Press, 2000).

Mark Peel, *Good Times, Hard Times: The Past and the Future in Elizabeth* (Melbourne: Melbourne University Press, 1995).

Greg Pemberton, *All the Way: Australia's Road to Vietnam* (Sydney: Allen & Unwin, 1987).

Scott Prasser, J. R. Nethercote and John Warhurst (eds), *The Menzies Era: A Reappraisal of Government, Politics and Policy* (Sydney: Hale & Iremonger, 1995).

Eric Richards, *Destination Australia: Migration to Australia Since 1901* (Sydney: UNSW Press, 2008).

Shirleene Robinson and Julie Ustinoff (eds), *The 1960s in Australia: People, Power and Politics* (Newcastle upon Tyne: Cambridge Scholars, 2012).

Tim Rowse, *White Flour, White Power: From Rations to Citizenship in Central Australia* (Cambridge: Cambridge University Press, 1998).

Tim Rowse, *Nugget Coombs: A Reforming Life* (Cambridge: Cambridge University Press, 2002).

Sean Scalmer, *Dissent Events: Protest, the Media and the Political Gimmick in Australia* (Sydney: University of New South Wales Press, 2002).

Michael Sexton, *The Great Crash: The Short Life and Sudden Death of the Whitlam Government* (Melbourne: Scribe, 2005).

Tom Sheridan, *Division of Labour: Industrial Relations in the Chifley Years, 1945–1949* (Melbourne: Oxford University Press, 1989).

Tom Sheridan, *Australia's Own Cold War: The Waterfront Under Menzies* (Melbourne: Melbourne University Press, 2006).

Paul Strangio, *Keeper of the Faith: A Biography of Jim Cairns* (Melbourne: Melbourne University Press, 2002).

Gwenda Tavan, *The Long, Slow Death of White Australia* (Melbourne: Scribe, 2005).

Stuart Ward, *Australia and the British Embrace: The Demise of the Imperial Ideal* (Melbourne: Melbourne University Press, 2001).

9   RECTIFICATION

Philip Ayres, *Malcolm Fraser* (Melbourne: William Heinemann Australia, 1987).

Stephen Bell, *Ungoverning the Economy: The Political Economy of Australian Economic Policy* (Melbourne: Oxford University Press, 1997).

Geoffrey Bolton, *The Oxford History of Australia*, vol. 5 (2nd edn, Melbourne: Oxford University Press, 1996).

Judith Brett, *Relaxed and Comfortable: The Liberal Party's Australia* (Melbourne: Black Inc., 2005).

Barrie Dyster and David Meredith, *Australia in the Global Economy: Continuity and Change*, (2nd edn, Cambridge: Cambridge University Press, 2012).

Grant Fleming, David Merrett and Simon Ville, *The Big End of Town: Big Business and Corporate Leadership in Twentieth-Century Australia* (Cambridge: Cambridge University Press, 2004).

Barry Jones, *Sleepers Wake!* (Melbourne: Oxford University Press, 1982).

James Jupp, *From White Australia to Woomera: The Story of Australian Immigration* (Cambridge: Cambridge University Press, 2002).

Paul Kelly, *The End of Certainty: The Story of the 1980s* (Sydney: Allen & Unwin, 1992).

Robert Manne, *How We Live Now: The Controversies of the Nineties* (Melbourne: Text Publishing, 1998).

George Megalogenis, *The Australian Moment: How We Were Made for These Times* (Melbourne: Viking, 2012).

Meaghan Morris, *Too Late Too Soon: History in Public Culture* (Bloomington: Indiana University Press, 1998).

Mark Peel, *The Lowest Rung: Voices of Australian Poverty* (Cambridge: Cambridge University Press, 2003).

Nicholas Peterson and Will Sanders (eds), *Citizenship and Indigenous Australians: Changing Conceptions and Possibilities* (Cambridge: Cambridge University Press, 1998).

Tim Rowse, *After Mabo: Interpreting Indigenous Traditions* (Melbourne: Melbourne University Press, 1993).

Susan Ryan and Troy Bramston (eds), *The Hawke Government: A Critical Retrospective* (Sydney: Pluto Press, 1993).

Peter Saunders, *Welfare and Inequality: National and International Perspectives on the Australian Welfare State* (Cambridge: Cambridge University Press, 1994).

Paul Smyth and Bettina Cass (eds), *Contesting the Australian Way: States, Markets and Civil Society* (Cambridge: Cambridge University Press, 1998).

Hugh Stretton, *Political Essays* (Melbourne: Georgian House, 1987).

Trevor Sykes, *The Bold Rider: Behind Australia's Corporate Collapse* (Sydney: Allen & Unwin, 1994).

Graeme Turner, *Making It National: Nationalism and Australian Popular Culture* (Sydney: Allen & Unwin, 1994).

James Walter, *Tunnel Vision: The Failure of Political Imagination* (Sydney: Allen & Unwin, 1996).

John Wiseman, *Global Nation? Australia and the Politics of Globalisation* (Cambridge: Cambridge University Press, 1998).

1 0   OUTCOMES

Chris Aulich and Roger Wettenhall (eds), *Howard's Second and Third Governments: Australian Commonwealth Administration 1998–2004* (Sydney: UNSW Press, 2005).

Chris Aulich and Mark Evans (eds), *The Rudd Government: Australian Commonwealth Administration 2007–2010* (Canberra: ANU E Press, 2010).

Mark Davis, *The Land of Plenty: Australia in the 2000s* (Melbourne: Melbourne University Press, 2008).

Wayne Errington and Peter van Onselen, *John Winston Howard* (Melbourne: Melbourne University Press, 2007).

John Edwards, *Beyond the Boom* (Melbourne: Penguin, 2014).

Ross Garnaut, *Dog Days: Australia After the Boom* (Melbourne: Redback, 2013).

Paul Kelly, *The March of Patriots: The Struggle for Modern Australia* (Melbourne: Melbourne University Press, 2008).

Malcolm Knox, *Boom: The Underground History of Australia from Gold Rush to GFC* (Melbourne: Viking, 2013).

Andrew Leigh, *Battlers and Billionaires: The Story of Inequality in Australia* (Melbourne: Redback, 2014)

Ian W. McLean, *Why Australia Prospered: The Shifting Sources of Economic Growth* (Princeton: Princeton University Press, 2013).

Robert Manne (ed.), *The Howard Years* (Melbourne: Black Inc., 2004).

David Marr and Marian Wilkinson, *Dark Victory* (Sydney: Allen & Unwin, 2003).

Ian Marsh (ed.), *Political Parties in Transition?* (Sydney: Federation Press, 2006).

George Megalogenis, *The Australian Moment: How We Were Made for These Times* (Melbourne: Viking, 2012).

Noel Pearson, *Up From the Mission: Selected Writings* (Melbourne: Black Inc., 2009)

Tim Rowse, *Rethinking Social Justice: From 'Peoples' to 'Populations'* (Canberra: Aboriginal Studies Press, 2012).

Rodney Tiffen and Ross Gittins, *How Australia Compares* (2nd edn, Cambridge: Cambridge University Press, 2009).

Patrick Weller, *Kevin Rudd: Twice Prime Minister* (Melbourne: Melbourne University Press, 2014).

INDEX

(Note: Page references in italics denote illustration)

CAMBRIDGE CONCISE HISTORIES

Titles in the series